A CULTURAL HISTORY
OF IDEAS

VOLUME 4

A Cultural History of Ideas
General Editors: Sophia Rosenfeld and Peter T. Struck

Volume 1
A Cultural History of Ideas in Classical Antiquity
Edited by Clifford Ando, Thomas Habinek, and Giulia Sissa

Volume 2
A Cultural History of Ideas in the Medieval Age
Edited by Dallas G. Denery II

Volume 3
A Cultural History of Ideas in the Renaissance
Edited by Jill Kraye

Volume 4
A Cultural History of Ideas in the Age of Enlightenment
Edited by Jack R. Censer

Volume 5
A Cultural History of Ideas in the Age of Empire
Edited by James H. Johnson

Volume 6
A Cultural History of Ideas in the Modern Age
Edited by Stefanos Geroulanos

A CULTURAL HISTORY
OF IDEAS

IN THE AGE OF
ENLIGHTENMENT

Edited by Jack R. Censer

BLOOMSBURY ACADEMIC

LONDON • NEW YORK • OXFORD • NEW DELHI • SYDNEY

BLOOMSBURY ACADEMIC
Bloomsbury Publishing Plc
50 Bedford Square, London, WC1B 3DP, UK
1385 Broadway, New York, NY 10018, USA
29 Earlsfort Terrace, Dublin 2, Ireland

BLOOMSBURY, BLOOMSBURY ACADEMIC and the Diana logo are trademarks
of Bloomsbury Publishing Plc

First published in Great Britain 2022

A catalogue record for this book is available from the British Library.

A catalog record for this book is available from the Library of Congress.

ISBN: HB: 978-1-3500-0747-5
       Set: 978-1-3500-0755-0

Series: The Cultural Histories Series

Typeset by Integra Software Services Pvt. Ltd.
Printed and bound in Great Britain

To find out more about our authors and books visit www.bloomsbury.com
and sign up for our newsletters.

CONTENTS

ILLUSTRATIONS

FIGURES

TABLES

GENERAL EDITORS' PREFACE

When Arthur Lovejoy introduced the field of the history of ideas to his listeners in the 1933 William James lectures, later published as *The Great Chain of Being*, he compared ideas to molecules. As he explained it, molecules combine and recombine to make compounds that vary over time. Yet the underlying stuff abides. The comparison gave him a way to capture the dynamic properties of ideas themselves and to forestall this or that thinker's eagerness to claim novelty. Further, since the periodic table has only so many elements, Lovejoy's conceit suggested that a person could, retroactively, make sensible statements about the whole.

In this book series devoted to the history of ideas, we hope to be able to make sensible judgements about the whole, but we are also convinced that the analogy needs rethinking. When Lovejoy accorded agency to the elements, with their pent-up interactive energies, he left out of focus the solution or medium in which those chemicals do their interacting. The non-noetic factors for which Lovejoy allowed come only from thinkers' internal dispositions, personal habits and preferences that might vary from person to person or from time to time. These volumes aim to widen considerably the intellectual historian's conception of how ideas emerge and move through the world.

A Cultural History of Ideas sweeps over 2,800 years of evidence. It proceeds on the premise that certain broad areas of inquiry have held humans' collective attention across a segment of the globe over all of this time. These nine topics are not presented as ideas in any simple sense. G. E. R. Lloyd's treatment of "Nature" in antiquity in volume 1 will already belie any confidence in a singular, perduring core even in this one-ninth of the terrain these volumes lay out. We propose this taxonomy instead as a set of general areas of investigation focused on comparable subjects across the ages. As historians of ideas, we aim to trace in this book series prominent lines of thought in each of these various realms—chapter by chapter, in the same order across volumes, from antiquity to the present—with close attention to constancy, change, and variation alike.

The first of these areas is "Knowledge" itself: what are we to make of the immaterial notions stored in our minds? Which ones count as true? How are such truths found, divided into new categories, conveyed, and used? After all, it is only in the twentieth century that anyone could speak meaningfully of the humanistic, social, biological, and physical sciences as distinct branches of knowledge. Many other systems came before. From "Knowledge," we turn to one of its central foci and the other starting point of this series: "The Human Self" in all its dimensions, physical, intellectual, emotional, and more. For it is the self that is the knower.

Then, moving outward from the singular self, we shift to "Ethics and Social Relations," or humans in concert with one another, and "Politics and Economies," or systems for organizing that collective existence legally and materially. "Nature" follows, including the human body, but also encompassing the earth that humans share with other animals, plants, and minerals, as well as the atmosphere and celestial bodies. Continuing to widen our lens, "Religion and the Divine" then takes the focus to the world beyond nature and to thinking about our origins, our afterlives, and our beliefs, which also means at times the limits of human knowledge.

The final categories take up, in close conversation with all of these previous domains, the realm of representation. "Language, Poetry, Rhetoric" concerns thinking about words in their many forms and uses. "The Arts" expands those questions into other symbolic systems employed in music, dance, theatre, fashion, architecture, design, and especially the visual arts, with a focus too on conceptions of beauty. Finally, "History" draws our attention to the representation of time itself, including notions of past, present, and future that simultaneously bring us full circle back to the understandings of knowledge and the self where we began.

Some specific ideas or concepts—freedom, dreams, power, difference, the environment, anger, to pick a random assortment—cross these many areas of inquiry and will appear more than once. But we take these nine broad categories to be proxies for some of the most fundamental areas to which humans in the domains of our focus—from so-called great thinkers like Plato or Locke or Einstein, to political leaders from Augustus to Charlemagne to Catherine the Great or Gandhi, to now-nameless scribes or teachers or midwives or bricklayers—have, over the centuries, applied their minds, alone and together.

But what is a *cultural* history of ideas? There are two distinguishing features of this approach, and both begin from the premise that the history of ideas is not, as some earlier historians including Lovejoy would have it, best understood as the record of a perennial conversation that largely transcends the specifics of space and time. Rather, we posit that just as the answers to big questions change depending on where and when we look, so do the questions themselves along with their stakes. "What is freedom?" means something very different to an enslaved Celt living in ancient Rome, a twelfth-century French monk, an aspiring merchant involved in transatlantic trade in seventeenth-century London, and a political theorist working in a US university in the era of late capitalism.

A cultural history of ideas is thus imagined, first, as a way to demonstrate the proposition that even the most innovative ideas to emerge from such queries, as well as the uses and impact of those ideas, have varied enormously depending on a host of contingent and contextual features extrinsic to the intellects that gave birth to them. These external features go well beyond other, competing ideas, or even competing texts in which other ideas are housed, despite the arguments of Quentin Skinner and much of what is thought of today as contextualized intellectual history. Cultural historians of ideas, to understand the thought of the past, necessarily look considerably more widely at a range of different domains of human life—or culture in the broadest sense.

Those cultural factors include changes in technology, media, and the economics of production and distribution; the authors in these volumes consider the evolution of ideas in relation to the emergence of alphabetic script and scribal culture, the printing press, photography, the computer, and other methods of communication that shaped their respective eras, as well as the commerce established around them. Our list also includes differing social structures and kinds of hierarchies and status markers, from race and gender, to estate, wealth, patronage, and credentialing, that have brought new kinds of thinkers to the fore and turned others into enemies or nonentities. In these pages we will meet, and also identify the support systems behind, philosophers, physicians, librarians, clerics, writers, artists, state officials, and only from the nineteenth century onward, "scientists," "experts," and, indeed, "intellectuals," as well as those denied these appellations. Other factors shaping ideas—including those of the most influential thinkers of every era—have been changes to laws; to religious practice and identity; to the distribution of resources; to patterns of migration, settlement, and urbanization; to notions of taste and manners; and to literacy rates, education, and intellectual life itself. So, too, do we need to study encounters between different peoples, whether through war, conquest, travel and exploration, exploitation, or peaceful cultural and commercial exchange. Then there is space in another sense. Historically specific settings, whether they be market places, monasteries, universities, salons, courts, coffee houses, medical clinics, port city docks, or think tanks, have inflected how ideas have been forged, disseminated, and debated and, ultimately, the form they have taken. So have modes of sociability. How can we understand the power of the ideas of Demosthenes or Horace or Lord Byron or Sarah Bernhardt without accounting for the social practices in which they were embedded, be that public oration, letter writing, listening to sermons or novels read out loud, or attending public performances, but also the material infrastructure behind those endeavors, from road construction to the microphone? And Scaffolding everything else in the realm of ideas have, of course, always been geopolitics and the apparatuses of power: empires, nations, regions, city states, kingdoms, dioceses, and villages, but also competition about and between ideologies, factions and parties, and policies, whether established by vote, by decree, or by physical coercion.

In approaching ideas in this deeply contextual way, the cultural history of ideas could be said to be borrowing from the subfield known as the sociology of knowledge. Both share an interest in uncovering the structures, including practices and institutions, that allow for the varied means by which knowledge has been invented, organized, kept secret, exchanged, transformed, and weaponized to accomplish various goals, from acts of radical imagination and liberation to keeping people in their place. Equally, though, the approach employed in these volumes could be said to draw on histories of reading, of looking, and of hearing, that is, of interpretation and reinterpretation, or hermeneutics and textual exegesis, across genres, languages, and eras—all modes long associated with histories of the arts and literature and philosophy. Moreover, a cultural history of ideas should equally be a history of dissent and of forms of censorship and repression instituted in response. Historians also need to establish the evolving boundaries between the sayable and the unsayable, the representable and the unrepresentable, and why and how they have been enforced or not. That means paying attention to conflicts and forms of violence over just these questions as well as networks and modes of intellectual collaboration. Part of the interest in looking at the history of thought embedded in ever-shifting contexts over such a long period of time is discovering how some ideas—say, ideas about gender difference or modes of seeing others—persist across moments of social and political fracture, such as major wars. Another part is discovering how ideas are transformed by— or help transform—larger movements in the worlds that produced them; consider, for example, how much the ideas of Jean-Jacques Rousseau shaped political and religious practice in the context of the French Revolution, from republicanism to the institution of a civil religion, but also how his conceptual innovations were blamed for the revolution's excesses and thus delegitimized afterward. Some ideas, of course, fail to create any kind of traction until long after their moment of invention. Or they never do. All this is of interest to the historian of ideas too.

Yet there is a second sense in which these volumes function as a *cultural* history of ideas. Grasping this aspect requires looking more to anthropology than to sociology or literary theory. It also demands taking seriously the ideas and representations that animate everyday life, which is another meaning of culture. This approach turns our attention at least partly away from the ideas associated with philosophers, famous thinkers, or even major social movements or modern "isms" like nationalism or communism in their larger contexts. It does so in favor of a focus on collective habits, rituals, patterns of speech and behavior, and customary forms of representation operative in social, political, and economic experience, seeing them as imbued with, and productive of, a vital, culturally specific landscape of ideas. Some scholars call these ideas, taken together, folk knowledge or folk logic. From the Annaliste tradition of history writing in France, others have adopted the term *mentalité*. Included under its purview are, potentially, studies of the history of collective memory, of values, of popular and mass culture, and of the senses and emotions and decision-making in all their historical particularity.

Importantly for our purposes, sometimes the realm or realms of *mentalité* have operated to uphold the dominant ideology of the moment or to boost an ascendant one; Jack Censer and Gary Kates's introduction to the volume on the Enlightenment, for example, highlights the way eighteenth-century advertising circulars, the so-called *Affiches*, subtly bolstered the intellectual currents associated with Enlightenment philosophy without ever drawing directly on the work of any of its key thinkers. But other times folk knowledge has worked to undergird marginalized people's efforts to resist, circumvent, or revise dominant thinking, whether that has been in order to preserve traditions under pressure or to try to break free of various forms of repression. Consider craftworkers or Black revolutionaries of various eras deploying vernacular notions and forms of protest to challenge those with political and material power, including those who own the means of production. Often these commonplace and quotidian ideas, even as they structure collective life, are so routine and taken-for-granted within the culture where they exist that they go largely unremarked upon in any of the standard modes of conveying thought that are the focus of most histories of ideas. It is only when such everyday ideas collapse or get deployed in new ways that we tend to see that they belong to history too—and bear some relationship to the better-known history of explicit ideas.

What this means is that a cultural history of ideas in the second sense must extend its source base well beyond great books or texts of any kind; relevant ideas are just as likely to be embedded in visual, material, or somatic forms as they are in writing. Coin collections, garden designs, bits of code, temple complex plans, dance patterns, even habits of greeting: all become potential sites for uncovering foundational ideas in past moments and varied places. It also means thinking beyond traditional notions of thinker or audience to encompass the voices, eyes, and ears of those traditionally excluded from the tribe of "intellectuals," including women, people of color, and the nonliterate, as they can be unearthed from these varied sources. The volumes and individual chapters of this series will have succeeded if readers come away with an ability to take recognizable ideas or ideologies (i.e., those of Karl Marx and, subsequently, Marxism) or recognizable moments in intellectual history (i.e., "the Middle Ages") and see them as doubly imbricated in culture as ideational context and culture as the realm of everyday meaning-making and representation.

One risk, of course, is that this collection, with its cultural approach to ideas, ends up reinforcing an obsolete ideological construction paid lavish attention, particularly in the last century: that of "Western Civilization." The primary focus of these volumes is indeed the part of the globe, the temporal range, and much of the subject matter that scholars have inconsistently labeled and identified with "the West." But not content just to reject this terminology, we aim in these volumes to avoid the trap of its logic too, and we do so in several ways. The authors of these chapters do not take their geography to be bounded in any *a priori* way; their terrain stretches variously beyond Europe to the Near East, to China and other parts of Asia, to Russia, to Africa, and, unevenly over the last half millennium to North, Central, and South America. It is also important that every volume pushes back on the idea that the subject at hand can be described as constituting some unified cultural ethos. Radical intellectual pluralism exists in every era, and links of commonality also reach across whatever temporal and geographical boundaries we might construct. At the same time, we advocate a kind of geographical awareness that keeps us from losing sight of the fact that the histories under primary scrutiny here have been both carefully constructed and profoundly shaped by fantasies about, as well as dehumanizations of, varieties of others, whether labeled barbarians, foreigners, exotics, or heathens, whether near or far. This kind of thinking, in turn, is inseparable from an often violent history of the extraction of resources and commercial practices around the globe, of missionary activity and evangelization within and well beyond Christendom, of the enslavement of, particularly, African peoples, and of the conquest and colonization of various Indigenous peoples from the Americas to the South Seas. Advocacy for social justice is a distinct project from this one, but exposing the blinding legacies of injustice stemming from every era is very much a part of it. These volumes embrace the idea that a cultural history of ideas is necessarily a "connected history," with a focus on circulation and hybridity, along with serious attention to disparities of power.

But even more, perhaps, a cultural history of ideas potentially offers a conceptual way out of the trap of Western Civilization precisely because it historicizes, indeed "provincializes" (to borrow Dipesh Chakrabarty's term), the very categories long used to bolster it. Of particular pertinence here is "progress." Rather than treat techno-scientific or moral-political progress across time as a given, this series sees conceptions of progress, as well as those of newness and modernity, as polemical claims invented to serve different purposes at different moments (see especially the introductions to the volumes on the Enlightenment and the Age of Empire, but also the Middle Ages). The same could be said for periodization, including the very terms into which these volumes are carved up; Jill Kraye, in her volume on "the Renaissance," starts off not by guiding a tour of this arena but by showing us how this category was invented in the first place and then exposing its retrospective ideological functions. Indeed, the authors in this collection uniformly work hard to take up the intellectual pillars of standard accounts of what has been called Western Civilization and embed them, as ideas, in history. In addition to the notion of progress, these include the idea of the individual genius thinker, the advent of intellectual tolerance, the mastery of nature, secularization or the ultimate triumph of scientific reason over the enchantment of the world, and a firm distinction between past and present.

Moreover, despite the fact that this set of volumes ties ways of thinking to particular circumstances in the past, it is also designed to make the case that no one era or people or place owns those ideas going forward. Even the pointed anxieties of today, which Stefanos Geroulanos lists in the introduction to the final volume as including "dehumanization, species extinction, climate catastrophe, economic indifference to individual suffering, and artificial [forms of] intelligence," are in some sense variants of old concerns. We can thus treat previous responses to them as a storehouse from which people anywhere can continue to build new answers even as those ideas' initial relationship to particular conditions and situations remains important to understanding their full complexity. If this collection of the work of sixty-two scholars from multiple humanistic disciplines has a central goal, it is to remind us that inherited ways of thinking and our ever-changing lived experiences are constantly pushing against one another in productive ways, generating refreshed responses or, indeed, ideas as a result. We all aim to continue this endeavor.

Sophia Rosenfeld and Peter T. Struck,
General Editors

ACKNOWLEDGMENTS

This collection received much from its contributors. Asked to write a synthesis, they were often the first to draw together an essay on a topic not yet well defined. Moreover, the sources of cultural history may be found almost everywhere in a variety of forms. Nonetheless, readers will find, thanks to our authors, both originality and broad mining of the sources, as well as coherent accounts of various facets of the Enlightenment. The authors also were involved in the selection of images. Likewise, the editors of the series were highly responsive, promptly answering queries and providing advice.

Enormously helpful was Dr. Jennifer Lansbury, a historian in her own right, who assisted the contributors in following the pattern laid out for submissions. She also supervised the overall trajectory from typed drafts to manuscripts ready for the publisher. Coordinating with ten different contributors, she secured permissions that were often difficult to obtain. Any project with so many involved can be challenging, and Dr. Lansbury made the process far smoother.

I would also like to thank my historian spouse, Jane Turner Censer, for many excellent suggestions and advice. And more generally, I appreciate the scholarly community at George Mason University for its willingness to answer numerous questions.

Jack R. Censer, Volume Editor

Introduction: The Sources and Circulation of Enlightenment Ideas

JACK R. CENSER AND GARY KATES

The Enlightenment's origins lie not only in the Scientific Revolution but also in the growing opposition to the final years of King Louis XIV's long reign in France (1661–1715). Both inside and outside the French royal court a nagging sense emerged that the old king had amassed too much centralized power, carried out useless wars, and favored high fashion and the arts at the expense of the welfare of his subjects. Pierre Bayle (1647–1706) and François Fénelon (1651–1715) both exemplify this new opposition, even though they had little in common and, indeed, saw one another more as adversaries than colleagues. Nonetheless, their joint impact as key role models for later Enlightenment philosophers is indisputable—and arguably as important as that of better-known figures such as Isaac Newton, John Locke, and René Descartes.

Bayle was raised in a small southern French town where his father was an impoverished Protestant minister. Through scholarships, Bayle acquired a good education and took a job teaching theology in a Protestant academy at the same time that France was cracking down on toleration for Protestants. Louis XIV's increasing punishment of Protestants, especially intellectuals such as Bayle, forced thousands to emigrate. By the mid-1680s, Bayle had joined a large French Protestant (Huguenot) exile community in Rotterdam, Holland, where he began a prolific publishing career. Although some of his books were scholarly tomes meant for fellow Protestant theologians, he also developed publications that reached beyond such a narrow circle, aiming for a broad-based European public that he termed the Republic of Letters. With some success under his belt, publishers were willing to back more expensive projects. During the 1690s, he put out a multivolume encyclopedia of his own opinions on politics, society, religion, and literature entitled the *Historical and Critical Dictionary*. Over the next century it became among Europe's best-used reference works.

Bayle's articles in the *Dictionary* were often subversive. For example, the article on the biblical King David seems safe enough at first; it is only when one looks at the footnotes that Bayle's critical stance is evident. There we read that while David was no doubt loved by God, he nevertheless raped, looted, committed adultery, and engaged in the mass murder of innocent victims. Bayle uses David to criticize absolute monarchy, especially one grounded upon divine authority. Whether God loved David or Louis XIV is His business, Bayle seemed to be suggesting, but ordinary people must resist any abuse of power, especially perpetrated in God's name. In this way, Bayle helped to lay the foundation stone for a modern liberalism that advocated religious toleration and limited political authority.

Unlike Bayle, Fénelon was a Catholic archbishop chosen by Louis XIV to educate his ten-year-old grandson, the intended heir to the French throne. As a moral primer for his young prince, Fénelon wrote up a juvenile sequel to Homer's *Odyssey*, focusing on the traveling adventures of Odysseus' son, Telemachus. Through visiting various types of countries, Telemachus learns that virtue is a monarch's most potent weapon and must always be used in ways that prevent war and corruption. A king's first duty, Telemachus is repeatedly told by his tutor, Mentor, is to look after the welfare of his people. Virtue is thus central to that project. At the same time, when Telemachus visits towns, he notices how social inequality caused by a vibrant trade in luxuries has led to the moral corruption of the wealthy and the impoverishment of poor workers, whose fate is little better than slaves. Luxury, warns Mentor, is the great corruptor of virtue. The only way for a king to

FIGURE 0.1 François Fénelon, engraving by J. Thomson, 1833. © Getty Images.

preserve virtue in society is for the kingdom's economy to focus on agriculture, growing plenty of food for everyone to eat, but also avoiding exotic luxuries from faraway lands. During a century in which Europeans were becoming increasingly addicted to coffee and sugar grown in Caribbean slave plantations, no wonder *Telemachus* became increasingly read for its rants against consumer luxuries.

Although Fénelon was among the most powerful archbishops in France, Louis XIV eventually exiled him from the royal court because he had become a ringleader in a mystical religious disturbance known as Quietism. Once Fénelon was gone from the political scene, *The Adventures of Telemachus* was published against his will (1699) and became an instant bestseller across Europe. Because Fénelon had been sent away for his deviant mysticism, and was now a political outcast, everyone read *Telemachus* as a cynical satire of the reigning king. Nothing was further from the truth. Fénelon had not criticized Louis XIV's political power or spoken up against Protestant harassment. Nonetheless, during the years following the deaths of both Louis XIV and Fénelon in 1715, *Telemachus* continued to be understood as a reform screed, and its author became associated with Bayle's call for a society based upon virtue, toleration, and monarchical constraint rather than their opposites. The Enlightenment had begun.

Both Bayle and Fénelon became Enlightenment icons during the period of Louis XV's regency (1715–1734), as their works influenced reform-minded statesmen and thinkers in French-speaking Europe. No one did more to spread their reputations than the great *philosophes* Montesquieu and Voltaire. Given that these men would set the foundation for a reformed monarchy that greatly limited the power of the Church in government and society, it is ironic that the founders they championed—Bayle and Fénelon—were both men of intense faith, one an irreverent Calvinist and the other an archbishop who supported Catholic mysticism.

Shortly after King Louis XIV died in 1715, Montesquieu (1689–1755) began work not on a formal political treatise, but on a novel with overt political themes, *Persian Letters*. Influenced both by the format and substance of Fénelon's *Telemachus*, one character asks another whether he thinks virtue is inherent to human beings. Montesquieu's mouthpiece, Usbek, answers: "There are certain truths which it is not sufficient to know, but which must be realized: such are the great commonplaces of morality." Just as Fénelon himself had used *Telemachus* as a popular device to channel serious political theory, so Montesquieu would now do something similar with *Persian Letters*. Not surprisingly, the book became an immediate bestseller and catapulted Montesquieu to instant fame from Dublin to Berlin. Likewise, Voltaire's *Philosophical Letters* (1733–1734) presented the young philosopher as his own Mentor visiting England. Using many of Bayle's ideas, Voltaire (1694–1778) painted an idealized picture of England as a land that combined religious tolerance, commercial prosperity, and limited monarchical authority. For Voltaire, England became a model for how states throughout Europe might reform their monarchies on the basis of religious toleration and commercial prosperity. To limit their impact, both books were heavily censored by French religious and political authorities.

Montesquieu would continue these progressive themes in his Roman history (1734) and in his magnum opus, *The Spirit of the Laws* (1748), which became the Enlightenment's bestselling political treatise. Nonetheless, Voltaire dominated the Enlightenment even more than Montesquieu, who died in 1755. From the 1730s through to his death in 1778, Voltaire always had several important books in print at once; even today one can argue that Voltaire has had more bestsellers than any writer in history. He also published across several different fields: history, political commentary, poetry, short stories, and

FIGURE 0.2 Voltaire, engraving (artist unknown), 1833. © Wikimedia Commons (public domain).

plays. In each of these genres he struck gold. Even before the era of mass literacy, at least everyone who knew how to read had heard of Voltaire. "The writings of Voltaire are quoted by the hairdressers and milliners of Paris," wrote one contemporary, "because they are written in the simple language of the country."[1] The success of the Enlightenment lay not only in liberal ideas that promoted toleration, freedom, and equality, but even more because these ideas were packaged in a language and style engaging to a developing reading public.

The Enlightenment may have begun in France over concerns about its monarchy, but by the 1760s, *philosophes* were contributing to the movement in various European countries. Perhaps nowhere was the Enlightenment more intense than in Scotland, which because of its high literacy rate and recent political union with England, played a cultural role in Europe well above its small size. When, for example, David Hume (1711–1776) moved to Paris for a two-year stay as the secretary for the British ambassador, he was feted as a celebrity along the lines of a Voltaire. After all, a French translation of his short book of political essays had become an overnight bestseller in 1752, and his *History of England* (1754–1761) was fast becoming recognized among the most important works of history of the eighteenth century. Only later would his first book, *A Treatise of*

Human Nature, overtake these others in securing his reputation as a brilliant philosopher. Likewise, Hume's close Scottish friend, Adam Smith (1723–1790), published only two books in his lifetime, but both were considered masterpieces before he died: *A Theory of Moral Sentiments* (1759) explained how virtue and sociable collaboration could thrive even in a modern world made of city dwellers who were largely strangers to one another; meanwhile his *Wealth of Nations* (1776) did more than any other single work to give birth to the new social science of economics, which for Smith and Hume lay at the foundation of any liberal society.

The Enlightenment reached its apogee—in France and across much of the West, from the North American and Caribbean colonies in the New World to Russia on the Asian frontier—during the period when the great 26-volume *Encyclopédia* was published (1751–1772) under the direction of Denis Diderot and Jean le Rond d'Alembert. Many of the great French *philosophes* participated in the venture, including Montesquieu, Voltaire,

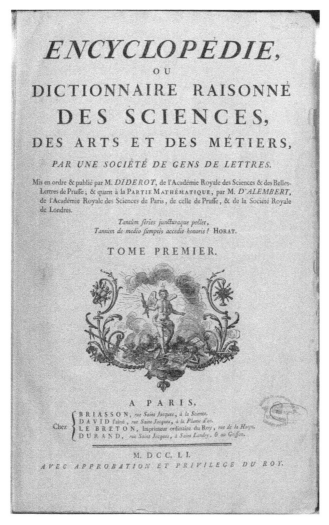

FIGURE 0.3 Title page, Denis Diderot, *Encyclopédie* (1751). © Wikimedia Commons (public domain).

and Rousseau. The *Encyclopedia* found its way across Europe and Great Britain—Adam Smith himself ordered a copy for the University of Glasgow Library when he served as its head librarian. Perhaps more important, this large publishing enterprise, always skirting with government and ecclesiastical censorship, signaled the Enlightenment as a movement of writers who hoped to connect directly to a larger, literate public through books, reference works, and journals.

The ideology and culture of the Enlightenment, which emerged first in France in reaction to the rise of royal absolutism and its emphasis on social privilege, continues to be influential to the present, even though challenged by populist, nationalist, and other collectivist norms since the late eighteenth century. In the Enlightenment, human activity rather than appeals to divine authority became the hallmark of the ideology of the *philosophes*, even as religious practices and thought remained important in many places as they do to this day. So did the idea of individuals endowed with basic, natural rights and tolerance for a wide array of different ideas and inclinations. In response, European culture gradually and subtly accepted and absorbed this new way of viewing the world, and many of its main ideas and practices have, for better and for worse, reshaped the extra-European world too.

However elusive the precise connection between ideas and culture, it is clear that we cannot explain the success of the Enlightenment only by looking at its greatest thinkers. Jürgen Habermas has argued persuasively of the engagement between the literate classes and a succession of monarchs who, despite varying degrees of reluctance, opened the door wider to "progressive" ideas, and who created by the eighteenth century a new "place" where educated and rising economic elites could contest royal and religious norms. Many nobles would also join in the debate. Habermas labeled this battleground the "public sphere" and described it as a realm in which those elites adopted, largely without any organized plan, customs and practices that reflected the contentions of the *philosophes*, as mostly French writers in this new tradition became known. This new set of beliefs and assumptions would, in the course of the eighteenth century, challenge and even displace many, if not most, royal habits.

Despite differences in wealth and often differences in manners, this elite—both noble and commoners—had in fact carved out a niche for itself. Although this amalgam might not have formed a cohesive social group, the participants shared much culturally. In a world of peasant illiteracy, they read. They often intermarried, to the social advantage of the commoner and the economic advantage of the noble. They shared a political position, sometimes even at the top of the social ladder, particularly in western Europe. And at first they probably formed a majority of those who straddled both older and new cultures.

As James Van Horn Melton has pointed out in wonderful detail, this elite group shared a multitude of cultural characteristics. Manners were softened. In England, the public rejected the harsh judgmentalism of Puritanism to embrace politeness practiced with wit. Addison and Steele's periodicals turned away from spartan attitudes toward "civility, order and liberty, learning and conviviality."[2] Commentaries on marriage critiqued matches made for gain in favor of those stressing companionship and the family, as they also discussed fashion and commerce. Even though the novel still received criticism as lacking piety, the press produced a welter of "moral weeklies" that decried social advantage in favor of domesticity.

Related in part to higher standards of sociability was the spread of salon culture. Although salons had been common in the seventeenth century, their purpose then was to educate and raise the bourgeoisie in "society." On the contrary, the Enlightenment salon, which generally convened once or twice weekly, beginning with dinner, focused on discussion as if its members were social equals, with outsiders needing a referral to join, though they were still involved. Suspended during the salon were "distinctions of rank, class, and nationality."[3] Rather than a school to discipline, the salon became a meeting ground where social privilege was temporarily erased.

Most significant was the conversational style of the salon, meant to contrast with the hierarchical nature of behavior at the court where kings judged subjects who, in theory, were subservient, to one extent or another. The salon was essentially collegial. Its participants discussed poems and essays and dispensed news, and established authors helped the struggling among them. Because the literary market grew increasingly open, aspiring writers needed less help from the privileged and the *salonnières*, privileged women who helped organize the cultural and intellectual life of the salons that sprung up in Europe's growing urban areas.

Other Western countries developed different norms. For example, German intellectual life more often resided in universities; and in German states military and fiscal affairs took precedence in contrast to fiction and speculation in England and France. Nonetheless, salons emerged there too with the interesting difference of providing an enhanced role for Jewish people in intellectual life. The Hohenzollern rulers welcomed Jews, who had accumulated fortunes, and some of whose wives presided over salons. In fact, the Prussian nobility, in need of funds, often married women from this echelon of society. Later, the rise of nationalist fervor, in the wake of the Napoleonic Wars, undermined what appeared to be a "cosmopolite" population. But salons in central and western Europe certainly had something of a heyday during the era of the High Enlightenment of the mid-eighteenth century and stimulated intellectual and open discussion of topics of social relevance. Further, with these ties of intellectual life and shared sociability, this subset of the wealthy distanced themselves to some extent from monarchical culture too. At the most, quiet resistance characterized this growth in independent thinking.

Despite much state and church censorship everywhere but Britain and the Netherlands, the press provided another alternative authority by delivering timely information to the public sphere and especially critics of royal government. An important indication of the power of this new medium was the explosion of the number of news outlets in the eighteenth century. Let us consider the French example, which was less vibrant than that of England but infinitely larger and more contentious than Russia, Austria, or Spain. As the international language of this era, French-language papers circulated well beyond their borders. Although only nineteen such newspapers existed in 1785, that number was nearly four times greater than fifty years earlier. Ineffective and inconsistent control of the press during its expansion had in this period already done much to enhance the public sphere's knowledge of other political approaches and even French difficulties in domestic political affairs, especially as the revolution appeared.

Growing up along with the political gazettes were other periodicals that focused on literature and those political tracts that provided readers with synopses of different authors. Published in France or just outside its borders to serve the country but avoid restrictions (although they still had to negotiate the French mail service), such periodicals numbered only nine in 1745, but had exploded to thirty-nine in the mid-1780s. To be certain, readers could consume many political tracts directly. Nonetheless, more depended on selections and summaries of the press. Considered together, these journals created a shared secular elite understanding of the intellectual, religious, and philosophical concerns of the era.

Nº. VI.

LE COURRIER

Du VENDREDI 20. Janvier 1741.

E NAPLES le 20. Decembre 1740. M. le Cardinal Spinelli, Archevêque de cette Ville, eſt de retour de Rome; & a déja été à la Cour rendre ſes reſpects à L. L. M. M. M. le Prince Borgheſe ſe couvrit Jeudi dernier devant le Roi, en qualité de Grand d'Eſpagne de la premiere Claſſe. On celebra Vendredi l'anniverſaire de la Fête établie en l'honneur de S. Janvier, lorſqu'il fut pris pour Protecteur de cette Ville & du Royaume, en 1631. à l'occaſion de l'Incendie du Mont Veſuve, dont cette Ville fut delivrée par ſon interceſſion. On porta devant le Chef de ce S. Martyr la phiole dans laquelle on conſerve de ſon Sang; & le Peuple eut la ſatisfaction de le voir liquefier, environ une demi heure après. On fit enſuite la Proceſſion ordinaire à cette occaſion. Le même matin le Roi tint Chapitre de l'Ordre, & donna le Collier à 12. nouveaux Chevaliers de la derniere promotion. Le Prince Octajano de Medicis, & le Prince Borgheſe furent du nombre. Ils ſont partis aujourd'hui de cette Ville, le premier pour Florence & le ſecond pour retourner à Rome. La Cour fut hier fort nombreuſe & très-brillante, à l'occaſion de l'anniverſaire de la naiſſance du Roi d'Eſpagne, Pere de notre Souverain. La Ville en Corps, les Tribunaux, les Miniſtres Etrangers; tout ce qu'il y a de Gens de diſtinction fut faire compliment à ce ſujet à S. M. qui admit tout le monde à lui baiſer la main. Il y eut le ſoir une triple décharge du Canon des Châteaux. On continuë en toute diligence les préparatifs pour l'armement des Troupes de ce Royaume.

De ROME le 25. Decembre. Le Pape aſſiſta Dimanche paſſé à la Chapelle pour le 4e. Dimanche de l'Avent & fut ſe promener l'après-midi dans les Jardins Gavotti & Guiliani. S. S. fut Mardi dire la Meſſe à la Minerve à l'Autel de S. Dominique. Elle admira beaucoup le Mauſolée qu'on a élevé à Benoît XIII. ſon Predeceſſeur & ſon Bienfaiteur, après quoi Elle ſe rendit à l'apartement du General des Jacobins, qui étoit malade. On conduiſit Jeudi dans les Priſons de cette Ville un faux Monoyeur, qui avoit été ſurpris avec des coins de Teſtons, Jules & autres monnoyes. On a commencé depuis quelques jours à ſonner toutes les cloches pour les Agoniſans, par ordre exprès de S. S. qui veut que pareille choſe s'obſerve tous les Vendredis à deux heures après-midi. S. S. ſigna ces jours paſſez pluſieurs petites Fermes, comme du papier, de la cire &c., dont M. le Tréſorier lui aporta les Baux.

De BERLIN le 2. Janvier. On a eu nouvelle des Frontieres de la Sileſie, que le 17. du paſſé le Roi y avoit harangué ſes Troupes au moment qu'elles alloient entrer dans cette Province. Le Roi étoit à la tête de ce Corps de Troupes qu'on peut apeller une Armée, ſon diſcours étoit conçu en ces termes.

FIGURE 0.4 Title page, *Courrier d'Avignon*, January 20, 1741. © http://www.gazettes18e.fr; Bibliothèque Municipale d'Avignon (public domain).

Inevitably, consolidated in this way, these periodicals also presented a landscape of notions that went beyond the thoughts of any individual *philosophe*. Literary journals also tended to treat the movement as a whole. This may have dissatisfied individual authors, but it spread a wide variety of different Enlightenment ideas. If governments compared their position with the past, they now faced more cacophony than had their predecessors in a time when publicity had been more strictly controlled by royal and religious adherents, either by the guidelines of government or by the timidity of publishers.

Curiously, the lowly advertiser (the *affiches*), at least where they existed, also significantly contributed to readers' positive reception of philosophic thought. Although the first of these began in Paris in 1751, growth was slow with only six imitators by 1760. An exponential flowering then occurred with the establishment of another twenty-eight *affiches* scattered throughout the realm. With each attached to its local region, such papers published advertisements, mainly for real estate, but also for books and a wide variety of retail goods, along with exchange rates and ship arrivals. The *affiches* borrowed material from other similar publications, and published the pieces that locals also submitted. Narratives of local activities, anecdotes, and a smattering of banal political news and other ephemera were crammed into these modest publications.

What makes such publications so interesting from the point of view of the Enlightenment is that much of their content furthered the goals associated with this progressive movement. Here, individual *philosophes* were scarcely mentioned, but some of the general outlines of the Enlightenment project as well as its subtexts were indirectly reinforced. Of course, these periodicals were in no position to challenge directly the government or the church. Nonetheless, in the avalanche of adverts, nostrums, and local items a strong message emerged: the existence of another "elite"—that inherent in small city life. Moreover, the papers pictured the modesty of family life characterized by humility, simplicity, hard work, and not surprisingly, presented a positive image of the "heartland." If not a Voltairean idea, this depiction of "noble" townspeople with different "honorable" values certainly was compatible with Rousseau's imagined society.

Such an emphasis on the bucolic family sat uneasily, as the editors themselves realized, with the commercial mayhem registered by the massive number of adverts there— advertisements for many products, based on wide variety of appeals. The "price for everything" message competed with the special privileges presumably possessed by the rich and ennobled. But whatever the seeming contradictions then and now, these two points (commerce and affection) constituted pillars of Enlightenment thought; aristocratic leisure and arranged marriages seemed to be overthrown by sentimentality and love. Unexpectedly, this sector of the press expressed most consistently, though indirectly, many tropes of the Enlightenment project, some of which contested one and another.

Of course, the French *philosophes* and their counterparts across Europe also authored many works directly troublesome for Old Regime government and challenging to Old Regime society. Making these ideas more accessible, beyond the reviews in the press, was the spread of reading clubs and, in Catholic Europe, clandestine publishing. Libraries too opened their doors to novelties, at least to some extent. In England and then its North American colonies, public libraries sprang up, and their collections increasingly included many Enlightenment books, which borrowers checked out. Great libraries that had been assembled by princes also began to open, if not lend, their collections to the public. Exceptional was the access offered by the Wolfenbüttel Library headed by the eminent philosophe Gotthold Lessing, which even allowed its holdings to circulate. Benjamin Franklin's Library Company of Philadelphia was another innovation that included virtually all of the Enlightenment canon. Compensating further were reading clubs and book lending operations that made books available even to working-class readers. New organizations collectively brought new publications to new audiences. Widening the public sphere still further were governmental efforts to suppress some works. Such efforts often backfired by creating *causes célèbres* that publicized notions that were challenging for the political and social elite to control.

Indeed, as the century wore on, government control of the public sphere seemed to wane. Particularly of significance in this regard were coffeehouses, where conversation was difficult, if not impossible, to regulate. Separate rooms and small tables secreted "dangerous talk" from watchful supervision of the police. Creating even more "room" for a range of ideas was the general informality of these establishments, which appeared

FIGURE 0.5 Wolfenbüttel Library, University of Göttingen, woodcut, 1885. © Getty Images.

to encourage egalitarian seating and frank exchange. Similarly, theaters enhanced the open expression of public opinion in much of Europe. Despite close censorship of productions everywhere but Britain, audiences gave a full-throated positive response and felt emboldened to opine on all aspects of the performance—including its point of view. The unusually mixed audiences—by class and even gender—encouraged unfettered opinions that increasingly seemed to determine which plays had long or short runs.

One additional organization that may have enhanced the role of the public sphere was the arrival and growth of Freemasonry. Beginning in the early eighteenth century, lodges of the Freemasons proliferated throughout Europe. A fraternal order, Freemasonry enjoyed a network of support that enabled mercantile connections and aided travelers. From 1771 to 1775, England sported 383 separate lodges. Although contemporaries worried that this network was a proto-revolutionary body, and some scholars have agreed, Freemasonry appeared in many different guises across a wide political spectrum.

Whatever the political inclinations of Freemasonry, it reflected, and likely enhanced, the growing sense of equality that was emerging throughout the West. Lodges ran on quasi-democratic principles including election of officers, majority rule, and public speaking. Meetings proceeded democratically as well. Furthermore, members referred to themselves as brothers, neglecting to use the labels and titles frequently attached to individuals in that era. One should not overemphasize the equality and see in these bodies some harbingers of socialism; Freemasonry was essentially dominated by the bourgeoisie, and membership fees and dues guaranteed that such organizations would exclude the working classes, foreshadowing the preponderant role of the middle and professional classes in the century's democratic revolutions. Masonry was, however, one more eighteenth-century phenomenon that seemed to undermine traditional social hierarchy. Freemasonry, like the press, wider distribution of books, an emphasis on

FIGURE 0.6 Freemason symbol—mystic eye with interlocking circle and triangle. © Getty Images.

politeness, coffeehouses, theaters, and other developments, too many to develop here, contradicted or at least evaded the social and intellectual inclinations of monarchical Europe and further publicized and projected new principles broadly into society and into the expanding polity.

ENLIGHTENMENT CULTURE

Emerging from the wide spread of Enlightenment, ideas provided a cultural echo—surely not as coherent even as the disparate views that made up its ideology. While the ideas were complex and prominent advocates argued over them, culture is a far more difficult matter to track. Scholars who study intellectual history commonly focus on formalized ideas debated by those who carefully define and debate specific notions. Cultural history expands the evidentiary field to include ideas that manifest themselves in everyday life as in public debate, polite and impolite customs, personal encounters, and much more. A commonsense interpretation might insist that Enlightenment culture consisted of a loosely linked group of concepts that were constantly in a state of rearrangement.

Culture, despite its evanescence, remains incredibly important insofar as it provides the skeleton of social life—perhaps an unwritten script that contemporaries understood to a greater or lesser extent and that allows millions of people to navigate in limited space without constant unanticipated confrontation. A modern example, though one that would penetrate far beyond the narrow Enlightenment, might be a modern fender bender on a busy street. Largely initiated with little knowledge of the minimal rules, thousands of times a day people get out of the cars, behave civilly, and provide contact and insurance information to each other. Surely aggrieved in this circumstance, people might quarrel—but they seldom do because they understand what is expected. Thus, like the behavior at the wreck, the focus of this volume, the cultural "script," remains somewhat illusory but potent. Though embedded or assumed, these notions govern societal interactions. To ferret them out, experienced scholars endeavor in this volume to find the customs that recur and provide the sinews of social interaction.

This volume, part of a series that seeks to explore culture in the West from antiquity to the present, considers, as do the other volumes, nine axes of cultural meanings important to general functioning of large groups of peoples. This is a difficult terrain for all the authors but an extremely important one as well if we are to comprehend how our predecessors lived. In fact, ascertaining a society's culture deserves equal status with the study of ideas. While a small elite has significant access to debates over ideas, the entire society imbibes shared understandings reflexively to function in daily life. Ideas and behavioral expectations interact, but some might describe the difference as that of an electrical grid compared to a thermostat. To further this end, this introduction briefly examines some of the key areas in which Enlightenment ideas developed and concludes by considering the interaction among these themes.

One qualification is in order. Although culture is omnipresent, it has boundaries. National cultures, regional cultures, linguistic cultures, and many other divisions are in evidence. Our primary focus remains the culture and ideas of the highly literate, which means almost exclusively the upper middle classes and the nobility. This group, with its sophisticated reading habits, has often been seen to constitute much of the eighteenth-century "public" as defined by Jürgen Habermas. But by the end of the early modern period, many commoners of substantial means intruded into the corridors of power and challenged the nobility and hereditary power in general. Women as well as men became central to the life of ideas in this era. People in colonial outposts, including the Indigenous and even the enslaved, helped to indirectly shape the thoughts of the Enlightenment too. So the social contours of the phenomenon we call the Enlightenment are at once narrow and broader than one might expect.

KNOWLEDGE

One of the primary preoccupations of the age of Enlightenment was knowledge itself: what was knowledge? Where was knowledge to be found? How could knowledge ever be organized and made useful? The first chapter by Chad Wellmon considers how "knowledge" was defined in the era of the Enlightenment. Limited by political and religious pressure, knowledge might be imagined as a coherent discourse that could be mastered by a single individual. Yet the explosion of information in the era of Enlightenment proved so great that mastery remained well out of reach of everyone, at least to some extent. In fact, knowledge, which had been previously construed as a somewhat manageable field of reliable information, took on new structures to make it accessible. As the number of texts exploded in the wake of the printing press and the growth of the book trade, efforts focused on systematized knowledge that could be arranged. However, this barrier proved porous as the explosion of information undermined all efforts at establishing limitations. Cultural gatekeepers endeavored to narrow the field by eliminating unreliable information, but this eventually gave way to the creation of indexes that simply provided a reference guide to sources. Heralding the much later internet, this new system was understood even contemporaneously as tentative, always renewing itself. Knowledge had changed from a set of discrete, authenticated, and authorized information to an open-ended field.

Most contemporary libraries possessed small collections of books that shared space with various artifacts and appeared more like museums. Collections were meant to reflect reality as contemporaries envisioned it. When the famous *philosophe* Gottfried Leibniz came to direct the Wolfenbüttel Library in 1691, books had been cataloged largely without systematic ordering. Leibniz' contribution was to group books together that shared similar topics. This departed from an approach that had little purpose except that it allowed the particular reader to locate a book that person already knew about and wanted. Leibniz' goal paralleled the developing notion of knowledge by congregating books of similar purpose. In nearby Göttingen, its great university soon ordered its library acquisitions around scholarly interests.

Despite such changes in arrangement to support better the creation of knowledge, libraries, like catalogs and indexes, eventually had to yield to the constant expansion and dynamism of knowledge. In fact, Enlightenment conceptions of the systematization of knowledge, begun in an era of order, came to point to an open-ended, always changing future. The effort at increasing flexibility and responsiveness led to a freer structure and greater creativity. Likely, the collapse of the old system contributed more to the future than an updating ever could have achieved. These uncontrollable phenomena presented an overwhelming challenge to cultural policing at first dominated by ecclesiastics. Only at the end of the nineteenth century would this problem find a new solution—research universities and their disciplines that would become "search engines" themselves.

HUMAN SELF

Even eclipsing the transformation of knowledge and libraries was the dramatic change of the notion of the "self" as it emerged in the Enlightenment. In the European West, social boundaries generally were strict and difficult to cross. Different formal social distinctions continued to matter greatly, whether one lived as a serf or as someone to whom others owed significant social deference. More common was a three-tiered system with nobles on top, often with legal inherited titles that provided hereditary benefits. For example, most nobles in France paid no land taxes and benefited in other ways as well. At the other end of the spectrum stood millions of peasants and urban laborers. Such individuals, especially in the countryside, had little chance of individual advancement, which was reserved for the educated middle classes and nobles. Group pressure could be maintained in part because most people had an identified social station that carried certain expectations.

Nonetheless, as Howard G. Brown shows in his chapter on the self, many factors coincided in the course of the eighteenth century to enhance personal identity and goals. Changes in the notion of consciousness began with the middle and upper classes but spread and have continued to spread all the way to the present.

To explain how the self's focus moved away from God, we can point to three especially critical factors: sensationalist psychology, imagination, and sympathy, all of which relate to experience. As society presented individuals with more choices, individuals came to feel they possessed more autonomy.

In the rise of individualism, we cannot neglect the thought of John Locke, who argued that it was the senses that activated the mind, which in turn led to consciousness. Accumulated over time, these feelings produced individuality and something that came increasingly to be known as the "self." The imagination in fact encouraged the individual to embrace a distinctive personal identity. Bernard Mandeville then added to this speculation. Brown summarizes the English philosopher's definition of sympathy as

> self-love and the basis for character formation within society. As an extension of self-love to others, sympathy serves to shape individual character by taming and directing passions. The resulting self is not a distinct entity, but a way of integrating signals from the senses and social experience into a single, moral agent. Thus, self-love is not evidence of the Fall, but a foundation for community in a complex commercial society.

Nonetheless, philosopher David Hume added that human "sympathy tempered this self centered notion of experience." When such personal attributes intersected with the consumer revolution and capitalism, the modern self had, indeed, been conceptualized.

Beyond philosophical interventions lay many political, cultural, and social practices of the era, which created a critical intersection between raw ego and opportunities for reflection. Increasing interiorization of both Catholic and Protestant practice allowed for personal reflection and a balanced self emerging from moral texts and personal self-centeredness. Combined with the open-endedness of knowledge, the autonomy of the self was reframing culture as less of a trap and more of an opportunity.

ETHICS AND SOCIAL RELATIONS

Contemporaries worried that even were "society" conceived as a secular entity, it had to be held together by divine authority. Otherwise it would never be able to cohere at all. Accompanying this anxiety was the explosion of consumerism for the middling and upper classes. Further, would luxury goods undermine middle-class morality? Although the Enlightenment created spaces for some social mixing, the *philosophes* focused their attention almost entirely on the educated, noble and bourgeois, at the top of society. Individuals were arranged on a ladder with the monarch at the top and the poor permanently at the bottom, without any consideration of exchanging places.

The Enlightenment was also a moment, as Sarah Maza explains, for the arrival of "society" as the place for interaction for human activity, with God seemingly uninvited. Contemporaries advocated new efforts to ensure social peace, including some that proposed the alternative of the market as a panacea. Adam Smith's notion of self interest as an automatic and invisible governor of social relations qualifies, but few endorsed it. Infamously, Bernard Mandeville, in his version of an autonomous society, *The Fable of the Bees* (1714), explained that some evil was, in fact, necessary for survival.

Other more convincing definitions of cooperation emerged. Fraternal societies and intellectual groups could, in the cities, create comfortable social space, and newspapers created social bonds. "Society" in general began to replace the highly differentiated social space that had been populated by guilds and vast social divisions. The academies, salons, and Freemasonic lodges all featured intellectual interaction and collegiality. Book clubs were also egalitarian. The introduction of coffeehouses promoted, at least to some extent, communal sociability, although they also were socially segregated. The "cures" seemed to apply little to the working classes.

What was seen as an escape valve for at least the peasantry was the concept of the wholesomeness of the countryside. The painter Jean-Baptiste Greuze encouraged this view by depicting rural life as a place of abundance filled with healthy and attractive young men and women—not to mention "adorable" livestock. Women, because of their virtue, could, according to contemporary belief, anchor the conjugal family. Associated with such domestic women were the emotions of sensitivity and sensibility. Family love could provide what once had been the dominion of the Almighty. Novels reinforced the emphasis on love through a focus on sensuality; and empathy toward other humans led to crusades against torture and brutal executions. Barbarity seemed on the wane. The limited impact of these cultural emanations, however, seemed to disappoint their adherents, but the revolution led to patriotism replacing the notions of the countryside and women as iconic.

In short, the anomie in the urban social sphere introduced by secularism and the absence of an activist God led to freelance solutions, far from anything seemingly codified.

POLITICS AND ECONOMIES

Related to and overlapping to some extent with the study of society was attention to the economy, as Gary Kates demonstrates. Most treatments of the ideology of the Enlightenment focus on the trajectory of criticism aimed at current governments, government-backed religion, and monotheist belief. Much writing of the time either advocated mixed government with divided sovereignty (Montesquieu); made brutal, sarcastic attacks on royal and aristocratic abuses (Voltaire); and/or advocated the possibility of direct democracy (Rousseau) as alternatives. In fact, all of these ideas received significant acceptance later in the revolutionary era. But equally important to the eighteenth century was the development of political economy—or as the term is more commonly used today, economics.

Interestingly, James Madison, later the American president, encountered in a college class on moral philosophy a work by the preeminent political theorist Montesquieu, *The Spirit of the Laws*, to which Madison repeatedly returned. Despite its more than one thousand pages, this volume went through more editions than any other such work in the eighteenth century and became a bestseller in its age. Even *The Federalist Papers*, a work designed to influence opinion in the adoption of the American constitution, cited *The Spirit of the Laws* more than any other work, including the great classics of political theory.

Innovatively, Montesquieu focused heavily on commerce in addition to his other philosophical concerns. He had given up on monarchy as a beneficial novel force and turned to commerce, which he believed improved manners and mores. Trade, in his opinion and that of many contemporaries, produced codependency among neighbors. Adam Smith followed Montesquieu in emphasizing the salutary effects of commerce. Although Rousseau disputed Montesquieu's praise of trade, others continued to rally to the latter's side. David Hume and Antonio Genovesi in Italy supported him. The well-known French revolutionary Mirabeau shared Montesquieu's general views, as he too

FIGURE 0.7 Joseph Louis Masquelier, *Mirabeau arrives at the Eliseum*, engraving, 1791. ©
Getty Images.

asserted that monarchy could advance property rights and investments in agriculture as
important reforms (Figure 0.7).

But a corrective conclusion emerged to the optimism expressed by Montesquieu and his
allies—including Adam Smith—in the justly famous book, Abbé Raynal's *A Philosophical
and Political History of the Settlement and Trade of the Europeans in the East and West
Indies* (1770). This work of 2,100 pages, which had expanded by a third edition (1780) to
5,000 pages (ten volumes!), described the spread of European trading to the entire world.
Considered a test worldwide of Montesquieu's optimism about trade, Raynal argued its
potential benefits to humanity as a whole. But Raynal's brutal attack on the Atlantic slave
trade and Diderot's criticism of European expansion as barbaric meant that Raynal's
impact was mostly a mixture of positive regard for commerce's economic impact but
horror regarding its means.

In sum, political economy proved an important part of the Enlightenment culture, but
it stirred up passions as well as emboldened elite readers. As Peter Gay has averred about
the ideas of the Enlightenment, its culture likewise encouraged ambivalence about its
boldest claims and complicated results.

NATURE

Notions of nature too were central to philosophical speculation in the Western world of
the early modern period, as Brian Ogilvie explains. The *philosophes* typically stipulated
an omniscient and omnipotent God who had created the universe. Attributed to this deity
was a purity that guaranteed the fundamental laws of nature to be commensurate with

godliness and thus necessary and desirable to discern and live by. Consequently, central to the Enlightenment were these laws, which were embedded in the creation and continued to eternity. This understanding conflicted with revealed religions of Judeo-Christian origins in which God showed himself to humankind and persistently intervened. In short, despite debate over the meaning of natural law, the belief in an impersonal God who manifested himself only in the basic workings of the world underpinned all of the other Enlightenment fields of speculation. Such optimism provided the foundation of what historian Carl Becker called the secular "heavenly city" of the Enlightenment.

Natural law itself, despite providing the bedrock for much of the Enlightenment, continued to be debated, even as philosophers came to draw a distinction between natural law, a set of universal moral principles rooted in human nature and accessible to reason, and the laws of nature, physical principles established by God that, for most, could be known through empirical investigation. The latter, mechanistic interpretations of the perpetuation of God's will on Earth proved problematic because such a theory opened the door to atheism. For a society where atheism was unthinkable for most, this was unacceptable. Hence, one debate centered on whether observable and extraordinary divine intervention was required, beyond the laws of nature, to maintain the cosmos in its ideal state. Miracles, and thus God, were perhaps necessary.

Despite the speculation about natural law and physical properties, natural law mainly involved morality: human beings' mutual obligations, impressed in their nature by their Creator. *Philosophes* were increasingly inclined to think instead in terms of natural rights, installed in individuals and, for some, capable of being alienated. The *philosophes* would go on to consider a whole host of related questions: was there a state of nature before society came to exist, and if so, how was society established? Were stages of social development arranged in precise chronological order? How did natural rights relate to society's positive laws? Further, and even more problematic, was the state of nature "good"?—an assertion that had underpinned reliance on nature as a sure guide to proper ethical behavior.

Despite such quandaries, *philosophes* and the educated public remained committed to natural law. Few were attracted toward atheism, though more wondered about this possibility than in previous periods. In fact, the *philosophes* in their speculations and arguments mainly assumed a rational and divine God whose creation and laws could inspire and justify the desire to discern God's law to guide human activity. Nonetheless, both *philosophes* and the public had an inkling that they might be whistling in the wind.

One very important corollary of the interest in natural law was vigorous scientific investigation that sought accurate understanding of the functioning of the universe as predictable through systematic laws. In fact, it was seventeenth-century René Descartes who managed to model the movements of the planets according to theoretical laws, revealing to contemporaries that coherent laws of physics governed the universe. Buoying astronomy was physics, but interest included other scientific areas. The impact on society was palpable as systematic laws came to explain natural disasters such as earthquakes and runaway fires.

RELIGION AND THE DIVINE

Scholars have generally agreed that the most consistent and formidable target of the Enlightenment was revealed religion in general and its most prevalent European form, Christianity, in particular. Although the *philosophes* and other Enlightenment thinkers ranged over a wider variety of subjects, consistently they envisioned belief and a reference to an active interventionist God as the opposition to an immense number of their goals. Specifically, at the bottom the Enlightenment elevated empiricism, documentation, and rationality, which they saw as antithetical to revelation. Much of their time was dedicated to undermining religious conviction as well as authority.

The treatment of religion in the *Encyclopédie* of the 1750s, the single most important compendium of mid-century Enlightenment thought, offers us, according to Jonathan Sheehan, an excellent way to gauge the *philosophes'* general view. Because attacking religion was, in fact, dangerous in that era, contemporary critics had to be cautious. Almost always they stipulated that God was real but had been understood by man in many different ways. Nonetheless, the *Encyclopédie* also strategically attacked the existence of God by using a careful approach that was apparently intended to thwart persecution by the authorities. Instead of denying God's existence, the *philosophes* chipped away at existing defenses of the existence of God. Thus, the *philosophes* could and did raise doubts under the rather cynical cover that they were merely endeavoring to strengthen such defenses. Many proofs depended on using the complexity of nature to demonstrate the necessity of an omnipotent first cause. For example, a baby has a mother; a mother has a mother; and so on. Only eventually was God the cause of this chain of events, with humans more directly responsible. But from the point of view of many religions, this effort proves problematic because other peoples held that revelation from God was direct to the prophets and central to the faith. This technique ultimately undermined claims about the superiority of Christianity.

Another method used routinely in the *Encylopédie méthodique*, the successor to the *Encylopédie*, was to treat God reverently but then to cross-reference his actions to other subjects that increased doubt. An interesting example can be found in the entry for heaven, as Sheehan asserts in his essay:

> Presumably of interest to someone wanting to know about God, [the entry for paradise] tells readers that nobody knows where it is, "in the third heaven, in the heaven of the moon, in the moon itself." "There is almost no part of the world ... where one has not searched, in Asia, Africa, Europe, America, the banks of the Nile, the Indies, China, the island of Ceylon, or the mountains of the moon in Ethiopia."

Likewise, the entry for revelation is nominally religious but then considers how the existence of one belief or another relies on dubious claims: "a modern author believed he proposed a substantial difficulty, remarking that revelations are always founded on previous revelations, 'Christ on Moses, Mohammed on Christ, Zoroaster on the religion of the mages, and so forth.'" Even more outrageous to believe was Rousseau's 15,000-word "creed of a Savoyard vicar," part of his famous *Emile*, in which he described the trajectory of a young man moving from doubt to piety. In it, Rousseau could not resist depicting a clergyman who threw in a few sex tips to Émile and his beloved Sophie.

In the end, the efforts of the *philosophes* terrified religious authorities, as neither churches nor universities could resist well. Enlightenment writers used different genres, with more or less gravity, and most important, a spontaneous use of materials that made countering them difficult. More devastating was that these provocateurs drew material from everywhere making an orderly response impossible. This was one of the lasting effects of the Enlightenment. But one may conclude that the *philosophes'* waffling between belief in a deity and thorough going cynicism reveals as well some uncertainty and less dogmatic views than other ideologies.

LANGUAGE, POETRY, RHETORIC

At the forefront of concern during the Enlightenment was the multiplicity of language barriers across the world, evidenced in part by Jonathan Swift's *Gulliver's Travels* where the protagonist observes a project designed to improve communication by shortening polysyllabic words as a reform that was intended eventually to abolish words entirely. Christy Pichichero notes that this improbable solution joined others, including the wildly impractical suggestion of carrying around the relevant object to eliminate nouns. Indeed, this "proposal" spoofed efforts by the British Royal Society, but more seriously constituted a complaint about the general impenetrability of individual languages to humanity writ large. Part of the solution might emerge from social organizations such as Freemasonic lodges, which hoped to produce sociability, knowledge creation, and knowledge sharing. Ideally, a universal language would develop, and highly ornamental language, as Petrus Ramus put it, would be eliminated.

A search for the sources of language also absorbed the *philosophes*. Essentially, two tendencies emerged: rationalist and sensationalist. The first (rationalism) depended on the notion that humans were endowed with a particular mental structure in the brain, predicating a shared language based on *a priori* rational cognition. Others believed that "sensation" created language. As language existed to convey thoughts, humans must have a shared structure. To explain this notion of sensationalism, a story emerged about two children, alone after the flood. Neither had ever met another of their own species. Lacking memory, they lacked imagination. In the words of the French *philosophe* Condillac, "their mutual discourse made them connect cries of each [as] natural signs." Traumatic experiences produced mutual sympathy. Consequently, "by instinct alone these people asked for help and gave it."

Beyond the polar opposites—rationalism and sensationalism—lay other studies of language and its close relations, rhetoric and poetry. Rousseau developed his plan for language as a powerful weapon in societal improvement. Focused on the frailties of humans, he tried to constrain or at least purge the selfishness natural to the species. He believed his system would, however, only work in an incredibly homogeneous society. In fact, his choice for such a place where such policies might work was Corsica, a selection that showed that he was expecting not only high morality but also ethnic similarity—and that on a primitive island separated from other social groups. Nonetheless, Rousseau would assert that language was not initiated around good will but, rather, fundamental self-interest, as in one of his most famous lines: "This is mine."

Debate around language contributed elsewhere to the culture of the Enlightenment. Within the theatre, a group of the artists (elocutionists) advanced arguments about the emotional power of spoken words. Against this endorsement of speech stood the view that the gestures that communicated meaning best were those of the "mechanical" school, which concentrated on oratory and content. Diderot was such an advocate of the mechanical school that he believed that even using earplugs, he could follow a performance as long as he could pay sufficient attention to gestures. Debate spilled out in other directions including the relative value of emphasizing the "Ancients" or the "Moderns" as the source for writing and performance. Questions of gender and natural language likewise roiled the literary world. Around language acquisition swirled many other issues, including efficacy of form. Arguing that rhetoric and elocutionary styles could stimulate affect in listeners, the *philosophes* noted differences that usually might depend on listeners. Specific styles were recommended with poetry perceived as a medium amenable to producing a range of reactions. Music might have a similar impact, but with less precision. Even political attitudes might be communicated effectively through the use of different styles of literature.

THE ARTS

Eighteenth-century Western visual art has sometimes been seen as a time marker midway between the great glory of Renaissance art and the innovations of the radically new departures of the nineteenth century. Beginning with an analysis of an explosive encounter between a South Pacific Islander and an English interloper, Douglas Fordham records the interpretation of the art of the period. Fordham notes that, in fact, it broke important new ground. At first eighteenth-century painting, drawing, and sculpture were relatively indifferent to what artists encountered overseas in "primitive" art, especially as it did not depend on classical perspective. But this interaction ultimately produced a very significant reaction. In fact, contemporary Europeans came to believe that primitive art might furnish the material for "naturalism" or the concept of revealing the world as the eye sees it. While this encounter did not produce a reevaluation of non-Western art, it had a significant impact on stylistic transitions within the European tradition.

At the same time, artists of this period embraced publishing multiple copies of an artwork. That involved innovation in materials and techniques, which in turn produced more accurate tones and colors in the processes of reproduction. Likewise, artists began to experiment with depicting unstable objects such as spinning tops and steam from a cup of tea. Nonetheless, naturalism could not be rendered with pure objectivity, as in fact it posed what Fordham calls "a constant and evolving set of challenges of those charged with its reproduction."

At the close of the eighteenth century, then, neoclassicism still reigned in stylistic terms, but important changes were emerging. Nude males, generally well-muscled and with clearly European visages, were prevalent. But even this central point did not go unchallenged—once again as a result of contact with non-European populations. An English painting of 1807, entitled *A Meeting of Connoisseurs*, features a group of "gentlemen" gathered to evaluate a painting that shows the classical proportions of the Apollo Belvedere. A closer look at the painting reveals that the model for the Greek god is a Black chimney sweep. Rapid imperial expansion along with debates about slavery further reduced the centrality of the white male model. The justly famous painting by Benjamin West, *The Death of General Wolfe* (1771), specifically complicated admiration for the central symbolic expression of Western painting. Here the nudes are Native Americans. How could the iconic nude remain ideal if enacted by a person of color?

Thus, in art we find the persistence of old forms, including the nude, whose context had already been under siege in the Old Regime. Redeemed, however, by the French Revolution, white male bodies show up in *The Tennis Court Oath* (1791), in a large number of delegates swearing allegiance to the revolution and its National Assembly. Still, David's preliminary sketches of floating heads for this painting remind the viewer that death in the revolution undermined the resurrection of the classic nude. And with that came devastating effects on the dominant political class of the Enlightenment as well as on the political culture that was to be built to replace the monarchy with a regime of male notability.

HISTORY

On the eve of the Enlightenment, history writing was still dominated by scholarship that focused mainly on lineage, royal and ecclesiastic, as well as details of battles. This scholarship reinforced the centrality of royal and noble efforts, whether secular or religious. But Caroline Winterer reveals that when the focus widened in the course of the eighteenth century, as historians began to write about the rise and fall of empires, a vision of different periods (or ages) whose character changed according to their purposes in culture and ideas emerged. In addition, over time historians' attention turned to progress, the idea that society and humanity gradually improved in tandem, evolving from barbarian to civilized behavior.

A number of factors drove this development. Among them was the dramatic rise of cities, which clearly indicate progress. By the second half of the eighteenth century, London (but also Paris and Amsterdam, among others) had become quite large. Persisting were the ruins of earlier ages, indicating by comparison that these cities were experiencing substantial growth. The evidence of change further suggested the notion of progressive stages of human development; long before Karl Marx inscribed a clear progression of steps, Europeans and especially Scots were beginning to think in similar terms.

Also revealed were remnants of the classical past, even in London, which had been a relative backwater in the era of Roman dominance. Progress received a particular boost from a retelling of the history of Rome, the greatest city in the West, which had begun from very unpromising beginnings. Greece too could be used to tell a similar story of strength rising out of prior weakness. Even its chief weakness—the division of the peninsula into numerous small city-states—had encouraged the growth of centralized government. Although classical history covered periods of strong leadership, it could also be employed to encourage anti-absolutist accounts of the past. Simultaneously and somewhat contradictorily, Greece as well as Rome had been democracies as well—and some people in the eighteenth-century West began to embrace this ancient form of government as an alternative to the present regime.

Further enabling the expansion of history in the age of Enlightenment was the creation of archives from many sources, including governments. These records not only made possible the writing of history but also gave it a solid evidentiary base that strengthened its status as a source of truth. With archives, historical accounts might be either substantiated or undermined, and the former became more able to survive skeptical readers.

Political change—particularly the rise of revolutions following the American and French examples—further encouraged a history that was necessary to explain these gigantic gyrations themselves, but also numerous developments that followed. Those included the rise of capitalism, individualism, and middle-class values. With the establishment of public libraries, middling social classes could become involved in reading history. History writing, in turn, increasingly took up everyone and everything. This avalanche of information led to incalculable cultural change that encouraged democratic participation in public life.

Clearly then, the general outlines and direction of historical writing about the West, especially enhanced rather than tempered Enlightenment enthusiasm. Sadly, though, beyond the chronological bounds of this book, it was the dreadful turn of history in the first half of the twentieth century that changed the common perception of our shared past as a story of progress into a dismal tale that was hardly inspiring.

OBSERVATIONS

Although cultures varied considerably in the eighteenth century across the entire West, from the European continent to well into the New World colonies, the Enlightenment produced certain shared modern values sharply at odds with the Old Regime governments that gave rise to it.

Many factors actually encouraged continuity and stability in this period. Although republics had existed in the past and still did in a few small places, for the most part monarchs and princes reigned everywhere until the revolutionary era. Hereditary nobility was normal, and while means of ascension existed, families who held positions for a long time occupied the peaks of society. In France, a "society of orders" stacked social and occupational groups in a clear hierarchy.

Moreover, much law was not statutory but simply enshrined tradition, and its authority depended on momentum. Many countries had intermediate bodies with power, such as diets or parliaments, but they too were often hereditary or depended on peculiar and particular historical rights. State churches also tended to hold this system in place. Belief in the divine included the notion that God had ordained all creation. By definition, this creation was good and should not be tampered with. Thus, though natural law emerged in response in part to contemporary debate, since it emanated from God, it could be used to ratify the existence of the clergy and divine-right kings. In many cases, including France, monarchs were understood to be God's representatives on Earth so that political chiefs had the authority to maintain position.

But, during the Enlightenment, natural law partially gave way to natural rights that invested all people with the spark of divinity that ultimately justified "human rights." In this period philosophers and their readers wrestled regularly with this issue, and by the end of the eighteenth century "rights" were enshrined in both American and French revolutionary documents. Such rights included in the French and American cases the notion that all humans are created equal—an astonishing claim for a society like France that had hierarchies undergirded by law, not simply practice.

What had caused this momentous cultural change? Scholars have wrestled with this seemingly spontaneous alteration of circumstances. Nonetheless, several seemingly inexplicable transformations occurred that ultimately embedded Enlightenment ideas and culture in the minds and social practices of Europeans well beyond the small public of highbrow readers. In fact, for some time a Marxist scholarly explanation had focused on worldwide trade and the growth of mercantile interests in the eighteenth century as the "cause." This new "bourgeoisie," according to this theory, sought to expand its interests in domestic commerce and international trade by changing the laws and the mores to accommodate this quest. While this interpretation has generally fallen into disfavor as much research questioned its findings, the rise in global trade is no doubt one factor in explaining the revolutionary transformations that convulsed the Atlantic at the century's close. Montesquieu was not alone in thinking that such commerce built trust among peoples looking for an alternative to endemic warfare. Instead of hierarchical governments and religious organizations, horizontal and equitable relations have been linked to the rise of the *philosophes* and also to their impact.

Whether or not trade was the cause, change was afoot from early in the century. This volume focuses on its nature and magnitude. In contrast to the particular interlocking cultural features that may have worked in tandem to produce a relatively fixed hierarchical culture, the Enlightenment synthesis as it formed feasted on alternate and complex understandings that became dominant as ecclesiastical and monarchical dominance receded. Unlike the social and economic factors that reinforced a traditional society based on monarchical principles and a rigid social structure, the arrival of a new "enlightened" and disruptive culture remains surely unpredictable and difficult to explain in retrospect. Although scholars have offered many suggestions—a growing population, weariness from constant wars in the early modern era, the impact of the age of exploration, the epistemological effects of the Scientific Revolution, religious pluralism in the wake of the Reformation, and lots more—the transformation of culture remains something of a mystery, the exploration of trade's impact notwithstanding.

In fact, without searching for a root cause or causes, one may begin almost anywhere among the topics featured here and observe the many connections, some convoluted, that reveal the new structure of Enlightened European culture. One important sign that change was in the air was the explosion of knowledge, so great that no one, not even great libraries, could maintain a stable approach to cataloging and shelf placement. Where knowledge had once to be sorted neatly into the trivium and quadrivium, new books swamped even the most assiduous librarians.

The disruption of a common knowledge base for the elite that might have received a thorough (for the time) education, changed the stable notion of self, which began to founder in a surfeit of information. Further undermining a fixed "self" was an expanded economy that produced not only new occupations but ones without clear, even legalized boundaries. Reaffirming these new realities was Lockean theory, which shredded the fixed social identity provided by corporatism and law as well as for elites and guilds in favor of personal development. The notion of sensation, in which every individual processed different information and had different experiences and acted accordingly, created a range of responses and more potential allowance for greater personal choice. To some extent, linguists disagreed by arguing that language development predicted otherwise. Linguists differed here by arguing that language development was consistent among individuals; otherwise communication would prove impossible. Encouraging this inclination among linguists was a strong theoretical desire to advocate for transparency as opposed to arcane models of speech that had been the fashion. The ultimate goal was consistent with other notions that promoted cooperation as a value that might help one understand how the new individualism could be modulated. Also different from the previous cultural regime were social and economic roles. Although the poor were generally consigned to fixed rungs on the ladder, their social superiors could achieve what they perceived as personal fulfillment. According to Adam Smith, trade proved to be a natural regulatory device; and Bernard Mandeville's *Fable of the Bees* proposed an economic system so organized as to allow elites to imagine themselves independent, even as they were in fact pursuing socially useful tasks. Even as women actually lost autonomy, they were still lauded as key to societal harmony. Adam Smith's economic theory reinforced the notion of autonomous behavior that was regulated through the workings of the market. Though manipulated, individuals might imagine personal achievement, not seeing themselves as cogs in the machine.

If God had retreated in the worldview of the *philosophes*, his role in nature had not. In fact, natural law created by God was assumed to have a moral and just purpose as opposed to serving as a prop for the status quo. The Enlightenment was most radical in relation to organized religion, which the French *philosophes*, in particular, saw as archaic and out of touch. However, though skeptical of a direct, observable divine role for God in daily life, the *philosophes* were very seldom atheists and promoted a practical, if cynical, notion that the unwashed needed the comforts and restraints of a God who had programmed into the system incentives and restraints. The deity who respected clockwork had created an ethical logic in place of his old role as miracle maker. This allowed the educated a new role in shaping politics and society.

Finally, notions about progress undergirded confidence in the rectitude of change ushered in by Enlightenment culture. The *philosophes* believed they were part of and witness to positive developments for individuals and for society as a whole. In fact, history as it came to be written in the eighteenth century emphasized improvement over time of which Europeans came to believe they were the progenitors as well as the beneficiaries. They did recognize that the peoples of newly discovered lands were exploited, as the Abbé Raynal revealed in detail in his bestselling *Philosophical and Political History of the Two Indies*. But interesting evidence for Enlightenment interest in natives, including their thoughts, appearances, and habits, emerged in art as well as philosophy. This subtle shift speaks loudly to a growing appreciation of the "other" in Enlightenment culture, though a sense of European superiority was hardly eradicated by the Enlightenment and forms of exploitation of non-European peoples, including slavery and colonialism, were only to grow in the next century.

Osmosis is the way most people learn culture. While contemporaries might never read a philosophical tract or even a pamphlet, they learn culture, for instance, language, from listening to others. Further, individuals do not learn in discrete packages like coursework in a university. Consequently, a short conclusion can only outline the way that these many conversations might have intersected and been received by men and women of the Enlightenment era. The chapters in this volume consider how the essence of the Enlightenment both stemmed from and seeped into the population at large.

Still, with seriously different new and increasingly accepted ideas, the new approach did mean a rupture with the past. The break regarding unquestioning belief in a creator and interventionist God, for example, remains too radical to be explained by evolutionary change. Why, in fact, did a God who could create observable miracles become relegated to working behind the scenes through nature? Scholars and contemporaries have in fact disputed too many explanations to be rehearsed here. Politics might be added to the explanatory mix. Revolutionary change swept through the West, introducing a radical reaction to the status quo, particularly the pyramidal society with an interventionist God and the hereditary elites on top. The more the aristocrats and king resisted, the more that challenges to the structure of the old regime, sustained by a creator God, crumbled. Such a superficial explanation cannot be developed in these few concluding sentences, but noteworthy enough is the fact that agnosticism, and even atheism, along with other potent doctrines spread somewhat, undermining past polity and encouraging the advent of the revolution. What is indisputable is that if this struggle for innovation began with the Enlightenment, it is far from over still. The cultural legacy of the Enlightenment was complex, consequential, and in the end, worldwide.

CHAPTER ONE

Knowledge

CHAD WELLMON

To search today is to Google—to use Google's search engine to find something on the Web. The search for meaning, love, purpose, or God—search as an existential feature of being human—has, in little more than a decade, been reduced to a secondary meaning. From its now almost apocryphal beginnings at Stanford in 1998, co-founders Larry Page and Sergy Brin described Google as a technology designed to "organize the world's information." In Google's first press release on June 7, 1999, Brin said that a "perfect search engine will process and understand all the information in the world."[1] In its first decade, Google focused on the former—processing and organizing information—by trying to map a World Wide Web that was essentially an ever-expanding and highly fragile set of documents connected by hyperlinks. Google's search engine helped people navigate the Web by modeling how web pages linked to one another. Google's search engineers thought of the Web as a medium of documents. Its search engine was, thus, document-centric, keyword based, and highly contextual. It returned search results whose key terms were embedded in particular texts, documents that, once you clicked on one, framed information in a particular way. Indeed, in its first decade, Google helped define "search" in two distinct ways: (1) as a set of navigational tools that orient people within some broader media environment, and (2) as a set of epistemologically creative technologies that adjudicate, evaluate, and (help) create knowledge.

In our contemporary world, though, we can easily forget that Google did not invent search. For our search technologies, as well as our own experiences of digital deluge and information overload, have a history.

Seeking to safeguard knowledge secured in the saeculum, early modern scholars devised note-taking strategies, maintained common books, and developed keyword-based reading strategies. In her landmark study of such techniques, historian Ann Blair described early modern scholars in dogged pursuit of information—"discrete and small-sized items that have been removed from their original contexts." She contrasts the "information" managed by early modern scholars to "knowledge," which, as she puts it, implies "an independent knower."[2]

But over the course of the eighteenth century, as both the quantity and quality—the various types of printed material, from lexica and dictionaries to the first specialized periodicals and journals and encyclopedias—of printed objects increased exponentially across Europe, it was the very notion of an "independent knower," at least as an ideal, that waned. By the nineteenth century, it had given way to a different set of epistemic ideals and virtues: communal, extra-individual, and shared. As intellectuals and scholars adopted and adapted these different ideals, they also began to conceive of what counted as authoritative and legitimate knowledge differently. *Knowledge* vacillated between more individual or personal notions and more objective, extra-individual notions.[3]

The eighteenth century is often studied as a watershed moment in the history of knowledge. Many scholars focus on the rise of new methods for ascertaining truths, as well as the expansion of the body of people who could be said to be knowers, to include, at times and in different ways, women, the Indigenous, and the nonliterate. In addition to this expansion lay the retraction of what was thought to constitute knowledge or even to be knowable. However, the history of knowledge in eighteenth-century Europe can also be productively told as the history of search, rooted in the technology of the book. Confronted with the proliferation of print and the transformation of institutions struggling to adapt to it, knowers of all sorts had to reassess and reinvent long-standing philosophical, scientific, and theological conceptions of what it meant to know. But they also had to learn how to navigate, filter, and search the material and media of knowledge— all the new and not-so-new forms that knowledge assumed between the late seventeenth and early nineteenth centuries. Conceiving of knowledge—a notoriously abstract term— in terms of search can focus our historical concerns on the ways in which "knowledge" entails not just heady concepts or personal beliefs but also a complex environment of objects, practices, techniques, and institutions through which people come to know. These eighteenth-century search technologies—books *about* books in particular—helped eighteenth-century readers make their way through a perceived surfeit of print.

In the end, considering the history of knowledge in eighteenth-century Europe is not just an exercise in antiquarianism. It can help us historicize practices and concepts that contemporary techno-utopians, in their breathless anticipation of perfect search engines and thinking machines, might have us forget; outline various technologies and practices of *making relevant* or *orienting*; and, finally, make better sense of our own digital cultures of knowledge and what it means to know in the twenty-first century. It also helps us make sense of the legacy of the Enlightenment.

We may imagine ourselves to be engulfed by a flood of digital data, but eighteenth-century intellectuals across continental Europe imagined themselves overwhelmed by books. Similar anxieties plagued readers in England as well, where Alexander Pope wrote in the *Dunciad* of "a deluge of authors [who] cover'd the land."[4] Late eighteenth-century German intellectuals saw themselves as having been infested by a plague of books, circulating contagiously among the reading public. To be sure the sheer number of texts in German lands did increase at a strikingly sharper rate between 1770 and 1800 than at any other time in the seventeenth and eighteenth centuries, an increase of about 125 percent.[5] But these fears of plagues and contagions were not merely quantitative anxieties—how many books exactly?—but more basically epistemological and ethical ones. They were anxieties about what counted as real, authoritative knowledge when information seemed ubiquitous and easily accessible, a question of continued relevance.

FROM KNOWING TO KNOWLEDGE

Looking back at the beginning of the nineteenth century at the semantic shifts that "knowledge" (*Wissenschaft*) had undergone over the course of the eighteenth century, an article in *Adelung's Lexicon* summarized the changes. At the beginning of the century, knowledge had been used to describe a subjective "condition in which one knows something"; it referred to the "clear and distinct ideas" of an individual knower.[6] By 1800, however, knowledge had come to refer not only to a subjective state or condition but "objectively" to describe "general truths that were grounded in each other." Knowledge no longer only referred to the mental processes of an individual. The first, more "antiquated" usage referred to a "particular insight" or mental capacity, whereas the second referred to an internal relationship among ideas themselves and, more broadly, an increasingly distinct realm in which these ideas had taken form—in objects, systems, media, practices, and institutions. Over the course of the nineteenth century, it was this second notion of knowledge that, in German-speaking lands at least, came to predominate. Knowledge referred not just to a particular mental state or capacity but also to a domain that increasingly exceeded any such states.

For much of the eighteenth century, German intellectuals and scholars associated authoritative knowledge with comprehensive or complete knowledge—what they termed *Vollständigkeit*. The concept oriented their design of and interactions with scholarly technologies such as lexica, encyclopedias, and related "finding aids" or "books about books." In the first half of the century, the quality of such books was judged to be a function of how "comprehensive" they were. But scholars rarely agreed on what counted as "complete" or "comprehensive" knowledge and how, if at all, it was to be achieved. By the end of the century many scholars began to pit "complete" knowledge against "systematic" knowledge. According to their critics, projects whose goal was "comprehensiveness" merely aggregated material stuff. "Systematic" projects, in contrast, created or represented coherent wholes. To use the language of the eighteenth century: should such scholarly and intellectual technologies facilitate aggregation or aim to constitute knowledge themselves? The story of "complete" knowledge—of what German scholars and intellectuals termed *Vollständigkeit*—and the epistemological and ethical questions that it raised can be told through a few exemplary projects.

First published in 1715, Christian Jöcher and Burkhard Mencken's *Compendious Lexicon of the Learned* was a lexicon of scholars and authors that, as Jöcher and Mencken put it, provided a "complete" and "coherent" account of learning from ancient Greece to eighteenth-century Germany.[7] The frontispiece offers a striking visual image of a "comprehensive" organization of knowledge. Extending from the bottom of the page to the top right side is a bookcase filled with books of all shapes and sizes. Its immensity is highlighted by a marked contrast with two much smaller men standing opposite it on the left-hand side of the page. One of the two men, cast in bright light, stands with an outstretched arm gesturing toward the towering shelf of books, whose spines are visible in a single glance. A vaulted ceiling extends across the top of the page and imbues the entire image with a sense of light-filled openness in which everything is illuminated and knowable. This image is a visualization of what Jöcher and Mencken claim their lexicon to be: an accessible, complete, and clear view of the entire scholarly world (Figure 1.1). It is an image of what eighteenth-century scholars referred to as the "empire of erudition" (*Reich der Gelehrsamkeit*)—a unified, homogenous realm of knowledge, theoretically accessible to all fellow scholars in print. The lexicon reveals, as though it were pulling back a curtain as suggested in the top left-hand corner, an already organized and established set of knowledge.

And yet, this particular image of knowledge or learning is one of book bindings, closed books shelved one beside the other. Further, the sheer immensity of the bookshelf, how it dwarfs the two men opposite it, is ominous. With the unlimited vertical horizon, the bookshelf could expand infinitely. With every newly published book, it could continue to grow upward, but the two men would be left to gesture in vain toward an accumulating mass of print. Furthermore, the shelf may well be visible, but there is no ladder, no way to actually reach the books. Would its shadow not ultimately obscure those two men gazing skyward? What was to prevent the bookshelf, teetering under the weight of

FIGURE 1.1 Frontispiece, Christian Jöcher and Burkhard Mencken, *Compendious Lexicon of the Learned* (1715). © Leipzig University Library, Litg.436-c.

ever-more print, from tipping over and crushing them? The image of a bookish scholar dying in his library was a common trope. An entry in Zedler's lexicon tells the story of Johannes Vossius, who "after climbing a book ladder, which suddenly broke and left him smothered in books, finally died on March 17, 1649 at the age of 72."[8] The proliferation of print was an existential matter. The metaphors of contagion and disease came later in the 1770s and 1780s.

If a reader were to have opened the *Compendious Lexicon of the Learned* and quickly leafed through just a few pages, he would have found a mass of bibliographic details about printed texts: titles, publication dates and locations, edition information, all arranged according to "learned" authors in alphabetical order. Little to no information or discussion about the content of the books is made available, just *metadata*.[9] Just like the frontispiece in which only the spines of the closed, shelved volumes are visible, Jöcher's "complete" account of learning only identified where knowledge may possibly be found or created. It provided an order not of knowledge per se but of print. It organized a textual tradition, what scholars carried over and passed on through time. Jöcher and Mencken's lexicon did not offer a comprehensive account of the content; there was almost no discussion of ideas, concepts, arguments, or anything other than bibliographic facts, nor were there any obvious judgments about the value of one book over another. The lexicon was critical in sense of its time; it analyzed printed material. The lexicon, its principled eclecticism—mass of information jammed together—assumes a certain epistemological stance: the purpose of search technologies such as itself is to help scholars navigate and locate texts so that they, not editors or technologies, can create knowledge and evaluate texts.

In addition to the lexicon, Jöcher also edited a journal called *Deutsche Acta Eruditorum*, whose subtitle—"or the history of the learned, who apprehend the current state of literature in Europe"—attested to the purported unity and cohesion of knowledge. Jöcher's journal was an amalgamation of previously distinct textual genres: book catalogs, trade fair catalogs, correspondences among scholars, and review periodicals. Together, Jöcher's journal and lexicon assembled the elements of what he termed "book history," an account of all knowledge available in print.[10] Both were to provide a "complete" account of the world of learning,[11] for Jöcher "completeness" meant material completeness: a full account of all available knowledge on a given topic or identification of every printed item on that topic.

And yet Jöcher repeatedly acknowledged his failure to achieve bibliographic completeness in practice. Already in the third edition of his lexicon (1733), he conceded that his lexicon "remains incomplete." In an almost pitiful tone, he complains that he just could not keep up. "Everyday," he wrote, he happened upon new books or colleagues who would inform him of a previously unknown scholar or author. In his preface, he even listed the names of over one hundred scholars about whom he had no knowledge beyond their name. He was acutely aware of the gaps in his "complete" account. Rather than abandoning his pursuit, however, he promised that each new edition would be "more complete" and contain more and more extensive entries.[12] The future offered the promise of fulfillment—a unity deferred. In the last edition that he edited (1750), Jöcher conceded that none of the previous editions had been "complete."[13]

The development of Jöcher's projects exemplified the basic epistemic ideals and virtues of the broader culture of German learning in the first half of the eighteenth century: a utopian desire to identify and locate *all* printed texts; a cultural belief that print technologies could sustain a homogenous, contemporaneous world of knowledge; a cultural confidence that printed objects lent knowledge an almost timeless presence (compared to more fundamentally historicist conceptions of texts and reading that emerged later in the century); and the idea that completeness did not imply coherence of ideas or concepts either within one book or among various books. Scholars such as Jöcher were the vernacular inheritors of early modern humanists such as Konrad Gesner for whom *ad fontes* suggested quite literally that all human knowledge was textual knowledge, and, thus, to know was to engage and to care for textual objects.[14]

In the first half of the eighteenth century, the authors and editors of similar projects across Europe dealt with similar concerns about knowledge in an age of media abundance. In his *Preliminary Discourse to the Encyclopédie*, which appeared at the beginning of the first volume (1751), Jean le Rond d'Alembert (1717–1783) wrote that the broader goal of the great French *Encyclopédie, ou dictionnaire raisonné des sciences, des arts et des métiers* was to accumulate and connect an "infinitely varied" human knowledge. But it did so in two different ways. As an encyclopedia, he explained, it set forth "as well as possible the order and connection of the parts of human knowledge," and as a dictionary it contained the "general principles that form the basis of each science and each art, liberal or mechanical, and the most essential facts that make up the body and substance of each."[15]

For Denis Diderot (1713–1784) and d'Alembert, the encyclopedic and dictionary functions of the *Encyclopédie* were designed to make the complexity of the world more manageable and navigable. Like their German contemporaries, they understood this complexity in starkly material terms. "The number of books will grow continually," noted Diderot, "and one can predict that a time will come when it will be almost as difficult to learn anything from books as from the direct study of the universe."[16] The unceasing production of printing presses filled "huge buildings with books" and threatened to create a second nature, a distinct world of print.

For Diderot, the prospect of the continued proliferation of print threatened to make any encyclopedic effort to comprehensively map all of knowledge futile. The perceived progress of knowledge, its continued growth in accord with print, rendered any such organizational efforts obsolete or, at the very least, provisional. What good, he asked, would the encyclopedias of the Renaissance be to us now in the middle of the eighteenth century?[17] With their cross-references (*renvois*) to other articles and to the general map of knowledge, the famous tree, the individual articles of the *Encyclopédie* were intended to alleviate this concern by encouraging active reading across articles and volumes. But the basic concern about the inability to provide a comprehensive account of knowledge remained.

Another of the eighteenth century's biggest books was Carl Linnaeus's *Systema Naturae*.[18] First published in 1735 in Leiden on the front and back of six folio sheets, the first edition of the *Systema* included eleven pages of observations and grids and in its first issue employed some of the largest sheets of paper to circulate in eighteenth-century print culture. But when its thirteenth edition was published in 1788 in (Liepzig), it had expanded from 11 to over 2,000 pages. Print could not contain all the knowledge that he and his colleagues kept producing. Linnaeus tried to manage the flow of information by keeping track of specimens sent to Uppsala from all over the world with a collection of small sheets of paper (the size of index cards) labeled by species, genera, and sexual system and stored in a cupboard.[19] But it proved too much for any one book. Each of these projects, from Linnaeus's *Systema Naturae* to d'Alembert and Diderot's *Encyclopédie, ou dictionnaire raisonné des sciences, des arts et des métiers*, implicitly and sometimes, as in the case of Diderot, explicitly acknowledged the impossibility of achieving "completeness." In 1750 Jöcher finally did as well. Capitulating to the futility of his pursuit of "completeness," he changed the title of his journal from *German Journal of Erudition* to *Reliable News on the Current State, Transformation, and Growth of the Sciences*. Because the journal's volumes had become "too numerous and confused," he admitted, he could no longer report on a homogenous, unified empire of erudition. By changing the title, Jöcher acknowledged that as print technologies changed so too did knowledge, but the imagination of a smooth, easily accessible world of printed knowledge remained stubbornly out of reach. Even intellectuals and scholars gradually abandoned *completeness* as an orienting goal. However, they then began to articulate another ideal—the notion that knowledge was not just a personal capacity but a material reality. Print did not simply undermine synthetic knowledge; it made it possible.

By 1750, then, German intellectuals and scholars had started to articulate other notions of *Vollständigkeit* and to create other different types of "books about books" and search technologies, such as Johann Sulzer and his *Brief Account of All Sciences*. In the first edition published in 1745 almost a decade before the French *Encyclopédie,* Sulzer argued that an encyclopedic book, which he defined as a complete account of learning, should fully and accurately represent the natural order of the sciences. "Order," he wrote quoting Pope, "is Heaven's great Law."[20] Like the rest of the divinely created order, knowledge, or the sciences (*Wissenschaften*) as he called it, also had its proper "Rang"—hierarchical order (xx). For Sulzer this *natural order* was grounded in the human faculties, namely, reason (*Vernunft*) and sensibility (*Sinnlichkeit*). A "complete" account of knowledge would be one that accorded fully and perfectly with the order of the human mental faculties.

In the 1745 edition, Sulzer described his "complete" and accurate account of knowledge would not simply collect the "material of learning" but organize and relate it to the human mental faculties. And, like Diderot and d'Alembert a decade later, he described this faculty-based order of knowledge as a tree. In the second edition (1759), however, Sulzer replaced the tree metaphor that echoed that Diderot and d'Alembert's because, as Sulzer wrote, "human knowledge constantly grows," the "material of learning is endless." Thus, he concluded, any efforts to fix the order of knowledge or provide a comprehensive account of it were epistemologically naïve and ethically dubious (arbitrary hierarchies). His new edition, as he put it, would simply "make do" by organizing all sciences according to eight classes: philosophy, history, arts, mathematics, physics, philosophy, law, and theology. He devoted a chapter to each category and suffused them all with discursive descriptions of each science and its underlying concepts. But he made no attempt to relate them to each other.

For Sulzer, previous finding aids and search technologies could indiscriminately collect as much information as they could because, he claimed, the store of human knowledge had been limited. Contemporary finding aids, in contrast, had to be more selective because they were being written in a "modern age" that produced an endless stream of new knowledge.[21] Given such an unprecedented expansion of new knowledge, so visible in print, modern texts had to filter out the "vain, useless, or outrageous" and eliminate the eclecticism that characterized previous eighteenth-century projects. With the second edition, Sulzer had given up on his initial attempts to offer a formal account of how the sciences and the different "parts" of knowledge related to one another. He had eschewed the bibliographic character of previous search technologies. What he was left with was the aggregation of discursive information into distinct categories, what he termed "containers."

In the final two decades of the century, a raft of broadly similar projects appeared across Europe, each one pursuing distinct notions of comprehensiveness but typically casting themselves as either formal or material, systematic or comprehensive, critical or archival. Material projects were crafted to collect and organize as much information as possible and present it in an accessible way, using preestablished categories. Formal projects, in contrast, were designed to highlight common methods or shared concepts and assumptions about what made knowledge cohere; to reveal the underlying concepts and ideas that bound knowledge together; and to discern "internal relationship" of all knowledge. Knowledge, in this second, more formal sense, was not reducible to its material forms, but it was also extra-personal. Ideas, propositions, thought, knowledge were now understood to exist outside of individual minds and, suggested some intellectuals, had an internal order of its own.

Many of the material projects tended to collapse under their own accumulating ambitions. *German Encyclopedia, or Universal Dictionary of all Arts and Sciences* began in 1778 and collapsed in 1804, having only reached the letter "K." Friedrich Martinis's

Universal History of Nature in Alphabetical Order managed over a period from 1774 to 1793 to produce eleven volumes that ended with the letter C. One reviewer noted in 1790 that "since the appearance of the first volume fifteen years have passed and two letters have yet to be completed. If this continues, there will be over 100 volumes and the last one will appear sometime in the middle of the twentieth century."[22]

But if the possibility of limitless content stymied many material projects, the profusion of possible categories and organizational schemas confused the more formal projects. With the ascendance of Immanuel Kant's so-called critical philosophy across Germany around 1790, many scholars believed they now possessed a basic set of categories that would "finally" allow for the complete organization of all knowledge. Instead, many of them succumbed, as one editor put it, to a "classificatory fury."[23] The philosopher Wilhelm Krug, for example, began his encyclopedia with a relatively standard classificatory scheme. But then he continued to divide these basic categories into evermore subcategories, and subdivide and subdivide. Krug's self-described "systematic" organization of the sciences repeated in its very form the hypertrophy of Enlightenment taxonomy projects that he mocked. *Vollständigkeit* was not just a question of quantitative comprehensiveness but also, perhaps even more fundamentally, cohesion.

SYSTEM AND TRUTH

Whereas the material projects (like their bibliographic predecessors) made few claims about the internal coherence of the information or knowledge that they collected, the more formal projects sought to create, or reveal, a "system of human reason."[24] The authors of these projects sought to discover what they considered the underlying principles of knowledge or, as they often put it, its "internal coherence," which they contrasted to a *mere* aggregation of facts, an arbitrary alphabetical arrangement of information, or a set of inherited (usually from early modern universities) institutional categories. These new projects, claimed their defenders, were concerned with pure, systematic, and true knowledge unbound from print. They typically distinguished themselves from the material projects and the earlier bibliographic projects by appealing to some criterion of truth. Knowledge was now not simply something that scholars needed to organize and represent in exhaustive acts of erudition; it was something that scholars had to evaluate and, ultimately, authorize as knowledge. Knowledge was, in other words, an honorific, a status bestowed upon information or what some scholars referred to as mere facts. A "system," as the philosopher and encyclopedist Wilhelm Traugott Krug (1770–1842) and other post-Kantian scholars understood it, represented a critical standard of truth or trustworthiness. "System" was the opposite of *Vollständigkeit*.[25] Whereas *Vollständigkeit* stood in for quantity and material completeness, system stood in for internal coherence and "truth." The aim of more formal projects was not simply to organize information about print and make print navigable; it was to constitute what counted as real knowledge.

THE SELF-ORGANIZING INDEX OF PRINT

But as the editors and authors of material and formal projects debated the proper aims of search and the purposes of knowledge technologies, the more bibliographic-oriented compendia common in the first half of the eighteenth century returned. Or perhaps they had never disappeared. As print proliferated and scholars grew ever more anxious about print plagues and floods in the last two decades of the eighteenth, scholars and intellectuals began to suggest, sometimes implicitly sometimes explicitly, that print had begun to assume an order of its own. Even some of the highly formal, Kantian-inspired projects were full of citations, discussions of editions, what they termed *Bücherkunde*—knowledge of books.

It is here, in the common turn to citational networks and the indexical forms of books and periodicals, that we can discern the emergence of a different approach to search and its technologies and practices: the idea that print was not only something to be managed by inventive humans or evermore complex encyclopedias, but that print had begun to manage itself. Scholars increasingly after 1780 referred to a "world of print" endowed with self-organizing capacities.[26]

The notion that printed knowledge was in some sense self organizing or internally coherent can be understood by the changing significance of that most banal of book elements: the index.[27] Index and indexical, in this context, refer to a much more capacious sense than might be common now. Indices are typically understood to be alphabetically arranged lists of topics, oftentimes located at the back of a book. These existed well before the eighteenth century and even before printed books or the Catholic Church's great *Index liborum prohibitorum*. An index was already understood to be a navigational tool to help locate a topic within a particular book. But over the course of the eighteenth century, the idea of an index took on a much broader function. Indices would help navigate not just particular books, collections, or libraries but, as one scholar put it, the entire "world of books" (*Bücherwelt*). Moreover, intellectuals and scholars increasingly conceived of the complex relationships of texts, readers, and knowledge in indexical terms. Indices would open up or make accessible not only individual books located physically in one place, such as a library or even a particular shelf; instead they would identify and locate *texts* that were scattered in many different places. They offered a virtual unit, as they were systems of metadata, representing not knowledge itself but knowledge about knowledge. In 1811, Johann Adelung's dictionary defined an index as a "register" (*Verzeichniß*) that locates the particular "page or place" where a certain name or term can be found; it helped readers navigate not just individual books by organizing topics—commonplaces—but by identifying particular pages within a print realm that was increasingly regarded as distinct and internally coherent. By the end of the eighteenth century, the continued growth of print was understood less as a problem of excess and overload and more as a challenge of making abundance searchable and navigable.

Consider, for example, the continued development of Jöcher's *Lexicon of the Learned*. In the 1726 edition, the "Aristotle" entry was just a few lines; it included a statement describing Aristotle as a philosopher, a student of Plato, and tutor to Alexander the Great. Almost sixty years later, the same entry from the 1784 edition describes Aristotle as the author of "scores of texts" and lists the bibliographic details of several modern, printed editions of individual works as well as those of several complete editions. Aristotle was no longer only a philosopher; he represented a node in the ever-expanding world of print.

Whereas Jöcher's lexicon focused on printed monographs and other types of books, Johann Heinrich Christoph Beutler and J. C. F. Gutsmuth's *Universal Subject Index* (1790) focused on periodicals, attempting to publish an index of every article published in a German periodical between 1700 and 1798. "In the countless hoards of periodicals," they wrote, "the best fruit of scientific thought" lay hidden, knowledge that was "otherwise only the possession of scholars and stored in books," which most people did not understand and couldn't read or didn't want to read. This scholarly knowledge was brought into "universal circulation through periodicals, purified, and translated into a general vernacular, and passed through people's hands like coins."[28] Periodicals allowed for everything that had lain "useless and meaningless" to be "searched and read and revealed." Periodicals provided for the gradual and distributed unveiling of knowledge.

But Beutler and Gutsmuth acknowledged that periodicals presented a particular problem to search.[29] They both distributed knowledge in the present as well as expanded it over time. Periodicals put new knowledge, according to Beutler and Gutsmuth, into a broader and more accelerated circulation because periodicals, like journals, were printed more regularly and more quickly; they changed the shape of knowledge by untethering it from individual monographs and their slower production times. This shift in the very shape of knowledge—of how knowledge is imagined—they suggested, made it more important than ever to know where to look. They facilitated this form of search by providing an even more stripped-down form of metadata than had their predecessors. Their "repository of human reason" (*Magazin*), as they described their periodical index, assigned each periodical an abbreviation (the *Berliner Monatsschrift*, for example, became B.M.), greatly shortened the names of months (*Dezember* became Dez.), and offered nothing more than bibliographic details.[30] Immanuel Kant's (1724–1804) famous 1784 essay "An Answer to the Question: What is Enlightenment" appeared like this: "*Was heißt aufklären*" Kant. B.M. J. 84. Dez. S. 481. Beutler and Gutsmuth identified particular topics and articles across the realm of print. In doing so, they treated print as a coherent, self-referential system. For them, the index achieved *Vollständigkeit* by modeling an order that was internal to the world of print itself. Readers needed only *Lokalkentnis* (vii), meaning exact coordinates by which to orient themselves in this particular world.

And yet, whom did Beutler and Gutsmuth imagine would read their *Universal Subject Index*, and how? Clearly, they designed it not to be read linearly, to sustain a transformation, but rather to mark paths and boundaries through a world that existed beyond any individual reader. The index was meant to orient possible readers and, thus, possible knowers within a realm that exceeded any single reader's capacities but that had become an essential condition of knowledge. It, and the range of epistemic media that followed, were indices for tilling the printed ground of authoritative information or truth.

The development of these types of print technologies contributed to the notion, increasingly common by the end of the century, that knowledge was not simply or even primarily a personal capacity or subjective state but also an extra-personal, objective reality that had taken a particular material form—in printed encyclopedias, monographs, or periodicals. The idea of a body of knowledge that was not necessarily bound to individual knowers raised the prospect that knowledge existed that had not yet been discovered or that had been forgotten. Knowledge could refer not just to a present capacity but a future potentiality and a common possession cultivated and shared among fellow knowers, scholars, or as would become the case in the nineteenth century, researchers. Knowledge, wrote Wilhelm von Humboldt in 1809, is a "never fully solved problem," an endless process of inquiry over time, a development embodied and transmitted in a community of fellow knowers who shared responsibility for it.[31]

INSTITUTIONS OF KNOWLEDGE: THE LIBRARY

These eighteenth-century debates about a comprehensive knowledge and the bibliographic, material, and formal ways to achieve it (or not) give us a sense of the rich conceptual history of search. But we also need to consider how these concepts and practices came to be institutionalized, that is, how they helped transform established institutions and also how these institutions helped transform these practices and epistemic ideas. Over the course of the nineteenth century, the most important institution for organizing knowledge became the research university, which had precedents in the University of Göttingen, established in the 1730s, though it only really rose to prominence in Germany in the first half of the nineteenth century and then in the second half in the United States. But crucial to the rise of the research university in the nineteenth century was, first, the development of the research library in the eighteenth.

According to Krug, a successful lexicon or encyclopedia would have provided not only an overview of all sciences but also "directions" for how to organize a big library.[32] Comparing an encyclopedic order to a well-organized library stretches back to at least Johann Alsted, who termed his encyclopedias "instar Bibliotheca philosophicae."[33] The shifts in the order of knowledge over the course of the eighteenth century, then, can be observed not only in the emergence of encyclopedics and periodicals of periodicals but also in the interrelations of books and cataloging practices of libraries from the late sixteenth to the early nineteenth century.

Few medieval university libraries contained more than one thousand individual titles, and their collections were constrained by a curriculum that itself was fixed by laws stipulating the texts to be read each semester.[34] Limited collections were also a function of the types of books printed in the first centuries of the printing press. The invention of movable type in Europe did not create immediate pressures on libraries to acquire a fundamentally broader range of titles. As book historian Lucien Febvre notes, "The immediate effect of printing was merely to further increase circulation of those works which had already enjoyed success in manuscript."[35] Print production in its first centuries focused on making Bibles more accessible, supplying students and teachers with the established canon, and providing prayer books and practical piety and devotional texts.[36]

But even beyond the fact that earlier libraries tended to have smaller collections of books, the libraries of the sixteenth and seventeenth centuries and the first part of the eighteenth century would have been difficult to distinguish from museums, cabinets of curiosities (*Wunderkammer*), or archives on other grounds. These libraries were spaces not just for books but for all that an individual collector deemed interesting. The library as a particular place restricted almost exclusively to books did not exist until well into the eighteenth century. Only over the course of that century did libraries emerge as the spatial counterparts of the printed *bibliotheca* and scholarly journals of the eighteenth century and, eventually, became essential features of the modern research university, not to mention urban public life.[37] In this sense, the evolution of libraries and catalogs parallels the developments traced in the last section toward a more objective account of knowledge.

Describing the public library of Hamburg in 1727, Kasper Friedrich Neickel offered a glimpse into one such library:

> On one side of the library one could see behind glass doors an entire row of human and animal skeletons, stuffed fish, snakes in jars of alcohol, snails, sea plants, stones, the head of a walrus and a bird of paradise, various aromatic timbers, urns, burial lamps, tanned human leathers, surgical, mathematical and physical instruments, a compass, a metal concave mirror and two globes; on the other side stood two book repositories; and on the pillars, which supported the entire gallery, were hung portraits of scholars.[38]

Like the stuffed animals and scientific instruments at their side, books were there to "amus[e] the curiosity of visitors,"[39] as J. J. Mascov, administrator of Leipzig's public library, put it in 1735. Such early eighteenth-century civic libraries provided space to be visited and observed. They were not primarily sites of the type of intellectual labor that would later come to characterize the research libraries associated with universities.

Before the mid-eighteenth century, the terms "library" and "museum" were nearly synonymous in German as well as in most other European languages.[40] Even the entry for *bibliotheca* from Zedler's early eighteenth-century lexicon describes a particularly well proportioned library, characterized by a "not insubstantial ornamentation" and a space that ordered "all kinds of mathematical instruments and works of art, architectural pieces and models, rare and beautiful paintings, small statures, ancient objects etc."[41] Compare this entry to the one for "museum": "art chamber [*ein Kunstkammer*], coin cabinet, rarity and antiquity chamber."[42] According to Jeffrey Garrett, both describe "rooms for interaction with stored objects, and book-objects arranged in libraries were treated no differently than any other place holder within the general taxonomy on display."[43] Books were, in other words, interchangeable with other objects contained in the library.

Moreover, like the other treasures arranged in such spaces, books in these libraries were often highly valued objects in their own right. In the late eighteenth-century novel by Friedrich Nicolai, *The Life and Opinions of Master Sebaldus Nothanker*, a fictitious book dealer named Hieronymus fondly remembers the days "of the beautifully thick postils, the extremely heavy medical reference books in folio, the *Opera Omnia*, the classical authors and church fathers in numerous folios. ... What are we given now instead of these important works? Small little books with only a few pages that pass from hand to hand—repeatedly read but rarely purchased."[44] Hieronymous laments the loss of these book objects to a modern, late eighteenth-century book market in which books had become mere commodities, one indistinguishable from the other. The importance of books as distinct physical objects was reinforced by the common practice of arranging them according to their page format; thus, their material size played a central role in determining their order on the shelves.

Despite how exotic some of these early eighteenth-century libraries seemed, they were not without their own order, whose form, function, and ends were simply different to those of most eighteenth-century libraries. These museums were akin to display rooms, which presented the visitor with a singular, unified order that was thought to reflect the order of nature. Describing his visit to the Wolfenbüttel Library in 1661, Herman Conring, one of the most famous scholars and polymaths of the seventeenth century, wrote admiringly of how this order could be grasped in one glance: "Truly it is greatly delightful, as it were, to learn in just one moment an almost infinite number of things, just as in fact often happens in other instances when much is suddenly given to be understood."[45] The order of books and objects in a library were presumed to "mirror the universe of knowledge" and the order of the sciences as laid out in encyclopedias or arranged in universities.[46] Mirrors that often lined the halls of the libraries provided sweeping glances of order. Such a visible order also meant that books and the other objects of the library were not stacked too tightly or hidden away on unseen shelves; that is, such an order presumed a limited number of objects, all accessible to sight. Furthermore, the order of the library was not thought to be proper to itself; rather, it was indexed to an external order presumed to correspond to a given natural world.

The most famous libraries of the Renaissance and the Baroque era were either private or based on the bequests of private collections and shaped by individual labors and proclivities.[47] University libraries in the same era, by contrast, generally had no acquisitions budget, and the majority of collections were based not on "title-by-title selection," but more on en bloc acquisitions of entire collections from professors or other private donors.[48] The renowned Altdorf Library, for example, bought the intact collection of Johann Wagenseil, Professor of History and Philology at Altdorf, in 1708. The collection included over six hundred titles and three hundred individual volumes (as well as a range of objects from a Lappland drum to various objects from a synagogue).[49]

These acquisitions presented those entrusted with the care of libraries with a range of problems, however. The sudden arrival of so many books overwhelmed staff: often new books were never fully integrated into the rest of the collection. Such acquisition practices also resulted in what today would be seen as an imbalance in coverage, since most librarians simply relied on what others had sought out for their own private collections.[50] These practices of accumulation, organization, and expansion tended to privilege the idiosyncrasies of the private collector over other schemes of acquisition. Library catalogs would often simply incorporate wholesale the newly acquired collection's catalog into itself. The Baroque library grew and expanded, as William Clark explains, as an "aggregated accumulation of the already accumulated."[51]

LEIBNIZ AS TEST CASE AND MIDDLE POINT

The seventeenth-century philosopher and polymath Gottfried Wilhelm Leibniz (1646–1716) was intimately familiar with the difficulties of organizing books and the limits of a universal library. When appointed librarian in Wolfenbüttel in 1690, he found the library had almost 26,000 print volumes and over 1,700 manuscripts. But, as was typical of the time, multiple titles were often bound together within a single volume, so it is now estimated that there were over 115,000 titles by over 56,000 different authors.[52] The collection's primary catalog was based on Gesner's classification with the addition of three supra-classes, including a *Manuscriptorum*, and the exclusion of four classes, including Metaphysics and Astrology. There were, then, twenty classes in all. Within each, books were further divided according to their format (folio, quarto, etc.) and numbered according to their location on the shelf. Newly acquired books were added to a shelf by placing decimals after the original volume, for example, 35, 35.1, 35.2, etc. The primary catalog, the book of books, was mainly a shelf list that recorded the physical location of the books.[53]

Soon after his arrival in Wolfenbüttel in 1691, Leibniz ordered the production of an alphabetical author catalog to supplement the systematic one (based on the organization of university faculties) already in use. He not only argued for the need of both but also for their mutual relationship. In so doing, he paved the way for the new eighteenth-century library. In his *New Essays* (not published until 1765, long after his death), Leibniz concluded his commentary on John Locke's *Essay Concerning Human Understanding* with a discussion of the division of the sciences and the difficulties of organizing a library. There are, argues the second interlocutor Theophilus (often understood to stand in for Leibniz), three ways of dividing the sciences. The first is a philosophical division of knowledge based on theoretical, practical, and logical arrangements. These divisions should not be understood as "distinct sciences but rather as different ways in which to organize the same truths."[54] The philosophical arrangement of the sciences, then, presumes not that sciences are distinct, internally self-contained bodies of knowledge, but rather that they are different forms of a more fundamental unity grounded in the singular truth. The second method is an administrative arrangement of knowledge, according to the faculty-based system of the university and the professions. This method is pragmatic and does not require one to have read a particular book to be able to place it in the system.

Then, in 1700, Leibniz sketched two schemes for a library classification system. The only plans that have survived are those more in accord with the latter organization and suggest that he saw the pragmatic advantages of the administrative catalog as more immediately essential. This set of plans is a more or less detailed version of a faculty-based arrangement according to the main classes: theology, jurisprudence, medicine, intellectual philosophy, philosophy of the imagination or mathematics, philosophy of the sensible or physics, philology or the things of language, and civic history.[55] "The accepted administrative division, according to the four faculties," wrote Leibniz, "deserves respect."[56]

Both the philosophical and university faculty-based methods of organizing sciences and by extension books were systematic and, thus, had certain limitations. Any strictly systematic method, contended Leibniz, led to a host of problems, the most basic being that individual book titles could reasonably fit within several rubrics. In a letter to the library secretary Johann Reinerding in July 1691, Leibniz wrote that he would prefer an "author catalogue in alphabetical order" (*Catalogum Autorum Alphabeticum*) over a systematic catalog because it would better facilitate working in the library—"one could then find the books without searching too much."[57] Given the limitations of a strictly systematic catalog, Leibniz' Theophilus concludes that the third and most ideal arrangement of books would be a systematic catalog that was supplemented by an alphabetical one.

But another one of Leibniz' critiques of these types of systematic catalogs had an even bigger effect on the modern catalog and organization of the library. He criticized Wolfenbüttel's plans to assemble a new systematic catalog from the books themselves (*ex ipsis libris*). Upon his arrival, Leibniz learned that a new catalog being developed was going to be based on the physical arrangement of the books on the shelves. Designing a catalog this way, he warned, would cost time and lead to innumerable mistakes. The already existing catalogs may not have been the most complete or efficient for finding the books, but they had been assembled with great care; therefore, reasoned Leibniz, any future catalog should be based on them and not on how the books were to be arranged on physical shelves. In effect, Leibniz intended to create a virtual library two steps removed from what he referred to as the "books in nature" (*büchern in natura*).[58] He proposed to displace the order of the local signature (*Lokalsignatur*), which tied the book to a physical place on a shelf, by a rationally (internally organized) system of knowledge.

Leibniz' key insight was to highlight the limitations of a shelf order of books and the difference between a shelf-based list and a systematic or alphabetical catalog. The former is constrained by the linear arrangement of physical books on a shelf.[59] Leibniz' interest in a systematic classification, one not tied to a shelf, is a claim that books have their own multidimensional relationships that can be traced better through cross-references and mutually interrelated catalogs. His suggestion to move away from a linear shelf list based on the physical arrangement of books and toward alphabetical and subject catalogs would have given the order of the library a more polydimensional objective form as represented in the material catalog. Library catalogs, as William Clark points out, became virtual libraries with their own internal logic independent of individual collector or librarian.[60] In this sense, Leibniz' vision of a systematic catalog freed from the actual bookshelf anticipated the distinct, objective world of books and its attendant technologies described in the previous section of this chapter.

THE ENLIGHTENMENT LIBRARY

The two largest Germanic book collections in the eighteenth century could be found in Vienna and Dresden, and both libraries started cataloging projects in the course of the century. Vienna began an alphabetical catalog in 1776 and a card catalog in 1780, but no catalog was ever completed. Dresden had a catalog dating from 1595 and had plans for an updated one in the 1740s with separate catalogs for each faculty, but it did not happen either. Similar problems emerged in Berlin. There, the Royal Prussian Library's collection had expanded from 50,000 volumes in 1750 to over 150,000 by 1786, but it was in notorious disarray. In 1790 four libraries were combined, but with no catalog or call numbers. Johann Biester, head librarian from 1784 to 1816, initiated an alphabetical catalog early on. A full-scale reorganization of the library did not begin until 1811, however.

It was the Göttingen catalog system that served as the model for all these others.[61] By 1800, the library at the University of Göttingen had over 200,000 volumes and was the largest academic library in the world, behind only the royal libraries in Vienna and Dresden in the German-speaking lands. It was distinguished not only by the size of its collection but also by the organization of its books. In the second half of the eighteenth century, as Naudé had anticipated, it became increasingly impossible to keep a library up to date.[62] Göttingen dealt with this problem by renouncing the *Bibliotheca universalis* ideal and confronting the limits of collecting books in the modern age.[63] The library in Göttingen never aspired to collect all book titles; instead, it sought to select titles in consultation with its university faculty. It became a research library, neither a *Bibliotheca universalis* nor a curiosity cabinet. Essential to its success, writes historian William Clark, was the "regular, serial acquisition of the now all too regularly producing academic market."[64]

According to Georg Heyne (1729–1812), who directed the library from 1763 to 1812, journals such as the *Göttingische Gelehrte Anzeigen* performed a "policing" function for the Republic of Letters by introducing a "normal law" for the rational order.[65] There was a "crucial synergy" between review journals and library acquisitions.[66] This was especially the case for the philosophy faculty, which created the library "in [its] image" by developing many of the library's organizational techniques and providing most of the librarians.[67] Philology professors (such as Friedrich August Wolf in Halle and Heyne's predecessor in Göttingen, Johann Matthias Gesner Göttingen) shaped other German libraries in their own academic terms.[68] The modern academic library developed out of this symbiotic relationship between philology and philosophy, with both realms assuming a differentiated and internally consistent empire of erudition. The university library became a supplement to the communal interests of the academic faculty, who were interested less in book format than in content. As one commentator put it in 1811, whereas private libraries were a function of a single person "who simply collects what mainly interests him," modern university libraries served the interests of "all."[69] In so doing, they helped constitute a distinct, objective realm of knowledge tied to books, similar to the journals and lexica of the eighteenth century.

Gerlach Adolph Baron von Münchhaussen, the Hannover minister who essentially ran the University of Göttingen for decades, enabled the library's new acquisitions policy by providing a comparatively generous library budget paid from tax surpluses.[70] Such a set, rational budget focused the acquisition efforts. Münchhausen regarded the library as an essential resource for Göttingen's scholars to bring fame to the university through their writing.[71] An acquisitions budget also rendered the older acquisition practices, primarily the reliance on gifts of entire collections, less important. After his visit to the University of Göttingen, Friedrich Gedike, a Prussian bureaucrat, reported that perhaps no other public library had "achieved as much as the one in Göttingen." The entire university, he continued, owed much of its "celebrity" to the library. The ever-expanding eminence of the scholars was a function of the library, which afforded them unparalleled tools for their work.[72] The success and prestige of the university was understood to be a direct result of the objectification of knowledge in the form of a library collection.

It was Göttingen's organizational schema, however, that made it the apogee of the early Enlightenment library. It cultivated an internal order distinct from the shelf lists characteristic of earlier libraries. Göttingen developed three catalogs: (1) an acquisitions catalog with bibliographic information that detailed the order of accession; (2) an alphabetical catalog not finished until 1789 that included the author's name, abbreviated title, place of publication, and date of publication; every author had a separate page; and (3) a systematic catalog developed between 1743 and 1755, which became the shelf catalog. The accession catalog was the only one to give full bibliographic information. It had twelve sections and it was arranged into four groups and three sizes. The alphabetical catalog had an academic category designation (*Fachbezeichnung*), but no individual numbers.[73] Heyne and his assistant librarian Jeremias Reuß created a systematic catalog that dictated a book's physical location in relation to other books, not in relation to a unique physical shelf space. This *Realkatalog* listed author, accession number, and title. It had six main parts and eighty-three subdivisions and "freed the systematic catalogue from the grasp of the physical arrangement of the collection."[74] The primary order of books, as William Clark points out, became less tied to their arrangement on physical shelves and more to the organization of citations and bibliographic data in a system. The library, then, had a double existence: physical books and shelves, on the one hand, and an internally coherent system that represented their organization, on the other.

In a historical sketch of Göttingen's acquisitions policy, written in 1810 while he was head librarian at the Royal Prussian Library in Berlin, Heyne summarized Göttingen's innovations in terms of science. The acquisitions policy was guided, he wrote, not by the "number of books," but rather by the "true value"[75] that they had for the plan and system of the library. The order of the library and its books embodied the order of a purposeful system. "In general," wrote Heyne, "only those books will be sought and chosen in which human knowledge ... has made an advance, progress or even a few steps forward." Those books that consist of mere "repetition, parroting, and compiling of what is already known or even the trivial" will have no place in the university library.[76] This is the imperative of science—the production of new knowledge over the display or representation of already-established knowledge—and the modern library is a material supplement to this progressive order of knowledge.

LIBRARY SCIENCE AS UNIVERSAL *WISSENSCHAFT*

In 1808, Martin Schrettinger, a librarian at the Royal Library in Munich, coined the term *Bibliothekswissenschaft*,[77] which he distinguished from bibliography and other forms of "book knowledge." In contrast to these purported sciences, he argued, library science is based on "firm" principles that make possible the "purposive" constitution of a library, whose main end is to facilitate "the speedy location of books."[78] Previous library catalogs had hampered this goal by continually expanding their systematic catalogs and thus allowing for the proliferation of the classes, categories, and rubrics designed to organize books. The "mass" and "growth" of books were a constant threat.[79] Echoing earlier concerns about the hypertrophy of systems and extravagances of some classification schemes, Schrettinger argued that a library catalog should be able to account for and accommodate two forms of "growth": books and the systems devised to order them. Furthermore, any organizational system, if it were to keep up with such growth, ought to function separately from the physical order of books on shelves. Books, he suggested, ought to be numbered and identified "independent of [their] location." Such a detachment was only possible through a "purposive-systematic compilation,"[80] an order inherent to the books themselves.

Unlike early modern accounts of libraries, Schrettinger made no effort to index his library science to a natural order. Instead, he described it as the "embodiment of all sciences and arts,"[81] that is, the system was the materialization of the order of the sciences. As a systematic account of the order of books, library science would be a science of the sciences. Revealing his Kantian influences, Schrettinger sought to sketch the "conditions of possibility of all order."[82] Moreover, anything other than books—coins, skeletons, and random objects—had no place in a library any more. A library, wrote Schrettinger, is a "substantial collection of books, whose arrangement puts anyone who longs for knowledge in a position to use every work contained therein according to his own needs and without unnecessary loss of time."[83] But the library is not merely a collection of books; rather, it is technology that supports the creation of knowledge by, as he puts it, "anyone who desires knowledge" insofar as it helps them quickly and efficiently locate books.[84]

As a systematic knowledge of the order of books, library science had to be free from any "local memory," by which he meant those early modern notions according to which the catalog, and thus access to the library, "existed only in the librarians' memory."[85] In German, this ability often went by the term *Büchertitelgelehrsamkeit* or erudition concerning book titles. But it also became an image of the incommensurability of such a system of organization and the proliferation of books. Echoing the broader semantic shifts in knowledge discussed in the first half of this article, Schrettinger argued that the organization and order of the library could not be bound to one person, but neither could it be a reflection of some external order (the cosmos, for example, as with early modern library schemes) nor a direct representation of a physical shelf order. To facilitate the finding of books, the organization of the library needed, as the historian Garrett explains, to take two distinct forms: one according to bibliographic information and the other the actual arrangement of physical books on shelves.[86] The former had to assume its own independent form as an internally coherent system that, in principle, could be accessed by anyone at any time. If a library is physically disassembled and moved to another location—its books scattered and separated from their shelf order—the system will remain intact and will allow for the reassembly of the books. With his systematic catalog, Schrettinger sought to differentiate and to objectify the order of the library just as Beutler and Guthsmut had done with journals and newspapers in their periodical of periodicals. But, as one reviewer put it, in a "Schrettinger library," if the catalog is lost, then the entire library becomes immediately "unusable."[87] The order of books was to be translated into a different material form—that of the systematic catalog.

As the title of Schrettinger's text suggests, however, the system was only an attempt (*Versuch*) and attested to what he considered the "impossibility of implementing a purely systematic arrangement."[88] No systematic organization could ever be complete, and thus no systematic catalog could ever be finished. While advising librarians to draft a plan "of the main subjects" of the sciences based on universal and particular encyclopedias, Schrettinger acknowledged that these categories and thus the systematic catalogs based on them would be "arbitrary."[89] No librarian should presume to order a library "from a higher standpoint" from which he might gaze out upon the "entire empire of human knowledge" and draw sharp and fixed distinctions between different areas of knowledge.[90] Undergirding the presumption of a dynamic order of books was the assumption that the order of knowledge and the sciences themselves were constantly changing. Because the borders and distinctions of the sciences were constantly changing, so too were the order of books. Scholars were constantly expanding and altering the "boundaries" of the literature of a particular science with new articles and books that did not easily accord with the established categories. Thus, for Schrettinger, the systematic catalog order of books should take precedence over the shelf order of books.

Schrettinger's post-Kantian insight was that if the order of the library could no longer represent the order of nature, then it must have an internal organization. The library is no longer a museum or curiosity cabinet that reflects or indexes the order of the universe. Like lexica, encyclopedia, and indices, the library itself, over the course of the eighteenth century, became a system, an order with its own internal logic, principles, and purpose.[91] It was in such new-style libraries that the scholar would, over the course of the nineteenth century, become the researcher, conversant in the "literature" of a particular field of knowledge and able to recognize its shape. These new libraries, imagined Schrettinger, would be the "ladders" upon which young, aspiring scholars could climb up "on the shoulders of the predecessors … in order to see even further."[92]

Yet, as noted above, Schrettinger was conscious of the limits of such a system of books; therefore, to facilitate the practical and efficient use of the library, he argued that systematic catalogs had to be supplemented by alphabetical ones. As we saw with the perceived failures of systematic registers for periodicals, systematic library catalogs all too often elided the particularity of individual books. They constructed opaque categories. Book titles did not match actual content, so they were easily miscategorized. Finally, because sciences were themselves in constant flux, systems based upon any clear divisions among and between them were often highly unstable.[93]

Schretttinger repeatedly acknowledged the difficulties inherent in a systematic catalog, but he remained committed to a systematic catalog that embodied a distinct order of books. He even based his own cataloging system on Krug's classification scheme and thus inherited many of the same problems of formalization that plagued post-Kantian encyclopedists.[94] As one reviewer wrote, despite Schrettinger's earnest critique of systems, his own textbook (*Lehrbuch*) managed to make "out of form a formality, and out of laws chains, and instead of a living and free organic whole … a patchwork of definitions and classifications laboriously strung together."[95] Schrettinger's library science had produced an objective system that, while it afforded a theory of totality, had very little to say about particular interactions with books in practice and even less to say about the ethics of knowledge—that is, the ends toward which all this collected knowledge should be put.[96] His textbook encapsulated the underlying tension between the dual notions of knowledge in the eighteenth century—the tension between knowledge as an objective reality and knowledge as a subjective capacity. As knowledge became an unwieldy second nature, humans increasingly struggled to develop search techniques and technologies to navigate it and orient themselves within it.

CONCLUSION

In 1809, Wilhelm von Humboldt wrote a memo sketching a proposal for a new institution of higher learning in Berlin. He proposed a university that would organize an array of related institutions, collections, and people devoted to the creation and cultivation of knowledge—from elementary and secondary schools to libraries, museums, and academies. This university, he proposed, would be the central medium for modern knowledge, gathering and unifying institutions, objects, and people for a common purpose, which he defined as connecting "objective knowledge with subjective development."[97] The task of the new university would be to bridge the gap that had emerged over the course of the eighteenth century between an objective, material world of knowledge—the bibliographic and print order discussed in this article—with the subjective formation of individuals. By the time professors delivered their first lectures at the University of Berlin in the fall of 1810, Humboldt had left his position in the Prussian bureaucracy. But he had helped reimagine the eighteenth-century German university, still characterized by its early modern guild-like character, as the modern research university and with it a new conception of knowledge as research and the scholar as researcher.

As research, the materiality, objectivity, and supra-individual notion of knowledge that had emerged over the course of the eighteenth century was reaffirmed. But that notion was also increasingly linked to a new and distinct epistemic persona: the researcher. The formation and legitimacy of this modern subject of knowledge was bound up with the modern research university and the methods, techniques, and practices it helped sustain. By the end of the nineteenth century, research universities would become the central technologies of knowledge around the world, organizing both the things and people of knowledge. They would, in sum, became search engines, determining what counted as authoritative and legitimate knowledge.

CHAPTER TWO

The Human Self: A Secular Alternative to the Soul

HOWARD G. BROWN

"To thine own self be true." This sixteenth-century statement has acquired a much different meaning three centuries later. In current popular thinking, "the self" is an immaterial entity that constitutes the core of personal identity, something interior and innate to be discovered and actualized. In contrast, early modern Europeans did not view personal identity in terms of autonomy, inwardness, or authenticity. The group had primacy over the individual, whether that group was a family, workshop, confraternity, guild, parish, village, neighborhood, or corporative body. Every person belonged to a variety of solidarities, both horizontal and vertical, that determined his or her identity. Moreover, it was the soul and its afterlife, not the self in this life, that needed attention. The period 1650–1800, by contrast, saw a more individualized and independent sense of self emerge to contest personal identity as the product of social roles.

What forces most compelled this process? Should historians emphasize the development of sophisticated new ideas or instead focus on social and cultural factors? There are no definitive answers to these questions. In fact, they are rarely posed quite like this. In this chapter, the self is not treated as an immaterial essence or as synonymous with personal identity. Rather, it is understood to be a cluster of psychological processes that increasingly came to sustain individuals in society. Thus, thinking about "the self" and experiencing it both have histories.

HISTORY AND TELEOLOGY

The history of the self is necessarily teleological, just like histories of the state or capitalism. Writing such histories depends on being clear about concepts and relating those to specific practices. The modern, enlightened self arose from an increase in the psychological work required to maintain a sense of personal identity. Such thinking is qualitatively different from simply having a sense of individuality, whether spiritual (the soul) or physical (the body). Rather, awareness of one's own individuality is to the self what trade is to capitalism: the latter is based on the former, but the complexity and cultural salience of the latter now largely determines the character of the former. As the pace of change accelerated and the array of choices in life grew increasingly varied between the fifteenth and twentieth centuries, individuals came increasingly both to reflect upon and to perform their personal identities. During this period, the role of dense social networks in shaping personal identities steadily lost ground. In their place arose forms of identity formation based on greater personal autonomy and intensified inwardness. Thus, the self developed as a psychological accompaniment and extension of individualism. A growing volume of trade brought on by increased agricultural yields or improved production methods may foster capitalism, but it is specific financial practices, such as double-entry bookkeeping, joint-stock companies, and bond derivatives, that magnified the economic consequences. Various social forces ranging from increases in literacy and consumerism to urbanization and companionate marriage all encouraged greater individualism from the sixteenth century onwards. Specific cultural practices, such as engaging in spiritual exercises, keeping diaries, reading sentimental novels, writing autobiographies—and, eventually, taking and posting "selfies"—all magnified the psychological consequences.

Understanding the self as the essence of personal identity is now a commonplace, but it is still rather vague as an idea. Efforts to be more precise about the concept are legion. Most of these engage with what Roy Porter has dubbed the "Authorized Version" of the rise of selfhood in the Western world. This is largely an intellectual history, one that links Socrates, Montaigne, Augustine, Descartes, Locke, Rousseau, Smith, Kant, Hegel, Nietzsche, Freud, Sartre, and other such luminaries in a long chain of writing about human consciousness. At the end of the chain lies not a heavy iron ball, but its supposed opposite: a personal identity based on an authentic, unified, and autonomous inner self capable of "self-esteem" and "self-actualization."

The historian Jerrold Seigel gave analytical clarity to his account of these developments by examining each thinker in this tradition in terms of three dimensions of selfhood: the bodily or corporeal, the relational or social, and the reflective or introspective. This resolutely modernist perspective deliberately marginalizes post-structuralists, such as Paul de Man, Jacques Derrida, and Michel Foucault; these late twentieth-century thinkers saw the Authorized Version as a "hagiography of humanism" and the Western individualist self as an illusion.[1] Seigel prefers a "common-sense understanding of individuals as centers of action and consciousness"[2] because he assumes that such an understanding promises more personal fulfillment in life. This assumption is a fundamental premise of modern liberal democracies and thus deeply embedded in contemporary Western societies.

Charles Taylor is more philosopher than historian and as such has written perhaps the most sophisticated history of the self.[3] Although his work is also largely intellectual history, Taylor claims that changing ideas generally reflect broader social and cultural developments. According to Taylor, the emergence of the self in Western societies is the product of changes in four ways of understanding individual significance based on (1) a sense of inwardness, (2) a sense of what makes daily life worth living, (3) forms of narrativity that stress personal development, and (4) individual agency within a network of social bonds. The most distinctive part of this approach is (2), which derives from Taylor's concerns as a moral philosopher. At the heart of Taylor's approach lies a sustained criticism of modern liberal understandings of the self because they have devalued the role of social context and institutions in shaping and sustaining personal identity, especially in moral terms. His basic argument emphasizes the importance to identity formation of having to choose between competing "goods" in life, by which he means values and sources of meaning. Thus, moral decision-making becomes central to his intellectual history of the self.

That said, the works of Seigel and Taylor, among others, make several things clear: that the self has been the subject of much discussion and disagreement in recent years;

that the seventeenth and eighteenth centuries generated foundational elements of the larger debate; that the conceptual fecundity of this period derives in large part from the search for a secular basis for human meaning and morality; and that the shift from the soul to the self derived from an increasingly empirical approach to human ontology. Moreover, these works also make it apparent that, over time, ideas about the self that were grounded in personal experience became the basis for psychology, whereas more speculative theories of the self, especially those that treated it as a fiction or an illusion, became isolated in the domain of philosophy.

All of these observations suggest that a cultural history of the self in the period 1650–1800 should emphasize how ideas about the self shaped and were shaped by how individuals constituted and experienced their personal identities. It is helpful, therefore, to define the self in ways that set aside philosophical speculation in favor of an understanding grounded in lived experience. Thus, the self is understood here as a cluster of *psychological processes* that maintains a sense of personal continuity, coherence, authenticity, and autonomy. Continuity comes from organizing one's own experiences into a narrative of personal development. Coherence is fostered by relating one's own thoughts and feelings to the observations and responses of others, even if these do not align well. A sense of authenticity develops through connecting one's motives to one's actions despite any inner struggle between sincerity and duplicity this may provoke. A sense of autonomy arises from being able to make major choices in life on the basis of personal perceptions of what is good and provides meaning or fulfillment in life. Together, these psychological processes, especially when stimulated by introspection, form a self. This unified self is experienced as a core identity that is inextricably linked with, but also distinct from, an individual body. Thus, the self takes shape as both the synthesizer and the synthesis that is personal subjectivity. "Ontologically there may be something illusionary here; experientially there is not," observes David Levin.[4] The more continuously, intensely, and consciously individuals engage in these processes, the more salient the self becomes. This definition asserts that the self is not innate, nor is it willed into existence. Rather, it is the psychological fruit of coping with the transition from the tightly knit, face-to-face communities of medieval Europe to the rising social anomie that characterizes modernity. This is a distinctly modern concept of the self, the telos in the historical teleology of selfhood.

How did the period 1650–1800 contribute to this development? Did the Enlightenment make a "breakthrough" to modern selfhood? To answer these questions, it is necessary to trace the most important developments in thinking about the self, especially those that provided the foundations of the secular, bounded self as an alternative to the Christian tradition of the soul. Augustine of Hippo taught Christians how to find God through intense introspection. A thousand years later, but only a half century apart, Descartes and Locke proposed radically different explanations for the relationship between the mind and the body. These two perspectives—dualism and sensationalism—provoked a seismic shift in western European thinking about the essence of an individual. Eighteenth-century discussions of personal identity focused on sensationalism, imagination, and sympathy. They dealt explicitly and extensively with interiority, but without a fixed or common vocabulary. In the process, the "soul" became naturalized and eventually fully secularized as the "self." Most contemporaries absorbed this shift without reading the major thinkers who articulated it. Nonetheless, revisiting the most significant and influential contributions to the debate helps to establish the basic parameters of thinking about selfhood as they evolved over the eighteenth century.

THINKING THE SOUL AND SELF

René Descartes (1596–1650) (Figure 2.1) responded to the scientific revolution in astronomy led by Copernicus and Galileo. An important mathematician in his own right, Descartes made even more important, if not so lasting, contributions to philosophy and epistemology. Always wary of the consequences of his claims, especially after Galileo had been condemned by the Papal Inquisition, Descartes, in his *Discourses on Method* (1637), developed an understanding of the self that largely fit with Christian teachings on God and the soul. Doing so, however, came at considerable expense to the durability of his epistemology. As famous as any phrase in philosophy, *cogito ergo sum* is both existentially and epistemically profound. At the most basic level, awareness of one's own thinking is evidence of an indisputable truth, namely, that one exists. Thus, consciousness became the essence of human existence. Augustine had expressed a similar idea, but he had not made it the necessary basis for all other knowledge. Descartes's premise also asserts that human reason, not divine revelation, is the guide to all true knowledge. Finally, and not incidentally, reflexive thinking was indisputable evidence of God as creator.

FIGURE 2.1 René Descartes, etching by Joannes Tangena, *c.* 1650. © Getty Images.

The boldness of Descartes's human ontology and consequent epistemology derives from the distinction he made between the materiality of the world and the immateriality of the mind. "The thinking substance" (*res cogitans*), interchangeably dubbed the mind, the soul, and even the self, is wholly different from the physical world (*res extensa*). Thus, in Cartesian dualism, the mind belonged to an ethereal universe that was utterly distinct from the body. This immateriality fit the traditional properties of the Christian soul, including survival after death. However, the radicalism of Descartes's dualism prevented him from developing a persuasive explanation for just how an individual consciousness related to its corporeal container. (He later unconvincingly claimed the "pineal gland" as a biological portal.) All the same, Descartes's emphasis on mind over matter dramatically enhanced the basis for personal independence. Making reason the foundation of being human put all forms of authority to the test; it also provided the means to control the passions. Thus, the battle between the spiritual forces of good and evil for dominance of an individual soul was replaced by a personal struggle to control one's own actions and shape one's own character according to deliberately chosen moral concerns. Here was a basic deism that dared not speak its name, at least not yet.

Cartesian dualism opened the door to the naturalization of the soul, but it was John Locke (1632–1704) who crossed the threshold into modern thinking about the self. Like his French predecessor, the English Locke wrote explicitly about the essence of personal identity, dubbing it the "self" in *An Essay Concerning Human Understanding* (1690, 1694) and thereby consolidating this neologism in the English language ("Self is that conscious thinking thing").[5] Locke could not accept the *a priori* nature of either the Christian soul or the Cartesian *res cogitans*. Locke sought to resolve the mind-body problem by inverting priorities and eliminating dualism. Rather than assume that consciousness was evidence of a preexisting immaterial entity, the English thinker crystalized an emerging emphasis among scientific thinkers on the role of the five bodily senses in determining human thought. Lockean sensationalism held that the mind begins as a *tabula rasa* and develops by processing a myriad of sensory impressions. Whereas human senses provide information in variable and sometimes misleading ways (optical illusions, echoes, etc.), the mind works to make the mass of data coherent. Being cognizant of this processing of sensory information is the basis for consciousness. Consciousness may be interrupted by sleep, delirium, and even drunkenness, but memory preserves continuity across these repeated interruptions. Thus, consciousness and memory combine to give the self coherence and continuity. Accumulated experience through life joins with a reflexive awareness of "Impressions, Thoughts, and Feelings" to give everyone a "self" that is not an ethereal substance, but an ongoing process experienced as the core of identity.

Various contributions to the so-called Scientific Revolution, notably those that stressed mechanics over metaphysics, made it difficult to persist in exclusively religious explanations of the natural world and human beings' relationship to it. Thus, the emergence of sensationalism became widely accepted because it fit especially well with Isaac Newton's mathematical explanations of physical motion and William Harvey's claims about blood circulation. By rejecting innate ideas, Locke effectively ruled out the soul as contemporaries understood it, even though he remained a committed Christian. Furthermore, his emphasis on sensationalism as the source of the self appeared to some as dangerously subversive because it destabilized the individual and, thereby, threatened religion and social order. Critics thought that if there were no original, timeless, and essential core of being, the prospect of divine rewards and punishments would no longer steer individuals toward morally upright living. As a result, as Seigel puts it, "Locke's psychology portended a major moral and cultural crisis."[6] However, this contemporary reaction largely ignored the role of morality in constituting Locke's understanding of the self. In fact, he viewed the concept of a unified self as both necessary and sufficient to make moral choices, otherwise individuals could not be held accountable for their actions, whether by man or by God.

Locke's sensationalist psychology provided the impetus for other, subsequent approaches to the self that further challenged the idea of the soul as the core of personal identity. Bernard Mandeville (1670–1733) shocked contemporaries with his bold assertion in the *Fable of the Bees* (1714–1724) that many traditional vices (pride, ambition, greed, love of luxury, etc.) actually served society by promoting achievement and trade. He argued that individuals acquire their unity and coherence not from reason and reflection, but from satisfying biological needs and natural passions. These are shaped by conscious and unconscious mental activities into socially acceptable behaviors, thereby disguising the reality that selfishness lies at the root of all human interactions. Moreover, moral behavior is merely social convention, not behavior needed to satisfy a distant God. Mandeville's ideas helped to secularize introspection. The complex relationship between personal desires and society's potential responses to them led to forms of individualized adaptation that formed the essential, wholly secular, self.

David Hume (1711–1776), writing in Scotland, took this emphasis on the social context for selfhood even further. In keeping with his commitment to total skepticism, Hume deemed the Lockean self a fiction because it only gave the appearance of unity. The mind received and processed such an overwhelming amount of sensory information that any semblance of coherence that resulted necessarily came from the most unreliable element of human thinking, the imagination. Although this aspect of Hume's criticism did little damage at the time, it inspired later post-structuralist critiques of the entire notion of a coherent, authentic self. More important to contemporaries was Hume's emphasis on the socially constituted nature of personal identity. The self is not a separate entity, but merely the means to process cognitive, emotional, and social stimuli. Hume devoted special attention to sympathy as a corollary to self-love and the basis for character formation within society. As an extension of self-love in the direction of others, sympathy serves to shape individual character by taming and directing passions. The resulting self is not a distinct entity, but a way of integrating signals from the senses and social experience into a single, moral agent. Thus, self-love is not evidence of the Fall, but a foundation for community in a complex commercial society.

Mandeville's promotion of self-interested individualism on economic grounds was further developed by another Scot, Adam Smith (1723–1790). Smith tempered the implications of his theory, however, through a Humean emphasis on sympathy as self-love extended to others. What is more, he made such sympathy an essential component of an individual's inner life. Emotions expressed by others, especially in response to suffering, provoke imaginative reflection on how one would feel in another person's circumstances. The process requires recognizing other individuals as sharing a similar subjectivity, if not identity, to oneself, as well as anticipating their judgments in response to one's own actions. By taking others' responses into account, the self becomes both the ultimate worldly judge of one's own emotions and the basis for maintaining society with others. This "impartial spectator" inside each of us is not as famous as "the invisible hand" guiding commercial society, but it expresses a central feature of Smith's overall theory, thereby sparing him from being as rudely dismissed as Mandeville had been. Moreover,

Smith's theory of the self in society as the basis for morality took him well beyond the limits of simple sensationalist explanations, with which he appeared uncomfortable.

Across the channel in France, the cultural significance of sensationalism in constituting the self owed much to the influence of Étienne Bonnot de Condillac (1714–1780). Condillac's popularization of Lockean sensationalism went even further toward making the self the product of sensory perceptions. Condillac's *Treatise on Sensations* (1754) presents the self as almost exclusively the product of sensory information acquired and interpreted through life experiences. In the process, individuals are enabled to use memory, imagination, abstraction, and reason as the basis for action. Such an understanding came close to pure materialism. However, by adding a complex theory of language as the basis for action and a God-given soul as the basis for morality and the foundation of consciousness, Condillac avoided the extreme materialist position presented in Jullien Offray de La Mettrie's scandalously atheistic *L'homme machine* (1747). Ultimately, Condillac did more to challenge Cartesian dualism than he did to provide an empirical understanding of the self. Moreover, his influence on Denis Diderot (1713–1784) also helped to spread sensationalist ideas. Diderot, as co-editor of the *Encyclopédie*, fully incorporated Locke's ideas into the article on the self. As one of the leading travelers on the road from deism to atheism, Diderot developed a radical materialist understanding of the self. Later works added the idea that every person is born with a distinctive character that determines his or her ability to control desires and emotional responses. He also emphasized the special role of memory, which he located in the brain (i.e., the body), and the damaging consequences of social interaction, which impaired moral judgment. The result was an overwhelmingly sensationalist and, more importantly, totally secular self.

Attempts to explain the essence of personal identity, whether termed the soul, the self, or the person, in largely secular terms meant confronting the issue of morality. Mandeville, Hume, Smith, and Diderot, in particular, found that establishing a secular basis for morality required developing more elaborate schemas to explain the mystery of the relationship between the mind and individual personality as expressed in society. In other words, these thinkers fostered a general trend toward theoretical psychology. Perhaps the most radical contribution to this trend came from Jean-Jacques Rousseau (1712–1778), a thinker from Geneva who shared few assumptions with his fellow *philosophes*, especially the more radical materialist tendencies of Diderot, Claude Adrien Helvétius, and the Baron d'Holbach.

Rousseau's contribution to understandings of the self departed from both the strict sensationalism and the prevailing deism of his day. His early novel *Emile, or On Education* espoused ideas about how children become conscious of themselves as individuals and develop a sense of personal morality in the process. At the core of moral choices, Rousseau asserted, are two kinds of self love, *amour de soi*, a natural and benign impulse to seek personal well-being, and *amour-propre*, an unnatural and malign drive to rise above others. Rousseau especially disparaged reason for its role in turning the opinion of others into a dangerous *amour-propre*, one that eroded personal independence and corroded social relationships at the same time. God the Creator made man naturally good and instilled a conscience in each individual to guide him. This moral independence is damaged and perverted by concern over the opinions of others. Much of Rousseau's *oeuvre* deals with creating conditions in society that would encourage individual autonomy and foster natural goodness in humankind. Above all, it is by looking inward, consulting one's own feelings and motivations, that one finds an authentic, unified self. Deep personal introspection becomes a means to unlock the goodness of nature, not a way to align one's soul with God's will. The epistolary *Julie, or the New Heloise*, provoked many readers to identity with the personal suffering and moral challenges faced by the young couple whose mutual love and personal virtue were so severely tested by social conventions. Exceptionally personal letters from readers, especially female ones, to the author testify to the powerful emotional responses and sustained introspection that the novel inspired. Its strong statements about natural differences between the sexes also helped to instill gender roles that separated the domestic sphere from the public sphere. Rousseau treated the self more as a psychological process than a distinct entity, though he did not make this explicit. Personal identity was corrupted and alienated by society, and so "self-discovery" became imperative.

Principal access to our true selves may be through introspection, but that meant confronting many inconsistencies and contradictions created by living in society. Rousseau illustrated this proposition with his astonishing and posthumous *Confessions* (1782) (Figure 2.2). Fully aware of Augustine's work of the same title, Rousseau, nonetheless, claimed that his work was unprecedented and inimitable. Above all, it was Rousseau's description of his own dishonesty, misdeeds, and unsavory sexual proclivities that marked the *Confessions* as an extraordinary exploration of the self. By mixing these offenses against standard morality with claims about having strong, natural impulses to lead a generous and virtuous life, Rousseau taught readers that it took psychological effort to achieve a coherent self, that is, something stable behind the masks presented to others in society. The apparent honesty and transparency of the *Confessions* inspired readers to reflect more actively on their own inner nature. Few writers have so profoundly influenced common understandings of personal identity and its implications for organizing society.

In the short term, Rousseau's turn away from reason toward feelings and nature did little to weaken the hold of sensationalism on understandings of the self. In Prussia, Immanuel Kant (1724–1804) joined the discussion with a complex, evolving, and sometimes incoherent series of arguments. Scholars remain divided over Kant's

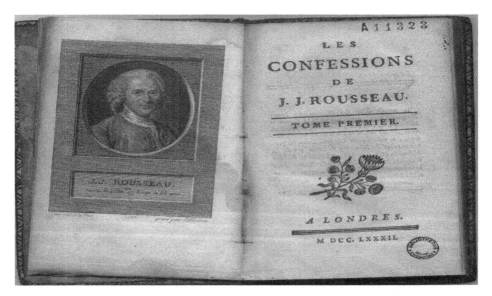

FIGURE 2.2 Frontispiece, Jean-Jacques Rousseau, *Les Confessions de J. J. Rousseau* (1782). © http://premiumtrade.info/house/rousseau-confessions.html (public domain).

metaphysical views on the subject. Central to the debate is whether Kant viewed the self, the referent of "I," as an entity or an activity. Being able to sustain either interpretation is made possible by Kant's distinction between phenomena (sensory experiences of physical objects) and noumena (intuitions that transcend the material world). For Kant, noumena cannot be reified, and yet together they permit the processing of experiences (not just sensory data) in ways that create personal identity, thus becoming the referent of "I" that resides within a single human body. Noumena transcend consciousness and memory, which Kant considered insufficient to constitute the self, and are transcendentally allied with the ultimate purposes of nature. In short, Kant reworked elements of Descartes's *cogito*, Locke's sensationalism, and Rousseau's moralism into a complex new amalgam that avoided pure dualism, materialist determinism, or claims about the innate goodness of man. Kant's highly elaborate conceptualization of the self served a simple purpose: to give individuals the scope for self-determination. Kant shared Augustine's lively awareness of evil as a part of human nature. However, despite repeated and confusing references to God, Kant situated evil in an essentially deistic universe in which humankind's rationality became the means to overcome wickedness. Kant viewed Rousseau as "the Newton of the moral world."[7] The moral maxims that underpinned benevolence and justice are to be discerned noumenally and then pursued rationally. In other words, only noumenal elements of the self could derive universal values from intuitive perceptions that made sense of personal experiences, and only a rational self could freely choose to enact those values. By invoking noumenal forms of knowledge, Kant supplemented sensationalism with a quasi-Christian source of morality. The intended result was to provide the individual self with the possibility of greater autonomy than even Rousseau had envisioned. Ultimately, Kant's conception of the self puts great stress on individuals using reason to engage in their own character formation (*Bildung*). Nothing could have been more German: a perfect stepping-stone from Pietism to Nietzsche.

Surveying the ideas of these intellectual giants unfortunately obscures the involvement of many others in the protracted debate over the relationship between mind and body or among consciousness, morality, and personal identity. Myriad eighteenth-century writers, whether producing books, pamphlets, magazines, newspapers, or private letters, engaged in a thorough rethinking of the soul as the most significant attribute of an individual. These varied and eclectic contributions, many from brilliant and not always reactionary clergymen, ensured that the path from a religious soul to a secular self was far from linear. They were, after all, dealing with the crooked timber of humanity. Nonetheless, this cacophony of conflicting voices largely accepted that life while it was being lived, not life after death, determined the essence of an individual. From this earth-bound perspective came another general consensus, namely, that consciousness, memory, and introspection combined to give individuals critical agency in constructing their own identities, including their own moral hierarchies.

Changing ideas of the self (the domain of intellectual history) are easier to trace than changes in the self as a psychological process and as an organizing principle for lived experience (the domain generally of cultural history). Discourses of the self and experiences of the self are distinct, though not unrelated, phenomena. Rather than search for the role of nominalism in shaping eighteenth-century selfhood, however, it is more helpful to explore a few of the other major tributaries that fed the widening stream. The most important stimulants in increasing the salience of the self included changes in religion, the rise of sensibility, and increased individualism, especially as encouraged by social mobility, consumerism, and rights-based polities.

RELIGIOUS CHANGE

Despite the importance of increasingly secular understandings of the self, personal experiences of a more salient self owed a great deal to changing religious teachings and practices across the early modern era. The Protestant "priesthood of all believers" introduced in the sixteenth century made individuals responsible for their own salvation. This included gaining a personal understanding of the Bible and basic theology, which literacy greatly facilitated. Disagreements between various Protestant sects over the relative importance of clerics or of performing good works did not erode their shared belief that every individual Christian needed to engage in "soul searching" and moral reform. Although much less obvious, this greater interiorization of piety had its counterpart in Catholicism as well. Various increasingly important Catholic practices, such as the examination of one's conscience, general confession, and meditative spiritual exercises, cultivated individual inwardness and a sense of personal development. Only a minority of Catholics took this approach to their own salvation in the early modern period, but those who did gained a stronger sense of self as a by-product of their attempts to find the love of God inside themselves. Baroque piety, which reached its height in the late seventeenth and early eighteenth centuries, democratized and popularized many of these practices. All the same, it is perhaps a bit exaggerated to speak, even tentatively, of "the Catholic priesthood of all believers."[8]

A variety of religious movements, both Catholic and Protestant, put even greater emphasis on the conscience and interior forms of piety that fostered the psychological process of the self. From the middle of the seventeenth century onward, Jansenism added a neo-Augustinian alternative to Catholicism in France and the Low Countries. The Jansenists' commitment to high standards of morality and personal piety, especially in preparation for Communion, stood in sharp contrast to the supposed casuistry and overall laxity of the Jesuits. The emergence of *convulsionnaires* (lay men and especially women who entered trances and performed "miracles") in Paris in the early eighteenth century revealed the hostility that most Jansenists felt toward any form of populist mysticism. This rejection of a strong emotional component to personal piety did not accord well with the age of Rousseau, and so the austerity of Jansenism lost most of its appeal after the 1750s. If there was a wider social residue, however, it was in the growing secular emphasis on civic virtue as a socially necessary form of personal self-sacrifice.

Protestantism experienced an even greater infusion of personalized piety. This came in the form of the multivalent Pietist movement in German states, the Netherlands, and North America, and its derivation, Methodism, in the British Isles. Both movements stressed personal salvation that depended, more often than not, on dramatic conversion experiences. The founders of Pietism in the late seventeenth century viewed it as a delayed completion of the Reformation at the personal level. Institutional churches, whether Lutheran or Calvinist, had acquired too much influence. Therefore, it was necessary to return to the practices of the early Church by cultivating the inner spiritual life in each believer. Some Pietist groups even accepted that God could reveal truth directly to the individual soul regardless of how well a believer grasped even basic theology. Such revivalist teachings proved exceptionally popular, and Pietism became a powerful force in central and northern Europe. Though not without intellectual and theological sophistication, the success of Pietism no doubt resulted from its endorsement of strong emotions as an integral part, if not absolute proof, of an inner spirituality. Admitting one's sinfulness, repenting past actions, and accepting Jesus into one's heart all cultivated much greater inwardness. The Moravian Brotherhood took such thinking to the American colonies, where it inspired the "Great Awakening" of the 1740s. John Wesley developed his own strand in England, where inner conversion and spiritual renewal challenged the ecclesiastical structures of Anglicanism. Methodism was criticized for its emotionalism and individualism, which is evidence in itself that it had a strong reflexive relationship with other emerging aspects of the age. That women made up a strong majority of members may also explain some of the condescension directed toward this new evangelicalism. However, advocacy of such novel issues as prison reform and the abolition of slavery shows that, under the influence of dissenting forms of Protestantism, many individuals came to believe that, as the repositories of God's love, they shared a basic equality and ought to work to relieve the suffering of others.

SENSIBILITY AND THE READING PUBLIC

Scholars agree that the practice of reading complex texts that explore human thought and action provide one of the greatest stimulants to the self. Just how common this practice may have become during the early modern period is hard to say precisely. Being able to sign an official document such as a marriage contract has been used as a proxy for literacy, and that ability increased very significantly in the eighteenth century in particular. For example, literacy rates in France grew between the 1680s and the 1780s from 29 percent to 47 percent of men and from 14 percent to 27 percent for women.[9] These millions of new readers did not all have the time or the attention span to read whole books; nonetheless, the emergence of a large reading public was of critical importance to developing a wider and deeper sense of self.

Changes in literature during the period 1650–1800 also engaged readers in more psychological ways than ever before. In fact, according to Philip Stewart, literature became "the domain in which psychological understanding developed before psychology."[10] In the period between Descartes and Diderot, sentiment emerged as one of the main subjects of literature, which increasingly sought to explore the human psyche in relatively realist ways. This focus on sentiment displaced classical treatments of the passions thereby adding subtlety and providing a more positive assessment of human emotions. Increased emphasis on sentiment paralleled the growing significance of the individual conscience, often stimulated by religious change, and increasing opportunities for privacy in daily life, at least among the expanding urban elites. (Of course, individuals who were surrounded at all times by their families and village had a very different understanding of "private life" and, therefore, the possibility of an identity outside their social context.) The Lockean emphasis on consciousness and sensationalism as the basis of the self encouraged literary reflection on emotions as an extension of the senses. Individuals were thereby encouraged to dwell on their own emotions as a form of sensory experience. The Abbé Prévost, for example, used a fictional autobiographical approach to explore the subjective emotional life of his main character, the Chevalier de Grieux (the seventh volume—*Manon Lescaut* of 1731—is the best known of this fictional multivolume "memoir").

The emergence of the novel as a dominant form of literature in the eighteenth century took the emphasis on inner emotions to new heights. The most successful of these were characterized by overt sentimentalism. The blockbusters of this genre were all epistolary novels: Samuel Richardson's *Pamela* (1740) and *Clarissa* (1748), Rousseau's *Julie, or the*

New Heloise (1761), and Johann Wolfgang von Goethe's *The Sorrows of Young Werthe* (1774). Scores of other novels and plays added to the sentimentalist idiom. In almost every case, the plot revolved around leading characters suffering misfortune and appearing as victims, often in the context of sexual relationships. A persistent preoccupation with the interior lives of the main characters, often but not exclusively female, also characterized sentimental literature. The aesthetic conventions of sentimentalism served to evoke emotional responses from readers collectively known as sensibility. As the cultural historian Cecilia Feilla explains, "Sensibility was the intuitive capacity for immediate moral and aesthetic responsiveness to others, and particularly to the suffering of others. Humanity, pity, and tenderness were among its privileged terms."[11] Smith, Hume, and Diderot had all presented important ideas on the role of sympathy in constituting the individual self as a reflexive response to social interaction. However, one scholar, John Mullan, has boldly claimed that "the novel was [the Enlightenment's] true imaginative enactment ... [because] it was in novels that the individual self—the experience of the self as individual—was most affectingly represented."[12] Thus, the sentimental novel developed more effective representations of the emotional experiences of others, thereby stimulating the ability of European men and women to imagine the emotional responses of others and to reflect on their own possible responses. The capacity to sympathize with family members, friends, and neighbors thereby expanded beyond parish boundaries and the common limits of social equals.

The historian Lynn Hunt has persuasively argued that the epistolary novels of Richardson and Rousseau became bestsellers because they enabled readers to experience vicariously the inner life of characters quite different from themselves. Such novels, therefore, implicitly "made the point that all people are fundamentally similar because of their inner feelings. ... In this way reading novels created a sense of equality and empathy."[13] Hunt further argues that the resulting ability of readers to identify with characters whose social identity differed radically from their own combined with the growing moral autonomy of individuals to inspire the basic idea of human rights that emerged in the late eighteenth century. Such an approach underscores important changes in the ways in which individual personhood was understood and experienced. Great thinkers had articulated ideas about interiority and the psyche, and led an evolution from the Christian soul to the secular self. Perhaps equally important, this shift in widely accepted understanding came equally from the greater emphasis that various Christian sects of the eighteenth century placed on the individual conscience, on the one hand, and the impact of sentimentalism as a stimulant for sensibility, which made man's moral dilemmas largely anthrocentric and increasingly individualistic, on the other hand.

INDIVIDUALISM

Increased individualism provided the basis for a more developed sense of self as well. The so-called "consumer revolution" that swept western Europe and the North American colonies in the eighteenth century proved a particularly powerful stimulus to both individualism and the psychological process of the self. The rapid proliferation of more affordable consumer goods is best explained by specific changes in the nature of demand. Supply came later. As Jan de Vries explains, consumer desires inspired an "industrious revolution" in which more people spent more time working for wages to buy material goods.[14] The resulting increase in disposable household income spurred a massive expansion of craft manufacture well before major technological innovations made the Industrial Revolution possible. The role of consumer demand in stimulating individualism and a more developed self fits with Charles Taylor's observation, highlighted earlier, that a growing sense of what made daily life worth living was an important stimulus to modern selfhood.

What did consumers want and why did they want them? Stockings and underwear, beds and linen, pottery and cutlery: these were the first priorities of most people. However, as the eighteenth century wore on, many Europeans, both at home and abroad, became able to acquire modest luxury goods such as pocket watches and fans. Moreover, material comforts were often less important than superfluities acquired to emulate elites. Large homes, fine furniture, luxury clothing, and jewelry had long been important to social ascendancy. The spread of wealth in society from the mid-seventeenth century onward, especially in urban settings, meant that changes in style came to influence how growing numbers of people expressed their status, as well as their social values, through household objects. In particular, style choices in clothing began to change more rapidly, largely due to the increasing availability of cottons (especially patterned calicoes from India), colored silk ribbons, and muslin stockings. Personal dress rapidly became essential to social mimesis—including the pursuit of gentility—and individual distinctiveness alike.

The pursuit of social status determined consumer-spending priorities well beyond clothing. Changes in architecture, furniture, and household wares point to an overall pattern of spending money on material goods that could create a simulacrum of gentility. Physical mobility often brought social mobility too. In communities that experienced little in or out migration, long-standing neighbors were well aware of one another's material worth. Such knowledge was much harder to come by wherever new arrivals accumulated in substantial numbers. There, style trends played a greater part in determining status and identity. Most notably, rooms that could serve as parlors became important places of sociability, even if they still contained a bed. By the middle of the eighteenth century, acquiring the accouterments needed to serve tea to visitors—including specialized furniture—indicated a conscious emulation of genteel living on the part of poor to middling householders (Figure 2.3). Thus, specialized rooms with fashionable furnishings provided the required setting for cultural performances in which etiquette and objects together spoke an international language of social status. Such arts of sociability swept northern Europe in the seventeenth and early eighteenth centuries. By the mid-eighteenth century, they had reached the edge of the North American wilderness. "For the privilege of taking tea in the parlor, more than a few families were content to continue pissing in the barn," observes Cary Carson.[15] Increasingly ornate furniture became important, joining silver bowls, candlesticks, and ceramic pottery as embodiments of wealth and status. An increasingly commercial society together with cultural emulation of gentility steadily eroded the traditional social order. The "great chain of buying" was replacing the great chain of being that assigned every individual a place in God's hierarchy for the universe.[16] This was an unmistakable cultural revolution achieved in but a few generations, as the intensive international debate about luxury (stirred by the likes of Mandeville and Smith) underscored.

Social emulation based on specific material acquisitions enabled migrants, whether to cities or across oceans, to participate in a relatively new set of conventions that gave them status wherever they went. Men and women who took coaches and wagons to Bordeaux or Paris, Liverpool or London, Brussels or Amsterdam, or boarded ships for Massachusetts

FIGURE 2.3 Portrait of John Potter and Family (artist unknown), *c.* 1740. Serving tea in the colonies: John Potter with family members and black servant, overmantle from his home in Matunuck, Rhode Island, *c.* 1740, oil on wood. © Newport Historical Society.

or Mexico City, treated the burgeoning world of fashionable goods as a means to secure the personal reputations that they had either lacked or left behind. Such thinking also imposed new cultural norms on the status conscious who remained stationary. In this way, style increasingly replaced substance in the making of personal identity. Belonging to "polite society" required distinguishing oneself from others through both objects and manners. Personal possessions, being generally few in number, held great significance because they expressed taste and individuality.

What needs to be underscored here is the scale and scope of these developments. The Renaissance had certainly provided novel opportunities for "self-fashioning." However, it was considerably more limited than Stephen Greenblatt has suggested. Only during the course of the eighteenth century did the possibility of transforming one's standing in society through apparel, manners, and household furnishings really begin to reach mass proportions. Material culture among the lower orders in Paris provides a good indicator. Domestic servants led the way in transmitting elite tastes to the broad base of the population due to their privileged access to quality used clothing and social proximity to employers characterized by their "respectability." The value of personal wardrobes among the popular classes tripled during the eighteenth century.[17] Moreover, for the first time, the value of women's clothing significantly surpassed that of men. In response, a new independent guild of "fashion merchants" was created in 1776. Kerchiefs, bonnets, and capes for women, frockcoats and three-pointed hats for men provided the means both to affirm and transform personal identities. That unmatched observer of Parisians and their mores in the late eighteenth century, Louis-Sébastien Mercier, repeatedly remarked on the use of manners and clothing to disguise origins and social rank, thereby turning the city into "a mix of individuals."[18]

The greater individualism to be found in urban settings also created aspirations for a sense of belonging and acceptance. Here is where all things fashionable played an important role in social integration. Participating in fashion trends and "good taste" made gentility culturally accessible. Towns and cities, most of which grew rapidly (some exponentially) after 1750, became the leading sites of "self-fashioning." Thus, during the course of the eighteenth century, as Maxine Berg notes, "politeness, civility, and taste became social markers more significant than material wealth."[19] Middling groups in particular created demand for consumer goods because they saw them as opportunities for personal choice that gave them both greater status and enhanced individuality. Under these conditions, fashionable clothing and household goods provided essential components of social cohesion, personal identity, and self-respect, all at the same time.

Nothing better exemplifies the identity-shaping power of objects than the household mirror. By 1700, owning a mirror in Paris was not a luxury, it was an urban necessity, and, therefore, already commonplace. And yet, the market in mirrors exploded over the following decades, quadrupling sales and creating a virtual mass market. By the 1780s, two-thirds of the popular classes had acquired more, larger, and fancier mirrors. Mirrors were more than evidence of status; they provided a fundamental tool in the psychological process of self-fashioning. Mirrors not only allowed individuals to contemplate their outward appearances, they enabled them to craft their public personas. This could mean improving posture or refining social gestures. Thus, mirrors became tools of integration into the world of superior social practices. As the historian Daniel Roche points out, "The mirror was, therefore, a means of progress for the individual conscience. It afforded everyone a way of discovering, seeing and duplicating himself."[20]

AUTOBIOGRAPHY

Further evidence for the emergence of a more salient self in the eighteenth century comes from the development and subsequent impact of autobiography. European elites had begun to generate ego documents such as *livres de raison*, travel accounts, and personal journals during the fifteenth and sixteenth centuries. However, very few writings provided any access to private thoughts or intimate feelings; Michel de Montaigne's *Essais* (1580) and the diary kept by Samuel Pepys (1660–1669) were glorious exceptions. In the second half of the seventeenth century, however, the writing and publication of personal memoirs emerged as an important means to preserve the past. Although a few of these revealed elements of self-reflection, the generally aristocratic genre of memoirs had "a horror of the self."[21] Women who wrote memoirs often included elements of private life only to find that this underscored their marginality. Even these memoirs differed significantly from true autobiography. Memoirs focus on the author's public roles and actions set in the context of larger events, whereas autobiography not only exposes the author's private life, including feelings, motives, and inner struggles, but also makes the development of the author's identity central to the narrative. Autobiography transforms intimacy into publicity and personal story into public history. Baring innermost thoughts establishes a writer's authenticity in the eyes of the reader. As Philippe Lejeune has observed, the "autobiographical pact" requires the reader to believe that the writer is sincere in trying to provide a truthful account of private matters to which he or she has exclusive access. Doubting the writer's sincerity turns autobiography into a form of fiction. In contrast, a reader who treats an autobiographical text as an authentic expression of the author's interiorized subjectivity is stimulated to introspection as well. Reading biography enables self-reflection; writing autobiography demands it. Because autobiography requires self-reflection, it has a greater capacity than mere biography to stimulate self-reflection in the reader. In these important ways, autobiography is an extension of the sentimental novel to real lives.

Rousseau's *Confessions* did more than any other book to establish the modern genre of autobiography. He wrote the book partly to justify himself to critics and partly to elaborate his anti-social perspective on the self. (An unconventional *arriviste*, Rousseau refused to adopt the sartorial trappings of elite status in France—stockings, wig, sword, etc.) Rousseau's novels had made him the object of a personality cult during his own lifetime. Avid public interest helped to establish the "autobiographical pact" that made the posthumously published *Confessions* so wildly successful. This required telling the truth about himself with complete sincerity: "I have shown myself as I was, sometimes contemptible and vile, sometimes good, generous, and sublime. I have laid bare my insides."[22] The private behavior that Rousseau describes (abandoning his five children, compulsive masturbation, and more) both scandalized readers and convinced them that they had joined a daring voyage of self-exploration and revelation. Thus, self-analysis was not a contingent element of the *Confessions*, but essential to both Rousseau's personal philosophy and his posthumous influence. The resulting intimacy encouraged readers to reflect more deeply on their own motives, misdeeds, and trajectory through life. The result was the consolidation of a burgeoning "autobiographical mentality" in which "a type of writing came to imply a mode of being."[23] The resulting change in subjectivity suggests that autobiography as a literary genre was the most obvious manifestation of a broader cultural development in which individual narrativity and interiority had become conjoined and conceptually reified. Much the same thing would happen after Freud when the ego and the subconscious gave denizens of the twentieth century new ways to understand and experience themselves.

Although also highly influential, Benjamin Franklin's *Autobiography* does not live up to its posthumous title. Its four sections were written many years apart (1771, 1781, 1788–1789). Not only did Franklin change considerably between bouts of writing, so did his purpose in writing. Moreover, he did not edit the four parts together for publication. As a result, what appeared in print shortly after his death in 1790 is more chronology than teleology: the foundations of his personal success are important, but his inner development is not. The messy history of the memoirs' publication also reveals that the authenticity of Franklin's actual words meant little to contemporaries. Franklin had been famous in Parisian high society for wearing a simple brown suit and fur hat as ambassador to France, but this had been intended to garner support for the Americans' cause more than to create a distinctive persona for himself. Moreover, there is good evidence that he shared early modern misgivings about singularity and individuality. He often remained anonymous and impersonal in his actions and publications, preferring the lessons of emulation to those of a uniquely original individual. Besides, his memoirs did not divulge secrets of his inner self, rather they painted a portrait of public success. In this sense, Franklin's *Autobiography* is the antithesis of Rousseau's contemporaneous *Confessions*. What is more, the term "autobiography" was, as Stephen Arch puts it, "a neologism that Franklin had probably never heard in his lifetime."[24] Only later, after the full publication (1818) and then renaming of his memoirs as an autobiography (1868), did Franklin become an outstanding example of a "self-made man" and an inspiration for nineteenth-century individualism.

According to literary critic Michael Mascuch, however, the Anglophone world did produce at least one genuine autobiography by the end of the eighteenth century: *Memoirs*

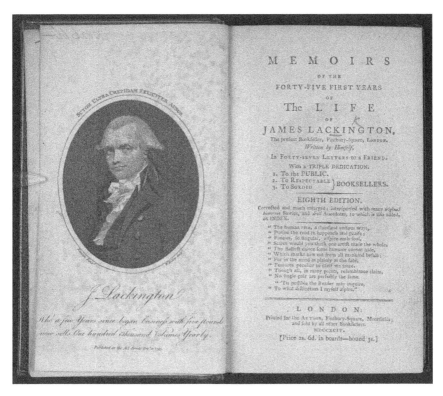

FIGURE 2.4 Frontispiece, James Lackington, *Memoirs of the First Forty-Five Years of the Life of James Lackington*, 8th ed. (1794). © The British Library Board / 1202.b.48.frontispiece.

of the First Forty-Five Years of the Life of James Lackington (London, 1791) (Figure 2.4). Lackington, like Franklin, was a printer and bookseller. He modeled his *Memoir* on contemporary biographies of weightier men such as John Wesley and Samuel Johnson. The *Memoir* also derived from other biographical genres such as the religious hagiographies of the seventeenth century and the criminal lives published by the Ordinary of Newgate in the eighteenth century. The former had been published to encourage emulation, especially through introspective piety, whereas the latter had been written to discourage emulation, especially when faced with similar temptations. Lackington's first-person narrative expressed great pride in its subject—his own rise from obscurity to "uncommon success"— and combined it with the sort of possessive individualism first embodied in the fictional Robinson Crusoe. Even more than Daniel Dafoe's novel, Lackington's *Memoir* contained a fully articulated plot that narrates the personal development of a bookseller (himself) whose fate was determined by his own particular thoughts and actions. Lackington emphasized his individual distinctiveness and personal genius, thereby rejecting the role of social institutions (parish, family, village, guild, etc.) in his development, and he presented his life as a "story" to enhance readers' engagement. Thus, Lackington's work constitutes a seminal cultural performance: an autobiography of an individualist self. It took at least a generation, however, for Europeans to realize that such an approach amounted to a new episteme of personal subjectivity, one that complemented both Kant's philosophy and Rousseau's *Confessions*.

FRENCH REVOLUTION

The French Revolution made extraordinary changes to collective and personal identities alike. Changes in vocabulary alone suggest the implications for human dignity even when material circumstances may not have improved. The abolition of seigneurialism officially turned peasants (*paysans*) into country dwellers (*habitants de campagne*), and in parts of eastern France even transformed serfs into tenants. Military service became the duty of citizen-soldiers, thereby transforming socially marginal soldiers (*soldats*) into patriotic defenders of the fatherland (*défenseurs de la patrie*). Destroying the entire corporative social order based on guilds, parishes, and noble lineage led to unprecedented social mobility, both upward and downward. At the broadest conceptual level, replacing a kingdom of subjects with a nation of citizens, each possessed of individual rights, made all adults equal before the law (though not equal in choosing lawmakers). Even the basics of human intimacy underwent radical change as no-fault divorce created a new economy of emotional fulfillment for women as well as men. These sweeping reforms in the structural underpinnings of traditional society were all associated with greater personal freedom, even as they brought new forms of vulnerability and dependency.

The French Revolution also gave millions of Frenchmen the opportunity to participate in politics. Doing so required them to craft public narratives of personal identity to be elected to any of the tens of thousands of new offices. By 1793, holding public office required obtaining a "certificate of civic conduct," which meant first explaining in detail one's conduct in the revolution thus far. Men who wanted to join a popular society had to answer similar questions posed in often raucous public meetings. The Reign of Terror multiplied the number of popular societies and intensified political factionalism. As a result, thousands of clubs went through internecine purification processes. Members often overstated their activist credentials and came to regret it once the political wheel of fortune turned against the Jacobins. Membership purges became legion by late 1794 and early 1795.

The overthrow of Robespierre in July 1794 further complicated the need for individuals to provide public explanations for their past political conduct. The changing opportunities and threats presented by the Revolution encouraged both multiple forms of self-representation and deeper self-reflection as individuals made what could be life-changing, even life-ending, choices. Throughout the protracted upheaval, individuals repeatedly found themselves forced to balance and blend their private interests and political principles, *paterfamilias* and *patrie*, hypocrisy and integrity, and so on. Private matters of conscience as well as public explanations of conduct intensified the need for self-reflection. The "law of suspects" adopted in September 1793 had made it exceptionally easy to imprison individuals. Perhaps 200,000 men and women found themselves locked up merely on suspicion of being dangerous to the fledgling republican regime. Many if not most of these individuals responded to their imprisonment by petitioning higher authorities for their release. These *mémoires justificatifs* generally contained carefully edited versions of their authors' lives to date. Many such "autodefenses" were printed to craft a particular identity in the eyes of the public, as well as those of civil and judicial authorities. These efforts to present a suitable public persona stimulated self-reflection. What were their deepest convictions? Were these worth dying for? Prisoners who made such thinking part of their narratives hoped to inspire greater empathy in their readers, who may have felt at risk themselves. General Moreau's published justification included the broad observation that, during revolutionary upheaval, "there is nobody who can be sure that one day he won't appear in the position of an accused. Therefore, let everyone do some self-reflection."[25]

Many *mémoires justificatifs* deployed the language and tropes of sentimentalism. Such was the case in the petition from Laurent Melloni, formerly the elected mayor of Bagneux (Indre), who made lachrymose claims about the extent of his misery. An official inquiry confirmed his age, infirmities, dependent children, modest property holdings, political principles, zeal and integrity in office, ignorance about the emigration of his sons, and the hardship caused by having his grain confiscated as political punishment.[26] Others used the discourse of transparency, including accounts of their private conduct, as evidence of their virtue and thus innocence. Turning inward for the sake of outward appearances was also tried. Authors who made claims about personal character, motives, and states of mind, aware that this might be seen as mere rhetoric, frequently added supporting attestations from members of their local community. The petition sent by Jean Gauzan offers a model. To support the brief moral portrait he sketched of himself, he provided a supporting document, signed by fifteen public officials and self-declared "notables" from his village of Réole, that corroborated his claims by noting that "he was always regarded as a good citizen, simple, peaceful, without ambition, seizing the opportunity to oblige, but timid and tranquil by nature."[27]

Autodefenses and petitions seeking relief from revolutionary repression proliferated more than ever during the Thermidorian period. They were also influenced by a wave of prison memoirs, either published by their authors or formed into compendia such as the *Almanach des prisons* (1794) and its trilogy of sequels. So popular were prison narratives that they virtually became a new genre of literature. Collections of prison letters mirrored the epistolary novel, and memoirs mixed sentimentalism with elements of autobiography. Victims commonly emphasized the profound emotional impact of being a suspect, spending time in prison, or losing relatives to the guillotine, thereby mobilizing the *sensibilité* and empathy that was expected of readers at the time.

As Thermidorian politics moved steadily toward revenge, thousands of *sans-culottes*, Jacobins, and former government agents became the target of purges and imprisonment. Spectacular lynchings and prison massacres proliferated across the south. As a result, many of the "perpetrators" of the Terror became themselves victims of violence and repression. Naturally, they too wrote autodefenses. The petition from Major Henry Maury illustrates how an official "terrorist" deployed the language of interiority and sincerity. Maury explains that he is in prison "for mistakes in which *my heart took no part*; my ordeal comes from having been a member of an Extraordinary [Military] Commission, and this ordeal, *I say with all the sincerity in my soul*, has as its cause the happiness of humanity, because ... I had the satisfaction of having contributed to saving a host of innocents."[28] As an army officer, Maury had probably done what was expected of him. But that was not his justification. Instead, he emphasized a clear conscience and virtuous conduct.

Autodefenses and prison memoirs written by victims of political repression of all stripes reveal the extent to which an enormous range of individuals had been forced to engage in extraordinary public encounters with their consciences and their reputations. If the autobiographical "I" is central to developing the modern self, as scholars generally acknowledge, then the French Revolution proved an especially powerful catalyst because it forced hundreds of thousands of Frenchmen to engage intensively, and very often publicly, with the tensions between inner motives and outer actions, between private fears and public emotions, to establish their personal identities. A comparison of Huguenot memoirs written in the wake of the Revocation of the Edict of Nantes in 1685 and the émigré memoirs written at the turn of the nineteenth century reveals a clear shift from establishing a *social* identity to forging a *personal* identity replete with modern elements of interiority, emotionality, and subjectivity utterly lacking only a century earlier. Here was yet another way in which the French Revolution capped the eighteenth century as a provocation to the interior subjectivity of modern selfhood. Lest we forget, however, the Romantic movement, truly mass consumerism, the social dislocations of industrialization, and even the invention of the term "individualism," all made their own major contributions to the development of the self in the decades after 1800.

CHAPTER THREE

Ethics and Social Relations: The Invention of Society

SARAH MAZA

It is not enough to say that the Enlightenment remade ideas about the social world; the eighteenth century actually saw the *invention* of what we call "society" as a concept distinct from the political and spiritual realms. This chapter explains why and how the idea of civil society emerged in eighteenth-century Europe from new ideas, new economic conditions, and new practices of sociability. It further explores responses to the dilemmas that arose from conceiving of society as an autonomous, secular sphere: if humans were not connected to each other through the divine, how would the social world hold together? Or, to put it slightly differently, if God did not guide the lives of men in society, where could one locate the sources of ethical behavior among humans? At the same time, concrete developments in the socioeconomic sphere led to different anxieties about social morality, as the rapid growth of towns and cities and a flood of new consumer goods available to persons of middling station triggered fears of social confusion tagged, in the eighteenth century, as the all-purpose scourge of "luxury."

The overarching solutions to such dilemmas were found in the closely related ideas of nature and sentiment: the natural world provided a template for ethical behavior through its most powerful human instantiation, the family, which had at its heart a newly defined relationship between men and women. The family, in turn, offered a model for relations in society at large, with humans presumed to experience a natural "sympathy" for their brethren within the wider kinship of humankind; compassion for other humans was often portrayed as a bodily reaction—tears, fainting—within the emotional style known as "sensibility." Ideals of natural human connection and familial empathy as a guide to social ethics flourished among educated Europeans until the 1790s, when the violence of revolution and warfare brought them up short.

Those only slightly familiar with the Enlightenment sometimes assume that eighteenth-century progressive thought included ideals of social "equality"; that is only true in a very specific and restricted sense. Although a few writers such as Jean-Jacques Rousseau theorized about radical social equality in a utopian natural state, most thinkers of the age shared in practice the views expressed in the article "Multitude" in that mid-century monument of Enlightenment thought, the *Encyclopédie* of Denis Diderot and Jean-Baptiste le Rond d'Alembert: "Beware the judgment of the multitude; in matters of reasoning and philosophy its voice is that of meanness, ignorance, inhumanity, folly and prejudice." The "multitude," the article continued, was only right after many years when its voice became "an echo that repeats the thought of a small number of men in the vanguard for posterity."[1]

Proponents of enlightened thought were firm believers in a social hierarchy that kept the poor and ignorant masses firmly parked at the bottom of society while themselves enjoying the comfortable lives of the social elite. The most famous embodiment of this disposition is Voltaire, known in his day as "the Seigneur of Ferney" after he bought an opulent manor on the Swiss border where he was attended by a flock of servants and benevolently lorded it over "his" peasants. But Voltaire, a commoner by birth, was also known for his scorching mockery of aristocratic claims and pretentions in the spirit of an age that prized talent and merit over inherited rank. As we shall see, in the places where progressive thinkers gathered—salons, literary societies, masonic lodges—aristocrats mingled in supposed equality with writers, artists, actors, doctors, priests, engineers, and other members of the non-titled upper classes. Both in theory and in practice, in short, proponents of Enlightenment were committed to creating equality only at the top of society, in congeries of the socially prominent and professionally successful known in the following century as the "notables."

The Enlightenment was therefore not in any way radically egalitarian. But the vast intellectual and cultural transformation that took place in eighteenth-century Europe did entail a deep revolution in how people thought about social relations. It did so by inventing our modern understanding of "society": a distinct sphere of human activity, ruled by its own laws, separate from the spheres of religion and government.

Prior to the eighteenth century, the idea of "society," a realm defined purely by the unofficial interactions of human beings with one another, would not have made much sense, as the human and the divine were presumed linked to one another in a series of mediated vertical relations. In early modern France, for instance, the different "orders" and "estates" of society were not imagined as having direct bonds with one another but as being indirectly connected through the monarch, himself God's representative on Earth: nobles served him in the army and at court, the clergy prayed for him, and the king gave legal existence to the realm's many occupational groups—from the Order of Barristers to the Corporation of Butchers—by granting them the "privilege" to carry out their occupation in return for their oath of loyalty to him. The social world was conceptually arranged as a ladder leading up to the king and through him to the deity rather than as a playing field where social groups coalesced or competed with one another on their own.[2] But by the late eighteenth century, the modern idea of an autonomous social world was widespread; this understanding, which today we take for granted, grew out of the century's intellectual developments, economic transformations, and new social practices.

The word "society" was before then used in both French and English to describe either a voluntary association or partnership (of merchants or men of letters, for instance), or the companionable bonds of "fellowship, consort, companie"—in either case a small-scale voluntary association formed by personal connections. In the eighteenth century, the word took off like a rocket as it acquired a new meaning. A database search of French books (from about three hundred in the seventeenth century to five hundred in the late eighteenth) shows *société* appearing 40 times in the period 1600–1610, 1,102 times in 1751–1760, and 1,811 times in 1771–1780. Over the course of those decades, while the older small-scale sense of "society" persisted, the newer meaning still in use today rapidly gained ground; the word came to signify, as Keith Baker puts it, "the basic form of collective human existence, at once natural to human beings and instituted by them, a corollary to human needs and a human response to those needs."[3] In the eighteenth century this newly conceived idea of "society" was increasingly imagined as not only the context but also the very rationale for human life. The *Encyclopédie*'s article *Philosophe* (man of letters, or intellectual) states that "civil society is to him, so to speak, a sort of deity on earth."[4] The imagined connection of all humans—usually on a national scale—was increasingly understood to be the setting, the means, and the end for the pursuit of earthly happiness.

INVISIBLE HANDS: SELF-REGULATION AND THE SOCIAL

The broad intellectual framework for the emergence of "society" in this sense is the one we are all aware of from our Western Civilization courses: the eighteenth-century secularizing impulse that, while otherwise respectful of religion, rejected the assumption that the divine directly regulated the world of humans. As the idea receded that God intervened in human affairs either directly or indirectly through his royal and priestly representatives on Earth, thinkers in the late seventeenth and early eighteenth century, such as Nicolas Malebranche and Gottfried Wilhelm Leibniz, struggled to reconcile the observed freedom of human social interactions with their belief in divine power over human affairs. God has introduced order into every particle of the universe down to the smallest grain of sand, Leibniz argued, but as limited knowers, humans cannot grasp His design. They fail to understand the infinity of causes and effects in our providentially wrought world because they are by nature unable to apprehend the whole of God's design.[5] As Alexander Pope put it most memorably in his 1734 *Essay on Man*, "All nature is but art unknown to thee / All chance direction which thou canst not see / All discord harmony not understood / All partial evil universal good."

Lurking just beyond the idea that God's design was inscribed in every shred of the universe, albeit in ways inaccessible to the limited understanding of humans, was the radical proposition that nature and human society might be entirely self-regulating organisms. For early eighteenth-century thinkers like Leibniz and Pope, providential design was, as Jonathan Sheehan and Dror Wahrman put it, "a shelter under which the ideas of self-organization could grow."[6] As the century progressed, so did speculation that both the natural and the human worlds could be entirely self-regulating, as theories of self-organization appeared simultaneously in several fields of inquiry. In the 1740s the English scientist John Needham carried out a series of experiments that appeared to confirm the possibility of epigenesis, the spontaneous differentiation of cells from an original spore, seed, or egg, leading to the appearance of new life-forms: thanks to a microscope Needham observed the seemingly miraculous generation of animal life, "perfect Zoophytes, teeming with Life, and Self-Moving," from a wheat concoction suspended in water. Around the same time the Swiss scientist Abraham Trembley caused a sensation by identifying the polyp, a hybrid plant-animal whose parts, when chopped up, came to life as a plurality of creatures. By appearing and multiplying on their own, Needham's "zoophytes" and Trembley's proliferating polyps posed an implicit challenge to the traditional creationist view that all life came to be at once by divine design.[7]

From early in the century, thinkers throughout Europe looked to the animal world as a metaphor for social organization. The beehive was an image often conjured up to describe social dynamics, especially in Britain: on the one hand, bees offered an image of purposeful, well-organized collective productivity, and on the other hand, the presence of a queen bee made the politics of the hive safely orthodox.[8] Early in the century, however, one writer took the hive metaphor in a dangerously heretical direction. The Dutch-British Bernard Mandeville argued in his scandalous 1714 *The Fable of the Bees: Or, Private Vices, Publick Benefits* that unethical behavior was necessary for human societies to flourish. The congruence between public and private virtue might make sense in an agrarian state, but as Mandeville saw it, a modern commercial society was dependent on the vice of at least some of its members: without vanity, envy, and competition, how would the market for consumer goods function? If everyone suddenly became virtuous, he argued, the whole economy of a place like England would collapse. The larger implication of Mandeville's argument, widely denounced in its day but also profoundly influential, was that modern societies functioned according to their own dynamics, which bore no necessary relation to a transcendent moral system.[9] In 1769 Diderot resorted to the image not of the hive but of the swarm of bees to conjure up provocative visions of biological and social autonomy. Imagine, he wrote in *D'Alembert's Dream*, a cluster of bees attached to one another by their feet; now take a pair of scissors and cut through the cluster at the point where the feet are attached. The outcome, he wrote, will seem like two separate organisms, or even more were one to continue cutting.[10] Such dangerously materialist visions of headless or mechanical nature could easily be transposed to the social sphere.

Although Mandeville elicited outrage for his provocative defense of the social utility of vice, the development of political economy as a science, and with it the conception of the economic realm as autonomous and self-regulating, moved apace starting in the late seventeenth century. In 1698 the English economist Charles Davenant urged his contemporaries to "trace all the Circuits of Trade, To find its hidden Recesses, To discover its Original Springs and Motions" so as to uncover the "Links and Chains by which one Business hangs upon another." As for governments, they should keep a benevolent distance from the economic sphere, "take a Providential care of the whole but generally let the Second Causes work their own way."[11] At mid-century two leaders of the dominant school of French economic thought, Physiocracy, posited that God had "bestowed on us as a father the principles of economic harmony," which amounted to saying that Providence had granted the economy its own self-regulating laws. The market might be subject to accidental disruptions, wrote one of their colleagues, but such events will be corrected "by a necessary effect of … competition."[12] The best-known metaphor for self-regulation appeared after mid-century in the work of Scottish economist Adam Smith: the image of an "invisible hand" that causes many individual quests for self-interest to result in the greatest good for all. The hand was not God's but the embodiment of the miraculous laws inscribed in the very dynamics of modern economies.[13]

As with the economy, so with society in general. In 1786 an English writer named Joseph Townsend published a pamphlet entitled *A Dissertation on the Poor Laws by a Well-Wisher to Mankind*, in which he argued that his government's attempts at regulations to alleviate poverty only worsened the problem they purported to solve. He offered, as a metaphor, yet another animal fable, that of two goats left on a South Sea island by a Spanish explorer. The goats mated and multiplied until their numbers outstripped the island's resources and the weakest among them died off, returning the population to equilibrium and abundant resources. One day, fearing that the island would become a magnet for pirates, the Spaniards planted on the island a pair of greyhounds who started to eat their way through the goat population. The goats retreated to a craggy high ground out of reach of the dogs, who nonetheless survived, and eventually multiplied, thanks to the folly of the occasional imprudent goat. Thus, wrote Townsend, anticipating aspects of both Malthus and Darwin, did the powerful dogs and vulnerable goats enjoy a self-sustaining equilibrium with each fulfilling their natural function.[14] That, of course, was how the human world was increasingly understood to work, with social and economic inequalities dictated not by divine fiat but by self-generated complementarities. Many a thoughtful observer would have agreed with Samuel Johnson's 1753 observation that in London, with one man's refuse being another's livelihood, he could not but "admire the secret concatenation of society, that links together the great and the mean, the illustrious and the obscure."[15]

URBAN LIFE, CONSUMER CULTURE, AND SOCIAL NETWORKS

Over the course of the eighteenth century, then, thinkers began to conceive of the natural world and, by analogy, the economic and social worlds as self-regulating aggregates whose "secret concatenations" typically functioned to the benefit of all, independent of divine design or royal decree. While ideas are much more than simple "reflections" of social "realities," there can be no question that this new understanding of human society as the complex, self-regulating, and generally beneficial setting for the pursuit of earthly happiness must be related to the extraordinary growth of urban populations and the surge in trade and consumerism in eighteenth-century western Europe and its overseas colonies. "Society" arose as a concept and an object of study at just the same time as European towns and cities were growing dramatically larger and more complex.

For a variety of interconnected reasons such as better climate, fewer epidemics, and improving agricultural productivity, the European population surged from about 120 million to 190 million over the course of the eighteenth century, drawing more and more people to towns in search of their livelihoods. Paris grew from 450,000 in the late seventeenth century to around 700,000 by the eve of the French Revolution; Berlin from 50,000 to 170,000 in the same period; Vienna's population increased from a few thousand to a quarter of a million; and London dwarfed them all, surging from 675,000 early in the century to almost a million. The proportion of people living in cities increased dramatically too, from about 15 percent to 30 percent in Britain, 16 percent to 19 percent in France, and 12 percent to 24 percent in the German-speaking lands. By 1750 London housed over one-tenth of the English population.[16]

This expanding urban population was both consequence and cause of Europe's booming economy, fueled by both domestic and overseas commerce. The circulation of goods, increased productivity, and the dramatic development of trade between Europe and its colonies, as well as between Europe and Asia, made life more pleasurable and comfortable for the middling and upper classes in Western cities. New goods proliferated: luxury items for the palate such as coffee, tea, chocolate, and sugar; useful everyday objects from clocks and mirrors to eyeglasses, fans, and board games; enticing consumer goods such as attractive printed fabric from India and porcelain from China, or imitations produced domestically for lower prices. In bigger towns and cities, living spaces and their furnishings became more intimate, attractive, and comfortable. In Paris, for instance, new apartments were built on a single level, with smaller and better heated rooms; upholstered seating, chests of drawers, brightly colored wallpaper and decorative knickknacks all made for easier and more pleasant living.[17] Further, for those who could afford them, consumer goods transformed all aspects of life: stylish clothing became cheaper, more abundant, and more attuned to fashion cycles; medical goods from pills and elixirs to prosthetic limbs and medicinal baths promised relief from bodily discomfort.[18] The pleasures and conveniences afforded by the eighteenth-century consumer revolution undoubtedly made it easier to imagine social life as an end in itself (Figure 3.1).

FIGURE 3.1 François Boucher, *The Afternoon Meal*, 1739. Oil on canvas. Louvre, Paris, France. © Wikimedia Commons (public domain).

Within these increasingly wealthy and populous towns and cities writers and thinkers also encountered institutions where the exchange of ideas and shared social practices among people of mixed—within limits—backgrounds offered aspirational models of life within a horizontal enlightened "society" in place of traditional status- and lineage-bound hierarchies. Some of these settings were quite informal. By the eighteenth century taverns had long been a fixture of European towns, providing an alternative living space for workers dwelling in cramped quarters as well as alcoholic beverages typically more salubrious than the local water. With their heavily male clientele mixed with prostitutes, entertainers, and police spies, taverns or *cabarets* were typically, on the continent, rowdy plebeian venues. In Britain, however, eighteenth-century alehouses (increasingly known as "public houses") evolved toward respectability by adding rooms for private gatherings of clubs, mutual-aid societies, and political associations. English taverns retained a plebeian clientele while also becoming centers for organized political activity by Whig and Tory politicians who mobilized their electorates by "treating" them to drink or food. The age of Enlightenment's most characteristic development was, however, the rapid spread in cities all over Europe of the coffeehouse, a more genteel alternative to the boozy tavern. The stimulating drink had been introduced to Europe as an exotic luxury from Turkey in the sixteenth century, and by the late seventeenth century elegant establishments devoted to its consumption had popped up in several European capitals. As early as 1686 the Italian owner of the Café Procope in Paris furnished his establishment with mirrors, marble tabletops, and candelabras, creating a venue for the well-heeled to enjoy the newly fashionable drink. By 1789 Paris had about nine hundred coffeehouses where respectable patrons could drop by informally to meet at communal tables, consult newspapers, and engage in "civilized" exchanges fueled by caffeine rather than spirits.[19]

Much more exclusive and structured were the social and intellectual gatherings known as salons that, in the larger European cities, brought together persons of learning and wit, while famously granting a starring role to the female *salonnières* who ran them. Salons first became popular in the later seventeenth century as alternatives to the strictly hierarchical, status- and etiquette-bound world of the royal court; as such they embodied an early physical and conceptual separation of "society" (in this instance, high society) from the state, or of the "town" side of *la cour et la ville* from the court. In seventeenth-century France, these Paris-based social gatherings run by high-born women were mostly aristocratic, devoted to gossip and flirtatious games but also to literary activities such as the penning of poems and group writing of novels. But their function was also to allow for some degree of social mixing at the top, since they provided a space where titled grandees could socialize with the upwardly mobile, the recently ennobled, and a sprinkling of upper-class commoners.[20]

By the eighteenth century, Parisian salons had become major cultural institutions. Their conveners were still women, albeit not escapees from the court and not even necessarily noble, and the intellectual component of their activities increasingly prevailed. Over the course of the century hostesses such as Madame du Deffand, Madame de Tencin, Madame Geoffrin, and Madame Necker vied to attract the wittiest and most celebrated writers to their (typically bi-weekly) gatherings, where letters from absent members reporting on developments abroad were read aloud and authors presented their ideas for debate and sometimes circulated their manuscripts. While blue-blood writers and guests still dominated, these gatherings devoted to literary life were later in the century frequently run by non-aristocratic women (Geoffrin and Necker) and had long opened their doors to talented commoners such as the cutler's son Diderot and the watchmaker's child Rousseau.[21] The mixing in salons was confessional as well as social; in these venues French Catholic high society embraced the Swiss Calvinist Rousseau and his compatriot the salon hostess Suzanne Necker, as well as numerous French and English Protestant writers. Berlin salons developed later than their French counterparts, and in the late eighteenth and early nineteenth centuries the most famous among them were run by the Jewish *salonnières* Henriette Herz and Rahel Levin, in whose homes famous writers and artists mingled with Jewish high society and with members of the nobility and royal family. Berlin's salons were thus daringly egalitarian, if only in the restricted sense typical of eighteenth-century elite culture.[22]

Such was the case as well with the most highly structured institutions for Enlightened sociability, masonic lodges. The trappings of Freemasonry and its very name harked back to a working-class culture, the legends and rituals of seventeenth-century English stonemasons' guilds (prominent symbols included builders' tools such as compasses, squares, and trowels). But eighteenth-century lodges, as they mushroomed all over

Europe, typically drew their members from the more prosperous segments of urban society. Lodges started in early eighteenth-century London as occupational associations with especial appeal to merchants, who used them for business and social contacts. Eighteenth-century masonry developed as a framework for (mostly) elite male sociability; lodges were settings for conviviality and philanthropy in which much energy was devoted to the rituals, rules, and governance of the organization. At the movement's height in the 1760s, London housed 184 lodges, with membership ranging from a dozen adherents to several hundred for any given one. Freemasonry spread from England to every country on the continent, especially the German states, the Low Countries, and France, which counted about six hundred lodges by 1789.

Although some French lodges started admitting women in the 1740s, Freemasonry was typically and overwhelmingly male, dedicated to brotherhood, business contacts, and intellectual activities—science especially—deemed beyond the grasp of the female mind. Lodges were socially exclusive as well; they recruited from the well-to-do, and while their membership might extend to the most prosperous among artisans, the steep initiation and membership fees, as well as the expectation that brothers would be well educated and financially independent, kept them culturally and financially out of reach of the poor, encompassing, in the words of one historian, the "modestly to greatly affluent classes."[23] The century's most famous representation of masonry, Mozart's opera *The Magic Flute*, features a prince, Tamino, whom the masonic high priest Zarastro invites into the brotherhood not on account of his rank but because he is "a man." While Tamino bravely undergoes ritual ordeals that will grant him access to higher wisdom and love, his servant Papageno turns down a challenge to do the same, stammering that he would much rather indulge in the simple pleasures of sleep, drink, food, and sex. The story's implication could not be clearer: "men" should be invited into the brotherhood of masons as equals, as long as their wealth, lifting them up above vulgar pursuits, allowed them access to enlightenment. Although masonic lodges embraced a much wider and more socially mixed population than did salons, they too leveled society only at the very top.[24]

Coffeehouses, salons, and masonic lodges were all very different institutions, but their simultaneous proliferation in eighteenth-century European urban settings is symptomatic of a deep cultural transformation: the novel assumption that social life could and should take place in settings where people elected to come together on the basis of shared interests and of projects freely embraced, rather than in the ancient, more formally organized structures of guilds, estates, and households. Elite urban sociability, with its emphasis on mixed, civilized social intercourse, offered an idealized template for a new sort of horizontally structured, self-regulating social world.

Institutions of sociability such as lodges and salons can also be seen as smaller, concrete embodiments of the much broader nexus of educated people that came into being with the proliferation of print culture. Literacy rates surged in most parts of eighteenth-century Europe. While historians acknowledge the problems inherent in measuring "literacy" (if a person is able to sign a will or a contract, does this mean she can read a pamphlet or novel?), there is no question that a dramatic change occurred in this period. In France average rates increased over the course of the century from 29 percent to 47 percent for men, 14 percent to 27 percent for women; national averages in Britain by century's end stood at around 60 percent for men and 40 percent for women. It was in this period that, as T. W. C. Blanning puts it, "the ability to read and write ceased to be the preserve of a small elite and became accepted as a desirable and realizable goal for everyone."[25] Contemporaries noted that new categories of people were now immersed in books. In

1783 the London publisher James Lackington observed that "the poorer sorts of farmers and even the poor country people" had their sons and daughters read current novels to them, "and on entering their houses you may see *Tom Jones, Roderick Random,* and other entertaining books stuck up on their bacon racks." Female readers in particular, Lackington recorded with satisfaction, had acquired expansive and discerning taste in books, "and there are some thousands of ladies, who frequent my shop, that know as well what books to choose, and are as well acquainted with works of taste and genius, as any gentleman in the kingdom, notwithstanding they sneer against novel readers."[26]

While only a subset of the literate population was equipped to tackle a book or newspaper, the supply of printed matter shot up over the course of the eighteenth century: reading material was a key item in the eighteenth-century consumer revolution, another means to the pursuit of pleasure and novelty. The sheer number of available books grew dramatically absent any change in printing technology. In Britain, for instance, around 6,000 book titles were published in the 1630s, 21,000 in the 1710s, and 56,000 in the 1790s. This was also true of periodicals. In the seventeenth century, London had only one daily newspaper, but by the 1770s readers could choose between nine dailies and a dozen other periodicals.[27] France had fifteen newspapers in 1745 and eighty-two forty years later, on the eve of the Revolution, with overall circulation figures quadrupling. The fastest growing among them were provincial papers known as *affiches* that, while mostly apolitical and commercial, allowed publishers to spread word of new books by enlightenment writers. While the number of paper titles and copies were modest by modern standards—the high-profile *Mercure de France* sold 20,000 copies of each issue in the 1770s—print matter was widely shared among institutions and individuals, with every copy of a paper reaching an estimated six or more readers.[28]

The same went for other forms of reading matter. Books were expensive items in the eighteenth century, costing the equivalent of a new pair of women's shoes; not until the nineteenth century did transformations in print technology that lowered prices make a mass reading public possible. While books were mostly purchased by the well-to-do in the century of the Enlightenment, more people had access to more of them through subscription and lending services. English readers formed book clubs whose members paid annual dues for a pool of circulating volumes and met for discussion; others set up subscription societies for access to potentially thousands of books. Hundreds of lending libraries from which one could check out a book for a small sum sprang up in the provinces as well as in London. The French too had their *cabinets de lecture*, where for an annual fee, patrons could either check out books or read in situ, and in towns more modest readers could even pay pennies to borrow a popular book, or even a lopped-off portion of one, by the day or even by the hour, from an enterprising bookseller or *bouquiniste*.[29] In sum, while the poor still encountered stiff cultural and financial barriers to readership, access to books and newspapers dramatically increased in European society for members of the prosperous middle classes: merchants, richer shopkeepers and artisans, teachers, clergy, and other professionals. Readers immersed in the same periodical or popular novel made up yet another social grouping that cut across traditional lines of status or occupation, albeit in most cases a virtual one, more diffuse and socially capacious than those associated with the salon or masonic lodge.

In the eighteenth century, then, the idea of "society" as the undifferentiated context and purpose for human association sprang from mutually reinforcing intellectual developments and material changes. In philosophy and in the natural and human sciences, thinkers theorized a world that, if still ultimately the expression of God's design, in practice operated and even evolved autonomously, animated by different versions of Adam Smith's "invisible hand." This conceptual revolution moved apace with the century's dramatic socioeconomic changes, as surging populations, greater wealth, and a new consumer culture blurred traditional hierarchies in urban environments. For the most optimistic observers, these new social formations seemed to function miraculously on their own, with the complementary needs of various elements (and in Mandeville's case, the vices of some) ensuring the well-being of all. For many other observers, however, especially as the century progressed, the absence of a divine or other transcendent binding force could be alarming, even downright terrifying.

FINDING MORALITY IN A SECULAR WORLD

If God was present but remote, leaving humans to their own devices in the wake of a benevolent act of creation, what would happen to men and women deprived of a daily moral compass? If a clergy, whose corruption had been exposed, no longer had the authority to dictate ethical norms, where would humanity find a collective moral guide and purpose? The most famous expression of this existential terror is Voltaire's 1759 tale *Candide*, the story of a naïve young man who in the course of his travels encounters every form of both natural and man-made evil, from earthquakes and floods to political corruption, wars, religious persecution, and torture. Through it all, Candide's mentor Pangloss mechanically responds to his pupil's mounting despair with the Leibnizian credo that all is for the best, we just cannot know God's larger design. Around the end of the story Candide and his battered companions, now living near Constantinople, consult a famous dervish, "the best philosopher in Turkey," begging him to explain why so much evil can be allowed to exist. "'What difference does it make,' said the dervish, 'if there is good or evil? When his highness sends a ship to Egypt, does he worry about whether or not the mice are comfortable on board?'"[30] Voltaire himself famously gave up on answering Candide's question and concluded that the best we can do is to make the world a bit less awful by coaxing produce from the small plots of our ruined Eden. God's remoteness, at best, from humanity had made moot the meaning of good and evil.

While Voltaire indelibly captured the anguish lurking beneath the optimism of the early Enlightenment—given an absentee God, where do we find morality?—many less celebrated writers experienced a similar sense of dislocation, which they tended to attribute to more concrete developments. Starting in the early eighteenth century, hundreds of writers in Britain and France churned out pamphlets and books that described the catastrophic effects of a plague they called "luxury." The concept was not a new one: denunciations of "luxury" permeate the Judeo-Christian tradition, from antiquity through biblical times to early Christianity and beyond. From the start, luxury was viewed, in the words of John Sekora, "as a fundamental and generic vice from which other, subordinate vices would ensue."[31] Some of the themes pervasive in eighteenth-century literature were present many centuries earlier in the writings of philosophers and theologians: luxury was the sin of wanting material objects and pleasures to which you were not entitled, including costly baubles and clothes, excessive food and drink, prostitutes and young boys. Self-centered and anti-civic, the vice of excessive desire was deemed by enlightenment and counter-enlightenment types alike a serious threat to the social order. Hence the proliferation of sumptuary edicts issued by early modern monarchs across Europe closely regulating the display of wealth and finery according to a person's rank. If the Great Chain of Being (the divinely ordained ranking of all creation and of humans in society) was the conceptual core of early modern sociopolitical life, "luxury," by putting resources and symbols in the wrong hands, fatally threatened the spiritual coherence of an ordered society. As Sekora notes, fears of luxury typically bubbled up in times of threat and disruption, during and after wars or drastic economic transformation.[32]

The eighteenth century in Europe was one such time, as we have seen. In the towns and cities where writers typically lived, the wealth pumped into society by overseas commerce, the riot of new consumer goods available to those of middling social standing, the population growth that brought a flood of strangers to town: all fueled thousands of pages of jeremiads about the threat of luxury. Since the seventeenth century, French writers had expressed fears of the socially corrosive effects of money, as newly rich financiers allegedly usurped the rightful place of the old nobility. By the middle of the following century, the rise of Madame de Pompadour, raised among merchants and bankers, as France's unofficial queen, prompted anguished and hostile commentary that the monarchy was literally in bed with finance.[33] In the eighteenth century, writers no longer saw the danger as confined to the upper reaches of society: people of all classes, it was claimed in apocalyptical warnings, were indulging in tastes beyond their station, and in doing so fatally undermining the natural order of society. Male domestic servants—gaudily dressed to serve the newly rich who, in employing them, allegedly robbed husbandry of crucial labor—were a favorite target. "The Dearness of Labour of all sorts, the Largeness of Wages and other Perquisites of Servants, their Idleness and insolence are all the effects of Luxury," George Blewitt wrote in 1725. Men drawn into service made up a "sort of idle Vermin by which ... the Kingdom is almost devoured."[34] Themes of catastrophic social aspiration pervaded French literature on luxury as well. "What a confusion in all conditions!" wrote one author at mid-century, "*les grands* want to imitate the magnificence of the sovereign; the citizens of moderate means want equal *les grands*; the poor want to imitate the middling, and by this dangerous chain the impulse for luxury is communicated from the highest rank down to the lowest classes of people."[35]

"Luxury" was shorthand for a whole nexus of social evils associated with incipient urban modernity. French writers described it as a scourge that led to various forms of "sterility" and incipient demographic and economic catastrophe: lured by the promise of material gratification, healthy peasants left the land, abandoning productive agricultural work for fruitless occupations such as domestic service. There, in imitation of upper-class rakes, they spurned marriage for a life of barren sensual enjoyment. Women of all classes were caught up in this frenzy as well; loath to take leave of social pleasures, they farmed out their newborns to "mercenary" wet-nurses who let the infants die. New consumer goods, fashionable clothing especially, had become available to all, but especially to the lower sort eager to ape their betters. The result was that it had become impossible to tell on sight who belonged to which social rank. Penned by writers of many different ideological leanings, from Catholic conservatives to Rousseauian radicals, denunciations of "luxury" expressed acute fears that material goods and the shallow pleasures of urban life would trigger social collapse and economic catastrophe.[36] In Britain, writers of all political persuasions, including such luminaries as Viscount Bolingroke and Henry Fielding, further warned that "luxury," having "descended from the highest to the lowest ranks of our people," undermined the state by encouraging idleness and insubordination among the lower orders.[37]

If the evils of modern life, as subsumed under the label "luxury," threatened to destroy the social order and the moral fiber of nations, salvation was regularly sought in luxury's symbolic opposite, the purportedly wholesome and fruitful world of the countryside.

The theme of social salvation through agriculture proved especially powerful in France, where it was most insistently expressed via the ideas of the influential economic school of Physiocracy. Physiocracy emerged in the 1750s, in the context of the disastrous (for France) Seven Years War, promoted by its adherents in part as a means of regeneration for a nation shattered by the loss of most of its overseas empire. In opposition to traditional mercantilist economic thinking, which understood national wealth to reside in a favorable balance of international trade and the accumulation of bullion at the expense of other powers, prominent Physiocrats, many of them noble landowners such as the Marquis de Mirabeau, argued that only agriculture could promote both prosperity and political stability. Physiocrats and their followers championed the creation of prizes and honors for farmers who increased their yields, and of agricultural societies where local landed elites gathered to discuss improvement. They enthused over the "productive" toil of the rural worker, while dismissing urban trades and services as "sterile" or "mercenary." Commerce might yield dramatic returns in the short run, but its profits were volatile and could vanish as quickly as they appeared. The land, by contrast, produced not only steadily increasing wealth but also social cohesion and moral values.[38] One writer urged priests to guide their flocks into agrarian work, "to make them love an estate that keeps them quite naturally from vice." Agriculture became, in the words of John Shovlin, "the symbolic ground on which it proved possible to reconcile wealth and virtue."[39] Throughout the century, French painters from rococo artists such as François Boucher to sentimentalists like Jean-Baptiste Greuze idealized the countryside as a place of abundance and innocent eroticism featuring healthy lads and comely lasses, mothers nursing their fat babies, and all manner of adorable livestock.

Such written and visual paeans to the countryside were symptomatic of the belief that "nature" could stand in for religion as a guide for social and moral norms. Where in earlier centuries the most powerful social and emotional connections could be with distant entities—God, a ruler or lord, an extended kinship network whose honor one was bound to uphold—eighteenth-century thinkers and commentators located the most viscerally "natural" bonds between humans in the intimate, physically proximate connections of the nuclear family. Central to the elevation of family love as the fundamental expression of, and model for, the most powerful social bonds, was a thoroughgoing redefinition of the nature and role of women. If women served as objects of hate and fear and as agents of corruption in certain settings—as power-mongering queens or mistresses, as avatars of destructive "luxury" through sex or consumption—the new "natural" woman, as most famously promoted by Jean-Jacques Rousseau, was to be the linchpin of that most natural and healthy of groupings, the intimate family.

GENDER, INTIMACY, AND ETHICS

Starting in the later seventeenth century, understandings of the difference between men and women began to change dramatically. Earlier conceptions of sexual difference in the Western world fit into the overarching schema of an unbroken hierarchy of beings from the divine to base matter, with humans at the midpoint. In this scheme of things women fell clearly below men on the ladder of creation, but the two sexes were essentially similar in nature. Early modern anatomical illustrations of human reproductive organs, for instance, portrayed the vagina as an inverted, outside-in penis, and the uterus as an internal scrotum (ovaries were sometimes labeled "female testicles"). As Thomas Laqueur has memorably shown, early modern anatomists believed that the woman's orgasm was as necessary as the man's for conception to occur. On the chain of being, women stood closer to matter than men and were therefore assumed to be, if anything, more lustful than their male counterparts.[40] Moreover, since sociopolitical power devolved from divine will and from kinship and household ties, women could on occasion wield legitimate power as rulers, consorts, regents, or the widows of powerful men; while male rulers may have been preferred, at the end of the day bloodlines and marital alliances trumped gender as the decisive criterion.

By the eighteenth century, however, the older scientific view of women as similar, if markedly inferior, to men had been swept away by new notions of the sexes as incommensurably different. Since the act of thinking came to be understood as radically separate from the material world, and, as a follower of Descartes famously put it, "the mind has no sex," the self-evident inferiority of women had to be firmly rooted in biology.[41] Female reproductive organs were now described as completely different from those of men, and the idea gained ground that a "virtuous" woman would have no inclination toward sexual enjoyment.[42] Eighteenth-century French writers such as Antoine-Léonard Thomas and Pierre Roussel posited that women's temperamental predispositions were governed by their acute nervous sensitivity, which allowed them heightened responses and greater imagination than men, but (pace Descartes) made sustained and focused thinking beyond the reach of their sex.[43]

Such physiological proclivities meant that women were uniquely suited to a domestic sphere, that of the intimate conjugal family, an arena where their extreme sensitivity would be naturally directed to spousal and maternal devotion. The "separate spheres" ideology dominant in the Victorian era first took shape in the eighteenth century, with male authors' fantasies of blissful households ruled by paragons of female love and devotion. The author of the article "Woman" (*Femme*) in the *Encyclopédie*, Joseph-François de Desmahis, sang the praises of his contemporaries' ideal woman: "Confined to the duties of wife and mother, she devotes her days to the practice of un-heroic virtues: occupied with running her family, she rules her husband with indulgence, her children with gentleness and her servants with kindness."[44]

The most influential advocate of the new cultural script that advocated the "natural" investment of women in their roles as wives and mothers was Rousseau. Equally popular with male and female readers, Rousseau promoted the sensual joys of the nuclear family as the proper locus for a displaced "polymorphous eroticism." His promotion of maternal breastfeeding (over the "mercenary" services of wet-nurses) earned him a rapturous following among upper-class women. Queen Marie-Antoinette, Rousseau's most famous if unlikely devotee, proclaimed herself a mother above all and promised to nurse her first child.[45] The heroine of Rousseau's extraordinarily popular novel *La Nouvelle Héloïse* (1761), Julie de Wolmar, turns away from youthful forbidden passion for her tutor Saint-Preux to settle into marriage and what the author portrays as a domestic utopia at Clarens, the couple's estate on the shores of Lake Geneva. There, Julie rules as queen of hearts over a large household where her spouse, children, servants, and laborers alike revere her thanks to the magnetic force of her kindness and the example of her virtue. To his enraptured readers, both female and male, Rousseau proposed a vision of sentimental familial bliss as the antidote to the corruption of modern life.[46]

The actual practices of upper-class family life appear to have changed significantly by the eighteenth century from early modern norms. In what remains the classic, if contested, exploration of the subject focused on England from the sixteenth to the eighteenth century, Lawrence Stone describes the evolution over three centuries from "patriarchal" to "companionate" marriages and families. The patriarchal model, which prevailed well into the seventeenth century, revolved around the strict enforcement of hierarchy and obedience. In the upper and upper-middle classes that are Stone's main focus, women were not free to choose their spouses and could be beaten by their husbands, while children were routinely subjected to harsh physical discipline and expected to show great deference to their parents, addressing them as "sir" or "madam" and never sitting in their presence. Upper-class spouses usually slept in separate bedrooms, Stone also reported; and children were mostly cared for by nurses and tutors and sometimes sent away from home at an early age as wards or apprentices. But over the course of the following century, expectations and behaviors slowly evolved toward more closeness, less formality, and open expressions of affection. Husbands and wives called each other "my dear," children were increasingly spared the rod except for the most grievous transgressions, and some began to address their parents as "mama" and "papa." Paintings, such as that of the Willoughby de Broke family (Figure 3.2) no longer showed children standing stiffly by their parents; instead they cuddled on their mother's lap or played at her feet while their father beamed at them. The expectation undergirding the model that Stone calls the "companionate family" was that domestic life with one's immediate kin should be a source of deep affective gratification rather than a formal arrangement in the service of reproducing family honor and status.[47] One study of eighteenth-century transatlantic

FIGURE 3.2 Johann Zoffany, *John, Fourteenth Lord Willoughby de Broke and his family*, *c.* 1766. 101.9 × 127.3 cm (40 1/8 × 50 1/8 in.), 96.PA.312. © The J. Paul Getty Museum, Los Angeles – Getty Open Content Programme.

correspondence shows family members adopting and encouraging a warm and informal "familiar" style in their letters to one another. In a 1769 letter to his brother in the Bahamas, Alexander Brown wrote, "You'll excuse all incorrectness, but such apologies are more becoming the formality of Courtiers, than the sincerity of Brothers so shall say no more."[48]

If some evidence suggests that the realities of family life—at least in the upper classes, where they are better documented—were evolving toward less formal and more demonstratively affectionate behavior, it is certainly the case that eighteenth-century art and literature portrayed the sentimental nuclear family as the single most powerful model of human, and therefore social, connection. Eighteenth-century French high culture in particular generated striking images of highly expressive, indeed melodramatic, family love. In the 1760s and 1770s, for instance, the much-admired paintings of Jean-Baptiste Greuze featured an idealized rustic family swooning and sobbing over a daughter's engagement or weeping and gesticulating at the deathbed of an aged father. Greuze's paintings were pictorial transpositions of a popular new form of theatre, known as the *genre sérieux*, featuring plays in which the action, unfolding in contemporary settings, was propelled by expressive, often cross-class, marital and familial love instead of by fate or duty as in classical drama.[49]

The plots of these successful productions by such writers as Michel Sedaine, Sébastien Mercier, and Pierre-Augustin de Beaumarchais most often involved tensions between characters of different social standing, resolved in the end by the revelation of a previously concealed biological family connection; they were known and appreciated for their highly demonstrative emotional style, with characters sobbing, fainting, and gesturing to convey extremes of feeling. Louis-Sébastien Mercier's 1772 *The Pauper*, for instance, a typical example of the genre, concerns a wretchedly poor family of spinners living in the basement of a hard-hearted nobleman. The aristocrat tries to seduce the virtuous daughter of the family who resists him but turns out, several plot twists later, to be his long-lost sister, adopted and raised by the paupers; in the end the upper-class onetime villain embraces his sister's kin (she is now set to marry her adoptive brother), tearfully acknowledging the power of family love. In the preface to another play in which the upstanding son of a peddler marries the daughter of a wealthy man, Mercier wrote that everything which "mingles the different estates of society and works to break down the excessive inequality of conditions, that source of all our ills, is politically good." The playwright was not calling for social revolution, far from it; rather, he was expressing a view common among literate elites of his time that the instinctive, natural love we feel for our closest kin by blood or marriage was the self-evident model and foundation for broader social connections.[50] Writers positioned the sentimental family, deemed the most authentically organic of social formations, as the best counterweight and remedy to the solvent of "luxury," the answer to the century's fears of social atomization.

Authors of plays in the *genre sérieux* proposed scripts that drew upon and reinforced a new emotional style increasingly popular among Europe's literate public.[51] These dramatists drew much of their inspiration from the single most popular literary genre of the eighteenth century, the sentimental novel. Prior to the eighteenth century, novels were few in number and aimed mostly at an elite readership able to understand their arcane classical references; they typically featured aristocratic historical protagonists or characters from ancient mythology. The genre was transformed in the eighteenth century, especially after the international success of Samuel Richardson's blockbusters *Pamela* (1740) and *Clarissa* (1748). Eight new novels were published in France in 1701, but 112 in

1789, and British presses churned out seventy new titles a year in the 1790s. Furthermore, novels now had "ordinary" protagonists, ranging from minor provincial nobility such as Rousseau's Julie de Wolmar to servants like Richardson's Pamela, and their mundane settings—country houses, middle-class drawing rooms, city streets—were recognizably familiar to their middle- or upper-class readers.[52] The most successful among them were written in epistolary form, recording their heroes' immediate, intimate experiences of heartbreak, amorous rapture, the threat of rape or the approach of death, in ways that provoked extreme, indeed, often somatic responses—tears, shortness of breath, dizziness, palpitations—among both male and female readers. Richardson's friend Aaron Hill wrote to the author after devouring *Pamela*: "I have done nothing but read it to others and have others read it to me, ever since it came into my hands … It has witchcraft in every page of it; but it is the witchcraft of passion and meaning." The death of Rousseau's heroine Julie at the end of his novel sent readers of both sexes into paroxysms of grief: "No, I was past weeping," one wrote to the author, "A sharp pain convulsed me. My heart was crushed." Another put the book away for three days because he could not bear to read the last letter describing Julie's final hours.[53] Some readers were convinced that the characters in novels were real people as they fell in love with them, sobbed over their misfortunes, and begged authors not to let them die.

Like lachrymose paintings and plays, these novels both reflected and shaped a new emotional style within the eighteenth-century reading public: the heightened affect, experienced and expressed in hyperbolic ways, known as "sensibility." Sensibility, as Sarah Knott notes, was both normative and prescriptive: it doubly described the way human beings operated—physiologically, emotionally, and cognitively—and a moral ideal, the ethical refinement of those who responded to the distress of others. Generally derived from Lockean sensationalism, sensibility (which contemporary English and Scottish thinkers also called "sympathy") rejected conventional distinctions between heart and mind, reason and passion; exposed to injustice or suffering, a properly ethical person would, from the vantage point of sensibility, react in ways simultaneously embodied and rational.[54] Bodily experiences too were central to the ideals of sensibility, both as the source of moral instinct in the man or woman of feeling, and as the quintessential arena for shocking abuse. The ravished woman, the tortured prisoner, the whipped slave all had iniquity inscribed on their bodies, which in turn demanded the intervention of the morally sensitive onlooker.[55]

SENSIBILITY AND HUMAN RIGHTS IN THE REVOLUTIONARY ERA

Lynn Hunt has argued that novels like those of Richardson groomed eighteenth-century readers to experience visceral identification with people they had never met, making possible the universalist sensibility that would lead to humanitarian ideals and legal standards. Hunt singles out as an example eighteenth-century crusades against extreme forms of bodily punishment—legal torture, whipping, branding, mutilation, and brutally protracted executions such as breaking on the wheel—that for centuries were deemed appropriate expressions of the judicial system. Somewhat paradoxically, she argues, it was as people developed a more bounded sense of selfhood—the idea that one's individual body was both sacred and separate from others—that revulsion against the infliction of gratuitous pain upon others began to take shape. This impulse culminated in campaigns against torture and cruel punishments, heralded by the 1764 publication of the Italian philosopher Cesare Beccaria's widely read indictment of judicial barbarism *On Crimes and Punishments,* which then resulted in the overhaul of most European penal systems by century's end. For most of the early modern period, the suffering and death of a criminal or heretic was understood as a collective rite, enacted as the erasure of sin from the body politic through a sacrificial ritual in which the condemned played an active role, his agony pressed into the service of collective redemption. But once bodies and pain became the sole property of individuals, critics no longer tolerated the infliction of bodily torture on other human beings with whom they had learned, over the years, to identify as people like themselves.[56]

"Sympathy" had political consequences too, according to Hunt, since the ideals and practices of sensibility ultimately led to enshrining the new concept of "human rights" as the ultimate rationale for government. Human rights were defined by their violation: it was revulsion against perceived outrages that led eighteenth-century thinkers to posit the existence of rights that were natural (inherent in all), equal (the same for all), and universal (applicable everywhere); implicit in the proclamation of universal rights by the Americans in 1776 and the French in 1789 was the idea that governments instituted to safeguard such rights through their laws could thereby secure cohesion and social peace.[57] Some groups were, of course, excluded from rights or included only in partial ways—children, the insane, the enslaved, religious and racial minorities, women, the poor (Figure 3.3)—and much political struggle in the nineteenth and twentieth centuries in the West aimed at reversing those restrictions. Ultimately, though, the legalization and politicization of empathy as the rights of "man and citizen" proclaimed a new framework for social connection: the nation.

Sentimental rhetoric and tropes of family love pervaded the American and French Revolutions. Ideals of sensitivity and brotherhood, as Sarah Knott has shown, shaped the language of officers fighting in the War of Independence who considered expressions of love for one another proofs of honor and loyalty. In 1782 lieutenant Ephraim Douglass wrote to General James Irvine a letter of concern about the latter's health: "I feel whatever the sympathetic heart of a sincere friend can suffer from the distresses of one to whom it is powerfully attached."[58] In France, the May 1789 convening of representatives from all over the nation as the Estates General elicited powerful feelings of love and kinship among participants such as the Marquis de Ferrières: "O love of my country, thou didst speak powerfully to my heart. I had not known how deep was the mutual tie that binds us to our soil, to men who are our brothers; I learnt it in this moment."[59]

Indeed, in the early months of the French Revolution, men like Ferrières still believed that a nation could be forged and held together by feelings of family love transposed onto a national scale. Rapidly unfolding events would, though, soon prove him and like-minded progressives wrong. The age of revolutions was one of wars and incipient class struggles that exposed the limits of Enlightenment beliefs in the possibility of harmoniously self-regulating societies and the power of sentimental kinship. The rise and consolidation through warfare of Western nationalism proposed a new model for the most effective large-scale human connection, one far more effective than eighteenth-century ideals of sociability and sympathy, but also far more dangerous.

A classic interpretation of eighteenth-century culture, prevalent some three or four decades ago, linked major changes in the European worldview to major socioeconomic changes and specifically to the "rise" of a secular, individualistic, and ultimately revolutionary "bourgeoisie." The eighteenth-century English novel, for instance, with its ordinary protagonists (Tom Jones or Pamela) engaged in individualistic survival or

C'eſt un pere une mère et trois petits enfans
Baignant des pleurs de la reconnaiſßance
La main qu'à leurs besoins ouvre la bienfaisance.

Adele D. Romance dite Romany, del.   *Delvaux sculp.*

Fig. 17. — Frontispice de *Mes Conventions,*

FIGURE 3.3 *Poor family begging for help*, engraving (artist unknown), France, late eighteenth century. © Getty Images.

self-fashioning (Robinson Crusoe or Moll Flanders), spoke to the experience of the striving middle classes.[60] The French Enlightenment, with its satires of idle aristocrats and paeans to tolerance and meritocracy similarly seemed to reflect the anti-noble ideals of a rising bourgeoisie. But this widely embraced Marxian perspective tended to reduce the culture of the Enlightenment to the offshoot of a broad, economically determined social dynamic. From the 1970s on, several generations' worth of revisionist scholarship has laid waste to this simplistic schema, pointing out, for instance, that many writers of the French Enlightenment and even more of their patrons were nobles, that blue bloods enthusiastically frequented salons and masonic lodges, and that monarchs and their agents, both in France and abroad, frequently protected and promoted allegedly "bourgeois" and "revolutionary" writers.[61]

Materialistic interpretations of eighteenth-century culture seemed doomed until a new generation of work on urban life, elite sociability, and the eighteenth-century consumer revolution offered novel and less rigid ways of linking culture to social change.[62] As this chapter has suggested, phenomena such as the spectacular growth of cities and the success of cross-class urban associations, such as freemasonic lodges went hand in hand with an understanding of "society" as autonomous and of the earthly pleasures of comfort and consumption as a central goal of human life.

By the same token, however, consumerism and the mixing of genders and classes in city life triggered anxieties about the effects of "luxury," leading writers of all stripes to seek morality and order in "nature," and in the quintessentially "natural" arena of the nuclear family bound together by the newly domesticated and idealized wife and mother. While scholars still debate whether or not to link these changes to a "bourgeoisie," recent scholarship with its emphasis on such matters as gender, the family, and material culture offers ever more complex and rewarding ways to consider the eighteenth-century relationship among material things, social practices, and ideological currents.

CHAPTER FOUR

Politics and Economies: The Making of Enlightenment Political Economy

GARY KATES

When the future US President, James Madison (1751–1836), attended the College of New Jersey (today Princeton University) in 1769, the class that perhaps made the greatest impression on him was an introduction to political thought taught by the college's president, John Witherspoon (1723–1794). A recent immigrant from Scotland, Witherspoon was certainly well prepared in moral philosophy, and scholars regard his course syllabus as a core reading list of canonical books in political thought at the height of the Enlightenment. (His list, in the order Witherspoon arranged it, is presented with additional bibliographical information in Table 4.1.)

This syllabus is perhaps most noteworthy for its modern bias. In marked contrast to their counterparts in today's introductory college course in political theory, eighteenth-century Princeton students were not required in this class to read anything from the

TABLE 4.1 Syllabus for John Witherspoon's Course in Political Thought[1]

Author	Edition Most Likely Read by Madison	Original Edition
Hugo Grotius	The Rights of War and Peace (London: W. Innys and R. Manby, 1738)	De jure belli ac pacis libri tres (Paris: Buon, 1625)
Samuel von Pufendorf	The Whole Duty of Man, According to the Law of Nature (London: R. Gosling, 1735)	De officio hominis et civis juxta legem naturalem libri duo (Lund: Junghans, 1673)
Richard Cumberland	A Philosophical Inquiry into the Laws of Nature (London: Samuel Powell, 1751)	De legibus naturae (London: E. Flesher, 1672)
John Selden	Table Talk (Glasgow: R. and A. Foulis, 1755)	(London: E. Smith, 1689)
Jean-Jacques Burlamaqui	The Principles of Natural and Politic Law, 2 vols. (London: J. Nourse, 1763)	Principes du droit naturel and Principes du droit politique (Geneva: Barrillot et fils, 1747 and 1751)

Author	Edition Most Likely Read by Madison	Original Edition
Thomas Hobbes	*The Moral and Political Works of Thomas Hobbes of Malmesbury* (London: n.p., 1750)	This is a compendium of two separate works originally published as *De Corpore Politico: Or, The Elements of Law, Moral, and Politick* (London: R. Martin and J. Ridley, 1650) and *Leviathan* (London: Andrew Cooke, 1650).
Niccolo Machiavelli	*The Works of Nicholas Machiavel*, 2 vols. (London: Thomas Davies, 1762)	*Discorsi di Niccolò Machiavelli cittadino, et segretavio fiorentino sopra la pima deca di Tito Livio* (Florence: Bernardo di Giunta, 1531)
James Harrington	*The Oceana of James Harrington* (Dublin: William Williamson, 1758)	*The Commonwealth of Oceana* (London: J. Streater, 1656)
John Locke	*Two Treatises on Government* (London: A. Millar, 1764)	(London: Awnsham Churchill, 1690)
Algernon Sidney	*Discourses on Government* (London: A. Millar, 1763)	(London: n.p., 1698)
Charles-Louis de Secondat, Baron de Montesquieu	*The Spirit of the Laws*, 2 vols. (London: J. Nourse, 1766)	*De l'Esprit des lois*, 2 vols. (Geneva: Barrillot et fils, 1748)
Adam Ferguson	*An Essay on the History of Civil Society* (Edinburgh: A. Millar, 1767)	Same

ancient or medieval periods. Notably absent from the syllabus are Plato, Aristotle, Saint Augustine, and Saint Thomas Aquinas. Indeed, except for Machiavelli's *Discourses*, all of these required books were first published within the century preceding Madison's reading. As an outlier, the case of Machiavelli is revealing. J. G. A. Pocock has convincingly demonstrated in his *Machiavellian Moment* that Machiavelli's *Discourses* inspired early modern readers to focus on the conditions required for maintaining and enhancing republican virtue and keeping corruption at bay.[2]

Indeed, the books on Witherspoon's list inherited civic republican concerns from the Renaissance. Yet at the same time, most of these works were preoccupied not with small republics, but with the rise of centralized and expansive monarchies during the latter half of the seventeenth century, from the English Civil War through the reign of France's Louis XIV. The central thread running through Witherspoon's syllabus seems to be less about preserving virtue and more about defining the rights of subjects vis-à-vis their sovereign rulers, and in turn, the rights of rulers in the international sphere in relation to one another. Louis XIV's expulsion of Protestants (Huguenots) from France in 1685 gave this theme special urgency, particularly in those countries that welcomed these Huguenots. Hugo Grotius and Samuel von Pufendorf were read from this perspective. Witherspoon wanted his students to understand these natural law theorists through the lens of Jean Barbeyrac (1674–1744), the exiled Huguenot, who translated Grotius and Pufendorf from Latin into French and included extensive notes that made their texts more relevant and explicit for grasping how the language of rights could be employed to restrain absolute monarchy.[3]

After Grotius and Pufendorf, Witherspoon's list focused mostly on writers who had adapted rights language and the natural law tradition to English politics. Richard Cumberland, Thomas Hobbes, James Harrington, John Locke, and Algernon Sidney all wrote under the shadow of Oliver Cromwell's Commonwealth. The same is true for John Selden, but eighteenth-century readers such as Madison would have known him through his popular *Table Talk*, a book compiled by his followers and only published posthumously in 1689. Updating this concentration on natural laws and political rights during the 1740s was Jean-Jacques Burlamaqui's *Principles of Natural and Politic Law*, which at least in its early reception, was closely associated with a book that appeared from the same publisher at the same time, Montesquieu's *Spirit of the Laws*. Rounding out the list was the *Essay on the History of Civil Society*, published in 1767 by the Scottish philosopher Adam Ferguson, whom Witherspoon probably knew personally before emigrating to America.

It would, of course, be a mistake to assume automatically that President Witherspoon's list reflects the consensus of public opinion on the period's most salient works of political theory. Like that of any professor today, it could well be that Witherspoon's syllabus represents works beloved by him but regarded by the reading public of his day as technical and arcane. Were these twelve books specialized works for training future lawyers, political leaders, and civil servants? Or were they regarded as foundational books that warranted familiarity among all general, if serious, students of politics?

Cultural historians, then, need a way to ascertain the popularity of the books on Witherspoon's syllabus. Of course, very few sales records exist for the eighteenth century. But given strides among scholars of book history, we know that print runs were fairly stable, usually ranging between 500 and 1,500 copies for an edition.[4] Table 4.2 reorders Witherspoon's syllabus according to the number of eighteenth-century editions.

TABLE 4.2 Witherspoon's Syllabus Reordered According to Eighteenth-Century Editions

Author	Title	Number of Eighteenth-Century Editions
Montesquieu	*The Spirit of the Laws*	97
Pufendorf	*The Whole Duty of Man*	69
Grotius	*The Rights of War and Peace*	55
Locke	*Two Treatises on Government*	29
Machiavelli	*Discourses on Livy*	25
Burlamaqui	*Principles of Natural and Political Law*	22
Sidney	*Discourses on Government*	13
Hobbes	*Leviathan* [and other political works]	10
Seldon	*Table Talk*	10
Cumberland	*A Philosophical Inquiry into the Laws of Nature*	7
Harrington	*The Commonwealth of Oceana*	7
Ferguson	*Essay on the History of Civil Society*	7

Not surprisingly, this analysis tells us that some on Witherspoon's list were immensely popular during the eighteenth century, while others were by and large unread except by specialists. First, Adam Ferguson's book never quite achieved the popularity of other Scottish Enlightenment works, such as David Hume's *Essays* or Adam Smith's *Wealth of Nations*. Second, the bottom half of the list reveals that the largely British theorists from the seventeenth century were by 1769 less read than their continental counterparts; only John Locke's *Two Treatises* in this group makes it into the top half. Of course, it is hardly surprising that Witherspoon was preoccupied with concerns that many eighteenth-century readers might find parochial. As a recent Scottish immigrant jailed by Jacobite rebels in the 1745 uprising, it was natural for him to view events from the historical perspective of British sectarian strife. But many younger Europeans and Americans had moved beyond this paradigm by the 1770s.

It is Montesquieu who dominates the picture. In her important study of James Madison's political thought, Colleen Sheehan notes that of all the authors on Witherspoon's list, even including Locke, it was the French nobleman Charles Louis de Secondat, Baron de Montesquieu (1689–1755) to whom Madison turned again and again for inspiration.[5] As Table 4.2 reveals, Madison's critical embrace of *Spirit of the Laws* was hardly accidental. For Madison's generation, from Virginia across Europe to Saint Petersburg, Montesquieu's *Spirit of the Laws*, first published in 1748, became by far the Enlightenment's most popular treatise on political thought. Comprising more than one thousand pages that were rarely abridged, and translated into Dutch, Danish, English, German, Italian, Polish, and Russian, the ninety-seven eighteenth-century editions of *Spirit of the Laws* made it more influential than similar works by Hume, Rousseau, Smith, or Voltaire. Montesquieu's contemporaries were well aware of the book's impact. As early as 1750, Felippo Venuti, an Italian church administrator and writer, judged it a "masterpiece," surpassing all other works of political thought: "There has never been a book, which like this one, in the same instant of its birth, is so prodigiously multiplied within its own borders and among foreign nations." Venuti was right. Montesquieu was not only among the most influential political theorists of the Enlightenment but also the first political theorist in European history to become a bestselling author among the reading public.[6]

At once elegantly written, immense in scope, and seemingly randomly organized, *Spirit of the Laws* discovered patterns among ancient, medieval, and modern forms of government, mainly in the West, but also in other parts of the world visited by Europeans (Figure 4.1). Montesquieu's overriding structure affirmed three basic types of government: republic, monarchy, and despotism. Within each form, Montesquieu found a psychological spring that motivated citizens in the public sphere: virtue in republics, honor in monarchies, and fear guiding most political behavior in despotisms. The combination of Montesquieu's light and graceful style, rarely seen in seventeenth-century political theory, and his mastery in finding colorful examples from throughout the historical record, helped make the work compelling and readable. And yet, readers were confused by the book's overall argument, and critics constantly complained about Montesquieu's muddled message. Was he a closet republican who hoped to undermine monarchy with radical change? Or was he a traditionalist who hoped to domesticate absolute monarchy with the aid of a strong nobility? Readers could find points to support either perspective. All could agree that whatever his strongest political leanings, Montesquieu despised despotism, fearing that France and other European powers were headed down that path. It is also clear that he wanted readers to come away from his book understanding why monarchy without political limits was inherently unjust, abusive, and perverse. And yet, the further

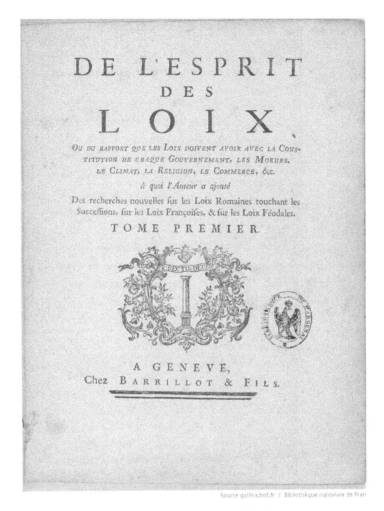

FIGURE 4.1 Title page, Montesquieu, *Spirit of the Laws* (1749). Title page of the first edition of Montesquieu's *Spirit of the Laws* published in Geneva by Barillot. Note the spelling error in the publisher's name and the absence of the author's name. © Wikimedia Commons (public domain).

one proceeds through his long book, the clumsier his organization seems, until finally by Book 19, Montesquieu appears to abandon the republic/monarchy/despotism triad altogether in an innovative and imaginative, yet frustrating, analysis of England. There is no question that Montesquieu admired England as the only government in history that had liberty at the basis of its constitution. Montesquieu attributed this emphasis on individual freedom to a separation of powers that prevented the type of unified sovereign typically found in republics, monarchies, and despotic states alike. Yet England did not seem to fit Montesquieu's definition of either a republic or a monarchy. Indeed, insofar as Montesquieu regarded England as emblematic of Europe's new commercial age, he seemed to suggest that his own structure—the division of states into three categories—had itself become obsolete. Readers were left wondering about Montesquieu's real intentions.

That such a long and imposing treatise—banned by the Catholic Church and censored in several Catholic countries—could become popular and remain so over many decades demands an explanation that moves beyond its ideas, argument, and style. Rather, the significance of the Montesquieu phenomenon lies in the changing context in which ideas about politics were disseminated during the eighteenth century. As explained by the twentieth-century German philosopher Jürgen Habermas, and adopted by many historians, the eighteenth century saw the rise of a literate public sphere filled with readers who hungered after books, newspapers, and periodicals, eager to discuss these texts with their friends in homes, cafés, libraries, reading clubs, and salons.[7] The result was a great expansion in the book trade and in periodical literature. While in raw numbers theological and devotional works may have risen too, in percentage terms they were replaced by secular genres such as history, biography, fiction, and political philosophy. Likewise, the number of titles published in Greek and Latin plunged, replaced by works in the vernacular. In this setting, French became the language of the educated classes in Europe. This last point is often misunderstood. More copies of *Spirit of the Laws*, and indeed, most of the writings of the Paris *philosophes*, were printed outside of France and sold throughout Europe than in France alone. Such books nonetheless were very often published in the French language. When Cesare Becarria's bestselling *On Crimes and Punishments* (1764) was translated from Italian into French, it did not mean necessarily that it was printed in France, given the restrictions imposed by state and church censors there. Likewise, when Becarria was translated into English, it was not from the original Italian, but from the French translation. The French Enlightenment was not only a movement in France, but simultaneously a European movement in the French language occurring outside of France's borders.[8]

English was the other great language of enlightenment, but often with a French connection too. The Enlightenment's Habermasian reading public came into full flower during 1787 and 1788, when thousands of Americans throughout the young United States assembled in small town meetings to debate whether their states should ratify the new constitution. These debates involved not simply elected politicians in state capitals but also delegates from hundreds of small towns all along the eastern seaboard. For example, the town of Richmond, Massachusetts held four separate meetings to debate the matter and decided against approving the new constitution. Which works informed these discussions? Madison, Alexander Hamilton, and John Jay's *The Federalist* (later known as *The Federalist Papers*) was simply the tip of the iceberg. Scholars once assumed that Americans were guided in these debates by English political thinkers, such as Locke, Hume, and William Blackstone. Now that the notes and reports of these ratification debates are available digitally, it is possible to see for the first time that *Spirit of the Laws* was cited in seventy-six instances, more than the work of any other modern writer. Blackstone's *Commentaries on the Laws of England* figured second, with fifty-one citations, followed by John Milton (thirty-two), Locke (twenty-six), Hume (twenty-two), James Harrington (nineteen), Jean-Louis de Lolme (twelve), Cesare Beccaria (eleven), Gabriel Bonnot de Mably (ten), and Grotius (ten). Perhaps more intriguing, both Federalists (arguing for the Constitution) and Anti-Federalists (arguing against it) relied upon Montesquieu. What these ordinary lawyers, ministers, businessmen, and civil servants could agree upon was that Montesquieu was an authority deserving consideration. These ratification debates demonstrate the widespread popularity and extraordinary reach of Enlightenment political thought near the end of the eighteenth century.[9]

After Montesquieu's death in 1755, his reputation as the Enlightenment's most important political philosopher was solidified in a long and laudatory essay that Jean-Baptiste le Rond d'Alembert appended to the fifth volume of the *Encyclopédie*, the central work of the Enlightenment. A vast enterprise of twenty-six volumes, with over ten thousand articles on every conceivable subject, the *Encyclopédie* spread across Europe partly because cheaper pirated editions soon became available. Montesquieu was referenced over five hundred times in the *Encyclopédie*, and he was the only writer to receive a special eulogy it its pages. Moreover, d'Alembert immortalized *Spirit of the Laws* as one of the classics of political theory and praised Montesquieu for his liberalism. D'Alembert's essay was itself republished and excerpted in various European journals and appeared often as a preface to later editions of Montesquieu's book and collected works.[10]

What made Enlightenment political thought—and particularly that of Montesquieu—distinctive in the historical development of European political theory was not only its ideas but also its engagement with the new Habermasian public. A comparison between Montesquieu and Locke demonstrates this change. Locke was born a half-century before Montesquieu, and both had written substantial works by the time they were fifty years old. The difference between them was that by middle age Locke had published none of his manuscripts while Montesquieu was already very well known for his *Persian Letters* (1721) and his *Considerations on the Greatness of the Romans and Their Decline* (1734). During the seventeenth century, membership in the Republic of Letters (a cosmopolitan network of intellectuals across Europe who mainly met through academies, salons, and especially correspondence) did not require publication. Indeed, in subtle ways, publication was discouraged. Latin was, moreover, still the dominant language, a barrier for any emerging vernacular public.[11]

Today we know that Locke composed his *Two Treatises of Government* in the wake of Restoration succession politics, probably completing it in 1683. Like his other essays written up to that point, he showed the manuscript only to a small group of influential leaders. It is likely that he never intended to publish what would become, of course, his political masterpiece. However, after he spent the bulk of the 1680s in self-imposed exile in the Netherlands, he saw firsthand how intellectuals there were affected by the emergence of a wider reading public. For example, Pierre Bayle's *News from the Republic of Letters*, a periodical notably published in French rather than Latin, was one very successful effort at widening the impact of philosophers, historians, and literary critics. In rather dramatic form, three of Locke's greatest works (his *Essay Concerning Human Understanding*, *Two Treatises on Government*, and the *Letter on Toleration*) were all first published in 1689. Nonetheless, even then Locke remained nervous about exposing himself to publication. He published *Two Treatises* anonymously, and at first he refused to take credit for it. Meanwhile, he agreed to publish his *Letter on Toleration* only in Latin, and he was angered when William Popple put out an unauthorized English translation. Locke considered publishing an inherently dangerous activity up to the end of his life.[12]

Montesquieu, too, was wary of publishing. He negotiated with publishers indirectly, through third parties, never allowing his name to be placed on the title page, although the authorship of his major works was an open secret until his death. Yet where Locke avoided literary recognition, Montesquieu coveted it, seeking at the same time to shield himself from state or church rebuke. Montesquieu was eager to publish at a relatively young age, and in 1725 parlayed his authorship of *Persian Letters* to garner entrance into that sacred temple of the Republic of Letters, the French Academy. Indeed, knowing how seriously Montesquieu took his overall career as a thinker, it is surprising, and yet indicative of the changing times, that a writer so absorbed in formal political philosophy would choose to publish a satirical novel for his first work. Clearly *Persian Letters* was aimed less at the inner core of the Republic of Letters and more at general readers untrained and uninterested in reading natural law treatises in Latin. During the second half of the eighteenth century, younger writers not only engaged with Montesquieu's ideas but also emulated the way that his books reached a wide readership.

Montesquieu has certainly not been ignored in Enlightenment scholarship, but he is nonetheless underappreciated today. Jonathan Israel's vast history of the Enlightenment mentions Montesquieu repeatedly, but usually in the guise of an obstacle to more authentic radicals such as Denis Diderot and Paul Henri Thiry, Baron d'Holbach. Montesquieu, writes Israel, was "a fundamental pillar of the West's moderate mainstream Enlightenment, the principal reply to the radical politics of the egalitarian materialists, *Spinosistes*, and democratic republicans," which Israel favors.[13] To be sure, Montesquieu was cautious and wary of offending church and state authorities. But Israel and other historians have minimized not only Montesquieu's popularity but also his radicalism. After all, Montesquieu's argument that the modern European monarchy was based not on virtue, but on honor—that is, egotistical self-interest—was deeply threatening both to conservative religious leaders and to progressives such as Jean-Jacques Rousseau (1712–1778). Together *Spirit of the Laws* and *Persian Letters* constituted a direct assault on the prevalent wish for a virtuous king portrayed so clearly in Archbishop François Fénelon's immensely popular *Adventures of Telemachus*.[14]

While Montesquieu became famous for his treatment of English liberty—a topic considered earlier by Voltaire as well—similar public interest was directed toward Montesquieu's treatment of commerce in Books 20 and 21 of *Spirit of the Laws*. There Montesquieu made three controversial claims, beginning with the assertion that modern monarchies spurred growth in trade and commerce. Small city-states may, he argued, trade for things they need, but monarchies hungered for novel and luxurious items that fed conspicuous consumption. "I know well that people ... have believed that the Romans greatly encouraged and honored commerce," he wrote in Book 21. "But the truth is that they rarely thought about it." Unlike the Romans, eighteenth-century Europeans were obsessed with Chinese porcelain and tea, Indian spices, Mexican chocolate, Canadian fur hats and coats, as well as sugar, coffee, tobacco, and cotton from their Caribbean and North American colonies. In this way, modern monarchies greatly expanded the material wealth of their subjects, igniting industry and growing a prosperous middle class. Here Montesquieu was weighing in on one of the most hotly contested debates of the Enlightenment, joining Bernard Mandeville, Hume, and Voltaire against the arguments of Fénelon and soon Rousseau. Second, Montesquieu argued that trade improved a people's manners, making them more polite and open to other cultural traditions. Commerce, Montesquieu insisted, "polishes and softens barbarous mores, as we see every day." Finally, Montesquieu argued that the result of this increase in luxury and the softening of manners would be a reduction in warfare between states. "The natural effect of commerce," he asserted, "is to lead to peace. Two nations that trade with each other become reciprocally dependent; if one has an interest in buying, the other has an interest in selling, and all unions are founded on mutual needs." Honor demanded ambition, distinction, and glory. If unchecked, it could produce a nobility intent upon constant war. Commerce, however, helped domesticate a ruling class, allowing it to distinguish itself through fashion and artifice rather than warfare. The result was an elite more interested in the arts, who also tended to mix with women in court and elsewhere more than their ancestors. "Everything is closely linked together," Montesquieu wrote. "The despotism of the prince is naturally united with the servitude of women; the liberty of women, with the spirit of monarchy." In this way, Montesquieu suggested, commercial life in the modern period would lead to less war and violence because "everywhere there are gentle mores [*moeurs douces*], there is commerce and that everywhere there is commerce, there are gentle mores."[15]

For most of the twentieth century, scholars focused more on the narrowly political themes in Montesquieu's writing, such as the use of intermediary bodies to limit sovereign power.[16] Although in 1939 John Maynard Keynes recognized Montesquieu as "the real French equivalent to Adam Smith, the greatest" of the Enlightenment's French economists, few treated his comment seriously.[17] However, in an influential book published during the 1970s, the economist Albert Hirschman recognized Montesquieu's ideas regarding commerce, claiming that many eighteenth-century readers found here the genesis of modern political economy, in which a global marketplace was understood to feed insatiable consumptive passions.

Hirschman also recognized that *Spirit of the Laws* was published during a period of rapid economic expansion, competition with England, and fiscal crisis in France. Between 1730 and 1770, trade between France and its neighbors grew by more than 400 percent, while income from colonial trade rose 1,000 percent. At the same time, government debt spiraled because of expensive mid-century wars.[18] Hirschman rediscovered Montesquieu's argument regarding commercial life as an exit from feudalism: commerce softened militarism; it increased women's status as consumers and cultural arbiters; it brought foreigners in contact with citizens, allowing both to compare habits and attitudes; and it made the cost of war between states appear much higher.[19]

Following Hirschman, more scholars began to appreciate how *Spirit of the Laws* became associated with the genesis of modern economics.[20] Many still think of economics as rising suddenly from the 1776 publication of Adam Smith's *Wealth of Nations*. But Smith's work was the culmination of an enormous wave of writing on political economy that began around the time *Spirit of the Laws* was first published. As Christine Théré has demonstrated, of the 4,265 books on political economy published between 1570 and 1789, over 75 percent flooded Europe in the forty-year period between 1750 and 1789, that is, immediately following Montesquieu's publication.[21] John Robertson has argued that the rise of political economy between Montesquieu and Smith constituted the most important development in Enlightenment political theory.[22] Enlightenment political economists suggested that a growing economy provided the centralizing state with more revenue, requiring government ministers to pay close attention to what today would be called macroeconomic policy. They also proposed that economic growth benefited individual subjects across class lines, resulting in improved public happiness, and they believed that sound public policy would help diminish war and conquest, relieving the burdens of government debt. While Montesquieu should not be given too much credit, his contemporaries realized that his book was at least partly responsible for how quickly notions of political economy spread across Europe. The *Journal of Commerce* summed it up this way in 1759: "We are indebted to M. de Montesquieu hardly less for the science of commerce than we are for philosophy and letters."[23]

The rise of political economy as a field of inquiry in mid-eighteenth-century Europe was also inextricably tied up with debates for loosening book censorship and allowing a free commercial press. Until then, economic policy had traditionally been regarded by the monarchy as a secret domain of the state, and, as with foreign policy, discussion among the public was kept to a minimum. For example, during the final years of Louis XIV's reign, when circles around Archbishop Fénelon proposed significant economic changes in France, none of those reform plans were published at the time. When the economic advisor Pierre le Pesant, Sieur de Boisguilbert dared to publish his ideas in 1707, he was immediately exiled. But two expensive mid-century wars that France fought against England (the War of the Austrian Succession [1739–1748] and the Seven Years War [1756–1763]) caused some in France's administration to question such secrecy. The French saw firsthand how public discussions of war financing had led the English to adopt innovative credit schemes to finance their military activities. Suddenly, French book publication regarding political economy took off, sometimes even with the encouragement of French ministers. "Around the year 1750," noted the witty Voltaire, "France, sated with poetry, tragedy, comedies, operas, novels, and adventure stories at last started philosophizing about grain."[24] There is a tendency to think that the eighteenth-century public described by Habermas made the novel its chosen genre, but the popularity of political economy rivaled that of fiction, and Montesquieu's *Spirit of the Laws* played a central role in that story.

At the time *Spirit of the Laws* was first published, Rousseau was employed as the secretary for Parisian Louise Dupin, wife of wealthy financier Claude Dupin. With Rousseau at their side, the Dupins spent a good part of 1748 and 1749 preparing an exhaustive commentary on *Spirit of the Laws*, subjecting it to various criticisms and discussion that focused on Montesquieu's notion of a commercial monarchy. Paul Rahe and Kent Wright have argued that Rousseau's first major essay, the *Discourse on the Arts and Sciences*, written in the Dupin home at this time, was produced as a response to Montesquieu. Where Hume and others embraced Montesquieu's championing of commercial society, Rousseau attacked it head-on. When Montesquieu compared ancient Greek virtue with modern European honor, his preference was toward the latter. Rousseau reversed Montesquieu's judgment, arguing that in comparison with the ancients, the insatiable appetite for goods among modern societies produced debt-ridden governments and neurotic individuals. Where Montesquieu had praised the commerce of luxury, Rousseau rejected a social system that made a few people rich and everyone else unhappy.[25]

In 1755, Rousseau's second essay, the *Discourse on the Origin of Inequality*, continued his engagement with Montesquieu's key ideas. Montesquieu's three political types— republics, monarchies, and despotisms—were abstracted, universalized, and reshaped into a historical stage theory based around inequality. Rousseau argued that what Montesquieu perceived was only a snapshot of a society moving in time. All societies, Rousseau insisted, transformed themselves first from republics into monarchies, and then into despotisms, with each stage exhibiting increasing levels of inequality. Where Montesquieu had argued that despotism was the only inherently *bad* form of government, Rousseau inverted his formula, arguing that a democratic republic was the only inherently *good* form of government because it was the only one premised on equality. Given that very few European states were either republics or despotisms, the real debate between Montesquieu and Rousseau was over the nature of monarchy. Where Montesquieu believed that a well-ordered monarchy could exhibit high levels of freedom and prosperity, Rousseau argued that the type of monarchy imagined by Montesquieu already exhibited despotic features that were unavoidable.

Rousseau followed up the second discourse with a third, the *Discourse on Political Economy*, originally published in 1757 as "Economy or Oeconomy" in Diderot and d'Alembert's *Encyclopédie* and renamed by Rousseau for separate publication afterward. This is a strange piece in which Rousseau pointedly rejected current economic themes in favor of political ones. While insisting upon strong private property rights, Rousseau nonetheless argued that governments should turn their backs on commerce and focus their attention on promoting virtue: "Do we want people to be virtuous? Let us begin then by making them love their country." The goal of politics was not to make everyone wealthy, it was to preserve freedom. As he put it, "A homeland cannot subsist without liberty, nor can liberty without virtue, nor can virtue without citizens." In a section that made explicit reference to Montesquieu, Rousseau warned against embracing "commerce and industry" because such economic growth only encouraged the oppression of the poor by the rich: "Are not all the advantages of society for the powerful and the rich? Are not all the lucrative posts filled by them alone? Are not all the privileges and exemptions reserved for them alone?" Rousseau's *Discourse on Political Economy* was nothing less than a full-throated revolt against modern political economy itself.[26]

Finally, the apex of Rousseau's political thought, his *Social Contract*, was published in 1762, and an abstract was included in his larger treatise, *Emile*, published the same year. Here Rousseau again inverted Montesquieu, advocating that all legitimate governments embrace virtue and equality—that is, the values Montesquieu had associated only with ancient democratic republics. Turning his back on modern commercial society altogether, Rousseau expected any decent society to curtail extreme wealth and to prevent poverty. Rousseau added a seductive innovation, distinguishing between government and sovereignty. Agreeing with Montesquieu that large countries are often better governed with monarchical or aristocratic forms, he insisted that such governments should nonetheless take instruction from a sovereign people, who themselves could legislate for the nation according to its will. Such a formulation seemed to collapse Montesquieu's various types of political societies into one, leaving no room for honor. While historians once believed that the *Social Contract* had little impact before the French Revolution, newer research has since documented the extensive popularity of Rousseau's political thought at the height of the Enlightenment.[27]

During the 1750s, French administrators courted a group of writers that clustered around the intendant of commerce, Jean Claude Vincent de Gournay (1712–1759). These men were not only permitted to propose major economic reforms but also, working in tandem with the new director of the book trade, Guillaume Chrétien de Lamoignon de Malesherbes, allowed and sometimes even encouraged to publish their proposals as books or as articles in new journals. The most prominent of Gournay's writers, François Véron de Forbonnais (1722–1800), published a chapter-by-chapter commentary on *Spirit of the Laws* while his 1754 *Elements of Commerce* served as a manifesto for the group. Gournay's writing workshop churned out various reform proposals, focusing on improving agriculture and loosening restrictions on the grain trade. It also advocated for more public discussion: a modern economy could only develop if policy-makers could sort through a variety of proposals that were based upon publicly available data and records. Forbonnais challenged the very essence of Old Regime secrecy, hoping to empower a new reading public. Montesquieu had already made this point. "The invention of printing, which has put books in everyone's hands," he wrote in his Roman history, "make men better acquainted with matters of general interest, and this enables them to become informed of secret activities more easily."[28] Forbonnais's influential *Encyclopédie* article, "Commerce," recycled what Montesquieu had described in Books 20 and 21 of *Spirit of the Laws* and specifically directed readers to that source (Figure 4.2). As

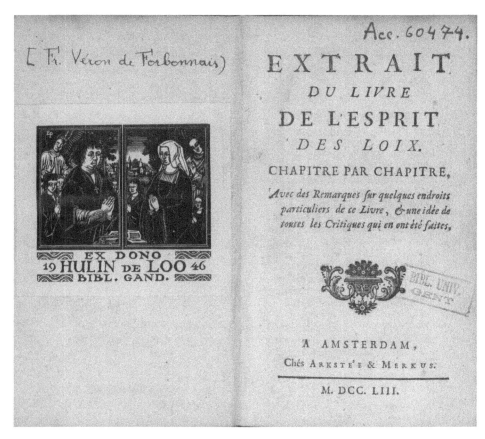

FIGURE 4.2 Title page, François Véron de Forbonnais's commentary on *Spirit of the Laws* (1753). © Ghent University Library, BIB.ACC.060474.

Forbonnais put it, "A nation that does not engage in commerce to its full capacity faces a gradual commercial decline."[29]

The adoption of the Scottish philosopher David Hume (1711–1776) by the Gournay group during the 1750s offers a striking example of how political economy became a thriving centerpiece of Enlightenment political thought twenty years before *Wealth of Nations*. Hume closely read *Spirit of the Laws* soon after it appeared and corresponded with Montesquieu about it. This relationship inspired him to focus more on political economy, and the result was the publication in 1752 of *Political Discourses*, a collection of sixteen short essays mostly on economic subjects. In essays such as "Of Refinement in the Arts," Hume weighed in with Montesquieu on the side of championing the growing market for luxurious goods in the modern global economy, viewing honor as a linchpin in the desire for such commodities.[30] In England, Hume merged *Political Discourses* into his other essay collections. But in Europe it was published separately, maintaining its own distinctive identity as a work contributing to economic thought (Figure 4.3). Indeed, the 1754 French translation by Jean Bernard, Abbé Le Blanc (1707–1781) was the first of Hume's works to be published on the Continent, and it immediately became a bestseller across Europe. Between 1754 and 1767, there were ten editions in French alone. By 1791 it had been translated, usually from the French, into Dutch, German, Italian, Spanish, and

FIGURE 4.3 Title page, David Hume, *Discours politiques* (1754). Title page from a French translation (though published in Amsterdam) of David Hume's *Political Discourses*, his first book to become a bestseller throughout Europe, composed of a dozen small essays on economic topics. © Antique Map & Bookshop, Puddletown, Dorset, UK (public domain).

Swedish. Le Blanc was a Gournay acolyte, and his 54-page introduction contextualized *Political Discourses* within the group's mission to discover a science of commerce. Such a science, Le Blanc explained, began with Montesquieu: "A work such as *The Spirit of Laws*, which contributes to perfecting the general wellbeing of a state, and consequently to public felicity, is certainly the highest and the greatest use of reason and enlightenment."[31]

This new interest in political economy stemming from Montesquieu also surged in Italian and German states during the 1750s. In 1754, Antonio Genovesi (1713–1769), who had taught metaphysics at the University of Naples since 1741, became the first occupant of a new chair in "commerce and mechanics," effectively the first professorship of economics in Europe. An admirer of the Gournay group, Genovesi was also part of a Neapolitan reading circle that met regularly to discuss and debate *Spirit of the Laws*, an experience that led directly to the establishment of his university chair. At his death,

Genovesi left a thoroughly annotated copy of *Spirit of the Laws* that formed the basis for critical notes appended to the Italian edition published in 1777.[32] Meanwhile, in the German states, the founder of Cameralism (a theory of political economy that influenced eighteenth-century German civil servants), Johann Heinrich Gottlob Justi (1717–1781) constantly engaged Montesquieu's *Spirit of the Laws* in his own published work. Both an acolyte and a critic, Justi agreed that embracing modern commerce could prevent monarchies from metastasizing into despotism, but he criticized Montesquieu for inflating the nobility's political role.[33]

The most popular expression of the new political economy came from the French writer Victor Riqueti, Marquis de Mirabeau (1715–1789), who in 1756, published his *Friend of Mankind or Treatise on Population*, which went through over twenty editions in its first decade. Filled with tangents and fascinating insights, Mirabeau argued that France's declining population, rooted in a lack of investment in agriculture, was the most salient cause of its ill social health.[34] Indeed, it was the prior publication of *Spirit of the Laws* that first prompted this wealthy nobleman to try his hand at a similar genre of writing, and with an ample share of false modesty, he compared himself to the Bordeaux master.

> In spite of the almost infinite subdivisions which he has given to his plan, readers complain for good reason that his progress is often tangled and usually difficult to follow. We certainly have that in common, him and me. His erudition is immense and sure; mine is very limited and faulty; his style is clear, noble, pure, and trenchant; mine is unequal, without taste, neglected, often diffuse, and mixed up; his mind illuminates and awakens the reader's intellect, mine tires him and stifles him; his ideas seem the flower of ideas, and in fact are the germ, mine are singular and trivial. He was a skillful workman, and totally devoted to this kind of study and work, and by his confession he consumed ten years in that one. I am none of that, and I have not used six months to cover all the territory that I have covered.[35]

While Mirabeau appreciated the significance of Montesquieu's work, he also disagreed fundamentally with the assertion, as Montesquieu put it, "that virtue is not the principle of monarchical government."[36] Reaching back to Fénelon's still popular *Adventures of Telemachus*, and building upon Rousseau's writing, Mirabeau countered Montesquieu by arguing that republics and monarchies were hardly distinct and their systems could be easily combined through a republican monarchy, in which "the prejudices that constitute honor make up a real part of the treasure of the state."[37] Mirabeau attacked an economy based on luxuries and rooted in serfdom; he expected the monarch to steer noblemen away from exotic consumption from far-away lands and more toward agricultural reform. He railed against landowners who spent lavishly on fancy carriages instead of improving agriculture. He insisted that monarchs reward noblemen only for improving the lives of their peasants.[38]

During the summer of 1757, Mirabeau was called to the Versailles Palace to answer the complaints of François Quesnay (1694–1774), the personal physician to King Louis XV's mistress, Madame de Pompadour, who was critical of Mirabeau's policy prescriptions. Mirabeau entered the conversation thinking Quesnay was something of an ignorant upstart, but within an hour, he reported, he realized he was in the presence of a master, and converted to Quesnay's outlook. Population growth, argued Quesnay, was the *result* of agricultural productivity, not its cause. Before the invention of agriculture, Quesnay had explained, populations were necessarily stagnant and impoverished. Only improved farming allowed the population to grow over the long term by enlarging a stable food supply. Instead of encouraging population growth, he believed, the focus should be on property rights and increasing the ability of landowners to improve their fields. From this point on, Mirabeau became Quesnay's junior partner, one of a stable of writers who became known as the Economists or Physiocrats.

Physiocracy was a strange and powerful union between these two very different personalities, combining new and old features of the Republic of Letters. On the one hand, Quesnay behaved like an old-fashioned courtier, completely dependent upon the good graces of his royal patrons and wary of publishing his work openly. He played an insider's game, shielding himself from the public, pushing his economic policies in the private circles of powerful actors, publishing articles and books only indirectly and anonymously, and sometimes withdrawing manuscripts from publication altogether. When, for example, he wrote "Remarks on the Opinion of the Author of *Spirit of the Laws* Regarding Colonies," using Montesquieu to make indirect criticisms of French colonial policy, the essay was published anonymously in the *Journal of Agriculture, Commerce and Finance*.[39] Mirabeau, on the other hand, was a publicity-seeking celebrity. From 1757 until Quesnay's death in 1774, Mirabeau willingly played frontman for a team that put out several books, including sequels and revised editions of his *Friend of Mankind*. While Mirabeau sought the public's adulation as an Enlightenment *philosophe*, his notoriety led to a short prison sentence when one of his books, *Tax Theory*, fell afoul of the government. One reason for Physiocracy's prominence was its dual ability to popularize ideas across a wide Habermasian public while never abandoning a secretive lobbying role near the apex of government policymaking. The Enlightenment was not simply an opposition movement that clashed with the political establishment, but often it was promoted by reformers and civil servants inside government circles.

An indication of the strong impact made by the writings of Mirabeau and company is the reaction of the Swiss-German historian Isaak Iselin (1728–1782). Writing to a friend in 1770 after reading a later edition of *The Friend of Mankind* that had incorporated several new insights from Quesnay, Iselin noted his enthusiasm for Physiocracy: "These truly generous men, real *viri fortes*, have restored my courage and taught me to regard both my own and my country's misfortunes with more fortitude." Among their most impressive accomplishments, believed Iselin, was replacing Montesquieu's "baroque" and "confused" picture of monarchy with a purer vision of how a virtuous royal administration could serve the public good.[40]

By 1767, when the publication of *Physiocratie* gave a name to this school of French economists, the doctrine had fully matured into Europe's first coherent system of political economy. Privileging the economy over war and conquest as a cornerstone of a monarch's success became a hallmark of Physiocratic thought born from engagement with Montesquieu. But the Physiocrats clashed sharply with Montesquieu over political issues. In a series of works Quesnay attacked Montesquieu's formulation that legitimate monarchy was limited and based upon a strong group of intermediary bodies, including the nobility and clergy. Like Justi, Quesnay argued that a recalcitrant nobility was responsible for France falling behind its competitors, such as England, and that modern monarchies needed to weaken the political clout of their nobility and clergy. Quesnay advocated "legal despotism," an absolute monarchy that operated wholly according to reason and natural rights, one that carried the best of both Fénelon and Isaac Newton, suggesting a king who embodied both ancient virtue and modern rationality. As one of Quesnay's collaborators, Pierre Paul Mercier de la Rivière, explained it in 1767: "Knowledge of the natural and essential order being public and evident, this government will benefit everyone by instituting a true legal despotism; arbitrary despotism is not true despotism because it is not personal, it is not legal, it fails to represent the interests of the person who exercises it."[41]

The Physiocrats may have inherited Montesquieu's interest in commercial society, but they had a profoundly different conception of monarchy, one that attempted to reconcile the liberties of individuals with the unlimited and unified sovereignty of the king. This was among the most controversial aspects of the doctrine, engendering much criticism within Enlightenment circles. "If these writers are the founders of the science of economics, as they modestly consider themselves to be, why do they not also call themselves the founders of the science of government?" one critic sarcastically remarked. "This glory belongs only to the immortal author of *Spirit of the Laws*."[42]

The Physiocrats refused to denounce Montesquieu by name and saw themselves as building upon his ideas. Pierre Samuel Du Pont's 1768 essay, "On the Origin and Progress of a New Science," charted a kind of intellectual genealogy of the Physiocratic school that began with Montesquieu, and led through Gournay to Quesnay and two of his collaborators, Mirabeau and Mercier de la Rivière. Du Pont highlighted as particularly influential Quesnay's articles "Farmers" and "Grain" for the 1756 volume of the *Encyclopédie*, and especially his "Tableau Economique" (Economic Chart), which visually represented the physiocratic model of agricultural productivity that was first published in various editions of Mirabeau's books. "The era of the revolution that turned our thinkers to the study of political economy goes back to M. de Montesquieu," Du Pont later wrote.[43]

If it had not been for Adam Smith's *Wealth of Nations*, the Physiocrats may have remained the most famous economists in Europe and recognized today as the new discipline's founders. But by the end of the eighteenth century, Smith (1723–1790) had usurped them as the Isaac Newton of political economy. First appearing in 1776, the publishing history of *Wealth of Nations* reveals a steady rise toward fame rather than an immediate and explosive surge. Smith's study of modern commercial society demonstrated how the domestication of self-interest by markets usually results in the improvement of society. Reversing classical republican notions that virtue required denial of the passions, Smith made clear that people may serve the needs of others not because of any learned sense of Christian virtue, but because their own hunger for self-advancement is dependent upon serving them: "It is not from the benevolence of the butcher, the brewer, or the baker that we expect our dinner, but from their regard to their own self-interest. We address ourselves not to their humanity but to their self-love, and never talk to them of our own necessities, but of their advantages."[44]

By the outbreak of the French Revolution, *Wealth of Nations* was among the most important and bestselling political treatises of the century. Its impact upon such revolutionary thinkers as Emmanuel Sieyès and Marie Jean de Caritat, Marquis de Condorcet is well known.[45] Smith had traveled to France in the mid-1760s, when the Physiocrats were at their peak, and *Wealth of Nations* cites their works and shows how indebted to them Smith was. However, in contrast to the Physiocrats, Smith warned against government policies that privileged agriculture over trade and industry, and he undermined Quesnay's political ideas. Smith believed, with Montesquieu, that economic conditions arose from the peculiar historical and social circumstances of a country, and he avoided the universal and abstract reasoning of Quesnay.

Contemporary readers invariably compared the impact of *Wealth of Nations* to *Spirit of the Laws*, since both books called for a political theory that incorporated principles of political economy. "The work of Smith must be epoch-making in the history of political science, like *The Spirit of the Laws*," commented one French reviewer. Similarly, another Frenchman reflected that "Great Britain, in bringing Smith into the world, has discharged its debt toward France, which has given birth to Montesquieu." The prestigious *Mercure de France* agreed, noting in March 1788 how everyone in England equated Smith and Montesquieu. Perhaps they were reflecting the widespread assessment of the popular Scottish moralist Hugh Blair, who noted that "since Montesquieu's *Spirit of the Laws*, Europe has not received any publication which tends so much to enlarge and rectify the ideas of mankind." Of course, Blair, who had heard Smith lecture, may have been echoing Smith's own sentiments. Sometime in 1753 or 1754—that is, early in Smith's career as a professor of moral philosophy at the University of Glasgow—one of his students jotted down this remark from the lectern: "Monsieur de Montesquieu is one of the most singular men that has ever been in the world, for he possesses four things which are never almost united: An excellent Judgment, a fine Imagination, great Wit, and vast Erudition." Nor did Smith's first biographer, Dugald Stewart, alter this assessment when he characterized the entire Scottish Enlightenment as "but a reflection, though with a far steadier and more concentrated force, from the scattered but brilliant sparks kindled by the genius of Montesquieu." The interest in equating Montesquieu and Smith reached its climax only three months before Smith's death in 1790, when the *Moniteur* reported that Smith was about to publish an important and comprehensive study of Montesquieu:

> It is claimed that the celebrated Mr. Smith, so favorably known through his treatise on the causes of the wealth of nations, is preparing and is going to publish a critical examination of *The Spirit of the Laws*. It is the result of many years of meditation, and what we have a right to expect from a head such as that of Mr. Smith is well-enough known. This book will be epoch-making in the history of politics and of philosophy; such, at least, is the judgment of well-informed men who are familiar with the fragments—which they speak of with enthusiasm for the most auspicious prospects.

This was, of course, wishful thinking; Smith never contemplated such a book, much less left a manuscript at his death. But such a fantasy reveals the public's keen interest in knowing the extent to which Smith endorsed or rejected Montesquieu's notion of limited monarchy and political economy outlined in *Spirit of the Laws*.[46]

Even more popular than *Wealth of Nations* was a work that appeared around the same time that also not only engaged with Montesquieu but also hoped to emulate his success. *A Philosophical and Political History of the Settlements and Trade of the Europeans in the East and West Indies* was first published in 1770 in a six-volume set of 2,100 pages; a second expanded version of 3,300 pages in eight volumes came in 1774, and in 1780, a third version of almost 5,000 pages spread over ten volumes was produced. Appearing under the authorship of Guillaume Thomas Raynal (1713–1796) (Figure 4.4), the work was in fact the product of a team of French writers, including Denis Diderot, who, as scholars discovered only in the twentieth century, secretly contributed over seven hundred pages to the project.

The *History of the Two Indies* is an encyclopedic history of European colonialism covering virtually all parts of the world where Europeans made contact with indigenous peoples. Its volumes include nineteen "books" subdivided into chapters. The first five books focus on European settlements in India, China, Japan, and Southeast Asia. Books 1

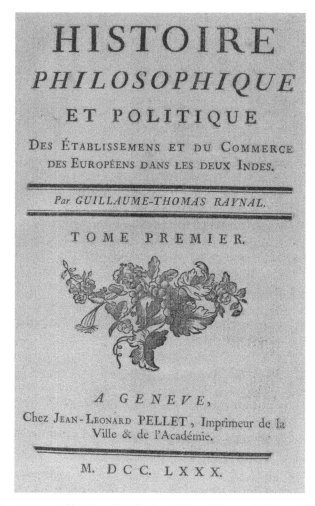

FIGURE 4.4 Frontispiece, Abbé Raynal, *Histoire Philosophique et Politique* (1780). Raynal's willingness to include his own portrait and name in the frontispiece of the 1780 edition of *Philosophical and Political History of the Two Indies* so angered French authorities that he was immediately forced into exile. © BnF.

to 4 are devoted to Portuguese, Dutch, English, and French colonies, while Book 5 spills over to small countries, such as Denmark. Books 6 to 10 turn to the New World, focusing especially on Spanish settlements in Mexico, Peru, Chile, and Paraguay. Book 11, among the most famous in the series, describes how Europeans came to use the coasts of Africa as a global center for purchasing slaves for its New World plantations. Books 12 to 14 then show in great detail the development of plantation economies, especially in the Caribbean islands, demonstrating how they became the crown jewels for the eighteenth-century British and French empires. Books 15 to 18 address British and French colonies in North America, and Book 19 includes a thematic recapitulation.

Raynal's *History of the Two Indies* is deeply engaged with Montesquieu, and it is not surprising that Montesquieu is mentioned in the work more than any other contemporary writer.[47] The entire project tests Montesquieu's theory regarding *doux commerce*. In Books 20 and 21 of *Spirit of the Laws*, Montesquieu predicted that even though global trade might make individuals anxious and competitive, it would benefit humanity as a whole, increasing overall wealth and discouraging wars and other forms of violence, leading humanity to more gentle mores. Raynal's work both accepts Montesquieu's ideal and rebukes Europeans for not realizing it. For example, early in the work, in Book 2, Raynal describes Dutch colonialism at the southern tip of Africa. Diderot intervenes with a section that angrily attacks Europeans for their treatment of native peoples. "But are they happy, you ask me?" Diderot's answer was unequivocal. "Are you fond of liberty? He is free. Are you desirous of health? He knows no other illness but old age. Are you delighted with virtues? He ... is a stranger to vice." Europeans might complain about how filthy the native keeps himself, but what may be dirty on the outside is clean on the inside. "Do you think," Diderot went on, that the corruption that manifests itself in "your hatred, your perfidy, and your duplicity" is anything worse than what your senses smell as "uncleanliness?" If their design had been to improve the life of the native, he suggested, then perhaps European knowledge and manners would have served some useful purpose. But, he concluded, Europeans had no such motive. "You have made a descent upon his country merely to deprive him of it. You have come near to his hut with the only view of driving him out of it. ... Your only intention has been to reduce him still nearer to the condition of a brute, and to satisfy your avarice." Diderot rhetorically warned the natives to "lay yourselves in ambush for them" before they "massacre you without mercy." There was no sign of Montesquieu's *doux commerce* here.[48]

Raynal's most passionate criticism was reserved for the transatlantic slave trade. "Nothing," claimed Raynal, "is more miserable than the condition of the Negro, throughout the whole American Archipelago. ... Deprived of every enjoyment, he is condemned to a perpetual drudgery in a burning climate, constantly under the rod of an unfeeling master." How could Europeans allow such an evil system to continue? African slaves "are tyrannized, mutilated, burnt, and put to death, and yet we listen to those accounts coolly and without emotion." How was it possible for intelligent and enlightened Europeans to ignore such inhuman practices? "The torments of a people to whom we owe our luxuries, can never reach our hearts."[49] Enslavement of Africans by Europeans, which coincided with the Enlightenment, undermined Montesquieu's faith in commercial progress. Montesquieu's notion of *doux commerce* was not simply naïve, but served as window dressing for one of the greatest crimes of humanity.

Despite being banned in many countries, including France, Spain, and the Austrian Empire, *History of the Two Indies* went through fifty-seven eighteenth-century editions, somewhat more than *Wealth of Nations* but less than *Spirit of the Laws*. Many compilations, anthologies, atlases, and abridgments were produced. In 1787, one 76-page compilation put selections from *History of the Two Indies* alongside Rousseau's *Discourse on Political Economy* and Montesquieu's *Spirit of the Laws*, allotting seven pages to Montesquieu, four to Rousseau, and over sixty to Raynal! Meanwhile, an excerpt reprinted from Boston to Dresden entitled *The Revolution in America* (1781), featuring chapters narrating that event, became the most popular history of the American Revolution circulating in North America during the early 1780s.[50] It is hardly surprising, then, to find Thomas Jefferson purchasing the work for James Madison, who designated it to be part of his library in Philadelphia.[51]

Raynal's *History of the Two Indies* seemed to sum up Enlightenment political thought for mainstream readers. Idealistic in its insistence on reforming repressive governments, advocating suppression of the slave trade and reversing the disastrous consequences of colonization, it nonetheless looked forward to a commercialized global economy in which increasingly tighter trade networks would reduce war by encouraging the pacific interdependence of all peoples. "Since *The Spirit of the Laws*, our literature has produced no greater work more deserving to be passed down to posterity as having produced our enlightenment and improvement," wrote Melchior Grimm of Raynal's book in his *Correspondance Littéraire*.[52]

A youthful Napoleon Bonaparte (1769–1821) was also inspired by the *Two Indies*. At age seventeen, Bonaparte devoured the work, constantly jotting down snippets into his notebook for future use. "I am not yet eighteen," he wrote in a letter to Raynal, "but I am already a writer; this is an age at which one must learn." Reading *Two Indies* made a young Bonaparte love history and want to write it himself. Bonaparte described himself as a "zealous disciple" who admired Raynal for "unmasking the prejudices of the great." A few years later, when General Bonaparte prepared for his Egyptian campaign, he gave specific instructions to include the entire ten volumes of *Two Indies* in his modest portable traveling library, alongside, of course, *The Spirit of the Laws*.[53]

In conclusion, what strikes one most about Enlightenment political thought was its popularity. For the first time in the history of European culture, large and difficult works of political theory became bestsellers, rivaling fiction, poetry, and theology. The Habermasian public who read Montesquieu, Hume, Rousseau, Mirabeau, Smith, and Raynal was not a mass public, as it would become a century later, but it included large sectors of the middling and elite classes. Books were still expensive, but they were also accessible, especially through new networks such as lending libraries. This new reading public read with a critical eye; reviews and diary entries are rarely wholly enthusiastic. Often readers engaged books that troubled them, spurred on more by an appreciation for the writer's eloquence than ideology. Finally, the infusion of economics into Enlightenment political theory was arguably the single most important innovation in the development of eighteenth-century political theory as a discipline, refashioning the goals of political life away from individual rights and legitimate authority and toward addressing the people's individual and collective happiness.

CHAPTER FIVE

Nature

BRIAN W. OGILVIE

Nature and Nature's Laws lay hid in Night:
GOD said, Let Newton be! And all was Light.

—Alexander Pope[1]

INTRODUCTION

In his *Dictionary* of 1755, Samuel Johnson began the definition of "nature" with characteristic bluntness: "An imaginary being supposed to preside over the material and animal world." Johnson left no doubt as to whether the Dame Nature of late medieval and Renaissance poetry and philosophy had a real existence distinct from the sovereign God who created and ordered the cosmos. But Johnson's ten other senses convey the breadth of the term in Enlightenment English. Nature could also refer to (2) "the native state or properties of any thing"; (3) "the constitution of an animated body"; (4) "disposition of mind"; (5) "the regular course of things"; (6) "the compass of natural existence"; (7) "natural affection, or reverence"; (8) "the state or operation of the material world"; (9) "sort; species"; or (10) "sentiments or images adapted to nature, or conformable to truth and reality." And last, oddly to a modern reader, we find the sense for which Johnson quoted Alexander Pope's epitaph for Isaac Newton (Figure 5.1): (11) "physics; the science which teaches the qualities of things."[2]

Nature's polysemy, already evident in Johnson's definition, shows even more clearly in the current *Oxford English Dictionary*, whose editors have determined fourteen senses of the word, many subdivided further, nearly all of which are attested before the sixteenth century. They group these, in turn, in four broad divisions: "senses related to physical or bodily power, strength, or substance"; "senses relating to mental or physical impulses and requirements"; "senses relating to innate character"; and "senses relating to the material world."

"Nature" thus has a fundamental duality. Depending on context, it refers either to the character, in some way or another, of an individual—the nature *of something*—or to the physical world as a whole. Enlightenment usage often slipped between the two: the fact that a particular behavior was in the nature of a being could be offered as evidence that the behavior was natural, and therefore sanctioned by Nature. As we explore the history of the concept and its place in Enlightenment culture, we must be attentive to such slippages.

Merely defining "nature" could take up this entire chapter; the *Oxford English Dictionary* entry, including usage examples, is over 18,000 words long. Instead, this

FIGURE 5.1 L. Desplaces, *An Allegorical Monument to Sir Isaac Newton and His Theories on Prisms*, line engraving after D. M. Fratta, J. B. Pittoni, D. Valeriani, and G. Valeriani, *c.* 1841. Wellcome Collection (public domain, CC BY).

chapter focuses on nature primarily in Johnson's sixth and eighth sense: "the compass of natural existence" and "the state or operation of the material world." Since that is still a vast canvas, it examines four points where nature took on significant salience in Enlightenment culture:

1. The first is the relationship between Nature and God. Despite the growth of modern atheism in our period, most Enlightenment thinkers, whether Christian, Jewish, or Deist, accepted that there was a Creator who had ordered the world in a legible fashion. Atheists in the line of the excommunicated Jewish philosopher Baruch Spinoza identified God with Nature. Toward the end of our period, this view was beginning to be challenged by an evolutionary account of the formation of the universe, the nebular hypothesis offered by Immanuel Kant and Pierre-Simon Laplace, but the notion of nature as Creation continued to hold sway. Hence,

statements and attitudes about nature often referred, at least implicitly but often implicitly, to conceptions of God.

2. The second is the concept of natural law and then natural rights. Roman jurists had offered the idea that in addition to the positive law of statute, human beings had access, through the exercise of reason, to "natural laws": certain ethical principles that were common to humanity and that could form the basis of the "law of nations" (*ius gentium*), that is, the foundational international law. This notion was developed at great length by scholastic writers from the thirteenth through the seventeenth century, contributing in fundamental ways to the development of modern international law. In this sense, "nature" provided a basis for establishing relations among peoples and for criticizing positive law. But from the seventeenth century, this idea of a natural law defined in terms of obligations common to all humanity was increasingly challenged by a distinct notion of natural rights possessed by distinct individuals who had to alienate some of them to form political societies.

3. The third topic is the laws of nature. The idea that natural processes generally followed a predictable order had existed in the Western tradition since the early Hellenic philosophers and was developed to a high state in certain ancient scientific traditions, most notably astronomy and statics. But the notion that nature followed certain highly specific principles that could be identified with laws emerged only in the seventeenth century in the work of the French philosopher René Descartes, who modeled his laws of nature on the "rules" (*regulae*) of mathematics. As we will see, this introduction required metaphysical underpinnings to clarify the obscure question of how inanimate objects could be said to "obey" laws. Over the course of the eighteenth century, laws of nature became a cultural commonplace, even as their metaphysical underpinnings were contested.

4. Finally, our fourth topic is the "state of nature." This notion offers an implicit contrast with the valuation of nature in the three previous aspects. If the nature created by God, made legible to reason in natural law, and given laws to follow, was valued positively, the state of nature often had a negative valence. In Catholic theology, it was opposed to a state of grace; nature, in this case, was the *fallen* nature of humanity after original sin. Thomas Hobbes emphasized another sense: the "natural condition of man" was a war of all against all, resulting in a life that was, infamously, "solitary, poor, nasty, brutish, and short." By nature, humans are immiserated due to their individual weakness, Hobbes insisted, and it is only in a state of organized society that they find some measure of security. The state of nature was thus understood as a state that was, happily, escaped in the founding of the first societies, even if for some thinkers, for instance John Locke, it still obtained among sovereign monarchs with respect to one another. By the late eighteenth century, this conjectural history had been elaborated in the stadial theories of the Scottish thinkers Adam Smith, William Robertson, and Dugald Stewart, in which the original primitive state of humanity, hunting in small bands, had been succeeded by pastoralism, agricultural civilization, and finally commerce. In these terms, the "state of nature" was contrasted with an improved or cultivated state—but unlike Catholic theology or Hobbesian political theory, it no longer applied to human beings.

As the fourth point makes clear, the concept of nature was under tension in Enlightenment culture. On the one hand, for some thinkers it was a divine creation, something for humans to obey and whose laws could be determined by reason (in the case of natural law) and experience (in the case of laws of nature). On the other, it was a primitive state that had to be escaped, whether through a sacrament, a social contract, or societal progress. Nature could be a term of praise or of opprobrium. But it could not be ignored.

These four areas were not merely subjects of intellectual debate. They had significant reverberations throughout Enlightenment culture. They were reflected in the literature of physico-theology, the practices of forming and displaying cabinets of natural history specimens, the demonstrations of natural philosophy (or as we would now say, science) that delighted aristocratic and bourgeois audiences—and in Europeans' increasing contempt for peoples who appeared to be in a state of nature, or close to it, due to their lack of political institutions or the weaknesses of their own innate natures.

NATURE AND NATURE'S GOD

We cannot understand nature in Enlightenment culture without understanding nature's God. A fundamental presupposition of most early modern thinkers was that nature, in the sense of the entirety of material things, was the product of a divine creator. For most, Christians and Jews alike, this was the God of Abraham. Deists, who rejected revealed religion, posited in that God's place a divine artificer who took no personal care of individual creatures but who had established a harmonious whole that was suited to the creatures it housed. A few radical materialists proclaimed that God *was* nothing more than nature, in the formula of Spinoza; by the second half of the eighteenth century, self-identified atheists were not afraid to claim the title, at least when among like-minded thinkers.[3] But they were still a tiny minority.

Though genuine atheists were few in number, they loomed large in the mind of their conservative opponents. The Flemish Jesuit Leonard Lessius claimed as early as 1613 that there were swarms of atheists threatening the entire world, led by that archfiend Niccolò Machiavelli.[4] (Never mind that Machiavelli had been dead for the better part of a century.) A century later, atheists were still rumored to be a threat; stories circulated about anonymous clandestine manuscripts defending atheist thought, such as the "Treatise of the Three Impostors," which allegedly argued that Moses, Jesus, and Muhammad had imposed a monstrous lie on their deluded followers. Dating back to the thirteenth century, these rumors ultimately led to the publication of two different books on the subject in the early and mid-eighteenth century.[5]

Still, even as late as the mid-eighteenth century, "atheist" was more a term of abuse than an accurate description of an individual's belief: an atheist was a freethinker whose beliefs threatened the religious foundations of society and the state. Most thinkers considered nature to be equivalent to the Creation, the "Six Days' Work" of Genesis. From the twelfth century onward, scholastic natural philosophers had granted some autonomy to nature, distinguishing between the primary cause of all things—God himself—and the secondary causes, the regular order of nature, that could be understood rationally.[6] God might intervene in that order from time to time; the result was a miracle. And particularly subtle intelligences—some humans, but especially demons—could use their knowledge of natural order to combine phenomena in rare and unexpected ways, producing "preternatural" phenomena: prodigies and wonders that, while out of the ordinary course of events, remained within the order of nature.[7]

The quasi-autonomous nature of the scholastic natural philosophers was soon personified. As "Dame Nature" or "Dame Kind" (in the sense of the kind of thing something was, its nature), she was represented in text and image as a regal woman ruling benevolently over the works of the creation.[8] The personification took on the classical notion of *lusus naturae*, "jokes" or "sports" of nature, a term used to describe monsters and marvels: though benevolent, Dame Nature was a bit of a trickster. You could never know exactly what strange thing she might produce. Her preternatural productions revealed her limited autonomy: as God's feudal vassal, she was granted latitude for action, though she was ultimately subject to his authority.

The Renaissance magus Robert Fludd (1574–1637) depicted this personified Nature as an intermediary between God and human arts. In one of Fludd's engravings from *The History of Both Cosmoses, the Macrocosm and the Microcosm* (1617), God, in the form of the Tetragrammaton, stands above his creation. The cosmos, in turn, is presided over by Nature as a mature woman clad in celestial objects and chained by her right hand to God. He is her superior, but she has leeway to act. Her left hand, in turn, holds a chain connected to an ape, who presides over human arts and crafts, reflecting the classical adage that "art is the ape of nature," namely, the arts are based on studying and imitating natural processes.

By the later seventeenth century, though, this personified nature was losing her personality. As we will see, new, more rigid conceptions of laws of nature that were always and everywhere in force were challenging her playfulness. Writing in the 1660s, the Dutch naturalist and anatomist Jan Swammerdam rejected the idea of jokes of nature, and the related idea that some animals arise through "spontaneous generation" of rotting organic matter into worms and insects, by insisting that "the Creator is so uniform in his works that chance has no place in them. For it is certain that God's works are based on constant and uniform rules" (Figure 5.2).[9] God's rules, not Nature's whims, determined the ways of the world.

A couple of decades after Swammerdam, the English virtuoso Robert Boyle offered a sustained assault on "the vulgarly receiv'd notion of nature."[10] In this work, he argued that Nature was not "that almost divine thing, whose works among others we are," but rather "a notional thing, that in some sense is rather to be reckoned among our works; as owing its being to human intellects."[11] Boyle rejected the received notion of Nature as a semi-divine being who does nothing in vain, never misses her goal, abhors a vacuum, and so forth, both because that notion attributed agency to an imaginary being and because it detracted from the honor and reverence due to the true Creator of the world. Analyzing the different senses in which the word *nature* was ordinarily employed, Boyle suggested that alternatives could be proposed to do away with the concept entirely. But if pressed to define it, Boyle would offer this definition:

> I shall express, what I called general nature, by cosmical mechanism, that is, a comprisal of all the mechanical affections (figure, size, motion, &c.) that belong to the matter of the great system of the universe. And, to denote the nature of this or that particular body, I shall style it, the private, the particular, or (if you please) the individual mechanism of it, that is, the essential modification, if I may so speak, by which, I mean, the comprisal of all its mechanical affections conven'd in the particular body, considered as 'tis determinately placed, in a world so constituted, as ours is.[12]

As is evident from this definition, Boyle offered a mechanical definition of nature. In the clockwork universe he imagined, there was no need for nature as a "plastick principle of all the mundane bodies" to intervene between God and the Creation. The universe was a divine clockwork; its nature was simply the design that God had followed when creating it.

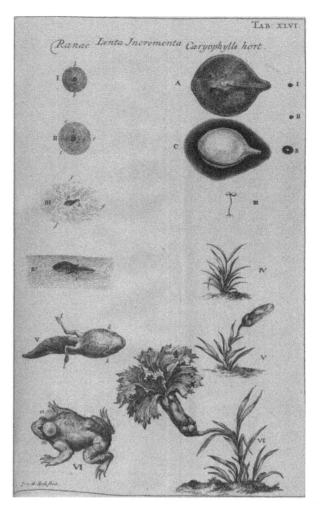

FIGURE 5.2 Jan Swammerdam, *Bible of Nature* (1737–1738). Biodiversity Heritage Library (public domain). Contributed by Naturalis Biodiversity Center. http://www.biodiversitylibrary.org/.

PHYSICO-THEOLOGY, NATURE'S MULTIPLICITY, AND NATURAL ORDER

In this view, rather than being an active power, nature was a passive plan. Not all of Boyle's contemporaries, even those who accepted the broad outlines of his mechanical natural philosophy, were willing to completely abandon the notion of plastic nature.[13] While Boyle's proposal to abolish the concept by resolving it into distinct synonyms obviously failed, his identification of nature with divine design became commonplace. We can see this in the tradition of physico-theology, the intellectual enterprise devoted to demonstrating the existence, omnipotence, omniscience, and benevolence of God through the study of his Creation. A significant movement in the Protestant world from the late seventeenth century to the early nineteenth, physico-theology spread widely the identification of nature with God's plan for creation.

In his eponymous *Physico-Theology* (1714), the English divine William Derham referred to nature and creation interchangeably. His dedicatory letter referred to "natural knowledge" as a path to understanding God, but in his text he referred to the natural world, interchangeably, as "the works of the Creation" and as "the works of Nature."[14] He sometimes used the term loosely (in a way that Boyle would have disapproved in a work originally delivered as a series of Boyle Lectures!), referring, for example, not only to the "course of nature," the "functions and operations of nature," and "nature's tendency"[15] but also in a way that quasi-personified the term. In various places, he referred to "the method nature takes in this great work," the "sagacity" and "artifice" of nature, and "nature's prodigious care."[16] He wrote that "Nature hath provided" the eyelid and eyelashes to protect the eye.[17] But Derham was aware that such usage was figurative, for he referred as well to "the great Author of nature," and at one point corrected himself: "Nature (or rather the great Author of nature)."[18] Summing up the principal argument of physico-theology, Derham suggested that atheism was irrational, and that it would be "monstrous" in a Christian "that hath studied Nature, and pryed farther than others into Gods Works."[19]

Physico-theologians and their fellow travelers emphasized the multiplicity of nature. For the English naturalist John Ray, the prodigious numbers of insect and plant species showed "how manifold" God's works were. The French abbé Noël-Antoine Pluche titled his immensely popular multivolume dialogue *Le Spectacle de la nature* (1732–1750), "The Spectacle of Nature," as if his characters and his readers were present at a theatrical performance. For Pluche, nature consisted of "all the bodies that surround us, the smallest as well as the greatest," whose "tendency toward a goal marks for us the intention of the Worker." Returning to the theme of the Book of Nature, beloved of physico-theologians, Pluche claimed that "nature is the wisest and the most perfect of all the books that are suited to cultivate our reason, because it encompasses the objects of every science and its comprehension is not restricted to any particular language or people."[20]

Physico-theologians could tout the multiplicity of nature because naturalists had been working hard to establish it. The sixteenth-century invention of natural history as a discipline had prompted Europeans to investigate, describe, collect, and organize plants, animals, and minerals on a hitherto unimagined scale. Between 1500 and 1700, the number of vascular plant species known and described leapt from several hundred to nearly twenty thousand.[21] In 1691, John Ray estimated that there were perhaps ten thousand insect species in the world. The following year he doubled his estimate.[22] These developments also encouraged attempts to define more precisely the concept of natural species and genus and to bring order to the apparently chaotic surfeit of God's creation. Late seventeenth- and eighteenth-century naturalists such as Joseph Pitton de Tournefort and Carl Linnaeus developed increasingly refined and extensive classifications of plants and animals.[23] At the same time, other naturalists like the French academicians René-Antoine Ferchault de Réaumur and his younger rival, Georges-Louis Leclerc, comte de Buffon, eschewed detailed taxonomies in favor of studying the dynamic processes of nature.[24]

Natural history collections—soon to become museums—could support either the Linnaean, taxonomic vision of nature or the process-oriented approach of Réaumur and Buffon. Denis Diderot preferred the latter. Writing in the *Encyclopédie*, Diderot wrote that "a cabinet of natural history is an abstract of all nature."[25] But he also pointed out that it cannot be ordered according to nature: "The order of a cabinet cannot be that of nature; in every aspect, nature shows a sublime disorder."[26] At the end, he promoted a grand, national collection:

> Might I be permitted to finish this article by proposing a project that would be no less advantageous than honorable to the nation? That would be to elevate a temple to nature that would be worthy of her. ... What a spectacle to have everything that the Almighty has scattered across the surface of the earth, displayed in a single place![27]

Diderot's phrasing reminds us that the Enlightenment, even in France, was not simply a story of secularization or disenchantment, but it also adumbrates how, for Romantic thinkers, nature might come to challenge or displace its Creator.[28]

Even as Enlightenment thinkers were disputing the proper order of nonhuman nature, others were turning to the question of human nature—also, of course, conceived as a product of divine craftsmanship. Alongside an earlier tradition of natural law arose a new, secular or secularizable, concept of natural rights. In both traditions, claims on nature were used to ground visions of social order.

NATURAL LAW AND NATURAL RIGHTS

Early modern definitions of natural law were broader than their Roman forebears. The Digest defined *ius naturale* (natural right) as the precepts common to all animals, not only humans: namely, procreation and care of their offspring. Those precepts binding on all human beings, regardless of political allegiance, were called *ius gentium*—the right of nations—by Roman jurists. Early modern jurists, on the other hand, did not regularly distinguish between *lex naturalis* (natural law) and *ius naturale* (natural right), and defined the latter as, in the words of Johannes Schneidewin in 1575, "knowledge or general rules, instilled in the human mind by nature or by God, which set out, through good morals, the best and most perfect way of life."[29]

Hence, natural law was that which was in accord with *human* nature, and it was accessible through reason. It had some sources in Aristotle's ethics, but it was particularly among Stoic philosophers that the notion of a rationally intelligible natural law was worked out in antiquity.[30] From the thirteenth through the early seventeenth century, scholastic thinkers from Thomas Aquinas to Francisco Suarez developed it into a rich tradition that provided the underpinnings for a universal ethic alongside the positive commandments of divine and human law, as well as a resource for challenging unjust aspects of the latter.[31] These arguments were not merely academic: Bartolomé de las Casas defended the natural freedom of native Amerindians in part on the basis of natural law, while Juan Ginés de Sepúlveda argued that their practice of idolatry and human sacrifice placed them outside natural law and justified their subjugation.[32]

The mainstream of scholastic natural law was associated with the intellectualist tradition of Aquinas and of the neo-Thomistic revival of the sixteenth century: good acts were intrinsically good, evil ones intrinsically evil. But even as strong a voluntarist as William of Ockham, who held famously (or infamously) that God could have made murder and theft moral according to his *absolute* power, held that in his *ordained* power, God had established a moral universe in which right reason was an infallible guide to natural law.[33]

In its emphasis on human beings' natural obligations to one another and their inherent sociability, the scholastic tradition of natural law was inherently cosmopolitan.[34] While it could be used to establish boundaries between human communities, those boundaries were permeable. In the face of religious war, the associated crisis of skepticism, and the collapse of the medieval imperial ideal, some seventeenth-century thinkers found this natural law to be hopelessly inadequate to addressing contemporary problems such as competing claims to political jurisdiction, whether a state could impose a religious settlement on its subjects—and whether subjects had grounds for taking up arms against an unjust ruler. These thinkers, from Hugo Grotius and John Selden to Thomas Hobbes, Samuel Pufendorf, and John Locke, focused instead on developing a concept of natural rights, then examining the extent to which those rights, possessed by individual human beings before political society had come into being, were limited, abrogated, or transferred in the state, or conversely, the extent to which their owners still possessed and could exercise them. At least to some degree, they strove to make reason, as well as custom, the basis for political order.

Like natural law, natural rights theories had origins in ancient Roman jurisprudence and scholastic legal thought.[35] The two were similar in taking as their point of departure human nature. But natural rights thinkers emphasized not the duties of people toward one another, but rather the rights they possessed before the institution of positive human law. As many natural rights theorists recognized themselves, rights and duties could be seen as two sides of the same coin: one individual's right to property, for instance, entails the duty of others to respect that right. But by starting with individual rights, and in particular, by conceiving of them above all as *property* rights, natural rights theorists developed a far more atomistic, and potentially radical, understanding of natural law than the scholastics. Hobbes developed "laws of nature" (his translation of *lex naturalis*), as a consequence of his initial "right of nature," defined as "the Liberty each man hath, to use his own power, as he will himselfe, for the preservation of his own Nature; that is to say, of his own Life; and consequently, of doing any thing, which in his own Judgement, and Reason, hee shall conceive to be the aptest means thereunto."[36] This apparently conflicted with Hobbes's first law of nature, the duty to seek peace, because self-defense is a natural right. To resolve the conflict, Hobbes deduced his second natural law, namely, that men must voluntarily renounce their natural right to everything, and his third, that they must keep their covenants with others, even if those covenants were made out of fear. A series of further deductions took Hobbes through a series of principles of equity, which he asserts can all be tested according to the Golden Rule:

> To leave all men unexcusable, they [the laws of nature] have been contracted into one easie sum, intelligible even to the meanest capacity; and that is, "Do not that to another, which thou wouldest not have done to thy selfe;" which sheweth him, that he has no more to do in learning the Lawes of Nature, but, when weighing the actions of other men with his own, they seem too heavy, to put them into the other part of the ballance, and his own into their place, that his own passions, and selfe-love, may adde nothing to the weight; and then there is none of these Lawes of Nature that will not appear unto him very reasonable.[37]

Hobbes was far more radical in his subordination of individuals to the Leviathan of the state than other natural rights thinkers. His materialism was even more shocking to contemporaries than Grotius's "impious hypothesis"—his startling claim that his principles would stand even if God did not exist or was indifferent to human affairs.[38] Much of Pufendorf's and Locke's intellectual energy went into refuting Hobbes. Natural rights thinkers did not all draw the same conclusions from their starting points: Grotius argued that the seas were the property of no one, a claim Selden went to pains to refute.

Their respective positions were not simply intellectual games; they were informed by Anglo-Dutch maritime rivalry. Some natural rights thinkers argued that insofar as an individual's liberty was their property, they could voluntarily sell it to another, namely, enslave themselves; others were horrified by the thought. Nonetheless, they agreed that natural law began with the rights of individuals and primarily involved negative restrictions on those rights. While the scholastic tradition had emphasized the accessibility of natural laws to synchronic reason, natural rights thinkers added a diachronic element: though human beings now live in political society, rights thinkers began by conjecturing about a hypothetical "state of nature" in which humans lived before the political state was invented. We will return to this concept momentarily.

Despite the challenge from natural rights theories, the notion of natural law as innate to human beings and discernible by reason persisted well into the eighteenth century. It was championed not only by scholastics but also by Protestants such as Gottfried Wilhelm Leibniz and Christian Wolff.[39] In his *Physico-theology*, the Protestant Derham quoted William King's observation that Christian monogamy is "more agreeable to the Law of Nature" than is polygamy.[40] It was also championed by many leading figures of the French Enlightenment as an alternative to custom—which was often antiquated, ridiculous, or unjust—and even divine law.[41] The many references to natural law in Diderot and d'Alembert's *Encyclopédie* treat it as a concept pertaining to moral philosophy and natural right: Louis de Jaucourt defined "natural law" as "a law that God imposes on all men, which they can discover by the light of their reason, in considering with attention their nature and state."[42] As we have seen, though, such considerations were increasingly taking the form of conjectural histories, and natural rights increasingly challenged natural law. Both natural law and natural rights were normative, moral theories: despite their differences, they set out to explain how human beings *should* behave. At the same time, a new concept of "law of nature," a law that was physical, not moral, and that could be discovered only empirically, had come into its own.

LAWS OF NATURE

The notion of "laws of nature" is so entwined with modern conceptions of science that its genealogy had received little attention until quite recently.[43] To be sure, the notion of regular, recurring phenomena in the natural world can be traced in the Western tradition to the Hellenic philosophers, and it was a prominent aspect of both Aristotelian and Stoic natural philosophy. But the modern idea of the law of nature is more precise. It involves a particular relationship obtaining in all circumstances, without exception, between specific aspects of natural phenomena: for example, Boyle's Law relating the pressure of a gas to its volume and temperature, or the Second Law of Thermodynamics. Such laws appeared first in the middle of the seventeenth century in the works of Descartes. By the end of the eighteenth century they were commonplace. Twentieth-century accounts of science often portray one of its central aims as the discovery of laws of nature.[44]

As we have already seen, we can trace back to the twelfth, thirteenth, and fourteenth centuries the idea that either the structure of the universe or God's ordained power established the natural laws that constrained human morality and the laws or rules governing the ordinary, regular behavior of the physical world. Historians of medieval science sometimes attribute the prominence of natural philosophy in the medieval and early modern university curriculum to this development.[45] What is striking about these regularities in scholastic thought from the thirteenth to the seventeenth centuries is that they admitted of exceptions. Aristotle had written that natural philosophy addressed phenomena as they happened "always or for the most part"; marvels and prodigies were not, properly speaking, part of natural philosophy.

As noted above, scholastic natural philosophers had elaborated on Aristotle's notion, holding that there were three realms of possibility: the natural, following the ordinary course of events; the preternatural, in which a highly unusual concatenation of natural causes, whether spontaneous or driven by human or demonic intelligence, produced unusual, wondrous outcomes; and the supernatural, in which divine intervention produced effects with no natural causes. In the fourteenth and fifteenth centuries, some natural philosophers and physicians, mostly outside of university settings, took an increasing interest in such "preternatural philosophy," cataloging the range of natural wonders and, in some cases, seeking philosophical explanations for them. These explanations were sometimes ingenious in their attempts to reduce preternatural phenomena to simpler causes, but they still left room for exceptions, including the so-called *lusus naturae*, "jokes of nature."

In contrast, the concept of law of nature as it was developed from the middle of the seventeenth century by Descartes and his successors did not admit exceptions. The post-Cartesian law of nature is "a specific and precise statement which codifies observed regularities in nature but which is also assumed to denote an underlying causal connection, and therefore can be said to carry explanatory force."[46] Descartes drew this notion from the realm of mathematics, where "rules" (*regulae*) had long been used to express such constant, necessary relationships. But in mathematics, rules had no causal force. As Descartes used mathematical tools to understand natural regularities, he turned rules into laws by adding a causal element.

For a mechanist like Descartes, who denied any active capacity for matter to respond to its surroundings and insisted, instead, on chains of efficient causation, it was initially difficult to understand how a causal law of nature could work. Laws require both legislators and subjects. It was easy to see how a divine Legislator might have established laws, but difficult to understand how entirely passive subjects could or would obey them. The historian John Henry has argued that Descartes turned to metaphysics to resolve this conundrum.[47] His solution was an absolute metaphysical distinction between inert, extended substance that was only reacted upon by other matter, on the one hand, and active, thinking substance, the stuff of the human soul and of the Creator, on the other. Extended substance "obeyed" the Creator's laws because He had made it thus and had imparted a fixed amount of motion to the entire system of the universe.

While a legislating divinity was necessary for Descartes to make sense of his system, atheist versions of his system soon appeared—versions that implied matter was active and self-organizing, most notoriously, Spinoza's "God, that is, Nature." To preserve orthodoxy, Christian and Deist philosophers writing after Descartes and Spinoza needed to keep physical matter inert and dependent on God. If matter were given any degree of autonomy, that opened the door to Spinoza's equation of God with nature. Moreover, to many anti-Cartesians, Descartes's own theism appeared suspect: Descartes grounded his physics in metaphysics, but he urged his followers not to seek purpose—final causes— in nature, on the grounds that the human mind was unequal to the task of discerning God's purposes. To Robert Boyle, John Ray, and others, that appeared to be a "pretend theism," not real belief. Their view was related to their objections to Hobbes's similar diffidence: in their view, Hobbes's "extreme voluntarism ... amounted to a denial that it was possible to find evidence of God's will in nature."[48]

Boyle was so alarmed by the active matter implied by the "vulgar" notion of nature that he rejected any discussion of laws of nature. In a 1685 publication, he admitted that he sometimes spoke carelessly of the "Laws of Motion and Rest," but when considered carefully, he observed, "to speak properly, a Law being but a Notional Rule of Acting according to the declar'd Will of a Superior, 'tis plain, that nothing but an Intellectual Being can be properly capable of receiving and acting by a Law."[49] What are loosely called "laws of nature" are, instead, "determinate Motions" impressed by God on matter at the Creation and ever since sustained by him.

Boyle's fundamental principle was accepted by most of his contemporaries, but not his scruples about the term. Following the example of Descartes, natural philosophers were increasingly using the term "law" to refer to regular, specific causal relationships between phenomena.[50] By the time Boyle wrote his inquiry on nature, the concept had received an immense boost from Isaac Newton's mathematical dynamics. In his 1687 *Mathematical Principles of Natural Philosophy* (in Latin), Newton had introduced three "laws of motion" (*leges motus*).[51] Newton was echoing Descartes, but the immense prestige he would come to have in the eighteenth century ensured the success and generalization of the concept. Further, Newton had underscored that laws of nature could be determined only empirically. Precisely because God could have chosen to create the world according to different laws, Cartesian cogitation was no way to discover the laws he had actually established.

G. W. Leibniz, too, was fond of referring to many different laws of nature. As Sophie Roux has observed, the concept of natural law, well established by 1715, combined the physico-mathematical idea of a specific relationship with the metaphysical idea of an established order: "The regularities of physics are also the principles according to which, following a command from God, things are organized—principles of order, constitutive principles, architectonic principles: other laws would have made another world."[52]

As the concept of law of nature was established, it was also applied retrospectively. In the *Encyclopédie*, d'Alembert referred to Kepler's "law," a term Kepler himself never used.[53] The inverse relationship between the pressure and volume of a gas, published by Boyle in 1662, is now commonly known as "Boyle's Law," but the term seems to have come into use only in the nineteenth century.[54] Once it was clearly formulated, it appears to have filled a need to the point where only recently have historians even thought to ask whether it had a history.[55]

By the middle of the eighteenth century, the reach of inviolable laws of nature had extended even to conservative Thomist theologians. While accepting in principle that there were realms of supernatural and preternatural phenomena, in practice they included almost all phenomena in the ordinary course of nature, subject to its laws.[56] However, if natural law remained as a normative principle, one that could be discerned by introspection and reason but that reprobates could willfully contravene, it was increasingly elbowed aside by laws of nature, iron-clad rules that governed both animate and inanimate substances, that admitted of no exceptions, and that could be discovered only by empirical inquiry.

The new concept of laws of nature circulated widely in Enlightenment culture. Over the course of the eighteenth century, natural philosophy (i.e., what we call science) became a popular pastime for the leisured classes alongside natural history.[57] Demonstrations of chemical reactions, electrical phenomena, and magnetism filled the salons of polite society, while the 1758–1759 return of Halley's Comet was a spectacular vindication of Newton's mechanics. Émilie du Châtelet's *Institutions de physique* (*Lessons on Physics*, 1740) presented a critical synthesis of modern laws of motion that she intended to be accessible to her teenage son, while her posthumously published translation of Newton's *Mathematical Principles of Natural Philosophy* (1759) made that seminal text available to readers of French.[58] Moreover, Buffon's multivolume *Natural History* (1749–1788), published in French as well as English, Swedish, German, Italian, and Russian translations and among the most popular books of the eighteenth century, broadly disseminated the idea that studying nature meant discovering the laws by which it operated.[59]

The consequences of this shift can be seen in one of the most dramatic events of the eighteenth century: the destruction of the city of Lisbon by earthquake, tsunami, and fire on November 1, 1755. Reactions to this first modern catastrophe were profoundly shaped by the concept of immutable laws of nature.[60] Disasters such as the earthquake that struck Basel in 1356 or the Great Fire of London in 1666, as well as lesser tribulations, had often been explained in providential terms, as punishments or warnings from God. Other explanations appealed to "the vagaries of Dame Fortune and the workings of an autonomous Nature."[61] By the 1750s, those explanatory resources were no longer available to those who accepted that the laws of nature were fixed and inviolable. Lisbon had been destroyed, tens of thousands killed, by the inexorable playing out of natural forces.

The earthquake challenged the easy pieties of those who held, with Leibniz and Alexander Pope, that God had ordained his inviolable natural laws as the constitution of the best of all possible worlds. In his 1756 *Poem on the Disaster of Lisbon*, Voltaire skewered the maxim, "Whatever is, is Right."[62] Though he professed that, understood properly, Pope's words were true, he held nonetheless that it was cold compassion to insist on it in the face of obvious human suffering. The existence of evil was a problem that no philosopher had solved, and "man's understanding is as weak as his life is miserable."[63] Voltaire's pessimistic irony was challenged by many.[64] But the notion that the laws of nature were indifferent to human misery served, at the very least, as a challenge to the idea that nature could be a source of guidance for our lives.

THE STATE OF NATURE

If "nature" had a positive valence when considered as the work of Creation, as the source of natural law, and as the source of the laws that govern the behavior of material objects (*pace* natural disasters), its role could be more ambiguous in some contexts: particularly that of the state of nature. To a Christian heritage in which the state of nature was contrasted negatively with a state of grace, and to a legal heritage that distinguished between natural and legitimate offspring, the seventeenth century added a new sense: the Hobbesian sense of the miserable state of nature before the social contract (or after it broke down). Eighteenth-century thinkers, in turn, added a further contrast: that between land or animals in a state of nature and those that had been improved or domesticated.

As William Gass observes, "The story of that state of nature … prefers to take us from our present place and time to another, earlier, indeed original, condition, and it plays continually on the differences. In a way, we always stand at the story's end."[65] The Christian and Hobbesian stories of the state of nature posit nature not as what is but what *was*, or what threatens to break out again. The stadial story, meanwhile, posits nature as that which has not been touched by human hands and improved—or, from a Romantic point of view, sullied. (As we will see, the Lockean version is more complicated.)

The idea that the original, natural state of human beings was in small family groupings, governed by no law (other than natural law), and that civil life had its origins in some sort of social contract, has a long pedigree. In *De inventione* and *De oratore*, Cicero had described the uncivilized state of human beings as one in which "greed, that blind and rash tyrant of the soul, abused the powers of the body to sate itself, with the most wicked accomplices." Conversely, he had praised the power of rhetoric as that which "was able to assemble scattered human beings in one place, to lead them from a savage and rustic life to this humane, civic cultivation, and to speak laws, judgments, and obligations to the now constituted citizens."[66] Cicero's contemporary Lucretius, too, had vividly described such a primitive state in book 5 of *De rerum natura*, lamenting the precarious condition of humans when they lived in small groups, threatened day and night by wild beasts, before they united and formed a compact.

Renaissance humanists took up this notion; indeed, some were profoundly shaped by it.[67] But as Richard Tuck has argued, they spent relatively little time thinking about the original human condition; their commitment to civic life drew their attention to the *ius gentium* and the civil law.[68] Moreover, another strand in the ancient tradition emphasized the golden age of humans before civil society, in which people lived in harmony with one another and with the natural world. Christian ethicists could reconcile the two accounts: the Fall had introduced sin, death, and strife into a previously harmonious world.

As we have seen above, the state of nature took on new importance in the work of natural rights theorists. Hobbes's well-known gloss in the *Leviathan* of this "naturall state of mankind" as a perpetual state of war in which human life is "solitary, poore, nasty, brutish, and short" scarcely needs to be repeated.[69] It is worth recalling, however, that Hobbes did not believe that people living in a "state of meer Nature" were necessarily always engaged in conflict. Rather, the lack of any law beyond the natural, which for Hobbes meant the duty of self-preservation, meant that conflict was always possible, and no magistrate existed to resolve it by means other than force.

Some of Hobbes's readers countered his account of the state of nature with the story of Eden. Aristotelians and Arminians, in particular, emphasized the perfection of nature. Even after the Fall, human beings retained notions of sociability and had access to natural law. Hence the occasional outburst of violence in the post-Edenic world, such as Cain's murder of Abel, represented an aberration, not a war of all against all.[70] Scholars have disagreed vehemently about whether Hobbes's own views of the state of nature were informed by, or compatible with, an Augustinian and Reformed interpretation of the Fall. It is clear, though, that many Reformed readers, approaching Hobbes from a tradition that assumed the total depravity of the reprobate, were capable of reconciling his philosophical history with biblical history—so long as the elect were excluded from the war of all against all.

Locke's conception of the state of nature, while related to Hobbes's, is both more complicated and less bleak. For Hobbes, one is either in or out of the state of nature, while for Locke, an individual might simultaneously be in a state of nature with respect to some people and outside of it with respect to others.[71] For Locke, in the *Two Treatises of Government* (1689), the state of nature is characterized by the absence of a common judge with authority to settle disputes between two persons. Hence, in Locke's day, two subjects of the same monarch are outside the state of nature, but sovereign rulers are in a state of nature with respect to one another.

In these early Enlightenment accounts of the state of nature, this notion appears primarily as a philosophical tool. By contrast, the "conjectural histories" of the later Enlightenment present it as a distinct historical stage in the development of human societies. Jean-Jacques Rousseau, Adam Ferguson, Adam Smith, and Dugald Stewart (who coined the term) offered imaginative accounts of the earliest stages of human society. These differed from the natural law tradition in certain key ways.[72] For our purposes, the most important is that they were both secular and non-contractual. Implicitly or explicitly, conjectural historians offered a narrative of the origins of human society and the causes of transitions between its stages as an alternative to sacred history. Furthermore, they recognized that, however the first social orders were established, it was not through any kind of formal, contractual arrangement.

These thinkers, and their contemporaries, did not see the state of nature as either a golden age or a Hobbesian war of all against all. For the Swiss thinker Jean-Jacques Burlamaqui, the true "state of nature" was not simply the human condition before civil society arose, but rather, as historian Robin Douglass puts it, "a normative ideal, that is, a state that is in accordance with the end and nature of man." Burlamaqui foreshadowed Rousseau in this: what Hobbes, Pufendorf, and others had considered to be a state of nature was defined instead by Burlamaqui as a "primitive state" that had to be overcome for human beings to fully express their nature in civil society.[73] Even Rousseau himself, despite the myth of the noble savage associated with him, thought that human nature could be developed effectively in a modern society through careful education that avoided its corrupting influences, as he explained in *Emile* (1762).[74]

This improved or cultivated state of humans in society finds its parallel in a final use of the term "state of nature" to designate land that was unimproved or plants and animals that were undomesticated. This sense had been foreshadowed in Locke's *Second Treatise on Government*, where private property is justified by the work the owner has done: an object "being by him removed from the common state Nature placed in it, hath by this labour something annexed to it, that excludes the common right of other Men."[75] However, the usage became common only in the late eighteenth century, both literally and, as in this example from Dugald Stewart, figuratively:

> I speak … of men destined for the higher and more independent walks of life, who are too often led, by an ignorance of their own possible attainments, to exhaust all their toil on one little field of study, while they leave, in a state of nature, by far the most valuable portion of the intellectual inheritance to which they were born.[76]

CONCLUSION

As developed by stadial conjectural historians, the notion of a primitive state of nature implied that Europeans' ancestors had once lived in small groups leading a nomadic life with few or no political institutions. The passage out of that stage involved progress. As Europeans were increasingly convinced of their superiority to other peoples in the world, this notion of progress served as an intellectual justification for their commercial and colonial expansion, in particular their dominance of peoples perceived as closer to nature and hence "without history."[77] Their apparent success in identifying ever more laws of nature and the technical mastery seemingly associated with that knowledge served as a further "proof" of superiority, especially when combined with the scientific racism that developed over the course of the eighteenth century, especially in its last decades: the idea that human beings could be grouped into clearly distinct "races," that intellectual differences existed between those groups, that those differences could be ranked hierarchically (with Europeans at the top), and that they were rooted in the natural essence of each "race."[78] The atomistic individuals posited by natural rights theorists, capable of alienating fundamental rights of autonomy and resistance, could be employed as an intellectual justification for absolutist states.

All this is true. Yet to acknowledge it is also to underscore the importance of the concept of nature in Enlightenment developments and debates, in the four areas this chapter has discussed and in many others. Like progress, commerce, and colonialism, nature was inescapable.

CHAPTER SIX

Religion and the Divine: The Encyclopedia's God

JONATHAN SHEEHAN

The study of the Enlightenment is a young field. Until the publication of Carl Becker's *The Heavenly City of the Eighteenth Century Philosophers* (1931) and Ernst Cassirer's *The Philosophy of Enlightenment* (1932), there was no "field" at all. The real growth phase only happened after the war. The repudiation of Becker in October 1956, at the conference celebrating the twenty-fifth anniversary of *The Heavenly City*, marks the emergence of a distinct project of intellectual inquiry confident about its methods and the story that it wanted to tell.[1] Above all, Becker's gloomy description of a cynical, scornful, and disillusioned Enlightenment was abandoned by a new generation of intellectual historians wedded to the modernization stories everywhere persuasive in the human sciences of the 1950s and 1960s.[2] This was true especially in the United States, where the study of the Enlightenment flourished. Although they diverged in many regards, Frank Manuel's *The Eighteenth Century Confronts the Gods* (1959) and Peter Gay's two-volume *The Enlightenment: An Interpretation* (1969), for example, both cheerfully depicted the party of reason winning the fight to replace a God-centered with a human-centered world.

In these early years, stories about religion in the Enlightenment were more or less couched in terms of decline, culminating in the great secularizations of the French Revolution. Since then, however, the field has grown more diverse in its methods, more inclusive in its cast of characters, and less confident in the story it wants to tell. Religion no longer graces the Enlightenment solely with its absence. Indeed, there is now a well-established cottage industry dedicated to the opposite proposition. Innovative monographs, edited volumes, surveys, articles, and review essays have made clear just how various the fate of religion was in eighteenth-century European life. Excellent works on the Jesuits in the Enlightenment; on the intellectual contribution of antiquarian and historical scholarship pursued within religious institutions; on the engagement of Europeans with Islam and the religions of the East; on the mystical roots of Enlightenment personhood; on the engagement and participation of Jewish intellectuals in wider Enlightenment discussions of reason; and many others have opened up rich veins of research that will likely be explored for years to come.[3]

That said, this outburst of creativity has not produced much historical consensus. This must in part have something to do with the complexity of the historical terrains in play. Plausible settings for the question "what happened to religion in the Enlightenment?" include: the end of the wars of religion, the growth of the early modern state, the emergence of the natural sciences, the rise of commercial society, and the expansion of

Europe abroad, not to mention the quickly transforming institutions of religious life. Simply identifying the proper context in which to address the question is no small matter.

Just as challenging to consensus, moreover, are the conceptual complexities inherent in the terms. The difficulty of defining with precision either "Enlightenment" or "religion," as Simon Grote has written, threatens to make "any discussion of religion and enlightenment… into either a frustrating exercise in equivocation … or an unresolvable quarrel over the definitions themselves."[4] There are ways to relax this conceptual knot, though they do not come without costs. One might use the terms to constrain each other, for example, and focus on "reasonable religion" as the Enlightenment ideal that stands at their intersection.[5] This captures the moderate theological perspective common to Protestant, Catholic, and Jewish normative thinkers from the period, and usefully isolates a set of conceptual commitments common to Christian and Jewish thought in the period. It hardly compasses what "religion" does, however, or what is done to "religion," in the Enlightenment.

These latter concerns are doubtless too big for intellectual history alone. Yet even if we restrict our gaze to the objects most proper to our discipline—concepts and ideas—we miss essential dynamics if we also limit ourselves to intramural theological debates. Seen in a longer-term perspective, what is most striking in the years after 1650 is the multiplication of the sources, genres, and forms of religious ideation. In the early seventeenth century, confessional churches still felt reasonably confident that they would have the last word about matters theological, not least because confessional states had real interests in guaranteeing this. By late century, this had decisively changed. Across Europe, states grew more assertive of their prerogatives vis-à-vis ecclesiastical establishments, on the one hand, and, on the other, the number of alternative post- or anti-confessional Christianities—Jansenism, Pietism, Quakers, Methodism, to name a few—skyrocketed.

As the power of confessional churches waned, so too did their ability to capture questions native to Christianity within the usual theological-ecclesiastical intellectual matrices. In what Amos Funkenstein called the "secular theology" of the late seventeenth century, for example, new natural philosophies developed powerful new answers to older theological questions. René Descartes, Isaac Newton, Baruch Spinoza, and Gottfried Wilhelm Leibniz all elaborated innovative vocabularies and forms of inquiry for addressing long-standing theological puzzles. This project was, as Funkenstein notes, secular insofar as it was written by laymen for laymen, but its audience would come to include exactly those professional theologians who had traditionally controlled the terrain of inquiry.[6]

From the middle of the seventeenth century onward, in other words, key concepts in the Christian imagination escaped the oversight of university-trained, ecclesiastically supported theological authorities. "Theology" became, as William Bulman has aptly written, "a disciplinary muddle, a space where the work of antiquarians, historians, philologists, Orientalists, philosophers, scientists, scholastics, and travel writers" worked out ways to think about God.[7] The conflicts that this produced are well known: struggles about the authority of the Bible, the origins of morality, the virtues of atheism, determinism and free will, and more. Theoretical positions aside, all of these unfolded in a newly heterogeneous ideational space. When Spinoza wrote, as a Jew and a philosopher, about the historicity of the Bible; when the literary entrepreneur Pierre Bayle offered a philosophical intervention into the theological issue of atheism; when the political philosopher Thomas Hobbes narrowed the compass of possible theological truths to the simple "Jesus is the Christ": each of these thinkers pulled a theological topic outside of its native habitat, subjecting it to new theoretical vocabularies, new techniques of analysis, and new argumentative priorities.

This dynamic of pluralization only accelerated with the dawn of the eighteenth century. Not only were the established churches forced to recognize new institutions and forms of Christian life—the establishment of dissenting academies in England after 1660, the German Pietists with their orphanage, printing press, and educational institutions in Halle from the 1690s, the support of various heterodox communities by Protestant princes in the Holy Roman Empire, the establishment of Jansenist convents in France, to name a few—but the very forms in which theological deliberation had traditionally taken place themselves began to change. The apologetic treatise and the learned doctrinal tome were at the least supplemented, if not in some cases replaced, by journals, newspapers, experimental essays, autobiographies, and much more.[8]

As the forms of deliberation and argument about matters theological grew in scope and variety, so too did ever more actors invite themselves into wider conversations about the nature of religion. In France, those who came to style themselves as *philosophes*, for example, did not come from inside the universities, some of them relying on patronage and some learning to live on the profits of their pen alone. Even in in the German lands, where learning was much more intimately tied to older institutions of academic learning, writers began to speak from more diverse positions. The Bible translators that I examined in *The Enlightenment Bible* (2005), for example, often spoke from beyond the world of church- and university-sanctioned theologians: scrappy religious enthusiasts, tutors, poets, literati, and small-town pastors went head-to-head with the more conventionally learned.

The proposal of this chapter is, then, that we take this new heterogeneity as the most fundamental historical condition under which religion and Enlightenment should be thought. The advantage of this pragmatic approach lies in its agnosticism toward any particular determinations, historical or conceptual, of its object. Whatever set of convergent circumstances produced this heterogeneity, whatever thing we take religion to have been for the many people who joined in conversation about it, whatever set of philosophical commitments they brought to the table: the intellectual space in which religious ideas were deliberated was fundamentally heterogeneous.

This heterogeneity, furthermore, I believe to be the best working description of the "Enlightenment" more generally. It was the deep structure that conditioned the intellectual ferment of the eighteenth century, that gave intellectual life its particular texture, that sanctioned the routine violation of boundaries between forms of knowledge, that encouraged playwrights to imagine themselves as scientists, musicians as political theorists, and poets as theologians. As such, our opening question can usefully be restated as this: what did it mean for those things taken to belong to Christianity (for this, really, is the "religion" chiefly at issue in western Europe) to be dispersed across the newly differentiated ideational space of the eighteenth century? What did it mean for Christian fundamentals to be deracinated, to come detached from older frameworks of adjudication and deliberation? What happens to the divine when it is freed of clerical oversight and allowed to roam free across the experimental intellectual spaces of the Enlightenment?

To bring this argument into focus, this chapter will pay careful attention to a very small intellectual object that tried to contain a very big intellectual topic: the article "God" in the French *Encyclopédie* edited by Denis Diderot and d'Alembert.

In 1754, God—*Dieu*—found a home in volume four of the *Encyclopédie*, nestled snugly between "diet" (*diète*) and "difference" (*différance*). His entry spans about eight folio pages. Even controlling for the idiosyncrasy of interests that produced its entries, God does not appear a special object for encyclopedic consideration. Describing Him takes about as long as it takes to describe consonants, *corvée* labor, and shells, but far fewer words than those needed for the French customs courts, or rope making.

This short encyclopedia entry is thus a minuscule (in both length and complexity) contribution to the innovative Christian library produced during the eighteenth century. Theologians from August Hermann Frank, John Wesley, William Law, and Johann Spalding to Emmanuel Swedenborg; philosophers from Christian Wolff, Jean-Jacques Rousseau, and Johann Herder to Immanuel Kant; philologists from Richard Simon to Johann Michaelis; even heterodox thinkers such as John Toland, Voltaire, Claude Helvetius, and Tom Paine: any one of these thinkers wrote in more depth and with more systematic concentration about God than the writer of this encyclopedia entry. So it might seem an unusual vehicle for reflection on the more general question of religion and enlightenment. But I hope to demonstrate here that, if short, it nonetheless captures crucial features of a new intellectual world in which organizing terms and questions in Christianity escaped from their theological and ecclesiastical stables and ran free across disciplines, genres, and perspectives.

To begin with, let us consider the author. The entry tells us at its conclusion that it was assembled from the papers of Johann Samuel Formey (1711–1797), the permanent secretary of the Prussian Royal Academy. Born in Berlin of Huguenot descent, Formey rose to prominence as a philosopher, journalist, and formidable correspondent, a go-between in the mid-century Republic of Letters connecting Berlin to writers diverse as Denis Diderot, Charles Bonnet, Voltaire, Claude Helvétius, Jean-Jacques Rousseau, and many others less storied. According to the preliminary discourse of the *Encyclopédie*, Formey was also one of the foundation stones upon which the project was built, someone who, Jean le Rond d'Alembert wrote, "had pondered a dictionary much like ours," and had "generously shared" the manuscripts that he had already completed in service of this new, and larger, work.[9] In fact, Formey sold the manuscripts—some 1,800 pages—for 300 livres to the encyclopedists, and presumably the entry for God was compiled from these. It seems certain that Formey had no say in the entry itself. As his correspondence indicates, by 1754 he had fallen out, especially with Diderot, publishing already in 1749 the *Reasonable Thoughts Contrary to the Philosophical Thoughts* of his more famous and radical Parisian counterpart.[10]

From the outset, then, the article was the product of the special media environment of the mid-century. The robust literary public sphere that was such a marked feature of the eighteenth century sustained, intellectually and materially, characters like Formey. One did not have to be a first-rate philosopher, for example, to participate at a high level in this intellectual culture. Formey made his fame largely as a popularizer of the metaphysics of Christian Wolff. *The Lovely Wolfienne* appeared in six volumes between 1741 and 1753, a jaunty work conceived, its author wrote, as "a diversion from study" during a happy September spent in the countryside in the company of women.[11] Its combination of anecdote, dialogue, pedagogy, exposition, and epistolary appendices were likely modeled after Francesco Algarotti's *Newtonianism for Ladies* (1737).[12] This genre of popular philosophy was a boom industry by mid-century, usually structured around "translations"—literal or figurative—of philosophical works into new languages or for new audiences.[13] Formey worked as a popularizer in other ways as well, serving in some capacity in the publication of some twenty (French language) literary journals between the 1730s and the 1770s.[14]

The "author" of the God article was, therefore, a kind of pastiche. Diderot and/or d'Alembert assembled, in some way unknown to us, materials gathered from papers written for a possible dictionary, papers compiled by a thinker whose major role was as functionary and intermediary between different languages and audiences, a role that afforded him in ways quite unique to the eighteenth century a commanding vision of the literary landscape across at least three European vernaculars.

Let us turn to the content of the article. To begin with, it is worth remarking on the difficulty of writing an entry on God for a work like the *Encyclopédie*. Leaving aside for the moment the perils of theological misstep, the first challenge must have been: what to include? The *Encyclopédie* was tagged a *dictionnaire raisonné des sciences, des arts et des métiers*, a *"reasoned* dictionary of the sciences, arts, and crafts." In contrast to regular dictionaries, the work followed an "encyclopedic arrangement, that is to say, the chain by which one can descend without interruption from the first principles of an art or science all the way down to its remotest consequences," and vice versa.[15]

The editors had in mind, as examples and contrasts, at least three previous dictionaries: Louis Moréri's *Great Historical Dictionary* (first edition, 1674), Pierre Bayle's *Historical and Critical Dictionary* (1697), and Ephraim Chambers's *Cyclopaedia: or, an Universal Dictionary of Arts and Sciences* (1728). In early editions of the first, an entry for "God" or *Dieu* is absent, but by 1718, the now much augmented dictionary included a short entry that took its definitional charge literally. God is "the name of the eternal being, infinite, incomprehensible, who created the world with his power, who governs it with his wisdom, and conserves it with his goodness," the Moréri entry began, mentioning names for God in different languages, and compressing a history of Christianity into little more than two hundred words.[16]

Bayle conceived his own work, at least in part, as a correction of Moréri, but Bayle avoided the word (and all such abstractions) altogether. The *Cyclopaedia* was a richer case. There the author conceded that an entry on God posed unique challenges for a dictionary. Dictionaries proceed by *definition*, the "Enumeration of the chief simple Ideas, whereof the compound Idea consists; in order to ascertain, or explain its Nature, and Character," Chambers explained.[17] But in the case of God, "no just Definition can be given of the Thing signified ... as being infinite, and incomprehensible."[18] What to do? Chambers resolved the quandary by changing the scope of the entry. *What is God?* became *How has God been defined?* Scripture defines him as "I am that I am"; philosophers have defined him as "a Being of infinite Perfection"; Isaac Newton defines him in terms of his "Dominion"; and so forth. The article does not stop there, however, recounting the names of God among the ancient Hebrews, the rabbis, the church fathers, and even the pagans, who after all had things that they called "God" as well. Practices of human deification; heathen star and sun worship; the various pantheons of Greeks, Romans, Syrians, Egyptians, and Persians; the philosophical theologies of Plato and Cicero: all received brief mentions. Because agreement on the definition of God did not emerge, definitions abound, creating exactly those effects of dispersion and multiplicity that I suggested above characterize the ideational space of Enlightenment.

The editors of the *Encyclopédie* had more systematic ambitions than Chambers did, however (Figure 6.1). These ambitions were signaled clearly in the oft-reprinted *System figuré des connoissances humaine*, the "tree of knowledge" that offered an at least imaginative unity to the many-volumed work. In the context of this "world map," as d'Alembert called it, the entry for God should be imagined along a path that led from "Reason" to the "Science of God" to "natural and revealed theology" and finally to "religion."[19] But even the editors insisted that to take this ideal as the real structure of the *Encyclopédie* would be a mistake. "The universe is but a vast ocean, on the surface of which

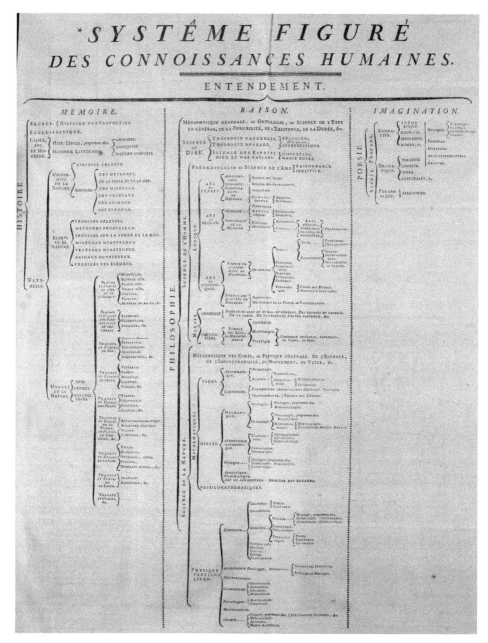

FIGURE 6.1 "Table of Knowledge," in Diderot, *Encyclopédie* (1751). © Wikimedia Commons (public domain).

we perceive a few islands of various sizes, whose connection with the continent is hidden from us," they ruefully acknowledged.[20] If we take it as the intended ideal, however, then an entry for God should offer more than a definition, even a paradoxical definition like the one found in Chambers. It should ultimately operate within a philosophical rather than a lexical horizon.

The entry did just this. It began with a confrontation of the same problem that Chambers faced, namely, how to put something that is, as Augustine wrote, "superior to all definitions" into an encyclopedia. But the entry restated the problem in philosophical terms: "however incomprehensible God might be, we should not infer that he is so in all respects." God resists predication, but the one predicate we can feel certain of affirming is that of existence, the author opened. "There is nothing easier than to know that there is a God," a line whose edge was sharpened by the polemical context of the eighteenth century, when skeptics (and dictionary authors) such as Bayle insisted that human statements about the divine could not even reliably include the predicate of existence. Bayle wanted "to prove that there was no possible demonstrative proof of the existence of God," the article lamented, especially none that depended on ordinary human experience or the consensus of history.[21]

The opening paragraphs of the entry were dedicated, then, to showing that the existence of God is "one of the first truths that forcefully seize any mind that thinks and reflects."[22] Proving something so self-evident, the article admitted sadly, should be beside the point. Indeed the very effort could be "injurious to man," since it suggests the opposite might be possible. Nonetheless, the article threw caution to the wind, and "to please all tastes" afforded its readers three additional proofs of the existence of God: a "metaphysical," an "historical," and a "physical" one.

In a general sense, the orientation of the article confirms the irony that the historian Alan Kors long ago observed about early Enlightenment philosophical atheism, namely, that its major arguments were first elaborated among Christian theologians. The refutation of the argument from "universal consent," Kors shows, was not original to Bayle, but was developed in hypothetical form by theologians hoping not to destroy but to "guarantee the faith."[23] We could profitably understand the article as an attempt to put this genie back in the bottle, mobilizing all of the arguments available to a middle-of-the-road pious philosopher worried about an ever more robust anti-clerical intellectual culture. The despairing tone of the article is perhaps a recognition of how difficult it would be to refute skeptical arguments that *even Christian theologians* had taken as persuasive.

That said, the article appears confident in its ability to cobble together adequate defenses against atheism. The first of its proofs, for example, it assembled from the English divine Samuel Clarke's *Demonstration of the Being and Attributes of God*, a series of eight sermons given as the Boyle Lectures in 1704. These lectures offered a bibliography of popular apologetics against atheism, beginning with the philologist and lay Newtonian Richard Bentley's *Confutation of Atheism* in 1692. Clarke's sermons, the title page announced, were directed "in Answer to Mr. Hobbs [*sic*], Spinoza, and their Followers," and they developed a version of what now is called the cosmological proof of the existence of God.

The proof has an ancient pedigree, with roots in Aristotle and Plato, but it gets its definitive Christian treatment in Thomas Aquinas's *Summa theologiae* (*c.* 1266–1273), where it is developed as one of "five ways in which one can prove that there is a God."[24] Characteristically, Thomas developed these proofs against doubters, the "gentiles" who might argue the nonexistence of God either from the existence of evil or from the adequacy of purely natural causes in explaining the world's phenomena. The second proof was

> based on the nature of causation ... In the observable world causes are found to be ordered in series; we never observe, nor ever could, something causing itself ... Such a series of causes must however stop somewhere ... Now if you eliminate a cause you

also eliminate its effects, so that you cannot have a last cause, nor an intermediate one, unless you have a first. ... One is therefore first forced to suppose some first cause, to which everyone gives the name "God."[25]

In Clarke's terms, "an infinite succession of merely *Dependent* Beings, without any Original Independent Cause; is a *Series* of Beings, that has neither Necessity nor Cause, nor any Reason *at all* of its Existence."[26] This original independent cause was, in Clark's terms, the unchangeable being that Christians call God, without which one would be forced into the absurd position that what exists might have "come into being out of Nothing, absolutely without Cause."[27] Clarke admitted that "we are infinitely unable to comprehend" *what* God is, but from the fact of his existence, he derived a series of attributes—his eternality, his singularity, his infinity, his intelligence, his liberty, and so forth—conformable to his own Christian view of the matter.[28]

From one perspective, then, Aquinas and Clarke were making largely the same argument about God and causality. From another perspective, however, the differences were stark. For Aquinas, the cosmological proof came at the *beginning* of his inquiry. It helped establish that there is an object for theology to explore, and the rest of the *Summa* explored that object in detail. Proofs of the existence of God were, in other words, preliminary to the main concern of the work: the elaboration of a systematic and comprehensive Christian doctrine. Clarke, by contrast, took the cosmological argument not as the beginning, but the *end* of his apologetic project. Having proven to his satisfaction that the "Adversaries of God and Religion have not Reason on their side," Clarke drew to a close. Subjects like Christology or the nature of Jesus, he concludes, "exceed the Bounds of my present Subject and deserve to be handled in a particular Discourse."[29]

Clarke deracinated this classical Christian proof, we might say, extracting it from one cultural-intellectual matrix and applying it to another, one with quite different stakes and contexts. His addressee was not the aspiring student of theology, but a wider literary public sphere assumed to be conversant with and perhaps favorable to the free-thinking works of Hobbes, Spinoza, Toland, and the like. It was, after all, in an effort to engage this wider public sphere that the Boyle Lectures were organized. As Boyle's will stipulated, the lectures were to be preached "against notorious Infidels, viz. Atheists, Theists, Pagans, Jews and Mahometans" but not to deal with any "controversies that are among Christians themselves."[30] In 1704, one proved the existence of God not to elaborate a normative vision of Christianity for those already assumed pious, but to defend a space for the divine against those presumed hostile to God himself.

How then shall we understand the transposition of the cosmological proof from the apologetics of Clarke to the systematic knowledge project of Diderot and d'Alembert? Here again a "content" became something else when inserted into a new cultural-intellectual form. The alphabetical order of the *Encyclopédie* could produce, as Diderot wrote, moments of "burlesque contrast," for example, in which "an article on theology would find itself quite superseded by one on mechanical arts."[31] A reader browsing the fourth volume would find the topic of God leveled, as it were, to the significance found in the surrounding entries. Dietetics and nutrition, on the one side, and *diffarréation*, the ceremony in which the Romans "announced the divorce of priests," on the other: these had a way of putting into perspective the grand metaphysics of the God entry.

Assuming that most readers did not approach the *Encyclopédie* like this, reading volumes cover to cover, the form of the work still powerfully reoriented its content. The meaning of "God" is, in the logic of the *Encyclopédie*, given an extraordinarily narrow compass. How narrow becomes clear if we glance at an encyclopedia apparently unknown to the editorial team, Johann Heinrich Zedler's *Universal Lexicon of Science and Art* (Hamburg, 1731–1754). There we can find a quite different way of imagining what an eighteenth-century reader should know about God. The anonymous author integrated philosophical defenses of the existence of God with scriptural proof texts, offered long bibliographies and summaries of different literatures Christian and pagan alike, described appropriate modes of worship, defended trinitarianism, recounted ancient heresies, gave detailed descriptions of the heathen gods, their names, their modes of worship, and much, much more over the course of nearly seventy-five folio columns.[32] In Zedler, in sum, we find a compendious description of God from many different theological, liturgical, polemical, and historical points of view.

For the *Encyclopédie*, by contrast, the only meaningful thing to say about God was that He existed. Here the difference in approach from that of Clarke is illuminating too. Clarke defended the existence of God to refute atheists, but he hardly thought that existence was the sole predicate one might attach to God, as his many treatises and sermons on Christian subjects well indicates. Even Chambers's nominalist approach in the 1728 *Cyclopaedia* produced a more robust semantic field inside of which God might operate. No matter how persuasive the *Encyclopédie* article might be, then, one is left, unusually, knowing only one (albeit important) thing about God. Formey's commonsense piety translates into something different in the space of the French encyclopedia.

Moreover, no entry stood on its own. The task of the *Encyclopédie* was to enchain, in the editor's terms, the entries into a network of knowledge. This "enchainment" took literal form in the cross-references (*renvois*) that the editors added to the articles to connect them to one another, "the most important part of our encyclopedic scheme," as Diderot wrote.[33] Cross-references

> suggest common ideas and analogous principles ... they give to the entire [work] that unity so favorable to the establishment of truth and conviction. But when necessary, they will also produce an entirely contrary effect; they will confront one idea with another; they will contrast principles; they will attack, undermine, and secretly overthrow those ridiculous opinions that no one would dare insult openly ... [From these latter] the entire work will receive an inner force and secret utility, whose silent effects will necessarily become sensible with the passage of time.[34]

There are ten cross-references in the God entry: demonstration, creation (twice), atheism, liberty, optimism, Manichaeism, Providence, chronology, and corruption. The article "Atheism," co-authored by Formey, is what one might expect: a description but mostly an attack on atheism on philosophical and political grounds. "Creation" takes the discussion implicit in Clarke—whether something can come from nothing—into the biological sciences, largely to conclude, with Clarke, that creation from nothing is "conformable with reason" and "elevates the power of God to the highest degree."[35] The article "Liberty," however, is something else entirely. A pastiche of the words of two authors—the Diderot collaborator, friend of the Baron d'Holbach, and fanatical atheist, Jacques-André Naigeon, on the one hand, and the mostly pious priest Claude Yvon, on the other—the article both offers a defense of Christian liberty against Spinozist determinism (Yvon) and a sympathetic elaboration of these same Spinozist views (Naigeon).[36] What a reader was to take away from such an article is not entirely clear, but at the very least it recast Clarke's confident affirmation that "the necessary being is thus a free being, for to act according to the laws of one's will is to be free." Our life is a "an enchainment of … necessary actions," our will "an acquiescence to be that which we necessarily are," and "our freedom a chimera," Naigeon wrote in the voice of Spinoza, leaving quite unclear what kind of moral freedom readers might expect to find either in God or in his creations.[37]

Interestingly, though, it was "Demonstration" and "Corruption"—both, like *Dieu*, in volume four—that caused most concern among critics. Authored by d'Alembert, neither article was self-evidently controversial. "Demonstration is an argument that contains invincible and clear proof of the truth of a proposition," the article opened, and distinguished between *a priori* and *a posteriori* forms of it.[38] To demonstrate *a priori* is to "prove an effect by its cause"; to demonstrate *a posteriori* is the opposite, in which "a cause is proved by its effects." To what kind of demonstration is the existence of God liable? This was a vexed question even for Clarke, who described his metaphysical proofs as *a priori*, but conceded that *a posteriori* arguments were "the most generally useful, most easy to be understood."[39] The *Encyclopédie* entry on demonstration took the same position:

> Philosophers, and even theologians are divided about *a priori* demonstrations, and some of the same reject them … [S]ensible proofs … are better. In the eyes of the people, and also the philosopher, an insect is a better proof of God than any metaphysical reason; and in the eyes of the philosopher, the general laws of nature prove the existence of God even better than an insect.[40]

Religion Avenged, a journal founded in 1757 and dedicated to outing secret skeptics, was unimpressed. There is an equivocation here, its anonymous author wrote, since the *a priori* demonstration that theologians reject—one that implies that "God had a producing cause"—is not the same as that described by d'Alembert.[41] The secret project to destroy these proofs and to blame it on theologians themselves is all too evident, the author argued. Nor can one demonstrate *a posteriori* on "the ruin of metaphysical demonstrations," since the former presuppose the latter.[42] "When, for example, one proves the existence of God by an insect, one proceeds from the principle that the wisdom found in the effect must be in the cause," and that "chance being nothing, it cannot be an efficient cause of this wisdom."[43] But only an *a priori* commitment to the notion that chance creates nothing, that all causes have an intelligent first cause, guarantees the validity of this proof. Once the "metaphysical proofs of the existence of God are knocked over," the Jansenist critic Abraham Chaumeix wrote, everything said in the article about God should be regarded "as nothing."[44] The argument of the cross-reference, in other words, rendered the article *Dieu* a worthless exercise in bad faith.

Insects also featured in the "Corruption" article, which boldly stepped into the debates about the generation of living organisms that crisscrossed scientific, literary, philosophical, and theological circles in the middle of the eighteenth century. Indeed, the final proof of the existence of God in Formey's article hinged on living organisms as conclusive demonstrations of the "will of an intelligent being who disposes matter according to its designs." As Formey explained, "All animals, even those suspected of coming from putrefaction … only came from as yet unseen seeds. … the same is true of all animals believed to be born from beyond the means of generation," and behind the formation of these unseen seeds is the wise hand of God.[45] The cross-reference to corruption that immediately follows this affirmation, however, might have given a reader some cause for doubt: "One cannot deny that, generally speaking, the particles that compose an insect could not be assembled by any other means than that of generation," noted the Corruption entry's author. "At any rate we know too little about the ways and mechanisms of nature to advance on this matter too exclusive an assertion. Certainly experience shows that in most cases where insects seem to have been created by corruption, they were created by generation; but is it demonstrated in all cases, that corruption can never create a living body?"[46]

Given the power of such materialist explanations of living organisms in mid-century, when a thoroughly impious writer such as Julien Offray de la Mettrie could write that an animal is "a living picture of perpetual motion" and matter has "the power to move by itself," the merest opening to arguments like these seemed, to critics, revelatory of the real aspirations of the *Encyclopédie*.[47] Diderot already, the authors of *Religion Avenged* noted, admitted the "duplicity" of the cross-references in his article "Encyclopedia," and references such as "Corruption" showed clearly that the "article *God* is likely nothing more ... than an *edifice of mud*."[48]

Let us take a step back now from the complexity of this short article in the *Encyclopédie*. In more synthetic terms, we can usefully coordinate our discussion with reference to: (1) the concepts unfolded in the article; (2) the relation of these concepts to the source material from which they were taken; (3) the articulation of the entry within a network of cross-references oriented by, though hardly determined by, the overall intellectual strategy of the *Encyclopédie*; and (4) the function of the work within an overall cultural intellectual terrain.

1. Insofar as the question "what happened to religion in the Enlightenment" turns on the history of theological concepts, we should observe that the article is unimpeachably pious in its orientation. At that level, we might assign the article to the camp of the "moderate Enlightenment," or even the "religious Enlightenment." Certainly Formey could easily stand as one of theological figures featured in David Sorkin's *Religious Enlightenment* (2008), someone who used "the new science and philosophy to promote a tolerant, irenic understanding of belief that could serve a shared morality and politics."[49] Formey would also fit nicely into the group of moderates who tried, in Jonathan Israel's recent telling, to split the difference between older theological and political orthodoxies, and the radical innovations offered by thinkers like Spinoza and Diderot.[50]

It is noteworthy, however, that the *Encyclopédie* author or editors chose a philosophical defense of the existence of God as the most relevant conceptual "content." This was by no means a foregone conclusion, as comparison with the English and German encyclopedias of Chambers and Zedler make clear. Further, this minimalist restriction of the terms of inquiry showed what could happen to "God" when driven from His native theological habitat. The God of redemption, the God who revealed himself on Sinai, the God become human, the God who died on Calvary, the God to whom Christians pray, the God whose sacrifice Christians celebrate: these correlates of the Christian divine, among others, are no longer in evidence. Readers would have to look elsewhere in the *Encyclopédie*—s.v.v. heaven, revelation, crucifixion, eucharist, and so on—to find any discussion of these (see below).

At a basic level, then, this enormous work disaggregated the concept "God," dispersing the cognate ideas and commitments that constituted the Christian God across its many volumes. One might plausibly describe this as an effort to "subordinate theology to reason," as Robert Darnton has argued.[51] But what seems even more characteristic of the *Encyclopédie*, and many of the intellectual projects of the Enlightenment, is the act of dispersion itself, the leveling of older hierarchies of knowledge and the rearrangement of their key concepts into new relationships. Encyclopedias do this in a quite literal way, especially for subjects/topics as historically and conceptually freighted as that of God. The tree of knowledge that d'Alembert appended to the *Encyclopédie* simply could not accommodate an object as big as God, whose attributes ranged across the various branches of the tree, from the theological sciences proper to the sciences of the soul, man, and bodies, to sacred history, the history of insects, and so forth. Such boundary transgressions were, however, not limited to the genre of the encyclopedia: many of the most generative intellectual projects of the era—think of Leibniz writing about mathematics, metaphysics, and mining; or Diderot experimenting with pornography, playwriting, and philosophy— were transgressing in just this way too.

By the end of the eighteenth century, things would change radically. Encyclopedic ambitions, for example, would be articulated in entirely different ways. Take the *Encyclopédie méthodique*, the much-expanded (and seldom read) encyclopedia published in over two hundred volumes between 1782 and 1832, as a successor to the original *Encyclopédie*. There, the entry "God" can be found inside a three-volume subsection (1788– 1790) dedicated to theology. Compiled by Nicolas-Sylvestre Bergier, royal confessor and Catholic apologist, the volumes served as a theological lexicon, a sourcebook for church history, and an introduction to Catholic dogmatics.[52] In this case, God was flanked by entries on "deacon" and "Sunday (*dimanche*), the day of the Lord." "We are leaving to the philosophers the task of proving the existence of God," the entry declared, affirming simply that, "we understand by this term the creator and sole governor of the universe, legislator of men, avenger of crimes, and remunerator of virtue."[53] This dictionary of theology would go on to enjoy a separate afterlife, republished and translated widely in the nineteenth century. For our purposes, however, it is most useful as a witness to the changing times. God would find a new safety in the confines of a theological discourse seen to be distinct from the wider intellectual culture, with profound long-term consequences for both theology and intellectual life more generally.

2. Looking behind the concepts to the source material from which the 1754 *Dieu* entry was built, we also see how Enlightenment intellectual practices reoriented the theological objects they encountered. Much of the content in the God entry was recycled from earlier, largely pious literature. Clarke's *Demonstration* supplied the metaphysical proofs of the existence of God; Isaac Jacquelot, the Huguenot opponent of Bayle, the historical proofs from his apologetic *Debates on the Existence of God* (1st edition, 1697), and Bernard Fontenelle, the physical proofs, from a short work published in 1724 entitled *On the Existence of God*.

As we already saw in the case of Clarke, the transposition of an argument from one context and genre to another changed the work an argument might do. Reading the *Encyclopédie* entry against its earlier sources can be interesting in other ways too. Like Formey, for example, Bernard Fontenelle was the permanent secretary of a royal academy (Paris), and a well-known popularizer of more difficult works of natural philosophy and history. Indeed, Formey was at times criticized as a "lame imitator" of his Parisian predecessor.[54] But however popular Fontenelle might have been, his work on the existence of God was an odd selection for Formey. It opened, for example, with the curiously elliptical argument that while "metaphysics furnish the most solid proofs of the existence of God," they are no more than "chimerical and purely imaginary" to those people who believe only what is "sensible and palpable," which was, in Fontenelle's view, most people.[55] For readers of Fontenelle's wider corpus, moreover, the short work likely seemed an outlier. It appeared in 1724, the same year as his *Of the Origin of Fables* was published in its most popular edition. This latter work was one of those amphibious works common to the early century, one that avoided any criticism of Christianity even as it attacked the ignorance and superstition of the ancient world that cradled Christ and his disciples.[56] Other thinkers—David Hume, for example—would make the connection more explicit, writing Christianity into his own version of Fontenelle's "the history of the errors of the human spirit."[57]

Assuming that Formey chose Fontenelle in good faith, still it must have pleased Diderot and d'Alembert to see such an ambivalent figure appear in the God entry. Indeed, Fontenelle would show up in Diderot's later *Dream of d'Alembert* (1769) exactly in the middle of an epicurean fantasy about spontaneous generation, the emergence of a world without divine plan, and the inevitable mistakes made by "transitory being[s] who believe in the immutability of things. ... Like Fontenelle's rose who said that so far as any rose could remember, no gardener had ever died."[58] Read one way, Fontenelle was a pious defender of the divine order of nature; read another, its pungent critic.

3. When we move from the "interior" of the article to the network in which the article was embedded, we can see even more clearly the dispersive energies of the Enlightenment. We have already discussed above the set of cross-references inside the article, but if we were to step back and imagine a reader trying to learn something about the traditional features of the Christian God from the *Encyclopédie*, the consequences are no less discomfiting. To take just a few examples: "Heaven" (*Paradis*), presumably of interest to someone wanting to know about God, tells readers that nobody knows where it is, "in the third heaven, in the heaven of the moon, in the moon itself." "There is almost no part of the world," the author wrote, "where one has not searched, in Asia, Africa, Europe, America, the banks of the Nile, the Indies, China, the island of Ceylon, or the mountains of the moon in Ethiopia," hardly a ringing endorsement of confidence in such a place.[59] The entry "Revelation" is pious, much like the entry for God: it includes a passionate defense of the truth of Christian revelation. But then it throws in a few skeptical comments if only for the purposes of their refutation ("a modern author believed he proposed a substantial difficulty, remarking that revelations are always founded on previous revelations," Christ on Moses, Mohammed on Christ, Zoroaster on the religion of the mages, and so forth).[60] The article "Eucharist" gave a long account of the sacrament, including a detailed examination of the conflict between Protestants and Catholics about the real presence and so on. Readers would find here a strong defense of the Catholic Church, no doubt. That said, they might read this entry differently if they came to it via the entry "anthropophage," defined as "people who live on human flesh," which included "eucharist" as one of its cross-references.[61]

4. The point is not only to reveal subversive, anti-Christian, or anti-religious views in the *Encyclopédie*. Certainly such views are important—and now we move to the wider cultural-intellectual terrain—especially when we observe the furor about the work inside more conservative theological circles in the 1750s. Already in 1752, the project was almost brought to an unceremonious end by accusations of impiety from religious conservatives. The volume containing the entry on God was published in the midst of heated public controversy, in which more moderate royal censors—especially the head royal censor, "director of the library," and friend of Diderot, Guillaume-Chrétien de Malesherbes—protected the work against its more ferocious critics. In 1759, Malesherbes's efforts failed. In March of that year, the French crown revoked the *Encyclopédie*'s publishing privilege, and in September, it was put on the Index of Prohibited Books and the Pope ordered extant copies burned. Fortunately for posterity, the text was already composed, and the final ten volumes were published under a false imprint.[62]

The God article was more than its practices of impiety, however. Even if the "demonstration" cross-reference *had never been added*, I would argue, simply putting God into this textual form transformed the kind of thing that He could be. The encyclopedic entry made theological topics necessarily vulnerable to unexpected triangulations, relationships, and histories. Disrupting the flow of theological reasoning, the entry might begin with a doctrine of God, say, and then have proceeded to explore His mysterious triune essence, the creation of the world, the nature of human salvation, and so on. Plucked from this matrix of ideas, "God" was then a lonely figure in the encyclopedia.

Nor was the encyclopedia the only form that displaced foundational theological concepts in unexpected ways in the eighteenth century: when Johann Jakob Scheuchzer published his *Physica Sacra* (1731–1735)—a massive work of German physico-theology that garlanded the entire Bible with 761 engravings packed with anatomy, botany, entomology, numismatics, geology, zoology, and much more—he reset the Bible into an entirely new constellation of knowledge (Figure 6.2). Certainly one could read his Bible piously, but it would be a new kind of piety, one that cared about the details of coins, shells, and flowers.[63] When Friedrich Klopstock wrote *The Messiah* (1748–1780), an epic poem about the life of Christ in a German hexameter that was published in serialized form in one of the era's new literary journals (aptly titled the *New Contributions to Delight the Understanding and the Wit*) and that was so sentimental it left his readers weeping, he created new possibilities for engagement with the biblical text unknown even to his hero John Milton.[64] When Jean-Jacques Rousseau inserted a 15,000-word "creed of a Savoyard vicar" into his educational treatise *Émile* (1762), personalizing the journey from skepticism to faith and suggesting ways to ease the way for the young, he improvised on the genre of the spiritual autobiography, even as he reoriented it within a work that ends with offering sex tips to the young couple, Émile and Sophie. The list could be expanded almost ad infinitum: major figures such as Isaac Newton, William Hutcheson, David Hartley, Edmund Burke, Joseph Priestley, Gotthold Ephraim Lessing, Johann Herder, Johann Hamann, and Moses Mendelssohn, jostled with scores of lesser-knowns whose works on matters theological populated new literary journals, new moral weeklies, poetry collections, published letters, in short, the entire media sphere of the Enlightenment. The result was a vast experiment with the materials of the Christian archive, creating unexpected, exciting, and disorienting connections and experiences for generations of readers.

To return at last then to our opening question—what happened to religion in the Enlightenment?—I would offer a few final suggestions and a caveat. First, the caveat. I have approached this question as an intellectual historian, not as an historian of Christianity. I have developed here some generalizations about the intellectual culture of the period and what it did to "religion," in other words, but not about the history of the churches, let alone the lived experience of eighteenth-century Christianity. These are not wholly distinct, of course. Not only were theologians active participants in this intellectual culture (as the many priests enrolled on contributor list to the *Encyclopédie* make clear), but they were also pioneers in the formal innovations that I have described above. The English Methodist John Wesley, to name just one, was someone whose most creative theological ideas took shape in letters, sermons, journals, hymns, and poems, rather than in learned or systematic treatises. Christianity was not simply a passive victim of intellectual change, but an active participant and contributor to this change as well. But the restriction of scope here—considering religion largely as an intellectual-historical object, and thus with special attention to key concepts and ideas—was made to isolate

FIGURE 6.2 Johann Jakob Scheuchzer, *Physica Sacra* (1731–1735), vol. 1, fig. 12. *Kupfer-Bibel, in welcher die Physica Sacra oder geheiligte Naturwissenschafft derer in der heiligen Schrifft vorkommenden natürlichen Sachen* (Augspurg und Ulm: gedruckt bey Christian Ulrich Wagner, 1731–1735). © ETH-Bibliothek Zürich, Rar 5864, http://doi.org/10.3931/e-rara-10140 (public domain).

what I believe to be special features of the Enlightenment and its effects on concepts taken to be "religious."

These features—and here are my suggestions about the broader frame of the chapter—included a radical deracination of theological concepts, their uprooting from earlier structures of theological reasoning, structures that had coordinated them inside the wider architecture of the theological imagination. No doubt these earlier structures themselves could change. Aquinas's demonstration of the existence of God did not do the same kind of work as Clarke's. Even seen from the inside, theology has its own robust history.

But what is remarkable about the Enlightenment is how even pillars of the theological imagination—like God himself—could be reset into new ideational frameworks. This experimentation with frameworks was not, of course, restricted to theological subjects alone in the eighteenth century. On the contrary, it was a feature of Enlightenment intellectual practice more generally. It was just these practices of experimentation that, for later commentators such as Immanuel Kant, made the philosophical projects of the earlier century seem unruly and undisciplined. Kant was a genius not just in his critical acumen, but also in his organizational skills, his ability to persuasively restrict the topics that philosophy was meant to address.[65] From this perspective, the philosophical project of the *Encyclopédie* would seem a jumbled mess, a mixing of things that needed to be kept separate. The great disciplinary projects of the early nineteenth century, including in theology, would then institutionalize lines of distinction that, fifty years earlier, it seemed imperative to blur.

So what finally happened to religion in the Enlightenment? It was, to put it briefly, dispersed and disaggregated, its conceptual archive reimagined in tandem with new genres of writing, new ways of telling stories, new practices of communication, and new philosophical commitments. What made this disaggregation so unusual, and at times so threatening to established churches, was its ad hoc, spontaneous, experimental nature. Churches no longer controlled their own theological materials, and universities did not yet control them to the extent they would in Protestant and Catholic Europe in the nineteenth century. Beyond the oversight of church and university, God migrated freely across disciplines and ways of knowing. This intellectual dynamic—more than any particular religious or philosophical commitment, more than reasonable religion or atheism or fideism or deism or materialism—conditioned what religion became in the Enlightenment.

CHAPTER SEVEN

Language, Poetry, Rhetoric

CHRISTY PICHICHERO

In Jonathan Swift's (1667–1745) fantastical picaresque satire *Gulliver's Travels* (1726), Lemuel Gulliver's third voyage brings him to Balnibarbi, a land somewhere near India whose primary occupation is financially ruinous and impractical speculative science. Gulliver visits the Academy of Lagado where he observes a number of preposterous experiments: one scientist attempts to extract sunbeams out of cucumbers to release them during rainy summers, another works to reconstitute food out of human excrement, and an "ingenious" architect pursues his unique construction method of building a house from the roof down taking bees and spiders as his inspiration. Gulliver then visits the school of languages where professors are engaged in efforts to improve the language of their country. Two projects are underway. "The first project was, to shorten discourse, by cutting polysyllables into one, and leaving out verbs and participles," relays Gulliver, "because, in reality, all things imaginable are but nouns. The other project was a scheme for entirely abolishing all words whatsoever."

Gaining insight into the rationale for this latter project, Gulliver then learns that "since words are only names for things, it would be more convenient for all men to carry about them such things as were necessary to express a particular business they are to discourse on." While women along with the "vulgar and illiterate" continued to insist upon using spoken language, many of the wisest, most learned men had already adopted the new, more efficient means of communication rooted in objects rather than words. Gulliver remarks, however, that this linguistic scheme has one primary inconvenience (Figure 7.1):

> If a man's business be very great, and of various kinds, he must be obliged, in proportion, to carry a greater bundle of things upon his back, unless he can afford one or two strong servants to attend him. I have often beheld two of those sages almost sinking under the weight of their packs, like pedlars among us, who, when they met in the street, would lay down their loads, open their sacks, and hold conversation for an hour together; then put up their implements, help each other to resume their burdens, and take their leave.[1]

Swift's thinly veiled critiques—of the British Royal Society, of the vogue of speculative science, and of linguistic projects in particular—reveal critical facets of the culture of ideas concerning language, rhetoric, and poetry in seventeenth- and eighteenth-century Europe. In the subsequent section of this chapter, Swift's Balnibarian academy and its experiments in language serve as a springboard for a discussion of the broad cultural trends that brought particular focus to questions of language, rhetoric, poetry, and aesthetics during the period spanning from 1650 to 1800. Following this overview,

FIGURE 7.1 "'Two of those sages ... like pedlars among us' (expressing themselves with things they carry around)," illustration by Arthur Rackham, 1909, from "Part III: A Voyage to Laputa, Balnibarbi, Luggnagg, Glubbdubdrib, and Japan" in Jonathan Swift, *Gulliver's Travels* (1726). © Hulton Fine Art Collection / Getty Images.

in the next three sections this chapter examines specific theories and ideas pertaining to language, rhetoric, poetry, and aesthetics developed during the neoclassical and Enlightenment epochs. These sections highlight the ways in which different philosophical schools of thought framed linguistic research and language reform projects of the era. In the seventeenth century, a Cartesian notion of *a priori* universal language shaped various initiatives, while during the eighteenth century empiricism and sensationalism constituted the primary conceptual approaches. The chapter concludes by gesturing toward the paradoxical legacy of these theories, whose intellectual value has perhaps been better studied than their role in perpetuating the cultural assumptions that fueled social class prejudice, discrimination against women, and the oppression of people viewed as ethnic "Others."

SWIFT'S BALNIBARIANS AND THE CULTURAL HISTORY OF LANGUAGE

The first thing to note in the above episode of Swift's novel is the location in which the series of outlandish experiments take place: a state-sponsored academy. In the fictional Balnibarbi, as in countries across the globe during the 1700s and 1800s, governments fostered what is often referred to as the "Scientific Revolution" by establishing or supporting academies and learned societies. The French Academy attending to language and literature was founded in 1635, and the French Academy of Sciences was inaugurated in 1666, six years after the creation of the British Royal Society. In the Holy Roman Empire, the Academia Naturae Curiosorum was formed in 1652, gaining recognition by Emperor Leopold I in 1677 and becoming the German National Academy of Sciences (Deutsche Akademie der Naturforscher Leopoldina) in 1687. The Prussian Academies of Arts and Sciences were instituted *circa* 1694–1696 and 1700 respectively. Numerous other academies engaging with language and the sciences, as well as military development, history writing, and more, were founded in the course of the eighteenth century in Spain, the Netherlands, Sweden, and the newly independent United States of America.

Within and outside of these academies, language was viewed as a subject of vital import from multiple perspectives. The first half of the seventeenth century witnessed the continuation of religiously motivated warfare across the European continent, and many believed that language was not only a cause of strife between Catholics and Protestants but also key to finding a solution. Language was also central to the absolutist political enterprise. France constitutes a noteworthy example of the linking of language and politics. French theologian and political theorist Bishop Jacques-Bénigne Bossuet (1627–1704) maintained that the monarch's word was a primary locus of his power. Basing his claims on biblical references to the commandments of kings, Bossuet insisted that the monarch's word must be unquestioned and uncontested—in short, absolute. The crown undertook an increasingly stringent series of policies to control "seditious" speech, to censor mail and printed texts, and to normalize practices regarding language, poetry, and rhetoric. The French Academy published its first dictionary of the French vernacular in 1694, thereby attempting to standardize the breadth and meaning of terms. The crown also designated the elite language employed by members of the royal family and aristocracy as the *bon usage* ("the appropriate usage") of French and thus as the officially sanctioned tongue of political, administrative, and high artistic discourse.[2] Squelching what was seen as the effervescent and effeminate *précieux* language associated with women of the literary salons and the Baroque aesthetic, King Louis XIV and his affiliates established a neoclassical linguistic regime that was masculine, socially elite, and intended to bring further prestige and control to the monarchy at home and abroad. In *Gulliver's Travels*, Swift brought to light the sexism and class discrimination inherent in many programs for language reform in France, Great Britain, and elsewhere in his reference to women and the "vulgar and illiterate" as posing supposed obstacles to the new linguistic schemes being developed at the academy in Balnibarbi.

Indeed, efforts to standardize national languages by suppressing regional dialects as well as "abuses" of language were widely discussed in this era. Many canonical writers of the early modern European philosophical tradition, from Francis Bacon (1561–1626) and René Descartes (1596–1650) to George Campbell (1719–1796) and Denis Diderot (1713–1784), suggested the need for controlling, redesigning, and revivifying language. Bacon condemned multiple abuses of language. These included the "Idols of the Marketplace," wherein everyday language was used imprecisely, and the excesses of the Renaissance rhetorical tradition whereby

> men began to hunt more after words than matter; and more after the choiceness of the phrase, and the round and clear composition of the sentence, and the sweet falling of the clauses, and the varying and illustration of their works with tropes and figures, than after the weight of matter, worth of subject, soundness of argument, life of invention, or depth of judgment.[3]

John Locke (1632–1704) warned of an ontological and epistemological crisis in semiotics since he believed that words are incapable of fully representing the things and ideas that they are meant to communicate.

Such critiques and warnings about crises were then amplified as literacy and education expanded across Europe and beyond, as did what historians Clifford Siskin and William Warner refer to as the new or newly important "cardinal mediations" associated with the rise of Enlightenment. Infrastructures for communication and voluntary social gathering blossomed during the seventeenth and eighteenth centuries: postal systems, salons, coffeehouses, taverns, inns, masonic lodges, social clubs, as well as academies and learned societies. These institutions and spaces fostered new types of sociability, knowledge creation, and knowledge sharing. They also produced new protocols for communication and generated ever more diverse, polymorphous publics (as opposed to a monolithic Habermasian bourgeois public sphere), along with cultures of publicity and celebrity that haunted and taunted monarchs and public intellectuals alike. Jean-Jacques Rousseau (1712–1778) was notorious for struggling with his own celebrity and the interpretations of his words and public image that he could never sufficiently control.[4] New genres and formats augmented the quantity and broadened the reach of the printed and spoken word. Despite censorship, newspapers, magazines, and other types of periodicals were launched and circulated across Europe and in colonial outposts treating a vast scope of different subjects from literature to military medicine to politics. These serial publications supplemented information flows in epistolary correspondence, dictionaries, almanacs, and encyclopedias. This expanding sphere of commercial print not only further democratized access to information but also, in combination with the developing practice of translation, facilitated transnational discourse and collaborations. What is more, Clifford and Siskin suggest that the upsurge in readers also led to an increase in writers, which meant a growth in the active consumption, production, and perhaps overall awareness of language, rhetoric, and aesthetic experience.[5]

In light of this novel communicative environment, the Balnibarbian language scheme of shortening discourse in *Gulliver's Travels* takes on greater meaning. Francis Bacon and François de Salignac de la Mothe-Fénelon (1651–1715), working a century apart, contended that language and rhetoric needed to become more scientific. Both men, along with many others writing in between and after them, disdained the figure- and trope-laden language associated with Renaissance humanist rhetorician Petrus Ramus (1515–1572) and his "Ramist" followers. This type of language obfuscated clear communication, manipulated the passions, and clouded the judgment, they believed, and was therefore in no way fit for the search for scientific and philosophical truths. Highly ornamental language was a waste of space on the page and of energy for writer and reader, speaker and audience. Fénelon and like-minded thinkers thus advocated for a classical emphasis on simplicity, clarity, and a natural style of speech that was more suitable for scientific communication and approachable for ever-growing writerly-readerly publics. This unadorned, logically driven "plain style" also held sway in the religious sphere and was championed in particular by Protestant rhetoricians.

The Balnibarbian language scheme of shortening discourse—and the analogue projects in European scientific circles to which it makes reference—also indicates an implicit critique of the elitism and fusty pedagogies of the traditional educational system. Across Europe, the foundation of all education from grade school through university-level studies was composed of the three arts of discourse, or *artes sermocinales*: grammar (the art of reading and writing), rhetoric (the art of speaking well to persuade), and logic or dialectic (the art of reasoning or discerning the truth). Since late antiquity, these arts were united as the trivium, and they needed to be mastered before one could progress to the study of the quadrivium (arithmetic, music, geometry, astronomy) and subjects such as law, theology, or medicine. Galileo Galilei (1564–1642), Bacon, Descartes, Locke, and others were indeed critics of the arts of discourse as traditionally taught and deployed. Yet, they also knew these arts intimately and as schoolboys had studied the eight parts of speech, labored through declinations, could immediately recognize a solecism in Latin, knew the tropes and different forms of syllogism, and had memorized passages of Cicero and Quintilian. Armed with this personal experience, these thinkers upheld the notion that knowledge of the language arts had become less useful than knowledge of the natural world or of the functioning of the human mind. Language was thus at the forefront of educational reform and scientific progress in the seventeenth and eighteenth centuries.

To take one example: Czech pedagogue, theologian, and philosopher Jan Amos Komenský (1592–1670), commonly known as Comenius and considered to be the father of modern education, reformed language pedagogy in several European countries to ensure that it was more thoroughly combined with gaining knowledge about the world. He also pioneered a more universal and practical style of instruction, instituted the use of vernacular languages rather than Latin, utilized pictorial textbooks, pushed for activities requiring logical engagement instead of rote memorization, and advocated for equal opportunity for women and children of poor families. The problem of fostering language learning in a modern, forward-thinking manner helped motivate the development of plans for universal languages and symbolic systems discussed later in this chapter.

A number of these systems were born of the aspiration to make language more efficient, thus Swift's reference to a language composed only of nouns. Philosophers also sought to discover or invent a language that was more universal and more accurately representative of the things and subjects being communicated. Swift satirized the Cratylist ambitions of the latter in the Balnibarbian language scheme of carrying around objects to cut out the imprecision and confusion that words, as mediators, could bring. Two primary influences fueled such endeavors, the first of which was globalization. A summarizing passage of John K. Noyes's book on Johann Gottfried Herder's (1744–1803) aesthetics and anti-imperialism describes the period of the late eighteenth century and the preceding century in terms of changing perceptions of the world:

> It was the time when, to speak with [historian] Dimas Figueroa, the three structural conditions that make it possible to speak of the beginnings of globalization were in the process of being fulfilled: the experience of the planet as a unitary whole, a real relationship between all regions of the planet, and "the inadequate regulation of this relationship by way of moral or political norms." This is the moment when the markets and trade routes established in the sixteenth century are being expanded throughout the world, while in the popular imagination the thread that ties them to

the conquests which originally established them is growing ever fainter. This period has been described by [sociologist] Immanuel Wallerstein as "the second era of great expansion of the capitalist world economy." It marks the transition between what is often referred to as the first and second phases of globalization. However we parse it, the result is more or less the same: The brutal conquests of previous centuries are making way for new forms of economic and political interaction, with their own characteristic modes of exploitation. The discovery of the world is rapidly approaching completion, and the conquest and enslavement of other cultures is meeting with ever more vociferous opposition, while at the same time the world market is becoming increasingly consolidated, and the diversity of world cultures is rapidly becoming a fact of life.[6]

Exposure to autochthonous language systems and the need to communicate effectively with economic and military partners in regions around the world helped to mold new horizons for linguistic reform and planning. Reports by Jesuit missionaries relating features of an extraordinary multitude of "exotic" languages brought about a sensitivity toward the diversity of languages and an interest in different writing systems. Mandarin Chinese was a particularly powerful stimulus as it was (somewhat erroneously) understood to be built of pictorial representations of "things" themselves as opposed to alphabetic spellings of words that in turn communicate things. While no scholar seriously proposed that people carry around giant bags of objects pertinent to their communicative needs, linguistic experiments with writing systems including shorthand and symbolic alphabets flourished in the second half of the seventeenth century. Efforts to create and teach language to deaf and/or mute individuals also encouraged reflection on the nature of human language and the development of nonverbal systems of communication.

The second stimulus behind projects of linguistic innovation during the seventeenth century was the intellectual revolution associated, in particular, with the philosophical ideas of Bacon and Descartes. Bacon had drawn a distinction between two types of grammar: "one popular [for learning languages] ... the other philosophical, examining the power and nature of words, as they are the footsteps and prints of reason." Descartes's emphasis on rationalism and *a priori* ideas in addition to his interest in universal language added methodological insight and further motivation for spearheading efforts to reconceptualize the relationship between grammar and philosophy, language and logic. Philosophical grammar dated back to antiquity, but its reemergence along with the invention of universal, natural, or philosophical languages became a significant trend in scientific inquiry.

Eventually, as Swift's novel attests, the above trends led to a number of proposals for language systems that were logically flawed, impractical, and in keeping with the idea of carrying around a large sack of objects to eliminate the need for speech, easily deemed ridiculous. New developments in philosophy, in particular sensationalism and its associated moral philosophy, ushered in a greater degree of doubt about universal language schemes in the course of the eighteenth century. Also, as globalization deepened, it fostered both greater awareness of cultural and linguistic differences *and* a subconscious or conscious tendency toward Eurocentric bias and white racial supremacy. These developments, too, led eventually to divestment in universalist considerations of language in favor of linguistic nationalist perspectives, as well as aesthetic theories that located the standard of taste in highborn men of European descent.

Overall, Swift's spoof of language experimentation in his time reveals the prevailing desire, shared with other domains of thought treated in this volume, for simplicity, rationality, and naturalness—in this case, in language. The pursuit of simplicity, rationality, and naturalness led to an obsession with origins, which framed many philosophical discussions of language, rhetoric, and aesthetic experience. The search for origins, in turn, placed a high value on authenticity and transparency and relied upon a pseudo-anthropological methodology, at times ethnographically based and in other cases more speculative. From the pulpit to the parliament, from cognition to intercultural communication, from the *je ne sais quoi* (ineffable attractiveness) to the sublime, the quest for authentic experience and connection—as well as genuine political, economic, cultural, and social domination—brings into relief the great paradoxes that characterized the early modern history of ideas concerning language, rhetoric, and poetry in the West. The rise of philosophical grammars and universal language schemes marked the first step in this evolution.

PHILOSOPHICAL AND UNIVERSAL LANGUAGE IN THE SEVENTEENTH CENTURY

"To us, who have the revelation of scripture," wrote Anglican clergyman and language planner John Wilkins (1614–1672) in his *Essay toward a Real Character and Philosophical Language* (1668), "'tis evident enough that the first Language was con-created with our first Parents, they immediately understanding the voice of God speaking to them in the Garden. And how Languages came to be multiplied, is likewise manifested in the Story of the Confusion of Babel."[7] For many seventeenth-century linguistic theorists, language had fallen from grace. During this era in which sacred and secular scientific projects were frequently coterminous, circumscribing universal or philosophical language was often considered an act of edenic recovery. The notion of a semiotically perfect, utterly transparent prelapsarian language of Adam inspired Wilkins and others, including George Dalgarno (1626–1687) who, in contrast to the former, believed that this language was of human rather than divine invention. Sacred and secular intermixed in such seventeenth-century projects of linguistic eschatology in that the pursuit of prelapsarian language was undergirded by the Cartesian philosophical concept of *a priori* rational language.

Descartes wrote little on language, but two of his thoughts led toward projects of philosophical grammar and language that dominated the middle decades of the seventeenth century. First, Descartes regarded language as something that distinguished humans and human rationality from animals, whose own communicative sounds could only convey the passions. Human language was, Descartes believed, uniquely composed of conventional signs formed by purposive and rational processes, while animal communication consisted entirely of simple, natural signs.

Secondly, Descartes was interested in the concept of a universal language built on *a priori* rational cognition. This language could be universally accepted and would be capable of eliminating the muddying of knowledge, judgment, and truth that Bacon had attributed to language. Philosophical grammar, an inheritor of certain antique approaches as well as medieval speculative grammar, emerged as a predominant trend in language studies of the seventeenth century. Philosophical grammars explored the connection between thought and language with particular attention to language as a rational, logic-based construct, general linguistics (as opposed to the structures of specific vernaculars), as well as semantics and its subfields.

The reinscription of logic into rhetorical and linguistic considerations began to take form in large-scale philosophical grammar projects by the 1630s. Gerardus Vossius (born Gerrit Janszoon Vos, 1577–1649), Dutch theologian and professor of classics and rhetoric, was a declared opponent of the narrow Ramist vision of rhetoric as style and delivery (*elocutio* and *pronuntiatio*) alone and published *De Arte Grammatica* in 1635. Vossius argued for the important role of logic in language and, somewhat reminiscently of Swift's satire, for the primacy of nouns and verbs over other word classes. An extraordinary scholar, Vossius wrote a grammar that contained a history of the subject, as well as his own discussion of the word categories in a monumental 1,400 pages. No less prolific, Juan Caramuel y Lobkowitz (1606–1682), the Spanish Catholic theologian, mathematician, and scholastic philosopher, wrote 262 works, which included his *Grammatica Audax* of 1654. Typifying the extraordinary erudition and hybrid sacred and secular concerns of scholars of his era, his "grammar" mixed together theology, metaphysics, logic, and grammar "to discuss philosophically, abstracting from all languages, the method and technical vocabulary ['second intentions'] of the art of grammar."

One of the most influential of these philosophical grammars was the *General and Rational Grammar* (*Grammaire générale et raisonnée*, 1660) by Antoine Arnauld (1612–1694) and Claude Lancelot (1615–1695), often referred to as the "Port-Royal Grammar" due to its authors' affiliation with the Port-Royal Jansenist abbey in Paris. Influenced by the Cartesian principle that ideas preexist their expression, the Port-Royal Grammar asserted that language arose from the need to convey human thoughts. Arnaud and Lancelot therefore claimed that all languages sprang forth from a rational basis; that they express "what happens in the mind"; and that grammar maintains a direct relationship to rational cognitive processes.

This relationship accounts for the universal characteristics studied in the *General and Rational Grammar* and allowed for the correlation between specific logical and grammatical structures. Arnauld and Lancelot utilized the three traditional categories of logic—conceiving, judging, and reasoning—as the structural basis for grammatical categories or parts of speech. Conception corresponded to nouns, judgment to verbs, and reasoning to syllogisms. The last category was relegated to a secondary importance in Arnauld and Lancelot's scheme because they viewed ratiocination as syllogistic, it being composed of two judgments.

The German philosopher Gottfried Wilhelm Leibniz (1646–1716) critiqued this categorizing in his own unfinished "rational grammar," most of which was unpublished until the 1990s. For Leibniz, traditional logical categories did not account for inferential thought and language, and he therefore critiqued Arnauld and Lancelot's understanding of reasoning as too restricted. However, despite such methodological differences, which plagued scholars who devised philosophical grammars and universal language schemes, the movement continued to blossom in the second half of the seventeenth century.

In addition to Cartesian philosophy, a number of other influences propelled the thinking of scholars who created philosophical and universal language schemes during the seventeenth century. These included the rediscovery of Adamic language, perceptions of Chinese characters, and Arabic numerals. The latter were of interest since the symbol for each numeral, such as "2," was invariably taken to indicate a certain quantity, though many words were used to express it in different vernaculars (two, dos, drei, etc.). Cave Beck (1623–1706) (Figure 7.2), an English clergyman and schoolmaster, Johann Joachim Becher (1635–1682), a German scientist, and Athanasius Kircher (1602–1680), a German

FIGURE 7.2 Frontispiece, Cave Beck, *The Universal Character* (1657). © Niday Picture Library / Alamy Stock Photo.

Jesuit scholar considered the founder of Egyptology, published writing systems based on "universal characters," in 1657, 1661, and 1663, respectively.

The two most oft-discussed schemes for universal languages today are those of Wilkins and Dalgarno. Colleagues at Oxford University, the two men had initially been collaborators in a project to create a philosophical or natural language. Both believed in the primacy of "things" over words. Both were also therefore keenly interested in pasigraphy or "real characters," though methodological differences had them part ways in 1659.

Dalgarno's work in Latin, *Ars Signorum* or *The Art of Signs* (1661), used the ordinary letters of the Roman alphabet to invent signs that represented simple notions and things called "radicals," of which there were one thousand. Compound signs were used for complex concepts, and the whole system was orchestrated upon Aristotelian categories or predicaments. He also offered a logic-based grammar for this language. Building a language that had greater conformity to principles of logic was indeed the primary philosophical focus of Dalgarno's system. In this way, his philosophical language could potentially function as a mechanism for communication, argumentation, and analysis, encompassing the three arts of the trivium at once.

Wilkins, on the other hand, was interested in creating a semiotic system that comprised both the trivium and the quadrivium, thereby representing an exhaustive, encyclopedic taxonomy of knowledge. He eschewed the use of any known alphanumeric system and took the path of developing a new system of real characters along with vocalizations that were intended to be closer to the things they were meant to designate. Consider colors for easily accessible examples of how his language functioned. The word for red was pronounced "gida": "gi" indicated that red was a thing classified as a sensible quality, "d" indicated a subclass of color; and "a" meant second species of this class (Figure 7.3). Green was gide, with "e" indicating the third species. Given his ambitious encyclopedic program, his lexicon contained many more radicals than that of Dalgarno, totaling in the environs of four thousand.

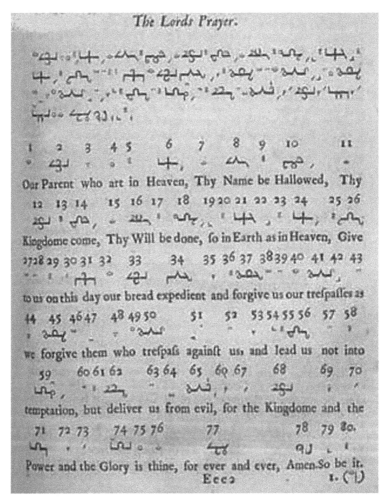

FIGURE 7.3 Lord's Prayer from John Wilkins, *An Essay towards a Real Character, and a Philosophical Language* (1668). © Historic Images / Alamy Stock Photo.

However, though a number of scholars continued to pursue the creation of philosophical language systems into the new century, public and scholarly interest waned drastically beginning in the 1680s. By then, Dalgarno himself had abandoned his original project, or rather channeled his interest into another sphere of linguistic innovation, that of communication for the deaf. Dalgarno insisted that teaching language to deaf children could occur following the same "natural" methods used to teach children who could hear; in his *Didascalocophus: Or, the deaf and dumb man's tutor* (1680), he proposed a system of finger spelling (Figure 7.4). At the same time, radically novel thinking about language, epistemology, and human nature were on the rise with John Locke and the growing philosophy of sensationalism. Striking down the Cartesian notion of *a priori* ideas in favor of an experience-oriented model based upon sensations and the impressions that they leave on the mind, Lockean philosophy challenged the very foundation upon which many seventeenth-century philosophical language schemes had been based. Étienne Bonnot de Condillac (1714–1780), Johann Gottfried Herder, and others rejected the premise that

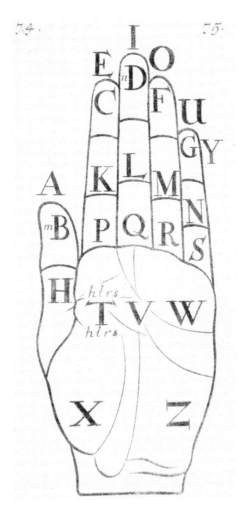

FIGURE 7.4 Finger spelling diagram from George Dalgarno, *Didascalocophus* (1680). © Beinecke Rare Book & Manuscript Collection, Yale University, General Collection.

thoughts existed independently and prior to language, believing to the contrary that it was language that produced thought.

In the eighteenth century, sensationalist philosophy was the new epistemological framing for investigations into the question of the origins of language. Enlightenment philosophers Condillac, Diderot, Voltaire (1694–1778), Jean-Jacques Rousseau, Adam Smith (1723–1790), James Burnett (Lord Monboddo, 1714–1799), and Herder sought not to create artificial language systems composed of "universal characters" or to rediscover and record a literal prelapsarian language. In fact, they took as their point of departure the hypothesis that language was not a divine invention bestowed upon human beings by God, but was instead created organically by humans due to their practical need to communicate. Therefore, instead of taking Adam as the figure through which they examined the origins of language, they posited a hypothetical post-lapsarian human not yet touched by language or civilization. This human was often based upon (pseudo)ethnographic studies of Jewish, African, Native American, Tahitian, Persian, and Peruvian peoples, as well as "Cannibals" in the case of Condillac. German thinkers such as Johann Heinrich Samuel Formey (1711–1797) and Johann Peter Süssmilch (1707–1767) notwithstanding, linguistic eschatology, with its innate ideas and its search for divine origins, gave way to anthropological or evolutionary linguistics that traced the rise and transformation of language over time.

While the philosophical foundations of these Enlightenment queries into the origins of language were drastically different from most of their seventeenth-century counterparts, a similar impetus ignited the search for natural languages. Bacon's century-old call for abjuring the abuse of any language that obscured meaning, thought, and communication continued as strongly as ever. In addition to this, the push against the Ramist division between logic and rhetoric also persisted into the eighteenth century. In fact, the division between the categories of language, rhetoric, and poetry were also blurred in the new focus on "natural" or "poetic" language and the assumption of a clear, energetic means of communication that the first humans—as well as "primitive" peoples—utilized. Philosophies of language, schools of rhetoric, and aesthetic theories all coalesced during this period, which saw one of the deepest, if not *the* deepest inquiry into human communication and emotion prior to the modern period.

LANGUAGE, NATURE, AND EMOTION IN THE EIGHTEENTH CENTURY

Sometime after the Flood, when the earth was reborn, there were two children, a little boy and a little girl. Each of them was lost alone in the desert, never having been exposed to another human being. Initially, they had virtually no memory, no ability to recall prior thoughts or experiences, and no capacity for imagination. They lived close to their immediate perceptions; their vocal sounds and gesticulations were instinctive responses to their sensations. One day, the two of them met and began living together. Subsequently, incidental reactive expression evolved into intentional language:

> Their mutual discourse made them connect the cries of each passion to the perceptions of which they were the natural signs. They usually accompanied the cries with some movement that made the expression more striking. For example, he who suffered by not having an object his needs demanded would not merely cry out; he made as if an effort to obtain it, moved his head, his arms, and all the parts of his body. Moved by

this display the other fixed the eyes on the same object, and feeling his soul suffused with sentiments he was not yet able to account for to himself, he suffered by seeing the other suffer so miserably. From this moment he feels that he is eager to ease the other's pain, and he acts on this impression to the extent that it is within his ability. Thus by instinct alone these people asked for help and gave it.[8]

Condillac's sensationalist fable of the origin of language, recounted in Part II, Section I of his *Essay on the Origin of Human Understanding* (*Essai sur l'origine des connaissances humaines*, 1744), followed a genealogy that had recently been proposed by English bishop and literary critic William Warburton (1698–1799) in his *Divine Legation of Moses Demonstrated on the Principles of a Religious Deist* (1738–1741). A French translation of Warburton's work was circulating in France at the time that Condillac was drafting his *Essay* and a part of the *Divine Legation* that treated Egyptian hieroglyphs and the history of language was translated and published in French in the same year that the *Essay* later appeared. Warburton theorized that hieroglyphs were representations of the world's first language, one of gestures and impassioned vocalizations like those imagined in Condillac's thought experiment. From this strongly expressive, transparent, and direct form of language that could be universally understood grew a poetic language—one of apologues, fables, and later similes and metaphors—by which humans apprehended the world and communicated their experiences. Only as human beings' mental capacities of reason, imagination, and memory expanded did a largely abstract language take shape, subdividing into particular idioms and losing its universal quality as well as the clarity and strength of the original *langage d'action* or language of action. In its transformation from natural reactions to abstract or arbitrary signs, language spurred the rise of thought and culture, but also resulted in losses.

Condillac's narrative, taken to some extent from Warburton, brings into relief the central tenets and points of debate surrounding the origins of language as hypothesized by thinkers of the eighteenth century. In addition to its foundation in sensationalist epistemology, Condillac took a position on what caused the first language. For him, humankind's natural sociability ineluctably drew the two children together. Their being of the opposite sex underscored their innate attraction in his heteronormative account. Once together, sensations of physical pain and need induced an initial communication and an overwhelming sense of compassion or sympathy caused a response in Condillac's harmonious vision of human mutualism. For Condillac as for Warburton, the results of the inexorable progress of human language were largely positive. Language was responsible for generating thought, since, as Condillac remarked, "the use of signs is the principle which unfolds all our ideas as they lie in the bud." In keeping with Warburton's conclusions, Condillac contended that the evolution of language toward the arbitrary sign also "produced all the arts that pertain to the expression of our thoughts" and placed language at the center of social, moral, artistic, and scientific progress.[9]

Rousseau, however, did not agree on any of these points. Rousseau unveiled his conception, at times contradictory, of the origins of language in his *Discourse on the Origin and Basis of Inequality Among Men*, or *Second Discourse*, of 1754 and in his *Essay on the Origins of Languages*, written during the 1750s and published posthumously in 1781. For Rousseau, the "noble savage" was naturally fearful as opposed to social, and his first act of communication was not incited by physical pain and want, but by "the moral needs ... and the passions ... love, hatred, pity, anger." Further, instead of viewing the rise of conventional language as the generator of human progress, Rousseau argued the opposite. The beginning of society corresponded with the concept of property and was manifested in a speech act by an individual: someone saying "This is mine." From thence, the rise of artificial or conventional language only fostered inequality in social and political structures. It became a tool of self-interest, deception, and domination for ruling elites who wielded words instead of swords to perpetuate their power and the unfair sociopolitical divisions that it entailed.

Rousseau indicted Northern languages, including French, as being the most culpable of these corruptions. French language and culture were not conducive vehicles for liberty. He bemoaned the fact that political modes of speech in French were largely written since there was no place for oral political debate. No matter their form, he insisted, political communications were devoid of content in the current world and were typically deployed to confuse and mystify rather than enlighten, a problem with modern language that Condillac also identified. What is more, Rousseau was doubtful that language could exist prior to thought as Condillac had contended. "For if men needed speech in order to learn to think," he commented wryly, "they had even greater need of knowing how to think in order to discover the art of speech."[10] Denis Diderot, who theorized on the origins of language in his *Letter on the Deaf and Dumb* (1751), also took issue with the notion that language formed thought and cast doubt on whether any conventional language could sufficiently express thought.

What Condillac, Rousseau, as well as Diderot and others agreed upon, however, was that the original natural form of language, the *langage d'action*, had admirable qualities that made it in many cases superior to conventional, artificial languages. Diderot celebrated the first poetic language of gestures and cries as capable of synchronically communicating a multiplicity of ideas to a multiplicity of senses, thereby resembling much more closely the richness of human thought. Conventional language, by contrast, had lost this simultaneously complex and transparent mimetic power. The *langage d'action* was more capable of expressing emotion and eliciting sympathy thanks to its representational capaciousness and "energy." Here, Diderot and the new school of epistemological rhetoricians, such as Scottish philosopher and professor of divinity George Campbell (1719–1796), followed Locke in marking vivacity of language as a key sign and cause of the vivacious perceptions and ideas that they prized.

Indeed, during the eighteenth century, projects of philosophers of language and those of rhetorical theorists in the epistemological (or psychological-philosophical) tradition overlapped. Both were ensconced in sensationalist philosophy, and both were ultimately interested in the means of effective communication writ large. Taking a broad view of rhetoric that likened it to the notion of the *langage d'action*, George Campbell, in his *Philosophy of Rhetoric* (1776), defined rhetoric as a "grand art of communication, not of ideas only, but of sentiments, passions, dispositions, and purposes."[11] For him, a system of rhetoric (i.e., communication) based on the psychological faculties of the human mind would allow readers to experience and understand an idea with the same "vivacity" as if they had experienced it with their own senses. Campbell believed, as had Giambattista Vico (1668–1744), Warburton, and others in the recent past, that the mind was essentially poetic, that is to say, the tropes and figures codified by rhetorical and poetic doctrine originated as structures through which the human mind apprehends the world. Viewing tropes and figures as scholarly inventions was thus to see things backwards. As Campbell wrote, tropes and figures "are so far from being the inventions of art, that, on the contrary, they result from the original and essential principles of the human mind." They were the universal structures of the human mind, "in all nations, barbarous and civilized," though "the simplest and most ancient tongues do most abound with them." Subsequently, it was "the natural effect of improvement in science and language, which commonly go together ... to range the several tropes and figures into classes, to distinguish them by names, and to trace the principles in the mind which gave them birth."[12]

In Vico's theory of poetic logic expounded in *The New Science* (1725), he had already expressed a similar notion, saying that

> all the tropes ... which have hitherto been considered ingenious inventions of writers, were necessary modes of expression of all the first poetic nations ... But these expressions of the first nations later became figurative when, with the further development of the human mind, words were invented which signified abstract forms or genera comprising their species or relating parts with their wholes.[13]

The history of language and the tropes were, according to Vico, part of tracing human history from what he called the age of the gods, of heroes, and of men. "Each stage, and thus the history of any nation," summarizes historian Timothy Costelloe writing about Vico, "is characterized by the manifestation of natural law peculiar to it, and the distinct languages (signs, metaphors, and words), governments (divine, aristocratic commonwealths, and popular commonwealths and monarchies), as well as systems of jurisprudence (mystic theology, heroic jurisprudence, and the natural equity of free commonwealths) that define them."[14]

In their own ways, all of these visions of the origins of the human species, endowed with poetic intellect and a transparent, natural language, were efforts to elucidate the history of human civilization, the workings of the mind, and the role that language could play in moral, intellectual, social, and political progress. Recovering the pure, emotive, effective *langage d'action* was thus a high stakes endeavor that influenced multiple sectors, including new schools of rhetorical theory. The elocutionary movement in England, for example, brought attention to the art of rhetorical delivery, a subject that Cicero, Quintilian, and classical rhetoricians had treated cursorily. The elocutionists believed that in spaces in which oral communication was vital—the theater, the parliament, and the pulpit—a renewal was desperately necessary. In his *Letter to a Young Clergyman* (1720), Swift derided the poor delivery of sermons, saying that

> you will observe some clergymen with their head held down from the beginning to the end within an inch of the cushion to read what is hardly legible; which, beside the untoward manner, hinders them from making the best advantage of their voice: others again have a trick of popping up and down every moment from their paper to the audience, like an idle school boy on a repetition day.[15]

Such ineffective speaking styles bred boredom and apathy, thereby diminishing possibilities for moral, social, and political improvement.

The elocutionists shared many of the same convictions as the eighteenth-century French, German, and Scottish philosophers of language previously discussed: that there was a natural language of gestures and tonal speech, that this language was emotive, clear, and universally communicative, and that the use of this language played a critical role in human progress. With this in mind, the elocutionists launched into a scrupulous exploration of vocal intonation, facial expression, and gesture in an attempt to theorize how to express oneself clearly and in a manner that would touch the minds and hearts of listeners. In the course of the seventeenth and eighteenth centuries, two opposing methodological approaches to this problem developed, one mechanical, emphasizing imitation and memorizing performative aspects in oratory and stage acting, and the other natural, focusing on increasing freedom and spontaneity of expression in the pulpit, the theater, and other spaces of public discourse.

Michel Le Faucheur (*c.* 1585–1657), a Genevan clergyman born of French refugees, is the largely unacknowledged father of the elocutionary movement. Indeed, English rhetorical theorists such as John Mason (1706–1763), John Ward (*c.* 1679–1758), and Charles Gildon (*c.* 1665–1724) all incorporated ideas from Le Faucheur's 1657 treatise *Essay upon the Action of an Orator; as to his Pronunciation & Gesture* into their own works. Le Faucheur was a declared naturalist, as had been Cicero and Quintilian in their few words on the subject of delivery. He recommended focusing on content rather than relying upon specific gestures or thinking too intensely about the rules of elocution as beneficial while giving a speech: "The very Thought of Rules and the Care of observing them would mightily distract and amuse. Besides that it would take off the Warmth and Spirit of his Discourse, perplex his Head, and disturb his Memory."[16] To maintain and strengthen a connection to an audience, he nevertheless offered astonishingly specific advice on the voice—his comments on speed, tone, volume, and other elements comprised eight of the fourteen chapters in his book. He also encouraged memorizing speeches, rehearsing them in front of an audience, and avoiding the pitfalls of off-putting postures and gesticulations of the head (throwing it backward), shoulders (shrugging), torso (thrusting forward one's belly), as well as awkward movements of the hands, eyes, eyebrows, mouth, lips, etc.

The theater was a primary place in which projects for natural gestural language and the battle between the natural and mechanical schools unfolded. In France, Diderot took a keen interest in the theater and acting techniques, having argued through examples drawn from the great playwrights William Shakespeare (1564–1616) and Pierre Corneille (1606–1684) that certain gestures could convey meaning that words never could. Demonstrating his typically playful impudence, he professed that he enjoyed watching plays while plugging his ears. Writers such as Louis-Sébastien Mercier (1740–1814) argued for the power of gestural language, as did actors, directors, and choreographers including Pierre Jean Baptiste Nougaret (1742–1823) and Jean-Georges Noverre (1727–1820) with his so-called *ballet d'action* (Figure 7.5). Indeed, a growing interest in pantomime marked debates and productions from the fairs (*foires*) to the Paris Opéra. Once again, "primitive" models of gestural dance were seen as sources for recuperating the natural and revitalizing modern European stages. European accounts of the dances and languages of Native Americans, Tahitians, Egyptians, and others were held up as examples (Figure 7.6). There were, of course, some skeptics. Ange Goudar (1708–1791), an Italian adventurer and man of letters, jeered: "It is much easier for a man or a woman to say I love you than to go search for this expression in *tours de jambes* (turns of the leg), which not being designed to explain love, cannot convey it."[17]

But across the channel, advocates of the natural and mechanical schools of elocution advanced their theories and attributed to them extraordinary, if at times inordinate, weight. Thomas Sheridan (1719–1788), an Irish actor, educator, and friend of Jonathan Swift, was a proponent of the natural school. In his *British Education* of 1756, Sheridan argued that proper fulfillment of juridical and ecclesiastical duties involved strong public speaking and making oratory essential to the health of the English Constitution. While many scoffed at this notion, Sheridan won a great following when he wrote and

FIGURE 7.5 A scene from the ballet of Jean-George Noverre, *Jason et Medée* (1781). © Hulton Archive / Getty Images.

created a lecture series entitled *Course of Lectures on Elocution* (1762). His ideal of rhetoric was derived from the strong emotiveness and conviction associated with natural speech, which would, he thought, engender authentic and convincing gestural and vocal communication:

> Let him speak entirely from his feelings; and they will find much truer signs to manifest themselves by, than he could find for them ... in order to persuade, it is above all things necessary that the speaker should at least appear himself to believe what he utters; but this can never be the case, where there are any evident marks of affection or art.[18]

In keeping with his interest in authenticity, Sheridan shunned all imitation, while those of the mechanical school suggested that even if nature provided the original language, the art of oratory must be learned. In his *Art of Speaking* (1761), James Burgh (1714–1775) included a thirteen-page catalog with a long inventory of "the principal passions, humours, sentiments, and intentions, which are to be expressed by speech and action."[19] Sheridan as well as John Walker (1732–1807), who was a fellow actor, a Ramist, and a proponent of the mechanical school, was influenced by Burgh's treatise. The elocutionary movement proliferated with the re-blossoming of physiognomy—the study of an individual's character based on his or her appearance—and gained a visual counterpart to

FIGURE 7.6 J. B. Scotin, *Illustrations of the American savages, compared to early mores*, engraving, 1724. © BNF Gallica.

Burgh's inventory of "passions, humours, sentiments, and intentions" in Swiss intellectual Johann Caspar Lavater's (1741–1801) illustrated *Essays on Physiognomy* (1772), which was popular at the time (Figure 7.7).

While the interest in gestural "natural" language continued to flourish, a countervalent tendency also developed in the later eighteenth century, taking form in a revaluation of conventional alphabetic language as particularly strong in its emotion-inducing, communicative capacity. "The proper manner of conveying the affections of the mind from one to another, is by words," wrote Irish philosopher and statesman Edmund Burke (1729–1797) in his *Philosophical Enquiry in the Origin of Our Ideas of the Sublime and Beautiful* (1757), thereby designating the primacy of words as communicative devices.[20] Others followed. Rousseau lauded natural gestural communication and enumerated its virtues, yet he ultimately argued that words and music were more powerful vehicles for conveying and inducing emotion. "Visible signs make for more accurate imitation," he wrote, but "interest is aroused more effectively by sounds."[21] Diderot attended to

FIGURE 7.7 Illustration by Thomas Holloway from Johann Caspar Lavater, *Essays on physiognomy, designed to promote the knowledge and the love of mankind* (1789–1798). © The Picture Art Collection / Alamy Stock Photo.

poetry and aesthetic experience and suggested artists try to "paint" thought in ways that mimicked the original structures of human cognition. Once again referring back to the tropes, he endorsed experimenting with metaphor, metonymy, and synecdoche to recreate the essence of natural communication that he believed could also be felt among actors and spectators, deaf-mute individuals, or Adam and Eve. Prefiguring pictorial poetic methods of the avant-garde, Diderot intimated that poets could innovate a literary hieroglyphics capable of activating multiple senses and faculties synchronically. This type of poetry would possess all of the elements of authentic natural language, be socially integrative, and also advance the progress of the human mind.

In these suggestions about the power of the word and of poetry, philosophers of language as well as theorists of another novel rhetorical movement, that of belletristic rhetoric, participated in the era's most significant discussions regarding aesthetic experience and critique.

LANGUAGE, AESTHETICS, AND POETRY IN THE SEVENTEENTH AND EIGHTEENTH CENTURIES

Aesthetic theory had been a part of philosophical discourse since antiquity. However, this branch of thought did not receive a name until 1735 when German philosopher Alexander Gottlieb Baumgarten (1706–1757) presented it as *epistêmê aisthetikê*, meaning the science of that which is sensed and imagined. During the seventeenth century, a new fervor for theorizing on these issues arose as artistic practices were increasingly codified in academies and treatises by leading literary figures. The year 1674 in France was a watershed in this regard. Poet and critic Nicolas Boileau-Despréaux (1636–1711) published a translation of Longinus' ancient essay on the sublime, as well as his own neoclassical treatise in verse, *The Art of Poetry* (*L'art poétique*). Both of these works proved to be extraordinarily influential, especially as French was supplanting Latin as the lingua franca of the Republic of Letters across the European continent. This was also the year in which Jean Racine (1639–1699) debuted his play *Iphigénie*, a tragedy that was inspired by Euripides' *Iphigenia at Aulis* (406–408 BCE) but did not resemble it, eliciting debate about to what extent the works of the ancients should be imitated.

These works, the polemics that they provoked, and the professional rivalries that surrounded them engendered a large-scale artistic, cultural, and eventually political controversy in the latter seventeenth and early eighteenth centuries referred to as the Quarrel of the Ancients and Moderns. In this quarrel, scholars debated whether antique literature, philosophy, and political systems (including those pertaining to official policies toward the arts) were superior or inferior to those of modern times. The dispute had begun during the sixteenth and early seventeenth centuries in Italy and France, but became more widespread later in the seventeenth century through the popularity of works of French and English writers: Charles Perrault (1628–1703), Bernard le Bovier de Fontenelle (1657–1757), Pierre Carlet de Chamblain de Marivaux (1688–1763), John Dryden (1631–1700), John Dennis (1658–1734), all in favor of Moderns; and Jean de la Fontaine (1621–1695), Jean de la Bruyère (1645–1696), Alexander Pope (1688–1744), Sir William Temple (1628–1699), William Wotton (1666–1727), and Richard Bentley (1662–1742), all in favor of antique traditions. Over time, the reputations and careers of those individuals involved in the quarrel became quite venomous and peppered with personal attacks. The pettiness and somewhat overblown character of the quarrel made it perfect fodder for Swift's satirical eye. He ridiculed it in his parodic epic "Account of a Battle between the Ancient and Modern Books in St. James's Library" in *A Tale of a Tub* (1704).

These writers, their works, and the cultural mediations discussed earlier in this chapter fostered a vibrant theoretical discussion of aesthetic experience and critique. Belletristic rhetoric appeared in this context. Rhetorical theorists who pioneered this tradition joined literary writers and artists, literati, and philosophers in attending to a series of questions with regard to beauty, the sublime, taste, genius, the picturesque, grace, the *je ne sais quoi*, and imitation in poetry and other art forms. Some questions were philosophical: what is the relationship between art and truth? What are the ontological structures of beauty, the sublime, and taste? What roles do sense perception, pleasure, pain, sympathy, the imagination, the association of ideas, memory, and rational judgment play in aesthetic experience? Other queries had a more socio-ethical or practical bent: is art essentially immoral and socially divisive or can it edify and unite? Is it possible to define a general standard of beauty or taste? If so, by what or whom can the standard be established?

Which of the artistic forms—painting, sculpture, poetry, music—is superior and how might one judge that? Which form or subgenre (tragic theatre in verse, satire, etc.) is most "natural," transparent in its semiotics, or capable of simultaneously carrying the emotions of the creator and touching the emotions of the audience? These and related inquiries occupied not only some of the most famous minds of the era in countries across the western hemisphere but also the publics who read their works, who frequented learned society meetings and lectures on belletristic rhetoric to hone their skills as critics and collectors, and who consumed literary and cultural criticism in the periodical press.[22]

In this grand canvas of eighteenth-century thought, several interventions on the subject of poetry connect directly to the theories of language explored in this chapter, especially as pertains to the search for a more highly communicative language that would strike the emotions vividly and with complexity, as some believed the language of "primitive" or "uncivilized" people could still do. Flying into the face of the century-long quest to make language more transparent and scientific, Edmund Burke advocated obscurity in language since "in reality a great clearness helps but little towards affecting the passions, as it is in some sort an enemy to all enthusiasms whatsoever."[23] In his *Meditations on Poetry* (*Meditationes philosophicae de nonnullis ad poema pertinentibus*, 1735) Baumgarten did not discard the utility of clarity in poetic language, but redefined it. He contended that poems aim for what he called extensive rather than intensive clarity. Poetry conveys a plethora of information contemporaneously, but it does not categorize this information as scientific, as logical discourse would require. Scholar Paul Guyer writes that according to Baumbarten, "poetry achieves its goal of arousing a density of images by portraying individuals in particular circumstances rather than by trafficking in generalities and abstractions. Thus Baumgarten turns what is a vice in scientific knowledge—connoting too many ideas without clearly distinguishing among them—into the paradigm virtue of poetry."[24] This "quantitative conception of the aim of poetry" resembles the kind of manifold and complete communication of which Diderot believed poetry to be capable in his vision of the modern poetic hieroglyph. Burke's and Baumgarten's ideas about conventional alphabetic language turn the long-standing insistence upon transparent and clearly circumscribed scientific language on its head.

In a similar vein, Herder and German Jewish philosopher Moses Mendelssohn (1729–1786) both rejected the cratylist perspective that prized "natural" language for its close semiotic relationship to the thing it represents. Instead, they championed poetic language precisely because of its "artificiality" and distance from that which it communicates. Mendelssohn argued that art forms that utilize natural signs—music, dance, painting, sculpture—are representationally constrained since they can only convey concepts and emotions that resemble the properties of the specific artistic medium in question. "Music," for example, is "the expression of which takes place by means of inarticulate sounds" and thereby can express exclusively the "inclinations and passions of the human soul which tend to make themselves known by means of sounds." The natural language of music cannot communicate specific objects such as "the concept of a rose, a poplar tree, and so on, just as it is impossible for painting to represent a musical chord to us." This is not the case for poetry, however. "The poet can express everything of which our soul can have a clear concept."[25] Mendelssohn referred to poetry and rhetoric as "beautiful sciences," comingling the scientific and artistic into a single aesthetic classification.

Herder agreed with Mendelssohn on this account, contending in his *Groves of Criticism* (*Kritischer Wälder*, 1769) that poetry's virtue was precisely that it was not constrained by the natural properties of its signs. In fact, the medium of arts other than poetry (the stone or marble of statues, the acoustic sounds of music, for example) could actually distract one from connecting to meaning in a work of art. German philosopher and critic Gotthold Ephraim Lessing (1729–1781) had made this argument in *Laocoön: An Essay on the Limits of Painting and Poetry* (*Laokoön oder Über die Grenzen der Malerei und Poesie*), published three years earlier in 1766. According to Lessing, the poet "wants rather to make the ideas he awakens in us so vivid that at the moment we believe that we feel the real impressions which the objects of these ideas would produce in us. In this moment of illusion we should cease to be conscious of the means which the poet uses for this purpose, that is, his words."[26] Herder continued this line of thinking about signifier and signified, positing that one must not focus on the sign itself, but rather on its sense (*Sinn*) and its force (*Kraft*). Though rather ill defined, force seems to have indicated the feeling of the essence of life that that the artificial signs of poetry best capture and transmit. "The essence of poetry," Herder remarked, "is the force, which adheres to the inner in words, the magical force which works on my soul through fantasy and recollection."[27] Poetry is thus capable of expressing anything and everything imaginable, presenting a broader range of truth than other art forms, and best touching the reader's soul by activating the imagination and memory.

Just as philosophers of language turned to the linguistic and artistic practices of "primitive" peoples as paragons of communication, Herder championed popular poetry and songs from across the globe in the *Correspondence on Ossian and the Songs of Ancient People* (*Auszug aus einem Briefwechsel über Ossian und die Lieder alter Völker*, 1773) and in his volume of popular songs from around the world (1778–1779). In the former work, he praised the cycle of epic poems by Celtic author-bard Ossian, whose work was discovered and published by Scottish poet James Macpherson (1736–1796) beginning in 1760. Referring to Ossian and to popular songs in general, Herder wrote exaltedly and nostalgically:

> Know then, that the more barbarous a people is—that is, the more alive, the more freely acting (for that is what the word means)—the more barbarous, that is, the more alive, the more free, the closer to the senses, the more lyrically dynamic its songs will be, if songs it has. The more remote a people is from an artificial, scientific manner of thinking, speaking, and writing, the less its songs are made for paper and print, the less its verses are written for the dead letter. The purpose, the nature, the miraculous power of these songs as the delight, the driving-force, the traditional chant and everlasting joy of the people—all this depends on the lyrical, living, dance-like quality of the song, on the living presence of the images, and the coherence and, as it were compulsion of the content, the feelings; on the symmetry of the words and syllables, and sometimes even of the letters, on the flow of the melody, and on a hundred other things which belong to the living world, to the gnomic song of the nation, and vanish with it.[28]

While Herder clearly intended to celebrate the "purpose, the nature, the miraculous power" of these songs, condescension (albeit perhaps unintentional) nevertheless looms in his romantic and essentializing view of people he describes as "barbarous" and "more alive, more freely acting." This dualism frames two concluding thoughts on the subject of this chapter.

First, the above passage conveys the ideals of liberty and authenticity that burgeoned during the seventeenth and eighteenth centuries in Europe. Freedom, genuineness, transparency, and corresponding communicational and poetic forms that are "more alive … more free … closer to the senses" were ardently cherished and perhaps overzealously pursued by the denizens of this first age of globalization when the informational environment was increasingly populous, dynamic, and complicated to navigate. The diligence, enthusiasm, and what can seem from our vantage point, naivety brought to universal language schemes and projects to recover "natural" language are rather striking to the modern reader. The Ossian poems make manifest the dangers of naively championing these ideals, especially since, unbeknownst to Herder and the numerous scholars and critics who analyzed these works, Ossian and his epic poems were a hoax. Macpherson had written them himself, inventing Ossian and his poetry from folktales and fraudulently attributing them to his fictional author. Innumerable scholars of the twentieth and twenty-first centuries have commented on the grand legacy of linguistic, rhetorical, and aesthetic thought of the period 1650–1800. Yet, the "natural," universal language championed by so many thinkers of the seventeenth and eighteenth centuries was also much like Ossian's great epic cycle: it was a fabulation, a hope, a dangerously seductive albeit noble dream … of something that never was.

Second, and far less noble, are the forms of "othering" and social exclusion involved in many Western linguistic, rhetorical, and aesthetic theories of the period. The exoticizing and instrumentalizing of non-European cultures, peoples, and languages—even when they are held up as paragons of "natural" communication (a back-handed compliment if ever there was one)—smacks of the ethnocentric bias and cultural imperialism that fueled the continuation of slavery, the civilizing mission, scientific racism, and the colonial projects of the nineteenth century. As Swift noted in his spoof of seventeenth-century language schemes in *Gulliver's Travels*, sexism and misogyny were also rampant throughout this period and in many of the works discussed in this chapter. Women philosophers, rhetorical theorists, and activists such as Mary Astell (1666–1731), Margaret Askew Fell (1614–1702), and Mary Wollstonecraft (1759–1797) worked to advance women's fundamental rights to access education, to participate in public discourse, and to have their intellectual contributions be taken seriously. Theories of taste in the belletristic rhetorical tradition and aesthetic discourse were likewise often openly disdainful of peasants and working-class people, as well as the growing bourgeoisie. In many cases, people from these groups were designated as having bad taste and were therefore scorned and systematically excluded from the self-selected cabal of "tastemakers." Scholars have long criticized Scottish minister and rhetorician Hugh Blair (1718–1800), for example, for his unquestioning Eurocentrism and complicity with class structures and prejudices. A few voices—notably Diderot, and especially Herder—were avowedly anti-imperialist in their political views, and Herder developed a theory of hermeneutics and translation predicated on deep respect for cultural, historical, and linguistic difference. Yet as the above passage on Ossian makes clear, these voices too had their implicit and explicit biases. These aspects of the story must also be understood as part of the heritage of thinking about language, rhetoric, and poetry of the neoclassical and Enlightenment eras.

CHAPTER EIGHT

The Arts: The Power of Pictorial Naturalism

DOUGLAS FORDHAM

On a sheet of cream paper two men face one another with outstretched arms. The figure on the left wears a long brown cloak, his face marked with tattoos and his hair gathered in a topknot. He holds a crayfish on a string, all ten appendages clearly demarcated. The man on the right wears European breeches, stockings, shoes, jacket, and a hat, and he holds a piece of white cloth. The watercolor is legible yet strange. Unmoored by perspectival space, the flattened figures with frontal eyes float near the top of the page (Figure 8.1).

This is an extraordinary work of art, a watercolor that captures with uncanny force the world in which "Western art" emerged. The man on the right is Sir Joseph Banks, future President of the Royal Society in London and one of the most important figures in the annals of Enlightenment exploration. He launched his reputation on the first Captain Cook expedition to the South Pacific in the 1760s, which is where we find him here, negotiating with a Maori man from New Zealand. In a letter written decades later, Banks recalled the following exchange that took place while the HMS *Endeavour* was docked in Tolaga Bay, New Zealand:

> Tupaia the Indian who came with me from Otaheite Learnd to draw in a way not Quite unintelligible[.] The genius for Caricature which all wild people Possess Led him to Caricature me & he drew me with a nail in my hand delivering it to an Indian who sold me a Lobster but with my other hand I had a firm fist on the Lobster determined not to Quit the nail till I had Livery and Seizin of the article purchased.

Banks remembers bartering with a nail rather than a handkerchief, but the description undoubtedly relates to this watercolor. Even more remarkably, we learn that it was the Tahitian priest and navigator Tupaia who painted the scene. Hailed as an ancestor by the Maori people he met, the Polynesian Tupaia helped to mediate between radically different worlds. With his facility for languages and a shared respect for tradition and ceremony, Tupaia enabled Cook and his men to communicate, however imperfectly, with communities across the South Pacific.[1]

As an *arioi*, a Tahitian high priest, Tupaia may have learned to paint ceremonial barkcloths with red, brown, and black ochres. We find a similar palette in the crayfish painting. Pictorial representation contained a powerful spiritual component in Polynesian culture, and Tupaia recognized that Europeans, too, placed a high premium on what they termed the arts. Fascinated by the sketches of Sydney Parkinson, one of the draftsmen on board the *Endeavour*, Tupaia dedicated considerable effort to emulating the visual codes and conventions of European art.

FIGURE 8.1 Tupaia, *Maori bartering a crayfish*, 1769. © The British Library Board / Add. MS 15508 (12).

Deeply wedded to symbolic systems of perspectival space and pictorial naturalism, Europeans found little to appreciate in alternative pictorial systems. Banks dismissed Tupaia's melding of Polynesian and European visual systems as "caricature," a term that became something of a catch-all for aesthetic difference. In 1813, J. P. Malcolm wrote *An Historical Sketch of the Art of Caricaturing*, which associated caricature with an ignorance of proper representational techniques:

> He that draws the human face divine for the first time is a caricaturist *per* force: he views the lines of the original, and, attempting to imitate them, produces a monster; and it is only by patience and perseverance he conquers his propensity to distortion: indeed, some industrious individuals are disappointed in all their endeavours, and caricature to the end of the chapter. This is also the case with certain ingenious natives of countries still in a state of uncultivated nature; and it must be acknowledged they excel all competitors antient [*sic*] or modern in the art I am treating of, and have done so from time immemorial.[2]

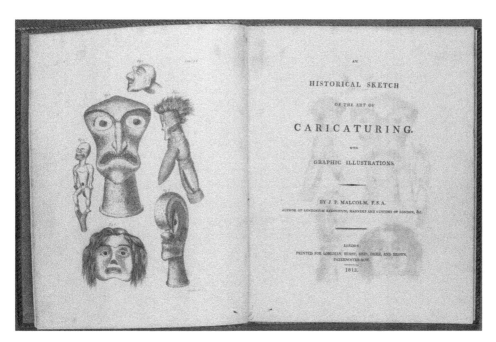

FIGURE 8.2 J. P. Malcolm, *An Historical Sketch of the Art of Caricaturing with Graphic Illustrations* (London, 1813). © The Lewis Walpole Library, Yale University (public domain).

Etchings in the book, made after Malcolm's sketches of objects in the British Museum, included sculptures acquired from the South Pacific, Asia, Africa, and even ancient Celtic objects uncovered in the British Isles (Figure 8.2). What defined this heterogeneous material as "caricature" was its deviation from Western pictorial naturalism. The rhetoric of naturalism wielded such power in the West that it would only be with "primitivist" artistic movements in the late nineteenth and early twentieth centuries that European artists began to break the spell. Even then hierarchies of race, culture, and pictorial technique persisted.

Tupaia's watercolor may seem like an odd place to begin an examination of visual art in a cultural history of ideas in the West. More sensible, perhaps, would be a history of artistic style, as artists transitioned from Baroque to rococo to neoclassical to Romantic forms. Allowing for significant overlap and recursion, this stylistic progression has been remarkably durable in the history books, and it tells us much about art produced in Europe. Many works do not fit within this narrative, of course, arriving either too early or too late, or appearing to be indifferent to the styles or themes of their historical moment. But even these disjunctions can be instructive.

Art historians have also placed great emphasis on national schools of art, particularly in the rapidly centralizing states of France, Great Britain, Prussia, and Russia. The Royal Academy of Arts in France was particularly well funded and influential, becoming a model for artists and rulers in other states. Through the auspices of the Academy, the French state commissioned and exhibited history paintings at Salons that came to be viewed as referenda on the health of the Old Regime. As the art historian Thomas Crow writes, "what might otherwise have been rather esoteric questions of artistic style and subject matter were often caught up in that struggle," referring to a struggle over political representation.[3] Artistic patronage in Great Britain was more decentralized, making use of public-private partnerships such as its own Royal Academy of Arts and the first Captain Cook expedition, both of which launched in 1768.

On a smaller scale, cities influenced the production and reception of Western art. Numerous studies have focused on artists, institutions, and audiences in major cities such as Paris, London, Rome, and Vienna. Studies relating to colonial towns have proliferated or faltered based, in part, on their relation to subsequent geopolitical developments. Colonial Philadelphia, New York, Boston, and Charleston have been swept into the history of American art. Art produced in Calcutta, Madras, and Bombay have garnered increasing interest due to their significance in the British Empire. Art produced in the Caribbean, including Cuba and Jamaica, are relatively new sites of art-historical interest. Far-flung outposts of the Spanish Empire, from Manila to Mexico City to the California coast, once considered by scholars to be in hopeless decline in the eighteenth century, are now discussed as vibrant cultural and architectural complexes. Many of these regions have benefited from comparative and transcultural studies, in which art and artists move between discrete cultural and geographic spheres.

With the exception of textbooks, rarely do art historians speak of European art or a single Western tradition.[4] More common are categorizations around nations, markets, or cultural exchanges. One place where "Western Art" has returned as a useful and critical category is in the pursuit of World Art history. The ambitious and controversial attempt by scholars to conceive of the history of art as a shared human endeavor across time and space has often compelled them to articulate characteristics that may be common to all "art"—such as the "facture" that comes from working with one's hands, or the way that humans experience architectural space—from the conventions of "Western art." Histories of World Art tend also to be wary of the terms upon which art-historical analysis has traditionally proceeded, finding assumptions and biases embedded in particular terms from centuries of European artistic practice and criticism.[5] The vocabulary for painting, for example, is often derived from oil painting on canvas rather than Aboriginal bark painting or Mesoamerican murals.

NATURALISM

"Naturalism" presumes that the aim of art is to replicate the world as the human eye sees it.[6] By the eighteenth century, naturalism was a deeply shared aesthetic commitment that cut across many local and national boundaries in the West. Indeed, its ubiquity makes it easy to overlook as a bedrock feature of European artistic practice. It became increasingly visible and self-conscious, however, as Europeans began to compare it to a much wider world of visual representation including Maori paddles, ancient Indian sculpture, Australian rock painting, and Celtic crosses. While European contact with the Americas dates back to the fifteenth century, the earliest accounts of encounter are overwhelmingly textual. The compulsion to represent *visually* the cultural, material, and ethnographic specificity of distant peoples and places developed only sporadically in the seventeenth century and then came to fruition in the eighteenth.[7] This visual turn helped to make naturalistic representation a potent marker of European identity. The perfection of pictorial naturalism came to be viewed as an index of European civilization.

The art of natural description was deeply embedded in a host of cultural practices, one of which was natural science. "Natural" representation often depended on the highly conventionalized use of optical devices that enhanced the naked eye, such as the

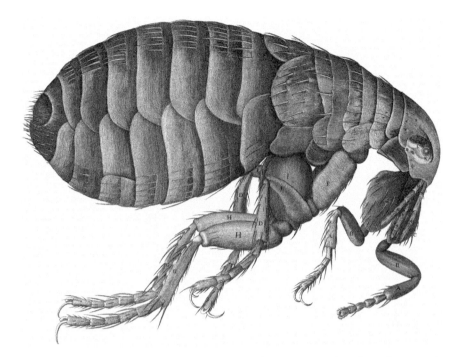

FIGURE 8.3 Robert Hooke, "The Flea" in *Micrographia; or, Some Physiological Descriptions of Minute Bodies made by Magnifying Glass* (1665). © Wikimedia Commons (public domain).

microscope, *camera obscura*, and telescope. The power of lenses to focus human vision is the subject of Robert Hooke's *Micrographia; or, Some Physiological Descriptions of Minute Bodies made by Magnifying Glass* (1665), in which he reproduced drawings of tiny living objects such as a fly's head and a flea in unprecedented detail (Figure 8.3). As Hooke made clear in his text, the printed image was not a simple, direct transcription of what he saw. First, Hooke had to understand what he was seeing before he could represent it: "I endeavoured (as far as I was able) to discover the true appearance, and next to make a plain representation of it."[8] Training the hand to work with the eye, the former fixing and translating the shifting impressions of the latter, entailed aesthetic judgment and critical discernment. This was equally true for drawing devices such as the *camera obscura*, which used lenses to project a scene onto a piece of paper through a pinhole camera.

Like the scientific method, techniques of visual transcription helped to standardize representational practices and subject representation to independent verification. This became increasingly important as artists traveled to distant parts of the globe and returned with representations of coastlines, plants, animals, and peoples that could then be compiled, ordered, and explained in the metropole. The Spanish Empire in South America, beginning to fade in the eighteenth century in the face of French and British competition, redoubled its commitment to botanical exploration and codification.

One particularly notable Royal Botanical Expedition, under the direction of José Celestino Mutis, produced over seven thousand plant illustrations over the course of three decades in modern-day Columbia, Ecuador, Panama, and Venezuela.[9] Mutis was one of a great many European travelers who contributed to a "cycle of accumulation" in which explorers gathered objects and information from around the world and then transmitted that material back to "centers of calculation" where it could be compiled, compared, and interpreted. These centers of calculation ranged from royal palaces and scientific societies to Joseph Banks's London townhouse. In the formulation of historian of science Bruno Latour, a successful cycle of accumulation depended on three factors:

> By inventing means that (a) render them *mobile* so that they can be brought back; (b) keep them *stable* so that they can be moved back and forth without additional distortion, corruption or decay, and (c) are *combinable* so that whatever stuff they are made of, they can be cumulated, aggregated, or shuffled like a pack of cards.[10]

Latour illustrated the power of this process through a cycle of accumulation initiated by the French captain J.-F. Lapérouse in 1787. Although Lapérouse vanished before returning home, he managed to transmit back to Europe cartographic information about the coastlines of China and Russia. The success of Lapérouse's voyage did not depend on *his* return, but rather on clear and systematic information that he transmitted back to Paris.

When Lapérouse landed on Sakhalin, off the coast of Kamchatka, a Chinese resident sketched a rough map of his island in the sand. Impressed with his knowledge but unsure of the scale, Lapérouse persuaded the islander to write the map on paper, and mark it with distances that corresponded to a day's voyage by canoe. Combined with bearings and soundings taken by Lapérouse's crew, these notes were transmitted back to Versailles and rapidly integrated into maps through a variety of metropolitan networks. Latour commented:

> On 17 July 1787, Lapérouse is *weaker* than his informants; he does not know the shape of the land, does not know where to go; he is at the mercy of his guides. Ten years later, on 5 November 1797 the English ship *Neptune* on landing again at the same bay will be much *stronger* than the natives since they will have on board maps, descriptions, log books, nautical instructions—which to begin with will allow them to know that this is the "same" bay.[11]

A similar account can be given of Tupaia, whose navigational expertise was indispensable to Captain Cook. Like so many other data points collected by the Cook voyage, it was sent back to London to be integrated into Western cartographic codes and shared with a variety of informational networks. Neither the death of Tupaia from disease nor the death of Captain Cook at the hands of the Hawaiians, on his third voyage, impeded the transmission of this information. Botanical images produced by Mutis and his colleagues, on the other hand, were not as well integrated into larger information networks back in Madrid, thrown into the tumult of the Penninsular War at the start of the nineteenth century, thereby delaying their influence.

DISCOVERY AND REPRODUCTION

The art of exploration has typically been viewed as a minor, mundane instance of art production in the eighteenth century. In their quest for accurate visual descriptions, traveling artists have been seen as the Aristotelian stepchildren to their more sophisticated metropolitan peers, who drew upon idealized Platonic forms. But this dichotomy is much too stark, for artists had yet to adopt Immanuel Kant's theory of the arts. In the *Critique of Judgment* published in 1790, Kant argued that freedom and play were the guarantors of the aesthetic, which was itself distinct from the utility of descriptive, scientific representation. Most eighteenth-century artists, on the other hand, operated on a continuum between acute visual description and elegant generalization. Lorraine Daston and Peter Galison note that even the most literal of scientific illustrators deployed a "truth to nature" paradigm.

> To see like a naturalist required more than just sharp senses; a capacious memory, the ability to analyze and synthesize impressions, as well as the patience and talent to extract the typical from the storehouse of natural particulars, were all key qualifications.[12]

Being truthful to nature, they suggest, was a culturally conditioned practice.

Air pumps, used to create an observable vacuum, and thermometers were some of the many tools that Enlightenment scientists used to objectify and to quantify the natural world. As historians of science have effectively demonstrated, the choice of instrument, indeed the very desire to quantify certain things in certain ways, strongly conditioned the facts that a scientific community accumulated and the conclusions that it drew from them. Artistic representations, like their scientific relations, were also the product of material and technological choices, which invariably inflected the nature of their insights.

In the visual arts, the eighteenth century is often viewed as a placid interregnum between the discoveries of the Italian Renaissance and the ruptures of the nineteenth century. Yet this underestimates the importance of aesthetic consolidation and cultural dissemination. The power of pictorial naturalism depended, to no small degree, on its replicability. Image reproduction was overwhelmingly accomplished in metropolitan printing houses that combined heavy machinery with specialized labor. Those printed images generated a kind of ad hoc encyclopedia of all that had been observed and recorded in the world. From those comparative and historical juxtapositions arose new disciplines with a modern, visual basis distinct from older exegetical traditions. Particularly notable beneficiaries included botany, zoology, geography, archaeology, and the histories of art and architecture.

The eighteenth century witnessed, in particular, a dramatic expansion of printmaking, which was largely produced from copper plates with rolling presses. European printmakers sought new means to reproduce the subtle naturalistic effects entrusted to them in sketches, watercolors, and oil paintings. Initially, these translations were made almost exclusively through etched and engraved lines, like the fine lines that delineate Hooke's flea. When Hooke translated what he saw through the lens of a microscope onto a sheet of paper, he surely understood that his task was not complete. He handed his drawing to an engraver who translated those marks onto a copper plate with yet another set of mark-making conventions. While these translations could be visually persuasive, artists and printmakers sought more refined means to represent tone and color on the printed page. Mezzotint printing offered one means of publishing subtle tonal prints, but the "bloom" of the mezzotint copperplate faded quickly, and the process was limited to expensive fine art reproductions. Another intaglio process, called aquatint, came into regular use in the 1770s and rapidly established itself as a popular means of reproducing landscape views. In the last decade of the century a relief process termed "wood engraving" and a planographic process called lithography both made their appearance, and we enter fully into what has been termed the "illustration revolution." Color proved more resistant to mass reproduction, and it was largely left to hand colorists prior to the invention of chromolithography in the mid-nineteenth century.

FIGURE 8.4 Jean-Baptiste-Siméon Chardin, *A Lady Taking Tea*, 1735. Oil on canvas. The Hunterian, University of Glasgow, Scotland. © Wikimedia Commons (public domain).

For Robert Hooke, illustration was not simply a means of transcription but also a part of the experimental process. To draw was to discover the essence and meaning of an object. The art historian Michael Baxandall has questioned whether painters might have approached the world in a similar frame of mind. To test this thesis, he examined a 1735 painting by Jean-Baptiste-Siméon Chardin of a *Lady Taking Tea* (Figure 8.4). Baxandall traced a number of ways in which Chardin's painting participated in a kind of vulgar Lockeanism, deploying the optical and cognitive theories of John Locke, particularly as they relate to the nuances and irregularities of visual perception.

Chardin is one of the great eighteenth-century narrative painters: he can and often does make a story out of the contents of a shopping bag. He narrates by representing not substance—not figures fighting or embracing or gesticulating—but a story of perceptual experience masquerading lightly as a moment or two of sensation: sometimes he jokes about this fiction with momentary substances like spinning tops or frozen steam from a tea-cup.[13]

Chardin's *Lady Taking Tea* reversed the logic of Hooke's flea, for it began with a well-known subject and then rendered it *as if* it were a fleeting visual impression. Both of these innovations became part of an expanding toolkit of pictorial naturalism in the eighteenth century.

FIGURE 8.5 Pierre Filloeul after Jean-Baptiste Siméon Chardin, *A Lady Taking Tea*, etching and engraving, 1759, published by Jacques Philippe Le Bas. © The Trustees of the British Museum.

Oil painting was uniquely suited, in many ways, to the subtlety of Chardin's observational insights. This did not prevent him from finding an engraver to reproduce the work in print (Figure 8.5). The limits of this translation are readily apparent in the curving, etched lines of steam that issue from the teacup like clouds from a witch's kettle. Emphasis is placed instead on the sentimental reverie of the woman, heightened by the poem at the bottom, which asks "if this boiling liquor could warm your heart." Naturalism was just one pictorial virtue among many, even as it underpinned most representations. At the same time, naturalism posed a constant and evolving set of challenges to those charged with its reproduction.

NATURALISM ACROSS GENRES

Naturalism was the diatonic scale of European art, we might say. As with the whole and half step conventions of Western music, naturalism was described by contemporaries not by its dominant feature, but rather by the styles and variations in which the standard scales were performed. Artists debated the relative merits of *disegno* (drawing) versus *colore* (color) in the production of portraits and history paintings. Representations of landscape

FIGURE 8.6 Paul Sandby, *Hackwood Park, Hampshire*, exhibited 1764. Oil on canvas. © Yale Center for British Art, Paul Mellon Fund.

were described as beautiful, sublime, or picturesque depending on a host of factors including paint handling, subject matter, scale, and level of detail. The richness of these terms paralleled the growing importance of landscape painting as a genre, particularly in Great Britain. A great many landscapes depict figures in the landscape looking, subtly cueing the spectator's own gaze. While landscape views of private property, such as Paul Sandby's view of Hackwood Park (Figure 8.6), dominated the first half of the century, touristic views of the Lake District, the Cliffs of Dover, and the Alps proliferated in the second half. While not everyone could enter the landowning classes, a confraternity of taste opened the doors to a wider public.

Stylistic choices and debates operated within a larger register of pictorial naturalism in which perspectival space and figurative representation were largely taken for granted. One challenge to this pictorial regime came with the elaborate adornment of elite interiors in a style retroactively and dismissively termed the rococo. This chapter is primarily concerned with two-dimensional representation, and it should be admitted that the arts of architecture, sculpture, ceramics, and textiles were not bound to the conventions of pictorial naturalism in the same manner as drawing and painting. With the rococo, painting was pulled out of its rectangular frame and inserted into a variety of irregular formats in which it became a functional part of interior design, which included stucco work, mirrors, and decorative wall painting. A stunning example of this can be found in the Parisian Hôtel de Soubise where the *Salon ovale de la princesse* includes canvases by

FIGURE 8.7 Gabriel Germain Boffrand, architect, *Salon ovale de la princesse*, Hôtel de Soubise, Paris, 1730s. © Chatsam—Own work, CC BY-SA 3.0.

François Boucher, Charles-Joseph Natoire, and Carle Van Loo (Figure 8.7). In addition to elite domestic interiors, the rococo also appeared in European palaces and churches, putting on a particularly exuberant display in Bohemia. In music too we find a variant of the rococo, sometimes termed the *style galante*, which was particularly influential in the opera houses of Naples, Venice, Dresden, Berlin, and Paris.

But even the paintings of Boucher, to take one of the most famous rococo painters, still largely adhered to conventions of perspectival space and human figuration. To be sure, many of his paintings were surrounded by decorative and design elements that undermined "picture window" borders that contributed to the autonomy and rationality of Western painting. But the "artificiality" of rococo painting soon brought censure upon it. This is how the French *philosophe* Denis Diderot opened his criticism of Boucher's paintings in the French Royal Academy Salon of 1765: "I don't know what to say about this man. Degradation of taste, color, composition, character, expression, and drawing have kept pace with moral depravity. What can we expect this artist to throw onto the canvas?"[14] Diderot championed paintings with either a rigorous classicism or an insistent naturalism. He died the same year that Jacques-Louis David completed the *Oath of the Horatii* (1784), a painting that Diderot never saw, but which offered an uncompromising commitment to both (Figure 8.8).

Diderot's Salon criticism, which circulated in manuscript across the Royal Courts of Europe, also makes it clear that pictorial naturalism was used and interpreted differently depending on a painting's genre. The French Royal Academy of Arts promoted a hierarchy

FIGURE 8.8 Jacques-Louis David, *Oath of the Horatii*, 1784. Oil on canvas. © RMN-Grand Palais / Paris, musée du Louvre / Gérard Blot / Christian Jean.

of genres, particularly in oil painting, that was widely adopted by art schools across Europe in the eighteenth century. Descriptive arts, such as still life and landscape, were at the bottom of this pyramid, while figurative arts, for instance, portraiture and scenes of everyday life, made up the middle ranks. At the top of the pyramid were complex multi-figure compositions, such as altarpieces and history paintings, which required literary sophistication as well as technical control. Generally speaking, the pyramid had straightforward Aristotelian description at the base and sophisticated Platonic ideation at the pinnacle. History paintings were not just technical feats, but lessons in contemporary virtue, illustrating stories from the Bible and the classical past that could educate and inspire the viewer. In France, the majority of these large-scale pictures were commissioned by the state through the patronage of the Director General of the King's Buildings. It was risky to try to criticize the French King in print with the potential for censorship or worse. More latitude was given authors to critique "official" art at the biannual Salons. In the right hands, art criticism could offer a subtle, veiled critique of not just state-sponsored art but also of those behind it.

Held at the Louvre Palace, the biennial Salon welcomed Parisians free of charge into the Salon Carré where they could view a spectacular series of contemporary paintings. Pietro Martini's engraving of the 1785 Salon provides a glimpse of the hierarchy of genres in action, with small-scale paintings and landscapes at the lower levels, rising to state-sponsored history paintings, which appeared "on the line," which was the line formed by

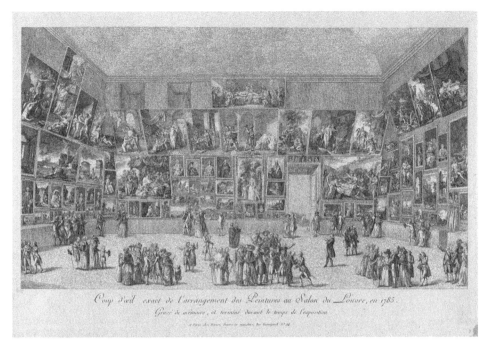

FIGURE 8.9 Claude Bornet after Pietro Antonio Martini, *A Precise View of the Arrangement of Paintings at the Salon du Louvre in 1785*, etching, 1785. © The Trustees of the British Museum.

the bottom edge of large history paintings in the Salon (Figure 8.9). Jacques-Louis David's *Oath of the Horatii* takes pride of place on the far wall, and even in the engraving we glimpse how its compositional simplicity, repetition of gesture, and broad swaths of un-modulated color enabled it to stand out among a cacophony of paintings. David represents an exchange that is just as fraught as the one painted by Tupaia sixteen years earlier. In this case, the power struggle takes place between generations of the same family. Three sons swear an oath on their father's sword to fight to the death for the glory of Rome. They will fight against three Curatii brothers, one of whom is secretly betrothed to a Horatii sister. Their oath to country is made, therefore, at the expense of domestic peace, as women and children collapse in a huddle on the right. To quote Baxandall, this is a painting structured by "figures fighting, embracing, and gesticulating." David's approach is far from the peaceful reverie and perceptual ambiguity of Chardin's lady taking tea.

But then again, David's insistent naturalism accomplishes something important in this painting. Sunlight streaming in from the upper left throws each muscle into soft relief, and the drape of fabric renders static poses more dynamic. While David's protagonists are absorbed in their own poignant drama, the viewer lingers over perceptual reality effects that enhance the painting's immediacy, persuasiveness, and vitality. Compared to other paintings in the Salon, David's canvas is stark and devoid of polite visual conventions; there are no naked putti, lush interior designs, or subtle variations in emotional response. David's painting glints hard as steel. *The Oath of the Horatii* is largely conventional, however, in its use of the heroic male figure. Studies of the male nude were the cornerstone of academic history painting, and David's virile oath-swearing was also a showcase for the heroic male form.

FIGURE 8.10 Léon-Mathieu Cochereau, *The Studio of Jacques-Louis David*, 1814. Oil on canvas. © www.lacma.org.

A student of David named Léon-Mathieu Cochereau helps us to visualize the importance of figure drawing to academic practice, painting a view of his master's studio in 1814 (Figure 8.10). After first learning to copy two-dimensional drawings and prints, aspiring painters were then encouraged to make two-dimensional sketches of three-dimensional sculptures, typically from plaster casts of Greek and Roman masterpieces. Having learned those skills, students were permitted to draw "from the life," which is what we observe in this painting. The students and nude model are all male, a prerequisite that ostensibly upheld moral standards while at the same time maintaining a male monopoly in the Academy. As in the *Oath of the Horatii*, sunlight is strictly regulated and musculature is subtly modeled.

CLASSICISM AND ITS DISCONTENTS

Formalized in the eighteenth century, the study of the naked male form has been a central component of artistic training in the West ever since, although the practice has waned recently in art schools. We may now be able to see Cochereau's painting as a visual record of a highly controlled, quasi-cultic cultural practice in which a select group of boys were

FIGURE 8.11 Thomas Williamson after John Boyne, *A Meeting of Connoisseurs*, hand-colored engraving, 1807. © The Trustees of the British Museum.

formed into a fraternity of sacred storytellers. In this rite of passage the boys became men by translating sense impressions of the naked male form into glorious heroes from the ancient past. We find the practice caricatured in an English print of 1807 titled *A Meeting of Connoisseurs* (Figure 8.11). Once again it is left to caricature to juxtapose Western aesthetics with ethnic and cultural difference. The print takes up a similar theme to that of Cochereau, but this time in the garret of an impoverished London artist. He has invited five gentlemen into his studio, a mixed lot with unflattering faces and physical proportions, to evaluate the preliminary drawing on his easel, which shows the ideal proportions of the famed classical statue, the Apollo Belvedere. The racist joke at the heart of this print is that the artist in the print is modeling his drawing on a Black sweeper, with broom in hand. Tall and well muscled, the sweeper is an excellent model for Apollo's physical proportions. Nonetheless, the joke is on any "connoisseur" who believed that such a comparison could be drawn between a contemporary Black Londoner and a Greek god. Subtle aesthetic judgments were useless, this print declared, in the midst of racial difference.[15]

In these two studio views, dating from nearly the same moment, we can discern some of the parameters around, and fissures within, a European set of cosmopolitan artistic practices. In both instances, we should not be surprised to find the male nude model transformed into idealized visualizations of the classical past. Neoclassicism was international in its scope, and it articulated European identity in the later eighteenth and early nineteenth centuries as an inheritance from ancient Mediterranean culture. Appeals to the classical pasts of Athens and Rome had been a central part of Western culture since the Italian Renaissance. Neoclassicism was an intensification of this cultural process, and one in which the visual arts played an outsized role. Material fragments of the classical past were avidly sought and highly praised, and painters, sculptors, and architects imaginatively combined and enlivened these fragments into vital, immediate works of art. One of the most influential theorists of neoclassicism was the German scholar and antiquarian Johann Winckelmann who declared in his *Thoughts on the Imitation of Greek Works in Painting and Sculpture* (1755) that "the one way for us to become great, perhaps inimitable, is by imitating the ancients." This seeming paradox would inspire and frustrate contemporary artists for decades to come, as neoclassicism blossomed into a pan-European movement. There was nothing dry or stale about Winckelmann's admiration for classical statuary, however, as it drew from the author rich, erotically charged passages of description and analysis. Winckelmann would go on to produce a monumental *History of Art in Antiquity* (1764) that would link the development of sculptural style with historical and political developments in ancient Egypt, Persia, Etruria, Rome, and above all, Greece. In the process, Winckelmann produced a generative template for the historical study of art in which trajectories of cultural rise and fall were mapped onto the expansion and constriction of political liberties and democratic institutions.

The cosmopolitanism of neoclassicism was severely tested, however, in the years between the outbreak of American Revolution in 1776 and the fall of Napoleon in 1815. The tumult of the French Revolutionary and Napoleonic Wars shattered European consensus on nearly everything, except perhaps the authority of classical culture. Caspar David Friedrich's religiously infused landscapes in Prussia, William Blake's mythical prints in England, and Francisco Goya's expressive history paintings in Spain can be viewed as reactions, at some level, to French political and cultural claims. Even so, official cultural channels and artistic institutions changed surprisingly little. The restored Bourbon monarch in Spain, Ferdinand VII, quietly placed in storage Goya's riotous paintings of Spanish resistance, including the gut-wrenching firing squad taking aim in the *Third of May 1808* (painted in 1814). The King then commissioned neoclassical history paintings in support of the Restored Monarchy.

Rapid imperial expansion and vociferous debates over slavery further challenged classicism's ability to articulate a single cosmopolitan, European cultural identity. The French Republic abolished slavery in its colonies in 1794 only to have Napoleon try to restore the institution in 1802. The British parliament abolished the slave trade in 1807, but did not pass legislation abolishing slavery as an institution until 1833. *A Meeting of Connoisseurs* draws its anxious humor from these debates. Cultural racism, like that seen here, became increasingly important in post-abolition Britain. As their humanity was legally restored, Black Britons faced a more insidious form of social and cultural pressure as "white" or "Western" Britons (a new category of subjectivity that did not always include the poor or the Scots-Irish) sought to limit the rights, privileges, and opportunities of Black people in Europe and in the colonies.[16] Overlaps in the discourses of aesthetics, racial theorizing, and caricature have only recently become subjects of academic inquiry, and yet Western pictorial naturalism became self-conscious, in many respects, in precisely those overlapping regions.[17]

FIGURE 8.12 Benjamin West, *The Death of General Wolfe*, 1770. Oil on canvas. © William L. Clements Library, University of Michigan.

Few paintings juxtapose the heroic male figure of history painting with the ethnographic figure of the imperial periphery as forcefully as *The Death of General Wolfe* (Figure 8.12). The American-born painter Benjamin West exhibited the painting at the Royal Academy exhibition in London in 1771. The painting represents Britain's conquest of French Canada in 1759 on the "Plains of Abraham" just outside the walls of Quebec. This was a climactic moment in what the American colonists described as "The French and Indian War," which they named for the two main threats that they faced on the Western and Northern frontier. The painting combines elements of the altarpiece, as General Wolfe expires Christ-like among devoted mourners, with classical history painting. Wolfe and his second-in-command Monckton reach weakly across the painting's central void to make contact, like a latter-day Achilles and Patroclus. The painting's innovative melding of epic form with contemporary dress prompted King George III to ask why the artist should "exhibit heroes in coats, breeches, and cock'd hats." The President of the Royal Academy of Arts, Joshua Reynolds, initially balked at the conceit, fearing that the painting entertained the exhibition public with a spectacular national victory instead of elevating the public's taste for classical forms and Platonic aesthetic values.[18] Particularly interesting is the displacement of nudity from the classical hero to the observant Native American. The Algonquin man's attributes, including his beaded pouch, tomahawk, and headdress were made after Native American objects in Benjamin West's personal collection, and they bolstered the painting's ethnographic accuracy. They also turned West's colonial American upbringing to his advantage. In a broader sense, the painting revealed a growing skepticism that heroic male nudes could signify in a modern, imperial world where nakedness was often viewed as a marker of "uncivilized" cultures. New tensions had begun to emerge between nakedness and nudity in art, overlain with the complexities of contemporary imperial experience.

David's painting of the *Oath of the Horatii* was meant to strip-down history painting to its bare essentials, to represent civic virtue in a visual language accessible to all. Yet it still relied on a complex analogy between the early Roman Republic and the monarchy of Louis XVI. It was a costume drama of the ancient past for a knowing segment of the Parisian public. With "contemporary history painting" by contrast, the audience no longer needed to know classical history or myth to grasp the virtues on offer. *The Death of General Wolfe* proclaimed victory for the "Moderns" over the "Ancients." To the imperial Grandeur of Rome, Great Britain would add the virtues of Protestant faith and mercantile wealth.

This optimism extended to France in the early stages of the French Revolution, and Jacques-Louis David embraced the moment with his own history painting in contemporary dress. The *Oath of the Tennis Court* commemorates an oath taken by members of the Third Estate to resist the dissolution of the Estates General. David exhibited the chalk drawing (see Figures 8.13 and 8.14) at the Royal Academy exhibition of 1791, and hoped to garner enough subscriptions for a reproductive print of a massive painted version. Finding few subscribers, David elicited the support of the National Constituent Assembly, which funded the painting in 1792 from the public treasury, backed in part by the anticipated sale of reproductive prints. A fragmentary canvas is all that is left of that commission, with each male figure sketched in heroic nude outline.[19] The ideological framework of the painting, David insisted, had to be classical and republican, and it had

FIGURE 8.13 Jacques-Louis David, *Oath of the Tennis Court*, 1791. Drawing and wash on paper. © RMN-Grand Palais / Gérard Blot / Versailles, châteaux de Versailles et de Trianon.

FIGURE 8.14 Jacques-Louis David, *Oath of the Tennis Court*, uncompleted fragment, 1791–1792. Black and white chalk and oil on canvas. © RMN-Grand Palais / Franck Raux / Versailles, châteaux de Versailles et de Trianon.

to draw upon an academic tradition of idealization that now, thrillingly, felt applicable to France's political moment. But the radical contingency of that moment soon passed with David finishing the portraits of just four legislators. As the French Revolution moved into the Terror, and as Girondins were ushered to the guillotine, the canvas became impossible to complete. Those floating heads became an eerie reminder of the fate of those swept before a Revolution they had helped to swear into existence.

THE END OF EIGHTEENTH-CENTURY CERTAINTIES

The "really modern times," E. H. Gombrich wrote in *The Story of Art*, "dawned when the French Revolution of 1789 put an end to so many assumptions that had been taken for granted for hundreds, if not thousands, of years."[20] To this story the art historian Ian McLean has countered that "Aborigines living around Sydney harbour faced a much more profound break in the assumptions of their civilization when the revolution of 1788 exploded on their shores."[21] That Revolution consisted of the "First Fleet" of 750 convicted British felons and the hundreds of marines and family members who were compelled to secure them there. White settler colonialism, as it came to be known, took place in other quarters of the world, and yet the contest between indigenes and colonists took on a particular charge in Australia, where Aboriginal history had unfolded for at least 60,000 years, largely on its own terms, prior to the arrival of Europeans.

This chapter suggests that the "Story of European Art" was profoundly shaped by exploration and empire. Processes and techniques of pictorial naturalism were honed on ships as well as in studios, and they contributed to conceptions of modern Western identity that were inextricably bound to the natural, cultural, and ethnic difference that traveling artists encountered. Tupaia's "oath of the crayfish" has much to teach us about the ethics and authority of David's *Oath of the Horatii*.

FIGURE 8.15 William Westall, "Blue Mud Bay, body of a native shot on Morgan's Island," pencil drawing, 1803. © William Westall, National Library of Australia, nla.obj-138891099.

Captain Cook's encounter with Australia in April 1770 set in motion a cycle of accumulation that would make the colonization of Sydney Harbor possible. Maritime exploration continued in 1802 and 1803 with the circumnavigation of Australia by Matthew Flinders and his crew. A pencil drawing by William Westall, official draftsman of the Flinders expedition, bears the inscription, "Blue Mud Bay, body of a native shot on Morgan's Island" (Figure 8.15). This haunting image represents a Yolngu elder from Arnhem Land wearing wrapped armbands. A small hole perforates his chest from which a thin stream of blood saturates a patch of ground below. The left foot is severed from the body and is represented next to it, possibly suggesting a dissection of some sort. This is the art of description at a disturbingly objective remove, as if the artist/witness bore no connection or responsibility to "a native shot on Morgan's Island." Turned upright, the drawing could be mistaken for an academic nude, although Aboriginal facial characteristics precluded such a reading for true "connoisseurs."

Westall surely did not expect the "natives" of Australia to survive colonial incursion and reassert their claim to the land. Yet the Yolngu people have shown remarkable persistence and adaptability, bringing into the present a tradition of bark painting that is second to none in aesthetic sophistication and narrative complexity. In 1996 Manydjarri Ganambarr painted an ancestral shark with earth pigments on bark, a work of art that makes claims on the land no less assertive than Paul Sandby's painting of Hackwood Park. Manydjarri represents the shark swimming in Buckingham Bay at the bottom of the bark painting (Figure 8.16). According to tradition, when the shark was speared by a harpoon it rushed onto shore, the shimmering cross-hatching revealing its power, as it gouged out watercourses in Arnhem land. Traces of the shark's form in the landscape can be seen in the upper half of the painting.[22] Here is a radical alternative to humankind's relationship to the land, as it articulates the ancestral claims upon which possession lies.

In the pluralism of today's global art world, the aesthetic certainties of Banks and Westall look decidedly untenable and frail. This is not to deny the power of naturalistic representation, which was mobilized at the centers of calculation to act on the world at a distance. But it is now possible to acknowledge the contingency and relativism of naturalism's conventions. It is also possible to ask how those values shaped European art and identity in the eighteenth century and beyond.

FIGURE 8.16 Manydjarri Ganambarr, *Djambarrpuyngu Marna*, 1996. Earth pigments on bark.
© The artist, licensed by Aboriginal Artists Agency Ltd © Milingimbi Art & Culture.

CHAPTER NINE

History: Narratives of Progress

CAROLINE WINTERER

During the period roughly 1650–1800, a new species of history emerged, called "philosophical" in its day and "Enlightenment" today. It molded the history of Europe and its empires into a narrative of progress from an irrational, barbaric past to a rational, civilized present epitomized by eighteenth-century Europe. Crowding out previous genres of history that had focused more narrowly on royal and ecclesiastic lineages and the detailed recounting of battles, philosophical histories offered something quite different and new. Their pages opened a sweeping narrative of rising and falling empires, of distinct ages characterized by certain defining cultural mores so palpably clear that they inspired eighteenth-century painters to represent them in vibrant color and detail. Philosophical history poured from presses in France, Ireland, the Holy Roman Empire, England, Spain, Sweden, and the Americas. Translated into modern vernaculars and disseminated in new genres such as encyclopedias, magazines, and newspapers, these new narrative histories schooled everyone from princes to farmers. An increasingly literate public read them alone or aloud to others in homes, academies, universities, salons, and coffeehouses.

Philosophical historians revolutionized Western thought by imagining that "history" was a largely secular, human-driven process that moved through universally shared stages from an age of barbaric unreason to one of civilized reason. Its revolutionary nature is best grasped by comparing it to the kind of history written before. In seventeenth-century France, for example, historians such as Henri de Boulainvilliers wrote a form of genealogical history that celebrated the roots of the French nobility in the feudal era and its ongoing noble rights, prerogatives, and connections to the royal family. The goal of this kind of historical research and writing was to maintain the political and social status quo, as well as to emphasize the importance of localities vis-à-vis the centralizing impulses of the monarchy.[1] By contrast, the "philosophic" histories of the eighteenth century were written not to support dynastic or parochial interests, but to illuminate the canvas of all of humanity within the context of nations and empires, or even all humankind.

As such philosophical history offered itself as the preeminent source of insight into human nature itself. Eighteenth-century historians hoped to paint a picture of human nature in its broadest strokes, as a universally shared characteristic of *Homo sapiens* (a category also invented in the eighteenth century). In this way, philosophical histories are also the parents of modern anthropology, a strain of thought that developed in the eighteenth and nineteenth centuries to explain the past and present of the whole of humanity. The philosophical historians also gave common people a powerful new weapon. Armed with a new notion of history as the story of humanity itself, ordinary people could strive not just for enlightenment and happiness, but even for revolution in the name of the natural rights and liberties that philosophical history told them was their birthright. It is no exaggeration to say that the age of revolutions could not have occurred without the inspiring new narrative frame provided by philosophical history.[2]

We can marvel at the ambition of these philosophical histories in setting the story of humanity on the grandest stage of time and space. A list of some of the most celebrated (in roughly chronological order, by author) would include Voltaire's *History of Charles XII* (*Histoire de Charles XII*, 1731), *The Age of Louis XIV* (*Le Siècle de Louis XIV*, 1751); David Hume's *The History of England* (1754–1762); William Robertson's *The History of Scotland, 1542–1603* (1759), *The History of the Reign of Charles V* (1769), and *The History of America* (1777); Catharine Macaulay's *History of England from the Accession of James I to that of the Brunswick Line* (1763–1783); the Abbé Raynal's *Philosophical and Political History of the Settlements and Trade of the Europeans in the East and West Indies* (*Histoire philosophique et politique des établissemens, et du commerce des Européens dans les deux Indes*, 1770); Edward Gibbon's *The History of the Decline and Fall of the Roman Empire* (1776–1788); Francesco Saverio Clavigero's *Ancient History of Mexico* (*Storia Antica del Messico*, 1780–1781); and David Ramsay's *The History of the American Revolution* (1789). Most people at this time hewed to a short, 6,000-year chronology for the creation of the earth and its peoples. So launching a narrative among the ancient Greeks and Romans meant that philosophical histories enfolded practically the whole of terrestrial and human history. No wonder readers gasped at the ambition and sweep of the new histories published in the eighteenth century: only the Bible itself offered a plausible rival as the great story of humanity. By 1757, the Scottish historian and philosopher David Hume proudly declared that history was "the most popular kind of writing of any."[3]

If we accept Hayden White's modern definition of history as "a verbal structure in the form of a narrative prose discourse," then the previous paragraphs pretty well capture the major historical achievements of the period 1650–1800.[4] But if we take a broader definition of history—as including not just the paper world of prose but also material artifacts and the totality of lived human experience—then a wider field opens. Embedded in a wider cultural context, philosophical histories shaped the world around them while in turn reflecting the social, economic, and political changes of their era. There was not one "history" but multiple "histories" that people in the period 1650–1800 created. These histories were experienced by ever-broadening publics in books, buildings, ruins, monuments, paintings, household furnishing, dress, and travel: in brief, in the many new venues opened by the expansion of literacy, communication, education, and political participation.

This chapter focuses on three major cultural sites that reveal in concrete ways the varieties of historical experience available to people in Europe and its colonies in the period 1650–1800: cities, classicism, and archives. None were new at this time, but all underwent profound transformations in size, scope, and purpose. That so many of the philosophical histories were published in major cities gives us a clue that urbanization played an important role in the creation, dissemination, and reception of the philosophical histories. In the period 1650–1800, people in European and American cities swollen by the new riches and functions of commercial empires began to rework the past to make sense of the present. Within this eclectic historicism, the classical past soon emerged as the visual lingua franca of communication across Europe and the Americas, channeling the past for multiple modern agendas from the political to the personal. With growing empires came a flood of paperwork as state and local archives attempted to collect and centralize knowledge from around the world. No previous generation had ever enjoyed such easy access to the record of the recent past. Archives now joined existing antiquarian cabinets as major sources of information that could be used to sew together the vast historical canvases that characterized "philosophical" histories. The age of revolutions occurred within these preexisting urban, classical, and archival contexts. While revolutionary rhetoric promised to sweep away an ignoble past of tyranny and tradition, in fact postrevolutionary histories built, as we will see, upon the intellectual and material remains of the prerevolutionary past.

CITIES

The place: 7 Bentinck Street in London, new home of the historian Edward Gibbon (Figure 9.1). The time: the decade of 1773–1783, when over half of Britain's American colonies won independence from the largest empire the world had seen since Rome.

FIGURE 9.1 Edward Gibbon, engraving by A. Chappel, 1873. Gibbon lived from 1737 to 1794. © Getty Images.

Seated in his London house after a Grand Tour that had taken him on a shattering visit to the ruins of ancient Rome, Edward Gibbon labored over what would become the six volumes of the *Decline and Fall of the Roman Empire*. The first volume alone proved a runaway success with both men and women. It lay "on every table, and almost on every toilette," according to the happy author.[5]

Eighteenth-century London was the incubator for the *Decline and Fall*, a project fundamentally urban in its conception and execution. His mind on ancient Rome and the world it had conquered, Gibbon stalked modern London's numerous learned societies and booksellers to fill his personal library. A seat in Parliament trained his sights on the empire beyond. "I never found my mind more vigorous, or my composition more happy, than in the winter hurry of society and parliament," Gibbon wrote of his London headquarters for the *Decline and Fall*.[6] The London publishing juggernaut of Strahan and Cadell ensured a wide audience for the great history that finally emerged between 1776 and 1788, twelve years to which the Declaration of Independence and the United States Constitution formed sobering bookends. For the lessons of Gibbon's *Decline and Fall* were as relevant as they were hard. Even the mightiest empires could be brought to their knees by unlikely forces, be they invading barbarians, rebellious colonists, or upstart cults that promised a better life in a world beyond.

Gibbon's London was one of many European cities being remade by over two centuries of global commercial empire building that turned them into financial, political, and cultural capitals. Enriched and enlarged beyond all previous imagining, cities now harnessed the past in new ways for the project of public enlightenment. Intellectuals across a range of topics converged on the idea that the path to progress lay in an educated public. In his essay "What is Enlightenment?" (1784), the German philosopher Immanuel Kant urged ordinary people to use their own reason as their guides, rather than slavishly hewing to received tradition. A knowledge of history was now deemed essential to public enlightenment. Lord Bolingbroke's popular *Letters on the Study and Uses of History* (1752) insisted on the utility of history to modern wisdom. "Whilst they narrate as historians, they hint often as philosophers," he wrote admiringly of historians.[7] Moreover, the idea of public enlightenment found expression not just in a rising tide of books but also in museums, palaces, boulevards, libraries, coffeehouses, salons, and gardens. Here, the past was slowly but surely reorganized for modern consumption. From Saint Petersburg to Rome, from Paris to Mexico City, the new historical sensibilities of the age of Enlightenment transformed imperial capitals and provincial cities by channeling the past as a total experience. The grandiose philosophical histories could not have been conceived, researched, written, published, and shipped without the cultural and financial might of modern cities now riveted on the past.

Though similar trends were afoot in other cities, London—in its sheer size and cultural reconstruction—exemplifies on the grandest scale the new historical sensibilities of the eighteenth-century city. The financial, cultural, and political nerve center of the British Empire, London had become Europe's largest city by 1750. Its 750,000 inhabitants now enjoyed museums, libraries, stately boulevards, and gardens that channeled the past as a total experience. The Great Fire of 1666 had instigated a massive rebuilding project, and London had become a city of the new. New roads crossed the city, new buildings pushed out into new suburbs, and new city gates replaced the narrow medieval openings perpetually clogged with traffic.[8]

Yet amid the new, the past was not only present but remade for modern needs. Old buildings were refurbished, disguising their antiquity. Christopher Wren's new dome

FIGURE 9.2 St. Paul's Cathedral, London. © Getty Images.

for St. Paul's Cathedral—originally a Roman basilica—replaced the crumbling medieval spire (Figure 9.2).[9] Horace Walpole's turreted Strawberry Hill House in Twickenham, London, was the first house to be built in a deliberately medieval style from scratch, rather than by using an existing medieval base. Hearkening to an idealized medieval past, Walpole's gingerbread confection presaged the larger-scale Gothic Revival of the nineteenth century. The new British Museum, founded in 1753, displayed antiquities plundered from Egypt, Greece, Rome, and the near East.

By the eighteenth century, history painting had risen to the top of the hierarchy of genres because it was thought to best reveal the universal essence of things, in contrast to lower genres such as still life that seemed to merely copy surface appearances. Previously confined mostly to palaces, cathedrals, and other stately venues, history paintings now became much more visible to the general public through a growing array of museums and public exhibitions. Some history paintings even began to reflect the narrative structure on which new philosophical histories hinged. Chief among these was the stadial view of history in which all human societies were thought to climb from hunting to pasturage to agriculture and then finally to the highest stage of civilization, commercial society.

This schema was especially associated with Scottish historians and philosophers who had seen their own nation rise from rags to something closer to riches through expanding commerce over the eighteenth century. Scots such as Adam Ferguson (*An Essay on the History of Civil Society*, 1767), John Millar (*Observations Concerning the Distinction of Ranks in Society*, 1771), Lord Kames (*Sketches of the History of Man*, 1774), and William Robertson found a wide audience of readers eager to set the dizzying economic changes of their era into a compelling narrative frame. Publicly displayed in London's Society for the Encouragement of the Arts, Manufactures, and Commerce (f. 1754), James Barry's

The Progress of Human Knowledge and Culture (1777–1783) captured the stadial view in a series of six enormous canvases. The sequence began with the Greek mythological figure Orpheus and ended in the afterlife, in Elyseum. In the mortal realm, Barry depicted Britain—and more specifically London—as the culmination of all human history. This narrative was especially clear in the fourth panel, entitled "Commerce, or the Triumph of the Thames." As Father Thames (Neptune) and nereids swim in the Thames, they are ferried along by various illustrious British seafarers such as Sir Walter Raleigh and James Cook, as modern British ships sail in the distance.[10] Gazing at Barry's painting, Londoners could see their nation and its capital city as the apotheosis of history and civilization.

London now also became a global center for history publishing. Several trends converged at once. First, with aristocratic patronage in decline, publishing a popular history book could supply a vital source of income. David Hume's *History of England* (1754–1762) became a bestseller, finally giving him the financial independence he had long sought.[11] Second, literate people began to read extensively (widely but more shallowly) rather than intensively (deeply in just a few books, chiefly the Bible and devotional texts).[12] London publishers responded to this shift in supply and demand. They published histories in small and large formats from folio to duodecimo that a variety of pocketbooks could afford. They shipped them to British colonies in North America, the Caribbean, India, and East Asia along with English translations from French, German, Swedish, and Spanish that ensured a wide audience in the empire.[13] One overwhelmed observer in the early eighteenth century guessed that there were over thirty thousand works of historiography in print.[14] Studies of other nations show a similar trend. In the German states for example, roughly 15 percent to 20 percent of all books published in the eighteenth century were on history, surpassed only by philosophy and theology.[15]

An increasingly literate public reached for new guidebooks to help them navigate a large city that mixed past and present in often confusing jumbles. *The Ambulator* (1774), a guidebook to London that saw thirteen editions over the next half century, led readers on a walking tour of London that explained the rise of the city from the age of "ancient, uncivilized Britons," through the medieval and Restoration periods, and into the period the author called "modern."[16] As the history-reading public swelled, so did the publication of printed chronologies in a variety of new shapes and sizes. Pinwheels, rivers, graphs, and other visual devices helped readers make sense of conflicting and confusing chronologies of rising and falling kingdoms from the biblical Creation to the present day. Children of both sexes were encouraged to copy passages from them, as history reading became an essential component of the moral education of children.[17] The most influential timeline of the eighteenth century was Joseph Priestley's *A Chart of Biography* (1765), which offered categories of influential people—including "Historians"—stretching from the biblical Saul through the eighteenth century. Priestley's chart culminated in King George III, whose royal library formed a cross section of eighteenth-century historical taste.[18]

CLASSICISM

Anyone walking through eighteenth-century London would not have failed to register the most obvious historical idiom of all: classicism. The symmetrical, columned buildings designed by Scottish architect Robert Adam in what became known internationally as the "Adam Style" evoked the monumental grandeur of ancient Rome at the height of its imperial reach. The Adam style was symptomatic of the enthusiasm for ancient Rome and Greece that now gripped Europe and its colonies. Building on the classical revival that began in the Renaissance, which had sought models of ethics, politics, and education that antedated the power of the Catholic Church, eighteenth-century Europeans and Americans rapidly deepened and widened their admiration for antiquity. More readers and a new class of consumers demanded an ever-growing supply of classical histories, classical public and domestic architecture, and classical home decoration and clothing. Philosophical histories could launch their narratives in Greece and Rome because their authors presumed the common fund of classicism among their educated readers.

The ancient Greeks and Romans had not known that they were "classical." The word was coined in English in the seventeenth century to describe not just Greco-Roman culture but also the social prestige it conferred (*classicus* in Latin referred to the highest class of citizens). Since the Renaissance, immersion in Greco-Roman texts had been encouraged as a direct preparation for public life. A classical education trained orators, statesmen, lawyers, scholars, ecclesiastics, and kings. At a time when Latin was the major language of scholarly life in Europe and its colonies, a classical education also greased the wheels of international relations. A common fund of texts, famous episodes, myths, and images pervaded the political language of the late seventeenth and eighteenth centuries. After 1500, books on classical themes were published in a growing number of modern European vernacular languages so that they could reach beyond the world of scholars.

Classicism was education for power. In France, Louis XIV fashioned Versailles in the late seventeenth century as a mythical-historical monument to French classicism in the service of absolutism. The Sun King liked to dress as Apollo, golden rays sprouting from the sides of his head. The throne room of Versailles, known as the Salon of Apollo, cast Louis as the symbolic center of the empire, his fawning courtiers only sighting him as the culmination of a series of gilded galleries featuring scenes from classical mythology.[19] But anti-absolutism could just as easily be wrapped in classicism. In 1699, François Fénelon, tutor to the young Duke of Burgundy (second in line to the throne of France), published *The Adventures of Telemachus* (*Les Aventures de Télémaque,* 1699) (Figure 9.3). This thinly veiled allegory follows the young son of Ulysses around the Mediterranean as he searches for his father with the help of a wise guide named Mentor. Immediately perceived as an attack on the absolutist policies of Louis XIV, this illustrated book became one of the runaway bestsellers of the eighteenth century. Its scenes even featured as the entryway wallpaper in the slave plantation mansion of American president Andrew Jackson as late as the 1830s.

In contrast to the exuberant and palpable physicality of classicism in urban architecture and mythological paintings, most formal classical education was almost entirely text based. Grinding through Greek and Latin was a form of virility cultivation through intellectual and sometimes physical punishment. Because the culture of eighteenth-century public life was highly oral, young people had to learn to bring classical texts to life through rhetorical performance. Boys memorized and then recited set pieces, such as the first fifty lines of Virgil's *Aeneid*. They publicly debated classically themed topics, such as whether Hercules had made the right choice by foregoing the pleasures of the flesh for the more difficult path to glory through physical hardship. Illustrated elocution manuals taught the proper classical poses and gestures that helped deliver the message to large audiences who might struggle to hear the speaker clearly.

To call this education "classical" is a misnomer, though, since that word implies equal coverage of all ancient societies. In fact, the main focus was the history of Rome. Lessons

FIGURE 9.3 Illustration from François Fénelon, *Les Aventures de Télémaque* (1793). © Getty Images.

from Roman history were deemed particularly useful for modern leaders in an age when cyclical history still commanded widespread assent. As Rome had risen and fallen through the rise and fall of each citizen's virtue, so would modern republics, monarchies, and empires. Roman lessons were drawn from a highly selective cast of characters and episodes that drove home the dogmas of civic humanism. The story of Rome's rise from huts huddled along the Tiber to its conquest of the Mediterranean in the first century CE was a treasure house of exempla. Livy, Virgil, Ovid, and Cicero provided models of oratory, martial valor, and stoic endurance in the face of misfortune. All these authors were believed to arm boys from both elite and middling families for a public life in a world so saturated by classicism that only a few thought it completely ridiculous for a modern politician to don a toga to make a speech or to pose for a portrait.

Even women, barred from public life, found inspiring exempla in the ideal of the Roman matron. Eighteenth-century paintings, engravings, books illustrations, stained glass windows, fans, and needlework samplers depicted exemplary figures such as the widowed Cornelia, mother of the Gracchi, who raised her two sons for service to Rome. Adopting the persona of the Roman matron even allowed a few highly educated eighteenth-century women to publish works of history, normally considered the domain of men only (the assumption being that you had to have participated in politics and war to write histories about them). The first English woman to become a published historian was Catharine Macaulay, whose *History of England from the Accession of James I to that of the Brunswick Line* (8 volumes, 1763–1783) told a republican-friendly story of England's ascent to its glorious age of Roman-style liberty under the seventeenth-century Commonwealth, "the brightest age that ever adorned the page of history."[20] Macaulay herself appeared in profile on the frontispiece of her history and in paintings in austere Roman costume. But as always, the classical knife could cut both ways ideologically. In his anti-revolutionary *Reflections on the Revolution in France* (1790), the Anglo-Irish statesman and philosopher Edmund Burke praised the imprisoned French queen, Marie-Antoinette, for enduring her humiliations with the stoic dignity of a Roman matron.[21]

Catharine Macaulay's history joined a raft of other histories of Rome published during the eighteenth century. Montesquieu's *Considerations on the Causes of the Greatness of the Romans and Their Decline* (*Considérations sur les causes de la grandeur des Romains et de leur décadence*, 1734) and Gibbon's *Decline and Fall* both took the causes of the "rise," "decline," and "fall" of the Roman Empire as their main subject. Like coroners dissecting a corpse, eighteenth-century historians studied the life cycle of the Roman Empire to guide their own imperial projects. Forgotten today, other eighteenth-century writers also produced Roman histories for a brisk market. The French Jansenist Charles Rollin's illustrated and often-translated *Roman History* (1738–1741) and *Ancient History* (1730–1738) were widely consulted not just by men but also by women and children, who could also learn about memorable episodes from its many copperplate engravings. The novelist, playwright, and spendthrift Oliver Goldsmith, now better remembered for the fictional *The Vicar of Wakefield* (1766) and *She Stoops to Conquer* (1773), turned to hack history writing with his *Roman History* (1769).[22]

Within this Rome-saturated culture, ancient Greece gradually began to reemerge in the eighteenth century. The rising appeal of Greece culminated in the broad cultural and intellectual movement of nineteenth-century philhellenism, which crafted a new political genealogy that made Greeks the ancestors to modern European and American democracies. But the seeds of philhellenism lay in the period 1650–1800. For the first time, Greece began to appear from behind the overwhelming cultural domination of Rome, providing historians and others with an array of imaginative possibilities for the reconstruction of self and society.

The reasons for Greece's relatively hidden position compared with Rome were both political and cultural. Mainland Greece and the Greek islands were largely inaccessible to Europeans until the middle decades of the nineteenth century because the Ottoman Turks ruled the area. What is more, democracy itself was, even at the close of the eighteenth century, deemed a more dangerous political experiment than representative republicanism, which could filter the suggestible voices of the giddy multitude from the political process. Finally, the many city-states of Greece provided an alarming example of why disunity and localism proved fatal to Greek political liberty. Having just helped to draft the United States Constitution, which substituted a strong centralized federal government for the weak and disunited Articles of Confederation, James Madison issued a wholesale condemnation of ancient Greece in essay #18 of *The Federalist* (1787–1788). He specifically cited the fragmented, warring city-states as a cause of their fall to Rome. "Had Greece, says a judicious observer on her fate, been united by a stricter confederation, and persevered in her union, she would never have worn the chains of Macedon; and might have proved a barrier to the vast projects of Rome."[23]

Another problem with Greece in the eighteenth century concerned historical narration itself. Unlike Rome, which offered a fairly tidy story with a beginning, middle, and end, the scattered city-states of Greece resisted narrative coherence. This problem was pointed out by the English writer Temple Stanyan, one of the first to publish a book whose title announced a coherent history of a place so long deemed incoherent: *The Grecian History* (3 volumes, 1707, 1743, 1749). It was easy to adopt the perspective of Rome, which could always remain at the center of the action as it relentlessly conquered the peoples around it, wrote Stanyan. But for Greek history, "it is no easy Task to marshal so many Events in due Order of Time and Place, and out of them to collect an intire unbroken Body of History."[24] Over the course of the eighteenth century, however, more and more historians naturalized the idea that ancient Greece possessed something so unitary as "a" history. This was achieved by the late eighteenth century by (in England) William Mitford, *The History of Greece* (5 volumes, 1784–1810), and (in Scotland) John Gillies's *The History of Ancient Greece, Its Colonies and Conquests* (2 volumes, 1786). Both Mitford and Gillies were monarchists skeptical of democracy. One of their signal achievements was, nonetheless, to pioneer a comprehensive narrative of ancient Greek history based on ancient sources.[25] Published in quartos, Mitford and Gillies reached a broad audience and set the stage for the major Greek histories of the nineteenth century that became pamphlets for modern liberalism and democratic politics. The British parliamentarian George Grote's *History of Greece* (12 volumes, 1846–1856), for example, assumed un-problematically that "a" narrative history of Greece could be written. By 1900, Greece would be cast as the political ancestor to what was christened "western civilization." This conceptual novelty transformed American higher education in the first half of the twentieth century and gave rise to the Western civilization course, a marvel of genealogical thinking that drew a straight line from ancient Greek to modern American democracy.[26]

The international market for antiquities now also helped to push ancient Greece into the limelight. The very infatuation with ancient Rome that sent hundreds of well-heeled Europeans to Italy each year on the Grand Tour also led them to discover what had been hiding in plain sight for two thousand years: the evidence for the ancient Greek empire in Italy known as Magna Graecia. Massive Doric temples south of Naples loomed picturesquely in the landscape, inviting new interest in the civilization that antedated the rise of the Roman Empire by several hundred years. Painters produced numerous landscape renderings of the temples at Paestum, which dated from the eighth century BCE (Figure 9.4). Antonio Joli's *A View of Paestum* (1759) showed modern travelers pausing among what remain even today the best preserved Greek Doric temples in the world. The moment also provided the opportunity for southern Italian scholars to assert their importance, even as the cultural gravity of Europe was shifting north. Eighteenth-century scholars in Naples, such as Alessio Simmaco Mazzocchi, now turned to Magna Graecia to locate a past greatness for the south of Italy, a region mired in poverty and relegated to the fringes of the historical narrative of ancient Roman triumph.[27]

The eighteenth-century recovery of Greek antiquity helped Europeans—and then later, Americans—to posit local, regional, and even national identities that skirted

FIGURE 9.4 Second Temple of Hera, Paestum, Italy. © Getty Images.

the harder edges of Roman militarism and imperialism. Just as classicism since the Renaissance had provided an alternative political and moral language to Christianity, now ancient history itself split along new geographical and chronological lines to meet modern needs. Greece's role was to become the representative of a sensual and palpable physicality, a pure aesthetics of beauty that would eventually come to stand as the authentic, individual voice of the citizen in a democracy. "Everyone should be Greek in his own way! But he should be Greek!" Johann Wolfgang von Goethe would insist.[28] The German traveler Johann Joachim Winckelmann helped to set the stage for the rise of the aestheticized Greek individual. His *The History of the Art of the Ancients* (*Geschichte der Kunst des Alterthums*, 1764) idealized ancient Greek beauty and periodized ancient Greek history according to aesthetic standards. The material artifacts of civilization, Winckelmann proposed, could tell a story of growth, maturity, and decline. Casting beauty as the highest achievement of art, Winckelmann delineated the political, social, and intellectual conditions that fostered or deterred the pursuit of beauty and creativity. With Winckelmann something like what we might call the "history of art" as a separate way of perceiving the past was born, with "art" now assuming its modern character as an aesthetic realm removed from and morally superior to markets or mere getting and spending.

ARCHIVES

Whether writing ancient or modern history, eighteenth-century historians increasingly believed that their histories should rest on archival research. Although archives first emerged in the ancient world as places to house government records (the Greek term *arkheion* means residency of the magistrates), they proliferated in the early modern period. The word *archive* first appeared in English in the 1600s.[29] A number of factors were at work: rising literacy among non-elites such as clerks, technological changes such as the printing press, communication improvements like the postal service, ballooning state and religious bureaucracies, and the record-keeping needs of a growing number of learned societies, joint-stock companies, and universities.

Archives facilitated a new kind of history writing in which documents could figure more prominently because vastly more accessible. Footnotes swelled in size as texts rested more and more on their authority. The growing focus on archival documents also reflected changing standards of what counted as reliable evidence. Verisimilitude—focusing on the natural and probable rather than the fabulous or trivial—now became an important task for the historian. More and more histories in the eighteenth century dispensed with the classical idea that the historian should have been a participant in the event he or she described. But the tradeoff now was that historians had to adhere to modern notions of probability and likelihood in a world governed by Newtonian laws of physics.[30] Voltaire's entry on "History" for Diderot and d'Alembert's *Encyclopédie* summed up the new dispensation. Voltaire devoted most of his entry to refuting the notion that history was an unreliable form of knowledge. "History is the narrative of facts presented as true, in contrast to the fable, which is the recitation of facts presented as false," he declared in the opening sentence of the entry.[31]

The greatest engine of archival growth now became European empire building in Asia, Africa, and the Americas. Colonial archives by the eighteenth century influenced the way history of both the West and the non-West was written, for archives could be used both to support and to undermine the territorial and political claims of empire builders. In the metropole and the colonies, administrators absorbed a growing river of information from a diversity of human societies, some entirely unknown to Europeans before 1492. The term *intelligence* began to be used after 1500 to refer to knowledge concerning recent events, especially information of military value. Desperate for up-to-date information about the colonies, administrators pioneered new kinds of documents that allowed for streamlined information retrieval. The questionnaire or "query," as it was known in the eighteenth century, became a favorite intelligence-gathering tool for imperial administrators, and historians were quick to see its advantages. The Scottish historian William Robertson's *History of America* epitomized the new quest for an empirically based historical method. Writing in Scotland for an English-speaking audience with limited direct knowledge of Spain's New World colonies, Robertson proudly detailed the enormous amount of research that he had done in the quest for what he called "scrupulous accuracy."[32] Striving for the fastidious new research standards set by Gibbon's *Decline and Fall*, Robertson tapped contacts at the British Embassy in Madrid to gain access to what he called "several valuable manuscripts" and to rare sixteenth-century Spanish books. He formulated forty-four queries about American Indian customs that his Madrid contacts distributed to Spaniards who had spent time in the New World colonies.[33]

Colonial archives, such as the ones Robertson consulted, profoundly shaped Enlightenment historical writing in several ways. At the most basic level, they added a whole new dimension of source material, with new languages, forms of writing and record-keeping that were pictorial rather than primarily linguistic, and new artifacts from the feathered headdresses of the Inca to the beaded moccasins of the Iroquois. All of these exotic objects found their way into European archives. Even European portrait paintings reflected the new interest in material culture. A 1644 portrait of the Electress Sophie of Hanover by her sister, Louise Hollandine of the Palatinate, shows Sophie dressed as a South American Indian, posed among palm trees with a red-feathered cloak.[34] These sources could also draw attention to the problems of bias in historical writing more generally, putting pressure on the Enlightenment's drive to craft universalizing narratives that applied to all humanity in all times and places. By the middle of the eighteenth century, Henry St. John, Viscount Bolingbroke, was already wondering about the problem of subjectivity in historical narration by conquered peoples.

> If we had the history of Canaan writ by a Canaanite, that of Carthage by a Carthaginian, or that of Mexico and Peru by a Mexican and Peruvian, figure to yourself how the hospitality, the fidelity, the innocence, and simplicity of manners, of all these people, would be exemplified in various instances, and what further proofs would be brought of the ferocity, the treachery, the injustice, and cruelty of the Israelites, the Romans, and the Spaniards, of the first and the last especially.[35]

The case of Mexico City in Spain's American colonies provided a stark example of these facts. Contrary to the "fall" narrative beloved of many philosophical historians, the Aztec (Nahua) imperial capital of Tenochtitlan was not destroyed with the Spanish conquest of 1521. At first contact, the city's native population had been roughly 200,000 to 300,000 (larger than any contemporary European city), and it stood as the capital of a vast Mesoamerican tribute empire. The invading forces of Hernán Cortés brought horrific destruction, as diseases such as smallpox decimated Indigenous populations and the Spanish actively destroyed the Nahua urban infrastructure, especially the great temples, which they disparaged as signs of Indian idolatry. Still, many features of the pre-conquest city endured in what the Spanish were soon calling Ciudád Mexico (Mexico City). Nahua geographical names, administrative buildings, aqueducts, rituals, and even the original axis of the city itself persisted in modified new forms for centuries after.[36] Thus, like London in the middle of the eighteenth century, Mexico City's urban landscape became a patchwork of new and old, of history and modernity.

A great deal of the pre-contact Nahua archival record also endured in new forms. Before the conquest, Nahua scribes in Tenochtitlan and other cities painted colorful pictorial manuscripts on bark paper (*amatl*) and animal skins. These formed a kind of collective memory for the Nahua, depicting everything from royal genealogies to founding narratives to solstices to dreams.[37] Called "codices" by Europeans, whose reference point was Greco-Roman manuscripts, the most beautiful and colorful Nahua manuscripts were shipped to Europe to decorate princely cabinets and church archives, and their modern names (such as the Codex Borbonico) reflect that Europeanization. In the century after the conquest, native Mexicans then generated a hybrid literary culture that mixed the Nahua pictographic tradition with Spanish script. Native scribes and thinkers, some directly descended from the pre-Hispanic aristocracy of central Mexico, learned not just Nahua but also Spanish and Latin, forming a vital administrative link between the small European ruling class and pre-Hispanic local traditions.

One Indigenous Mexican archive in particular shaped the many histories of New Spain that were published in Europe and the Americas in the period 1650–1800. This Indigenous archive culminated in one of the most influential philosophical histories of the Americas in the eighteenth century, the Mexican-born Jesuit historian Francisco Saverio Clavigero's *Ancient History of Mexico* (1780). In contrast to other popular histories of New Spain written by Europe-based authors who had never set foot in the Americas, Clavigero's history was deeply rooted in the native archive and so was able to dispute the dismal view of the New World propagated by a cadre of leading European intellectuals. The Comte de Buffon's *Natural History* (*Histoire Naturelle*, 36 volumes, 1749–1788), for example, had maintained that the cold and humid climate of the Americas caused animals to degenerate into smaller and less fertile versions of their European cousins. The Dutch geographer and philosopher Cornelius de Pauw applied this insight to human beings in his *Philosophical Research on the Americans* (*Recherches philosophiques sur les Américains*, 2 volumes, 1768), heaping scorn on the "tasteless and rude" codices of the pre-contact Mexicans. Even the Scottish historian William Robertson's *History of America*, which conceded that the empires of Peru and Mexico had ascended higher in civilization than the "rude" tribes of North America, concluded that the hostile climate of the Americas stifled the life force. In this view, even the most civilized, enlightened Mexicans had not been able to rise to the level of European society.[38]

The Indigenous Mexican archive laboriously assembled over 250 years proved to be the key to undoing the dismal narrative propagated of American degeneracy popularized in so many European philosophical histories. This archive began to be assembled in the early seventeenth century by the mestizo chronicler Fernando de Alva Cortés Ixtlilxóchitl (*c.* 1578–1648). As his surname suggests, Ixtlilxóchitl was the descendant of the rulers of the major Mesoamerican city of Tetzcoco, which had been the cultural center of pre-conquest Mexico. The city had then had a botanical garden, baths, a zoo, and a renowned library housing Indigenous manuscripts from around the Valley of Mexico. The Spanish had torched most of the library in their attempts to eradicate native idolatry. Casting himself as the preserver of the pre-conquest past of Tetzcoco, Ixtlilxóchitl saved what he could from what he called the "royal archives": fragments of the codices, maps, and other materials that were spared the flames. To these he added new materials created in the immediate post-conquest period. He also recorded the testimonies of local elders with direct knowledge of the period they called their "ancient histories."[39] From these documents, Ixtlilxóchitl wrote histories that attempted to shed light on the pre-Hispanic past.

This was a remarkable feat of historical preservation and imagination. Less than a hundred years after the devastations of the 1520s, already an archive was forming, along with the effort to link the present to an "ancient history" of America through documentary evidence. What happened afterward was equally important. After Ixtlilxóchitl's death, the archive passed to the Mexican historian and intellectual Carlos Sigüenza y Góngora (1645–1700), who like his predecessor saw the archive's contents as a way to write the history of what he called "the ancients."[40] After Sigüenza y Góngora's death, the archive passed to yet a third person, the Italian antiquarian Lorenzo Boturini Benaducci (1702–1735). Boturini had arrived in Mexico from Spain in 1735 to trace the historical origins of the Virgin of Guadalupe, spending seven years studying Nahuatl and Indigenous Mexican culture, and amassing numerous Indigenous documents, including those preserved by Ixtlilxóchitl and Sigüenza y Góngora. In 1746 Boturini published a list of the manuscripts in his collection, and deposited the collection at the College of Saint Peter and Saint Paul in Mexico City.[41]

It was here, finally, over 250 years after the Spanish conquest, that the pre-Hispanic archives would enter the realm of European "philosophical" history and the reading of the international learned public. This was thanks to the Mexican-born Jesuit Francisco Saverio Clavigero, who used this laboriously maintained local archives to write his internationally renowned *Ancient History of Mexico* (*Storia Antica del Messico*, 1780), the first history to lay out sympathetically and exhaustively the ancient history of the pre-Hispanic peoples of Mexico. Studded with engravings of ancient Mexican marvels such as the Great Pyramid in Tenochtitlan, Clavigero's history rebuked European philosophical historians' assertion that the Indians of the New World were barbarians stranded low on the ladder of civilization. Using the Indigenous Mexican archive assembled by his predecessors, Clavigero mocked the armchair European philosophical historians who used only European archives and painted the American canvas in broad strokes while knowing nothing of the local terrain. He explained in his preface that he had lived in Mexico for thirty-six years, had learned Nahuatl, had studied ancient Mexican manuscripts, and had consulted with relevant locals. Rebutting the argument that only a few of the pre-Hispanic codices had been spared the flames of the Spanish missionaries, Clavigero insisted that huge numbers of codices had survived to undergird the many histories of Mexico written to date, not just by the Spanish but by Mexicans themselves, whose names he listed for the benefit of ignorant Europeans. Grounded in local evidence, these works could rebut what Clavigero called the "massive blunders" of writers such as Buffon, de Pauw, and Robertson. Warming to the idea that American evidence was the best evidence, Clavigero patiently walked his readers through a detailed examination of the content and current location of the precious Mexican codices.[42] Clavigero's work was soon translated into French, English, and other languages, enjoying a wide circulation around the Atlantic world for at least half a century. It even went on to influence nineteenth-century US historians such as William Prescott, whose *History of the Conquest of Mexico* (1843) still drew on Clavigero—and by extension, the Indigenous American archive assembled in the late sixteenth century.

More broadly, Clavigero's *Ancient History of Mexico* formed part of a trend that grew much stronger in the nineteenth century and especially the twentieth century: of writing histories from the subject position of common people, whether these were the colonized, the enslaved, the working class, or other groups that had lurked at the fringes of philosophical histories. In this development, the eighteenth-century novel proved to be a close ally to history writing. The novel prioritized individual experience and dignified the daily dramas of women, servants, and children. The archive of the eighteenth-century epistolary novel was—like so many eighteenth-century histories—the humble letter. Both eighteenth-century histories and novels strove for a kind of realism, the first through the renunciation of "fable," the second through an attempt to capture the particular idiosyncratic truths of an individual's ordinary experience.[43] In these ways, eighteenth-century history both shaped and was shaped by the culture around it.

REVOLUTIONS

In July 1776, American revolutionaries tore down the gilded lead statue of George III in New York City and soon after changed the name of King's College to Columbia College in honor of the invented new goddess of American republican government. Fewer than twenty years later in 1793, the French beheaded their king Louis XVI and then, some months later, their queen, Marie-Antoinette. Everywhere revolutionary Parisians tried to eradicate the hated symbols of what was now given a new, historical name: the *ancien régime*.

Antimonarchical iconoclasm signaled the fundamental historical rupture of the age of revolutions. In the United States, France, Haiti, and Latin America, "revolution" came to signify that the present age would be sharply separated from the past. What made a revolution revolutionary was not just political and social disruption, but a new sense of possibility that time itself was accelerating into a better tomorrow.[44] Revolutionaries around the Atlantic committed themselves to a new political language of relentless futurity and progress, one that painted the prerevolutionary past as an age of primitive and barbaric darkness to be scorned and left behind.

Historians became engines of modern rights-based revolutions by publishing new histories that anticipated human-directed progress away from a benighted past of aristocratic and ecclesiastical privilege and toward an "enlightened" future of universal human rights based in the natural order. The abbé Raynal's *Philosophical and Political History of the Settlements and Trade of the Europeans in the East and West Indies* (1770) developed the history of European colonies in the Americas and the East and denounced European cruelty, religious intolerance, and arbitrary authority over colonized peoples. Though it bore Raynal's name as author, the *Histoire des Deux Indes* was in fact a compilation from numerous hands, with many of the more radical historical interpretations penned by the *encylopédiste* Diderot.[45] In the midst of their eight-year war against Britain, American revolutionaries eagerly read Raynal, quoting the French *philosophe* in letters as an authority on their historic rights and liberties. From Paris in 1778, John Adams pressed his American friends for facts that would help Raynal revise his history in light of modern standards of archival accuracy. "The Abby Reynel [*sic*] is writing an History of this Revolution, and is very desirous of obtaining authentic Documents. Can you help him to any?" John Adams asked his fellow Bostonian Thomas Cushing in 1778.[46] Adams's efforts paid off. In 1780, a revised edition of Raynal's *Histoire des Deux Indes* appeared that included a new section on the American Revolution; that section was then published in London and translated as *The Revolution of America* (1781). Drawing heavily on Thomas Paine's incendiary pro-revolutionary pamphlet, *Common Sense* (1776), Raynal declared that the American Revolution fundamentally ruptured history itself. "The present is about to decide upon a long future," wrote Raynal in *The Revolution of America*. "All is changed. ... A day has given birth to a revolution. A day has transported us to another age."[47]

Everywhere new histories of national revolutions soon appeared, many written by partisans actively involved in the cause. Haiti's revolution was covered in *An Historical Account of the Black Empire of Hayti* (1805) by Marcus Rainsford, a British soldier who became an admirer of Toussaint L'Ouverture, the former slave who led the uprising. In the United States, the South Carolinian David Ramsay's *History of the American Revolution* (2 volumes, 1789) showed how virtuous American farmers, merchants, mechanics, and fishermen won independence from the corrupt British. From Massachusetts came Mercy Otis Warren's *History of the Rise, Progress, and Termination of the American Revolution* (3 volumes, 1805), which cast the revolution as the story of rising American liberties.

But it was the French Revolution that caused the most cataclysmic rupturing of what it meant to write "history." Major histories of the French Revolution that appeared in the nineteenth century included Thomas Carlyle, *The French Revolution: A History* (3 volumes, 1837), Jules Michelet, *History of the French Revolution* (*Histoire de la Révolution Française*, 7 volumes, 1847–1853), and Alexis de Tocqueville, *The Old Regime and the Revolution* (*L'Ancien Régime et la Révolution*, 1856). Karl Marx, whose own history of the French Revolution was never completed, nonetheless thought that it was the most important revolution in world history. Its underlying logic, according to Marx and his many scholarly followers, was a class struggle of bourgeois property against the old feudal interests, and therefore a victory for the new social order of modernity.

For these observers, the French Revolution was the great fissure in the eyes of most Europeans that separated the premodern world from the modern world of capitalism, individualism, democracy, and bourgeois values. As Tocqueville put it, "The French made, in 1789, the greatest effort that has ever been made by any people to sever their history into two parts, so to speak, and to tear open a gulf between their past and their future."[48] The French Revolution's causes and effects were to be read universally. As the opening sentence of Charles Dickens's novel *A Tale of Two Cities* (1859) phrased it, the French Revolution could only be received "in the superlative degree."[49]

Classicism—that international language of verbal and visual communication—was also pressed into the service of revolution, becoming the first major language of modern, secular propaganda. It was precisely the familiarity of classicism that allowed it to cloak the new in the most ancient and comforting motifs. Revolutionaries stripped classical motifs to their bare minimum—a style later dubbed "neoclassicism"—claiming that they were purging the world of the secretive and degenerate ostentation of monarchy's gilded and ornamented classicism. The clean, simple lines of neoclassicism would be the visual incarnation of the commonsense clarity of equality based on natural law. All around the Atlantic, revolutionaries converted classicism into the banner of kingless, republican government. In France, Jacques-Louis David's great paintings *Oath of the Horatii* (1784) and *The Death of Socrates* (1787) led the way with a scoured, linear aesthetic that dwelled on themes of stoic self-sacrifice. One of the great paradoxes of the Industrial Revolution was to elevate the classical aesthetic of self-abnegating civic virtue into a consumer commodity. Neoclassicism thereby became the first international style that consumers could buy to cultivate that self-abnegating political persona. Josiah Wedgwood's pottery factory in England, named Etruria to evoke the rustic simplicity of pre-Roman Italy, churned out a stream of teacups and serving platters that spread the new gospel of republican classicism even to nations only grasping faintly at republican principles, such as Sweden. The most extensive refashioning of classicism in the service of republican revolution was the new American city of Washington, DC. One of the first planned cities of the modern period, it rose from the swamps of Maryland and Virginia with a Roman-style grid plan and white neoclassical buildings that declared the innocent republican aspirations of the new United States.

Cities became repositories for new, postrevolutionary archives that facilitated the writing of histories that described the inexorable rise of the modern nation-state. The challenge of new national archives was to preserve the records of the now-discredited *ancien régime* while also differentiating that archive from the paperwork of the postrevolutionary regime. In Paris, the National Archives were founded as the parliamentary archives of the National Assembly, and then in 1794 developed into the central archives of the French state that would help to consolidate the documentary past leading to republican France. In the United States, the Library of Congress, founded in 1800 in Washington, DC, aimed to become both a depository of all "American" publications but also to school sitting legislators in the United States Congress. Its origins as the private library of Thomas Jefferson dramatize the shift from history writing as a private, gentlemanly activity to an activity performed in service of the nation-state. Archives also set about publishing volumes of their contents to disseminate them to publicly minded citizens eager to write amateur national histories.[50] In the United States, the first documentary editions of what would soon be called "the founding fathers" allowed for the formation of a hero-worshipping national cult. Jared Sparks, the first person to hold a chair in modern history at Harvard University, published edited—and in the view of some critics, bowdlerized—editions of the writings of George Washington and Benjamin Franklin.

The professorship of Jared Sparks at Harvard testified too to a larger transition in which the writing of history moved into universities. What had been the province of a genteel elite with the education and means to write history for broad publics now became the specialized craft of professionals trained in new, more "scientific" methods. Scientific history was born in early nineteenth-century Germany, where scholars hoped to remake German cultural institutions as a substitute for the wholesale political revolution that had transformed France but bypassed them.[51] German professors emphasized a new pedagogy of self-culture, or *Bildung*, a kind of inward revolution by which studious individuals— rather than the alarming armed collectives of the French Revolution—attained a higher wisdom and sense of wholeness. At Göttingen, Heidelberg, Leipzig, Freiburg, Berlin, and other German universities, professors pioneered an array of techniques for plumbing the past: philology, numismatics, epigraphy, paleography, and sigillography, all pursued with laser-like rigor aimed at uncovering "what really happened." The rise of scholarly professional journals, professional historical societies, and other professional rituals eventually bifurcated the project of writing history into general and scholarly branches, each finding their own readerships.

Today, few people, whether scholars or the general public, read the philosophical histories of the long eighteenth century. Receding behind the "scientific" histories that superseded them in the nineteenth century, the philosophical histories now appear charming but factually unmoored and aphoristic rather than authoritative. Much of the political and cultural context that made them gripping to their readers has likewise disappeared. Classicism is no longer a political, ethical, or aesthetic model; cities are no longer the only major sites of historical memory; and modern anthropology has discredited the hierarchical barbarity-to-civilization ethnological model on which many of these narratives hinged.

Yet Voltaire, Gibbon, Macaulay, and others still whisper to us today. The Enlightenment's biological framing of a national and imperial rise and fall, as well as the narrative of inevitable progress, both seem so ordinary today that many people are incredulous and even offended when these are revealed as the inventions of the Enlightenment rather than as laws of nature. Perhaps most importantly, the historians of the Enlightenment bequeathed to us the germ of the idea that history could be about everyone and for everyone, a legacy that continues to unfold today.

NOTES

Introduction

1 *The Aberdeen Magazine* 3, 1788–1790, 35.
2 James Van Horn Melton, *The Rise of the Public in Enlightenment Europe: New Approaches to European History* (Cambridge: Cambridge University Press, 2001), 96.
3 Melton, *The Rise of the Public in Enlightenment Europe*, 206.

Chapter 1

1 Brin quoted in "Google Receives $25 Million in Equity Funding," Google Press, June 7, 1999. Available online: http://googlepress.blogspot.com/1999/06/google-receives-25-million-in-equity.html (accessed January 23, 2022).
2 Ann Blair, *Too Much To Know* (New Haven, CT: Yale University Press, 2010); see also, Helmut Zedelmaier, *Werkstatten des Wissens zwischen Renaissance und Aufklärung* (Tubingen: Mohr Siebeck, 2015).
3 Gygory Markus, "Changing Images of Science," *Thesis Eleven* 33, no. 1 (August 1992): 1–56.
4 Pope, *The Dunciad, Variorum 1729* (Leeds: Scolar Press, 1966), 21; see, Paula McDowell, *The Invention of the Oral: Print Commerce and Fugitive Voices in Eighteenth-Century Britain* (Chicago: University of Chicago Press, 2017).
5 This percentage increase is based on the number of listed titles in the Leipzig Book Fair catalog, which went from 755 titles in 1740 to 1,144 in 1770 and then to 2,569 in 1800. See Rudolph Jentzsch, *Der deutsch-lateinische Büchermarkt* (Leipzig: Voigtländer, 1912).
6 "Wissenschaft," in Johann Christoph Adelung, *Grammatisch-kritisches Wörterbuch der hochdeutschen Mundart* (Vienna: Bauer, 1811), 4:1582–3. For a more extensive discussion, see Chad Wellmon, *Organizing Enlightenment: Information Overload and the Invention of the Modern University* (Baltimore: Johns Hopkins University Press, 2015), 3–4.
7 See Wellmon, *Organizing Enlightenment*, 45–6.
8 Johann Heinrich Zedler, *Grosses Vollständiges Lexicon aller Wissenschaften und Künste* (Leipzig: Johann Heinrich Zedler, 1746), 50:1393.
9 Helmut Zedelmaier, "Suchen und Finden vor Google: Zur Metadatenproduktion im 16. Jahrhundert," in *For the Sake of Learning: Essays in Honor of Anthony Grafton*, volume 18, edited by Ann Blair and Anja-Silvia Goeing, 423–40 (Leiden: Brill, 2016).
10 "Vorrede zu der vorigen Auflage," in Christian Gottlieb Jöcher, *Compendiöses Gelehrten-Lexicon* (Leipzig: Friedrich Gleditsch, 1733), 1:4.
11 "Vorrede zu der vorigen Auflage," in Jöcher, *Compendiöses Gelehrten-Lexicon*.
12 "Vorrede zu der vorigen Auflage," in Jöcher, *Compendiöses Gelehrten-Lexicon*.
13 "Vorrede zu der vorigen Auflage," in Jöcher, *Compendiöses Gelehrten-Lexicon*.
14 Compare to Adrian Johns, *The Nature of the Book* (Chicago: University of Chicago Press, 1998).
15 Jean le Rond d'Alembert, *Preliminary Discourse to the Encyclopedia of Diderot*, trans. Richard N. Schwab (Indianapolis, IN: Hackett, 1963), 4.

16 D'Alembert, *Preliminary*, 314; Denis Diderot, "Encyclopédie," in Denis Diderot and Jean le Rond d'Alembert, eds., *L'Encyclopedic ou dictionnaire raisonnee des sciences, des arts et des metiers* (Paris, 1780; reprint as compact edition, New York, 1969), 644.

17 Quoted in Daniel Rosenberg, "An 18th-century Time Machine: The *Encyclopédie* of Denis Diderot," in *Postmodernism and the Enlightenment*, edited by Daniel Gordon, 45–67 (London: Routledge, 2001).

18 See Bradley Pasanek and Chad Wellmon, "The Enlightenment Index," *Eighteenth Century Theory and Interpretation* 56, no. 3 (Fall 2015): 357–80.

19 Staffan Müller-Wille, "Collection and Collation: Theory and Practice of Linnaean Botany," *Studies in History and Philosophy of Biological and Biomedical Sciences* 38 (January 2007): 541–62, 558.

20 J. G. Sultzer, *Versuch einiger moralischen Betrachtungen über die Werke der Natur* (Berlin: 1745), 22.

21 Sultzer, *Versuch einiger moralischen Betrachtungen*, 6.

22 "Naturgeschichte," *Allgemeine Literatur-Zeitung*, May 22, 1790: 409. For a more extensive discussion, see Wellmon, *Organizing Enlightenment*, 77–107.

23 Jonas Maatsch, *Naturgeschichte der Philsopheme* (Heidelberg: Universitätsverlag Winter, 2008), 39.

24 Wilhelm Traugott Krug, *Versuch einer neuen Eintheilung der Wissenschaften* (Sulechów, Poland: Darnmann, 1805), iii.

25 Kant's definition of system: "the unity of mannigfaltigen Erkenntnisse unter einer Idee" (KrV B 860).

26 Compare the notion of the self-organization of print to the various forms of self-organization described by Jonathan Sheehan and Dror Wahrman, *Invisible Hands: Self Organization and the Eighteenth Century* (Chicago: University of Chicago Press, 2015).

27 Pasanek and Wellmon, "The Enlightenment Index," 357–80. The Multigraph Collective, "Index," in *Interacting with Print* (Chicago: University of Chicago Press, 2018).

28 Johann Heinrich Christoph Beutler and Johann Christoph Friedrich Gutsmuth, *Allgemeines Sachregister ueber die wichtigsten deutschen Zeit- und Wochen-schriften* (Leipzig, 1790), ii–iii.

29 Beutler and Gutsmuth, *Allgemeines Sachregister*, 1:iv.

30 Beutler and Gutsmuth, *Allgemeines Sachregister*, 1:vii.

31 Wilhelm von Humboldt, "Über die innere und äussere Organisation der höheren wissenschaftlichen Anstalten in Berlin," in *Wilhelm von Humboldts Gesammelte Schriften: Volume 10, Politische Denkschriften*, edited by Bruno Gebhardt, 250–6 (Berlin: B. Behr, 1903), 251.

32 Wilhelm Traugott Krug, *Versuch einer systematischen Enzyklopädie* (Leipzig: Winckelmann & Barth, 1796), 13.

33 Ulrich Dierse, *Encyklopädie. Zur Geschichte eines philosophischen und wissenschaftlichen Begriffs* (Bonn: Bouvier Verlag, 1977), 117.

34 Hugo Kunoff, *The Foundations of the German Academic Library* (Chicago: American Library Association, 1982), 8–9.

35 Lucian Febvre and Henri-Jean Martin, *The Coming of the Book* (New York: Verso Classics, 1997), 249.

36 Roger Chartier, *The Order of Books: Readers, Authors, and Libraries in Europe between the Fourteenth and Eighteenth Centuries* (Palo Alto, CA: Stanford University Press, 1994).

37 William Clark, "On the Bureaucratic Plots of the Research Library," in *Books and Sciences in History*, edited by Marina Frasca-Spada and Nick Jardine, 190–206 (Cambridge: Cambridge University Press, 2000).

38 Neickel, *Museographia, oder Anleitung zum rechten Begriff und nützlicher Anlegung der Museorum, oder Raritäten-Kammern* (1727), quoted in Georg Leyh, "Die deutsche Bibliotheken von der Aufklärung bis zur Gegenwart," in *Handbuch der Bibliothekswissenschaft*, vol. 3, pt. 2, edited by Georg Leyh, 1–491 (Wiesbaden: Harrassowitz, 1957), 63. On Neickel's *Museographia*, see Tony Bennett, *The Birth of the Museum: History, Theory, Politics* (London: Routledge, 1995).

39 Leyh, "Die deutschen Bibliotheken," 64.

40 See Eric Garberson, *Eighteenth-Century Monastic Libraries in Southern Germany and Austria: Architecture and Decorations* (Baden-Baden: Valentin Koerner, 1998), 41.

41 Zedler, *Grosses Vollständiges Lexicon*, 3:568.

42 Zedler, *Grosses Vollständiges Lexicon*, 22:705.

43 Jeffrey Garrett, "Redefining Order in the German Library, 1775–1825," *Eighteenth-Century Studies* 33, no. 1 (1999): 103–23, 105.

44 Friedrich Nicolai, *Das Leben und die Meinungen des Herrn Magister Sebaldus Nothanker*, vol. 1 (Berlin: Friedrich Nicolai, 1776), 113–14.

45 Quoted in Garrett, "Redefining Order in the German Library," 109.

46 Kunoff, *Foundations*, 122. The rest of this paragraph is based on Kunoff's argument here.

47 Leyh, "Die Deutschen Bibliotheken," 12.

48 Kunoff, *Foundations*, 98.

49 Clark, "On the Bureaucratic Plots," 191.

50 Clark, "On the Bureaucratic Plots," 99.

51 Clark, "On the Bureaucratic Plots," 192.

52 Hans Schulte-Albert, "Leibniz and Literary Classification," *Journal of Library History* 6, no. 2 (1971): 133–52.

53 This is confirmed by a firsthand account that criticizes the original Wolfenbüttel catalog because it was devised according to the number and physical location of the book. See Herrn Zacharias Conrad von Uffenbach, *Merkwürdige Reise durch Niedersachsen, Holland und Engelland* (Ulm, 1754), 356.

54 G. W. Leibniz, *New Essays on Human Understanding*, trans. Peter Remnant and Jonathan Bennett (Cambridge: Cambridge University Press, 1996), 525.

55 Leibniz's sketch (*Idea Leibnitiana: Biblotheca ordinandae contractior*) is reproduced in E. I. Samurin, *Geschichte der bibliothekarisch-bibliographischen Klassifikation* (Leipzig: VEB Bibliographisches Institut, 1964–1967), 348n.

56 Samurin, *Geschichte der bibliothekarisch-bibliographischen*, 526.

57 G. W. Leibniz, *Sämtliche Schriften und Briefe* (Berlin: Akademie Verlag, 1970), 1:6, 56.

58 Leibniz, *Sämtliche Schriften und Briefe*, 1:57.

59 Schulte-Albert, "Leibniz and Literary Classification," 144.

60 Clark, "On the Bureaucratic Plots."

61 This new cataloging process is detailed in Adalbert Hortzschansky, *Die Königliche Bibliothek zu Berlin: Ihre Geschichte und ihre Organization* (Berlin: Behrend, 1908). Perhaps not coincidentally Wihelm von Humboldt had been a student of the philology professor and librarian Christian Heyne at Göttingen.

62 Kunoff, *Foundations*, 12.

63 See William Clark, *Academic Charisma and the Origins of the Research University* (Chicago: University of Chicago Press, 2006).

64 Clark, *Academic Charisma*, 321.

65 Clark, "On the Bureaucratic Plots," 201.

66 Clark, *Academic Charisma*, 323.

67 Kunoff, *Foundations*, 67. Göttingen's first three librarians were Gesner, Michaelis, and Heyne. Kunoff points out that this was in part the case because of economic reasons. Philosophy faculty members were the lowest paid and, unlike members of the higher faculties, had little opportunity to earn a living outside the university.

68 Kunoff, *Foundations*, 68.

69 Friedrich Ebert, *Ueber öffentliche Bibliotheken besonders deutsche Universitätsbibliotheken* (Freyberg: Commission der Craz und Gerlachisch buchhandlung, 1811), 22.

70 Kunoff, *Foundations*, 52.

71 Leyh, "Die Deutschen Bibliotheken," 116.

72 Friedrich Gedike, *"Der Universitäts-Bereiser,": Friedrich Gedike und sein Bericht an Friedrich Wilhelm II*, edited by Richard Fester (Berlin: Alexander Duncker, 1905), 27.

73 Leyh, "Die Deutschen Bibliotheken," 128.

74 Clark, *Academic Charisma*, 320. As Clark writes, Göttingen "rationalized the bibliotheca universalis into a bibliotheca virtualis" (323). See also Markus Krajewski, "Zwischen Häusern und Büchern: Die Domestiken der Bibliotheken," in *Museum, Bibliothek, Stadtraum: Räumliche Wissensordnungen 1600–1900*, edited by Robert Felfe and Kirsten Wagner, 141–52 (Berlin: Lit Verlag, 2010).

75 "Heynes Bericht von 1810," in *Vier Dokumente zur Geschichte der Universitäts-Bibliothek Göttingen*, edited by Karl Julius Hartmann, 14–18 (Göttingen: Häntzchel & Co. 1937), 15.

76 "Heynes Bericht von 1810," 16.

77 Martin Schrettinger, *Versuch eines vollständigen Lehrbuchs der Bibliothek-Wissenschaften oder Anleitung zur vollkommenenen Geschäftsführung eines Bibliothekars in wissenschaftlicher Form* (Munich: Lindauer, 1829). See also Albrecht Christoph Kayser, *Über die Manipulation bey der Einrichtung einer Bibliothek und der Verfertigung der Bücherverzeichnisse* (Bayreuth, 1790). Schrettinger draws on this text throughout. Bibliothekwissenschaft was first institutionalized as a science later in the nineteenth century, with its first chair in 1886. For a broader history of the term, see Krystof Migon, *Das Buch als Gegenstand wissenschaftlicher Forschung: Buchwissenschaft und ihre Problematik* (Wiesbaden: Otto Harrassowitz, 1990), 21–41.

78 Schrettinger, *Versuch*, 80; 2:12.

79 Schrettinger, *Versuch*, 1:46.

80 Schrettinger, *Versuch*, 1:14.

81 Schrettinger, *Versuch*, 2:25.

82 Schrettinger, *Versuch*, 1:25.

83 Schrettinger, *Versuch*, 1:11.

84 Quoted in Garrett, "Redefining Order in the German Library," 116.

85 Clark, *Academic Charisma*, 303; Garrett, "Redefining Order in the German Library," 6.

86 Schrettinger, *Versuch*, 1:15; see Garrett, "Redefining Order in the German Library," 118.

87 "Bibliothekwissenschaft," *Jenaische Allgemeine Literatur-Zeitung* 70 (April 1821): 79.

88 Schrettinger, *Versuch*, 1:49.

89 Schrettinger, *Versuch*, 3:61.

90 Schrettinger, *Versuch*, 3:15.

91 Clark, "On the Bureaucratic Plots," describes this process and everything else related to the emergence of the modern research university as the triumph of the bureaucratic and thus a "move from the material and visible to the formal and rational. It dematerialized books, whose covers became incidental and whose contents essential" (205). The systematic catalog's location of "a book, along with the page number in the catalogue, could give each book a unique signature or trace in the system. In other words, a book's virtual or literary

location or signature in the systematic catalogue—in the system of knowledge—dictated its physical location in the actual order of the library. That reversed the traditional relationship of catalogue and books. The catalogue as a virtual library achieved supremacy over the actual library, the physical order of books" (320).

92 Schrettinger, *Versuch*, 1:15.

93 The arguments to which Schrettinger alludes had been made repeatedly in the last decades of the eighteenth century. See, for example, "Bücherverzeichniß und Bibliothek," in *Deutsche Enzyklopädie oder Allgemeines Real-Wörterbuch aller Künste und Wissenschaften*, edited by Heinrich Köster, Martin Gottfried, and Johann Friedrich Roos, vol. 4, 570–2 (Frankfurt: Varrentrap Sohn & Wenner, 1780); see also Albrecht Kayser, *Ueber die Manipulation bey der Einrichtung einer Bibliothek und der Verfertigung der Bücherverzeichnisse*, edited by Heinrich Köster, Martin Gottfried, and Johann Friedrich Roos (Bayreuth, 1790). Kayser, in particular, argued that an alphabetical catalog was more efficient than a systematic one.

94 Such as Michael Denis, *Einleitung in die Bücherkunde* (Vienna: John Thomas von Trattner, 1778).

95 *Jenaische Allgemeine Literatur-Zeitung* 70 (April 1821): 75.

96 *Jenaische Allgemeine Literatur-Zeitung* 71 (April 1821): 83.

97 Wilhelm Von Humboldt, "On the Internal Structure of the University in Berlin and its Relationship to other Organization," in *Rise of the Research University*, edited by Louis Menand, Paul Reitter, and Chad Wellmon (Chicago: University of Chicago Press, 2017), 108.

Chapter 2

1 Roy Porter, ed., *Rewriting the Self: Histories from the Renaissance to the Present* (London: Routledge, 1997), 11.

2 Jerrold Seigel, *The Idea of the Self: Thought and Experience in Western Europe since the Seventeenth Century* (Cambridge: Cambridge University Press, 2005), 5.

3 Charles Taylor, *Sources of the Self: The Making of the Modern Identity* (Cambridge: Cambridge University Press, 1989).

4 Jerome David Levin, *Theories of the Self* (Washington, DC: Taylor & Francis, 1992), 205.

5 David Wootton, "Unhappy Voltaire, or 'I shall never get over it as long as I live'" *History Workshop Journal* 50 (2000): 137–55. Pages 152–3 have an appendix showing the introduction of "the self" and derivatives such as "self-consciousness."

6 Seigel, *Idea of the Self*, 89.

7 Carl J. Friedrich, ed., *The Philosophy of Kant: Immanuel Kant's Moral and Political Writings* (New York: Modern Library, 1949), ix.

8 Moshe Sluhovsky, *Becoming a New Self: Practices of Belief in Early Modern Catholicism* (Chicago: University of Chicago Press, 2017), 142–3.

9 T. C. W. Blanning, *The Pursuit of Glory: Europe 1648–1815* (London: Viking, 2007), 476.

10 Philip Stewart, *L'invention du sentiment: roman et économie affective au XVIIIe siècle* (Oxford: Voltaire Foundation, 2010), 7.

11 Cecilia Feilla, *The Sentimental Theater of the French Revolution* (Farnham, UK: Ashgate, 2013), 12.

12 John Mullan, "Feelings and Novels," in *Rewriting the Self: Histories from the Renaissance to the Present*, edited by Roy Porter, 119–34 (London: Routledge, 1997), 121.

13 Lynn Hunt, *Inventing Human Rights: A History* (New York: W. W. Norton, 2007), 39.

14 Jan de Vries, *The Industrious Revolution: Consumer Behavior and the Household Economy, 1650 to the Present* (Cambridge: Cambridge University Press, 2008).

15 Cary Carson, "The Consumer Revolution in Colonial British America: Why Demand?" in *Of Consuming Interests: The Style of Life in the Eighteenth Century*, edited by Cary Carson, Ronald Hoffman, and Peter J. Albert, 483–697 (Charlottesville: University of Virginia Press, 1994), 505.

16 Colin Jones, "The Great Chain of Buying: Medical Advertisement, the Bourgeois Public Sphere, and the Origins of the French Revolution," *American Historical Review* 101 (1996): 13–40.

17 Daniel Roche, *The People of Paris: An Essay in Popular Culture in the 18th Century*, translated by Marie Evans (Berkeley: University of California Press, 1987), 162.

18 Quoted by Roche, *People of Paris*, 129.

19 Maxine Berg, *Luxury and Pleasure in Eighteenth-Century Britain* (Oxford: Oxford University Press, 2005), 205.

20 Roche, *People of Paris*, 154.

21 Adelaïde Cron, *Mémoires féminins de la fin du XVIIe siècle à la période révolutionnaire: Enquête sur la constitution d'un genre et d'une identité* (Paris: Presses Sorbonne nouvelle, 2016), 13.

22 Jean-Jacques Rousseau, *Les Confessions: Texte du manuscrit de Genéve* (1782; Ebooks libre et gratuit, 2004), 4. Available online: https://ebooks-bnr.com/ebooks/pdf4/rousseau_les_confessions.pdf (accessed February 5, 2022).

23 Nicholas D. Paige, *Being Interior: Autobiography and the Contradictions of Modernity in Seventeenth-Century France* (Philadelphia: University of Pennsylvania Press, 2001), 4.

24 Stephen Carl Arch, "Benjamin Franklin's *Autobiography*, Then and Now," in *The Cambridge Companion to Benjamin Franklin*, edited by Carla Mumford, 159–71 (Cambridge: Cambridge University Press, 2008), 163.

25 Lise Andries, "Récits de survie: les mémoires d'autodéfense pendant l'an II et l'an III," in *La Carmagnole des Muses: L'homme de lettres et l'artiste dans la Révolution*, edited by Jean-Claude Bonnet, 261–73 (Paris: Colin, 1988), 273.

26 Archives Nationales, AD^{III} 112, d. 12.

27 Archives Nationales, D^{III} 102, d. 17.

28 Archives Nationales, D^{III} 94, d. 6; emphasis added.

Chapter 3

1 Denis Diderot, "Multitude," in *Encyclopédie*, ARTFL Project, available online: https://artfl-project.uchicago.edu/,mytranslation (accessed January 31, 2022).

2 Georges Duby, *The Three Orders: Feudal Society Imagined*, trans. Arthur Goldhammer (Chicago: University of Chicago Press, 1980), 1–9; Sarah Maza, *The Myth of the French Bourgeoisie: An Essay on the Social Imaginary, 1750–1850* (Cambridge, MA: Harvard University Press, 2003), 15–21.

3 Keith Michael Baker, "Enlightenment and the Institution of Society: Notes for a Conceptual History," in *Main Trends in Cultural History: Ten Essays*, edited by Willem Melching and Wyger Velema, 96–108 (Amsterdam: Rodopi, 1994). See also Daniel Gordon, *Citizens Without Sovereignty: Equality and Sociability in French Thought, 1670–1789* (Princeton, NJ: Princeton University Press, 1994), ch. 2.

4 Baker, "Enlightenment and the Institution of Society," 95–6.

5 Sheehan and Wahrman, *Invisible Hands*, ch. 1.

6 Sheehan and Wahrman, *Invisible Hands*, 45.

7 Sheehan and Wahrman, *Invisible Hands*, 157–64.

8   On the popularity of "bee" texts see Dror Wahrman, "On Queen Bees and Being Queens: A Late Eighteenth-Century 'Cultural Revolution'?" in *The Age of Cultural Revolutions*, edited by Colin Jones and Dror Wahrman, 251–80 (Berkeley: University of California Press, 2002).

9   E. J. Hundert, *The Enlightenment's Fable: Bernard Mandeville and the Discovery of Society* (Cambridge: Cambridge University Press, 1994). The first edition of the *Fable* was first published in 1714 but only with the expanded second edition of 1723 did it come to wide attention.

10 Denis Diderot, *Rameau's Nephew and D'Alembert's Dream*, trans. Leonard Tancock (London: Penguin Books, 1966), 168–71.

11 Sheehan and Wahrman, *Invisible Hands*, 57–8.

12 Sheehan and Wahrman, *Invisible Hands*, 250–1.

13 Sheehan and Wahrman, *Invisible Hands*, 264–9.

14 Sheehan and Wahrman, *Invisible Hands*, 225–8.

15 Sheehan and Wahrman, *Invisible Hands*, 239.

16 T. C. W. Blanning, *The Culture of Power and the Power of Culture: Old Regime Europe, 1660–1789* (Oxford: Oxford University Press, 2002), 123–6.

17 Berg, *Luxury and Pleasure in Eighteenth-Century Britain*; Annick Pardailhé-Galabrun, *The Birth of Intimacy: Privacy and Domestic Life in Eighteenth-Century Paris*, trans. Jocelyn Phelps (Philadelphia: University of Pennsylvania Press, 1992).

18 Daniel Roche, *The Culture of Clothing: Dress and Fashion in the Ancien Régime*, trans. Jean Birrell (Cambridge: Cambridge University Press, 1997); Daniel Roche, *A History of Everyday Things: The Birth of Consumption in France, 1600–1800*, trans. Brian Pearce (Cambridge: Cambridge University Press, 2000); Jones, "The Great Chain of Buying."

19 Melton, *The Rise of the Public in Enlightenment Europe*, ch. 7.

20 Carolyn Lougee, *Le Paradis des Femmes: Women, Salons, and Social Stratification in Seventeenth-Century France* (Princeton, NJ: Princeton University Press, 1976).

21 Dena Goodman, *The Republic of Letters: A Cultural History of the French Enlightenment* (Ithaca, NY: Cornell University Press, 1994), chs. 2–3. An important challenge to Goodman's argument is Antoine Lilti, *The Worlds of the Salons: Sociability and Wordliness in Eighteenth-Century Paris*, trans. Lydia Cochrane (Oxford: Oxford University Press, 2015).

22 Deborah Hertz, *Jewish High Society in Old Regime Berlin* (New Haven, CT: Yale University Press, 1988).

23 Margaret Jacob, *Living the Enlightenment: Freemasonry and Politics in Eighteenth-Century Europe* (Oxford: Oxford University Press, 1991), 8.

24 Melton, *The Rise of the Public in Enlightenment Europe*, 261–2.

25 Blanning, *The Culture of Power*, 111–14.

26 Quoted in Blanning, *The Culture of Power*, 137 and 153.

27 Blanning, *The Culture of Power*, 137–57.

28 Censer, *The French Press in the Age of Enlightenment*, intro. and ch. 2.

29 Melton, *The Rise of the Public in Enlightenment Europe*, 104–10.

30 Voltaire, *Candide*, trans. and ed. Daniel Gordon (Boston: Bedford/St. Martin's, 1999), 118.

31 John Sekora, *Luxury: The Concept in Western Thought, Eden to Smollett* (Baltimore: Johns Hopkins University Press, 1977), 48.

32 Sekora, *Luxury*, 65–77.

33 Shovlin, *The Political Economy of Virtue*, 26–38.

34 Sekora, *Luxury*, 81.

35 Jean-Baptiste Beauvais, cited in Ellen Ross, "The Debate on Luxury in Eighteenth-Century France: A Study in the Language of Opposition," PhD Dissertation, University of Chicago, 1975.

36 Maza, *Myth of the French Bourgeoisie*, 53–7.

37 Sekora, *Luxury*, 63–100.

38 Shovlin, *Political Economy of Virtue*, 49–92; Maza, *Myth of the French Bourgeoisie*, 36–40.

39 Shovlin, *Political Economy of Virtue*, 75, 51.

40 Thomas Laqueur, *Making Sex: Body and Gender from the Greeks to Freud* (Cambridge, MA: Harvard University Press, 1990), chs. 2 and 3.

41 Londa Schiebinger, *The Mind Has No Sex? Women in the Origins of Modern Science* (Cambridge, MA: Harvard University Press, 1991).

42 Laqueur, *Making Sex*, ch. 5.

43 Liselotte Steinbrugge, *The Moral Sex: Woman's Nature in the French Enlightenment*, trans. Pamela E. Selwyn (Oxford: Oxford University Press, 1995), ch. 3.

44 Cited in Steinbrugge, *The Moral Sex*, 32.

45 Madelyn Gutwirth, *The Twilight of the Goddesses: Women and Representation in the French Revolutionary Era* (New Brunswick, NJ: Rutgers University Press, 1992), 178–84.

46 Steinbrugge, *The Moral Sex*, 63–82.

47 Lawrence Stone, *The Family, Sex, and Marriage in England, 1500–1800* (New York: Harper & Row, 1977), chs. 5–9.

48 Sarah Pearsall, *Atlantic Families: Lives and Letters in the Later Eighteenth Century* (Oxford: Oxford University Press, 2008), 78.

49 Emma Barker, *Greuze and the Painting of Sentiment* (Cambridge: Cambridge University Press, 2005); Mark Ledbury, *Sedaine, Greuze, and the Boundaries of Genre* (Oxford: The Voltaire Foundation, 2000).

50 Maza, *Myth of the French Bourgeoisie*, 61–7.

51 William Reddy, *The Navigation of Feeling: A Framework for the History of Emotions* (Cambridge: Cambridge University Press, 2001), ch. 5.

52 Blanning, *Culture of Power*, 145–54; Hunt, *Inventing Human Rights*, 38–45.

53 Hunt, *Inventing Human Rights*, 45; Robert Darnton, "Readers Respond to Rousseau: The Fabrication of Romantic Sensitivity," in *The Great Cat Massacre and Other Episodes in French Cultural History* (New York: Basic Books, 1984), 243.

54 Sarah Knott, *Sensibility and the American Revolution* (Chapel Hill: University of North Carolina Press, 2009), 4–6.

55 Thomas Laqueur, "Bodies, Details, and the Humanitarian Narrative," in *The New Cultural History*, edited by Lynn Hunt (Berkeley: University of California Press, 1989), 176–204.

56 Hunt, *Inventing Human Rights*, ch. 2.

57 Hunt, *Inventing Human Rights*, 19–34.

58 Knott, *Sensibility and the American Revolution*, 161.

59 Charles Élie de Ferrières, *Correspondance inédite* (Paris: Armand Colin, 1932), 43. On the meaning of brotherhood in the French Revolution see Lynn Hunt, *The Family Romance of the French Revolution* (Berkeley: University of California Press, 1992), ch. 3.

60 The classic statement of this interpretation is Ian Watt, *The Rise of the Novel: Studies in Defoe, Richardson, and Fielding* (Berkeley: University of California Press, 1957).

61 For an overview of the changing scholarship on Revolutionary origins, see William Doyle, *Origins of the French Revolution*, 3rd edition (Oxford: Oxford University Press, 1999), 5–34. For new approaches to cultural change in the period, see Sarah Maza, "The Cultural Origins of the French Revolution," in *A Companion to the French Revolution*, edited by Peter McPhee, 42–56 (Chichester, UK: Blackwell, 2013).

62 The most influential "post-revisionist" statement on the matter is Colin Jones, "Bourgeois Revolution Revivified: 1789 and Social Change," in *Rewriting the French Revolution*, edited by Colin Lucas, 69–118 (Oxford: Clarendon Press, 1991).

Chapter 4

1 Source: Dennis F. Thompson, "Bibliography: The Education of a Founding Father. The Reading List for John Witherspoon's Course in Political Theory, as Taken by James Madison," *Political Theory* 4 (1976): 523–9. The list originally included only names of writers. Thompson argues for titles and editions most accessible to Americans like Madison; I have also included the original edition of the work. I have omitted Barbeyac because clearly Witherspoon means not those books he authored, but those he edited, such as Grotius and Pufendorf. See also John Witherspoon, *Lectures on Moral Philosophy*, edited by Jack Scott (Newark: University of Delaware Press, 1982), 187, which differs slightly from Thompson. In his introduction, Scott notes that "of the 469 graduates during Witherspoon's administration (1768–1794) ... six were members of the Continental Congress, twenty-one were United States senators, thirty-nine were representatives, three were justices of the Supreme Court, and one became president" (15–16).

2 J. G. A. Pocock, *The Machiavellian Moment: Florentine Political Thought and the Atlantic Republican Tradition* (Princeton, NJ: Princeton University Press, 1975).

3 David Saunders, "The Natural Jurisprudence of Jean Barbeyrac: Translation as an Art of Political Adjustment," *Eighteenth-Century Studies* 36 (2003): 473–90; Edouart Tillet, "Jean Barbeyrac, or the Ambiguities of Political Radicality at the Dawn of the Enlightenment," in *The Internationalization of Intellectual Exchange in a Globalizing Europe 1636–1780*, edited by Robert Mankin (Lewisburg, PA: Bucknell University Press, 2018), 31–54.

4 Richard B. Sher, *The Enlightenment and the Book: Scottish Authors and Their Publishers in Eighteenth-Century Britain, Ireland, and America* (Chicago: University of Chicago Press, 2006), 87. The expansion of WorldCat from a cataloger's database used initially by librarians in Ohio to a global online database that includes the holdings of virtually all major libraries in Europe, Canada, and the United States, now allows easier quantification of eighteenth-century editions for any published work.

5 Colleen A. Sheehan, *The Mind of James Madison: The Legacy of Classical Republicanism* (Cambridge: Cambridge University Press, 2015), esp. 63–77. Montesquieu may also have been Witherspoon's favorite author. See Witherspoon, *Lectures on Moral Philosophy*, 139.

6 Felippo Venuti, *Il trionfo letterario della Francia* (Avignon: Alessandro Giroud, 1750), 27n. Editions for Montesquieu are derived from counting the editions listed in Cecil Patrick Courtney, "*L'Esprit des lois* dans la perspective de l'histoire du livre (1748–1800)," in *Le Temps de Montesquieu*, edited by Michel Porret and Catherine Volpilhac-Auger (Geneva: Droz, 2002), 65–96.

7 Jürgen Habermas, *The Structural Transformation of the Public Sphere: An Inquiry into a Category of Bourgeois Society*, trans. Thomas Burger and Frederick Lawrence (Cambridge, MA: MIT Press, 1989). Melton, *The Rise of the Public in Enlightenment Europe*, is especially helpful here. See also Dena Goodman, *The Republic of Letters: A Cultural History of the French Enlightenment* (Ithaca, NY: Cornell University Press, 1994), 12–15, 142–8; and Keith Michael Baker, "Defining the Public Sphere in Eighteenth-Century France: Variations on a Theme by Habermas," in *Habermas and the Public Sphere*, edited by Craig Calhoun (Cambridge, MA: MIT Press, 1993), 181–211.

8 For the growth of periodicals, see Jack Censer, *The French Press in the Age of Enlightenment* (New York: Routledge, 1994); and Antonio Forster, "Review Journals and the Reading Public," in *Books and their Readers in Eighteenth-Century England: New Essays*, edited by Isabel Rivers (London: Continuum, 2001), 171–90.

9 John P. Kaminski, Gaspare J. Saladino, Richard Leffler, Charles H. Schoenleber, and Margaret A. Hogan, eds., *The Documentary History of the Ratification of the Constitution*, digital

edition (Charlottesville: University of Virginia Press, 2009), available online: http://rotunda. upress.virginia.edu/founders/RNCN (accessed May 16, 2014). Pauline Maier, *Ratification: The People Debate the Constitution, 1787–1788* (New York: Simon and Schuster, 2010); does not include Montesquieu.

10 Jean le Rond d'Alembert, "Eulogy for President Montesquieu," in *Encyclopedic Liberty: Political Articles in the Dictionary of Diderot and D'Alembert*, trans. Henry C. Clark and Christine Dunn Henderson (Indianapolis, IN: Liberty Fund, 2016), 122–38; Dan Edelstein, Robert Morissey, and Glenn Roe, "To Quote or Not to Quote: Citation Strategies in the Encyclopédie," *Journal of the History of Ideas* 74 (2013): 223–4.

11 Anne Goldgar, *Impolite Learning: Conduct and Community in the Republic of Letters, 1680– 1750* (New Haven, CT: Yale University Press, 1995).

12 Richard Ashcraft, *Revolutionary Politics and Locke's Two Treatises of Government* (Princeton, NJ: Princeton University Press, 1986).

13 Jonathan Israel, *Enlightenment Contested: Philosophy, Modernity, and the Emancipation of Man 1670–1752* (Oxford: Oxford University Press, 2006), 289.

14 Patrick Riley, "Fénelon's Republican Monarchism in *Telemachus*," in *Monarchisms in the Age of Enlightenment: Liberty, Patriotism, and the Common Good*, edited by Hans W. Blom, John Christian Laursen, and Luisa Simonuttti (Toronto: University of Toronto Press, 2007), 78–100.

15 Montesquieu, *The Spirit of the Laws*, trans. Anne M. Cohler, Basia Carolyn Miller, and Harold Samuel Stone (Cambridge: Cambridge University Press, 1989), 316, 338, 382; Istvan Hont, "The Early Enlightenment Debate on Commerce and Luxury," in *The Cambridge History of Eighteenth-Century Political Thought*, edited by Mark Goldie and Robert Walker (Cambridge: Cambridge University Press, 2006), 379–418.

16 For example, Elie Carcassone, *Montesquieu et le problème de la constitution française au XVIIIe siècle* (Paris: Presses universitaires de France, 1927).

17 John Maynard Keynes, "Preface to the French Edition," in *The Collected Writings of John Maynard Keynes, Volume 7: The General Theory*, edited by Elizabeth Johnson and Donald Moggridge, xv–xvii (Cambridge: Cambridge University Press, 1978), xxi–xxiv.

18 John Shovlin, *The Political Economy of Virtue: Luxury, Patriotism, and the Origins of the French Revolution* (Ithaca, NY: Cornell University Press, 2006), 113; James C. Riley, *The Seven Years War and the Old Regime in France: The Economic and Financial Toll* (Princeton, NJ: Princeton University Press, 1986).

19 "The most influential exponent of the doctrine of *doux commerce* was Montesquieu." Albert Hirschman, *The Passions and the Interests: Political Arguments for Capitalism Before its Triumph* (Princeton, NJ: Princeton University Press, 1977), 60.

20 For example, see Catherine Larrère, *L'Invention de l'economie au XVIIIe siècle: du droit naturel à la physiocratie* (Paris: Presses universitaires de France, 1992); Céline Spector, *Montesquieu et l'émergence de l'économie politique* (Paris: Champion, 2006); and Michael Sonenscher, *Before the Deluge: Public Debt, Inequality, and the Intellectual Origins of the French Revolution* (Princeton, NJ: Princeton University Press, 2007), esp. 95–179.

21 Christine Théré, "Economic Publishing and Authors, 1566–1789," in *Studies in the History of French Political Economy from Bodin to Walras*, edited by Gilbert Faccarello, 1–56 (New York: Routledge, 1998), 11.

22 John Robertson, *The Case for Enlightenment: Scotland and Naples 1680–1760* (Cambridge: Cambridge University Press, 2005), esp. ch. 7: "The Advent of Enlightenment: Political Economy in Naples and Scotland, 1730–1760."

23 Quoted in Paul Cheney, *Revolutionary Commerce: Globalization and the French Monarchy* (Cambridge, MA: Harvard University Press, 2010), 51.

24 Cheney, *Revolutionary Commerce*, 52.

25 Paul A. Rahe, "The Enlightenment Indicted: Rousseau's Response to Montesquieu," *Journal of the Historical Society* 8 (2008): 273–302; Johnson Kent Wright, "Rousseau and Montesquieu," in *Thinking with Rousseau, from Machiavelli to Schmitt*, edited by Helena Rosenblatt and Paul Schweigert, 63–91 (Cambridge: Cambridge University Press, 2017).

26 Jean-Jacques Rousseau, *Discourse on Political Economy* in *The Basic Political Writings*, 2nd edition, trans. Donald Cress, 123–52 (Indianapolis, IN: Hackett, 2011), 134, 135, 147. See Ryan Patrick Hanley, "Political Economy and Liberty," in *The Challenge of Rousseau*, edited by Eve Grace and Christopher Kelly, 34–56 (Cambridge: Cambridge University Press, 2013).

27 Carla Hesse, "Revolutionary Rousseaus: The Story of His Editions," in *Media and Political Culture in the Eighteenth Century*, edited by Marie-Christine Skuncke, 107–28 (Stockholm: Kungl. Vitterhets Historie och Antikvitets Akademien, 2005).

28 Montesquieu, *Considerations on the Causes of the Greatness of the Romans and Their Decline*, trans. David Lowenthal (Ithaca, NY: Cornell University Press, 1965), 199.

29 François Véron de Forbonnais, "Commerce," in *The Encyclopedia of Diderot & d'Alembert Collaborative Translation Project*, trans. Nelly S. Hoyt and Thomas Cassirer (Ann Arbor: Michigan Publishing, University of Michigan Library), 2003, available online: http://hdl.handle.net/2027/spo.did2222.0000.145 (accessed April 13, 2018). Originally published as "Commerce," *Encyclopédie ou Dictionnaire raisonné des sciences, des arts et des métiers* (Paris, 1753), 3:690–9. Scholarship on the Gournay group has mushroomed. See in particular Loïc Charles, Frédéric Lefebvre, and Christine Théré, eds., *Le Cercle de Vincent de Gournay: saviors économiques et pratiques administratives en France au milieu du XVIIIe siècle* (Paris: Institut National d'Etudes Démographiques, 2011); Henry C. Clark, *Compass of Society: Commerce and Absolutism in Old Regime France* (Lanham, MD: Lexington, 2007); Robin J. Ives, "Political Publicity and Political Economy in Eighteenth-Century France," *French History* 17 (2003): 1–18.

30 Ryu Susato, "Hume's Nuanced Defense of Luxury," *Hume Studies* 32 (2006): 175.

31 David Hume, *Discours politiques*, trans. Abbé Le Blanc (Amsterdam [Paris]: Lambert, 1754), xi–xii.

32 Philippe Audegean, "Genovesi, Antonio," trans. Philip Stewart, in *A Montesquieu Dictionary* [online], directed by Catherine Volpilhac-Auger, ENS Lyon, September 2013, available online: http://dictionnaire-montesquieu.ens-lyon.fr/en/article/1367160245/en (accessed January 23, 2022). See also Till Wahnbaeck, *Luxury and Public Happiness: Political Economy in the Italian Enlightenment* (Oxford: Oxford University Press, 2004), 59–66.

33 Ulrich Adam, *The Political Economy of J.H.G. Justi* (Bern: Peter Lang, 2006).

34 Mirabeau was mistaken about France's so-called population decline. See Carol Blum, *Strength in Numbers: Population, Reproduction, and Power in Eighteenth-Century France* (Baltimore: Johns Hopkins University Press, 2002), 11–20, 43–4, 48–9.

35 Victor Riqueti, Marquis de Mirabeau, *l'Ami des hommes ou Traité de la population*, nouvelle edition, 6 vols. ([Avignon], 1759), 3:408–9.

36 Montesquieu, *Spirit of the Laws*, 25.

37 Mirabeau quoted in Shovlin, *Political Economy of Virtue*, 67.

38 Michael Kwass, "Consumption and the World of Ideas: Consumer Revolution and the Moral Economy of the Marquis de Mirabeau," *Eighteenth-Century Studies* 37 (2004): 187–213.

39 [François Quesnay], "Remarques sur l'opinion de l'auteur de l'Esprit des Loix concernant les Colonies, bk. 21, ch. 17," *Journal de l'agriculture, du commerce, et des finances*, 5 (April 1766): pt. 1, 3–34.

40 Isaak Iselin to Jean Rodolph Frey, April 14, 1770, quoted in Sonenscher, *Before the Deluge*, 191.

41 Pierre-Paul Le Mercier de La Rivière, *L'Ordre naturel et essential des sociétés politiques* (London: Nourse and Densaint, 1767), 78, quoted in Liana Vardi, *The Physiocrats and the World of the Enlightenment* (Cambridge: Cambridge University Press, 2012), 170.

42 "Review of Le Mercier de la Rivière, *L'Ordre naturel*," *Journal de l'agriculture, du commerce, et des finances* (September 1767): 102. See also Loïc Charles and Philippe Steiner, "Entre Montesquieu et Rousseau: La physiocratie parmi les origines intellectuelles de la Révolution Française," *Etudes Jean-Jacques Rousseau* 11(1999): 83–160; and Loïc Charles and Christine Théré, "The Writing Workshop of François Quesnay and the Making of Physiocracy," *History of Political Economy* 40 (2008): 1–42.

43 Pierre-Samuel Du Pont de Nemours, "On the Origin and Progress of a New Science," in *Commerce, Culture and Liberty: Readings on Capitalism Before Adam Smith*, edited by Henry C. Clark, 564–97 (Indianapolis, IN: Liberty Fund, 2003); final quotation from Cheney, *Revolutionary Commerce*, 52.

44 Adam Smith, *An Inquiry into the Nature and Causes of the Wealth of Nations*, 2 vols. (London: Strahan and Cadell, 1776), 1:17.

45 William H. Sewell Jr., *A Rhetoric of Bourgeois Revolution: The Abbé Sieyes and What is the Third Estate?* (Durham, NC: Duke University Press, 1994); and Emma Rothschild, *Economic Sentiments: Adam Smith, Condorcet, and the Enlightenment* (Cambridge, MA: Harvard University Press, 2001).

46 This paragraph relies heavily on the quotes found in Henry C. Clark, "Montesquieu in Smith's Method of 'Theory and History'," *The Adam Smith Review* 4 (2008): 133. For a related perspective, see Istvan Hont, *Politics in Commercial Society: Jean-Jacques Rousseau and Adam Smith*, edited by Béla Kapossy and Michael Sonenscher (Cambridge, MA: Harvard University Press, 2015), esp. 72–8.

47 Muriel Brot, "Montesquieu dans l'Histoire des deux indes," *Revue Française d'Histoire des Idées Politiques* 35 (2012): 123–33.

48 Abbé Guillaume Thomas Raynal, *A Philosophical and Political History of the Settlements and Trade of the Europeans in the East and West Indies*, 8 vols. (London: Strahan and Cadell, 1788), 1:309–12.

49 Raynal, *A Philosophical and Political History*, 5:267–8.

50 *Les trois philosophes sur la nature de la monarchie* (London, 1787); Abbé Guillaume Thomas Raynal, *The Revolution of America* was first published in London by L. Davis in 1781, and went through thirteen editions by 1783.

51 Colleen A. Sheehan, "Madison and the French Enlightenment: The Authority of Public Opinion," *William and Mary Quarterly* 59 (2002): 933.

52 *Correspondence Littéraire*, July 1774, 10:454–5; cited in William R. Womack, "Eighteenth-Century Themes in the *Histoire philosophique et politique des deux Indes* of Guillaume Raynal," *Studies on Voltaire and the Eighteenth Century* 96 (1972): 133.

53 Andy Martin, *Napoleon the Novelist* (Cambridge, UK: Polity, 2000), 13, 17–18, 61.

Chapter 5

1 Alexander Pope, *The Works of Alexander Pope, Esq: Volume 2, Containing His Epistles and Satires* (London: printed for L. Gilliver, 1735), 160.

2 Samuel Johnson, *A Dictionary of the English Language: In Which the Words Are Deduced from Their Originals, and Illustrated in Their Different Significations by Examples from the Best Writers: To Which Are Prefixed, a History of the Language and an English Grammar*

(London: Printed by W. Strahan, for J. and P. Knapton; T. and T. Longman; C. Hitch and L. Hawes; A. Millar; and R. and J. Dodsley, 1755), 1350.

3 Michael J. Buckley, SJ, *At the Origins of Modern Atheism* (New Haven, CT: Yale University Press, 1987); Michael J. Buckley, SJ, *Denying and Disclosing God: The Ambiguous Progress of Modern Atheism* (New Haven, CT: Yale University Press, 2004); Charles Taylor, *A Secular Age* (Cambridge, MA: Harvard University Press, 2007).

4 Leonardus Lessius, *De providentia numinis et animi immortalitate libri duo adversus Atheos & Politicos* (Antverpiae: Ex Officina Plantiniana, apud Viduam & Filios Io. Moreti, 1613); see Brian W. Ogilvie, "Stoics, Neoplatonists, Atheists, Politicians: Sources and Uses of Early Modern Jesuit Natural Theology," in *For the Sake of Learning: Essays in Honor of Anthony Grafton*, edited by Ann Blair and Anja-Silvia Goeing, vol. 2, 761–79 (Leiden: Brill, 2016).

5 Silvia Berti, Françoise Charles-Daubert, and Richard H. Popkin, eds., *Heterodoxy, Spinozism, and Free Thought in Early-Eighteenth-Century Europe: Studies on the Traité des trois imposteurs*, International Archives of the History of Ideas/Archives internationales d'histoire des idées, 148 (Dordrecht: Springer Netherlands, 1996).

6 Edward Grant, *God and Reason in the Middle Ages* (Cambridge: Cambridge University Press, 2001); Robert Bartlett, *The Natural and the Supernatural in the Middle Ages* (Cambridge: Cambridge University Press, 1980).

7 Fabián Alejandro Campagne, "Witchcraft and the Sense-of-the-Impossible in Early Modern Spain: Some Reflections Based on the Literature of Superstition (ca. 1500–1800)," *Harvard Theological Review* 96, no. 1 (2003): 25–62; Lorraine Daston and Katharine Park, *Wonders and the Order of Nature, 1150–1750* (New York: Zone Books, 1998).

8 C. S. Lewis, *Studies in Words* (Cambridge: Cambridge University Press, 1960), 24–74; Clarence J. Glacken, *Traces on the Rhodian Shore: Nature and Culture in Western Thought from Ancient Times to the End of the Eighteenth Century* (Berkeley: University of California Press, 1967), 387.

9 Jan Swammerdam, *Historia insectorum generalis, ofte Algemeene Verhandeling van de Bloedeloose Dierkens* (Utrecht: by Meinardus van Drevnen, Ordinaris Drucker van d'Academie, 1669), Naa-reeden, 5; Jan Swammerdam, *Historia insectorum generalis, in qua verissimae mutationem, seu lentae in membra epigeneseos rationes, duce experentia, redduntur, recepta vulgo insectorum metamorphosis solide refutatur* (Utrecht: Ex officina Otthonis de Vries, 1685), 153.

10 Robert Boyle, *A Free Enquiry into the Vulgarly Receiv'd Notion of Nature; Made in an Essay Address'd to a Friend* (London: H. Clark, for John Taylor, 1685/6); Robert Boyle, *Works* (London: Pickering & Chatto, 1999–2000), 10:437–581. On the genesis of the work, see Michael Hunter and Edward B. Davis, "The Making of Robert Boyle's 'Free enquiry into the vulgarly receiv'd notion of nature' (1686)," *Early Science and Medicine* 1, no. 2 (June 1996): 204–71.

11 Boyle, *Works*, 10:445, orthography modernized.

12 Boyle, *Works*, 10:467, orthography modernized.

13 Hunter and Davis, "Making of Boyle's 'Free enquiry.'"

14 For example, 2nd edition, 1, 33 n. 2.

15 William Derham, *Physico-Theology: or, a Demonstration of the being and attributes of God, from his works of creation: Being the substance of sixteen sermons preached in St. Mary le Bow-Church, London, at the Hon.ble Mr. Boyle's Lectures, in the years 1711 and 1712: With large notes, and many curious observations*, 2nd edition (London: Printed for W. Innys, at the Princes Arms, in St. Paul's Church-Yard, 1714), 45 n. 4, 68, and 78.

16 Derham, *Physico-Theology*, 76, 312 n. 5, 334, and 338.

17 Derham, *Physico-Theology*, 88.

18 Derham, *Physico-Theology*, 217 n.

19 Derham, *Physico-Theology*, 441.

20 Noël-Antoine Pluche, *Le Spectacle de la nature, ou Entretiens sur les particularités de l'histoire naturelle qui ont paru les plus propres à rendre les jeunes gens curieux et à leur former l'esprit* (Paris: Vve Estienne, 1732–1750), 1 (2nd edition, 1737): iv–v. On Pluche as a Jansenist physico-theologian, see Ann Blair, "Noël-Antoine Pluche as a Jansenist Natural Theologian," *Intellectual History Review* 26, no. 1 (2016): 91–9.

21 André Cailleux, "Progression du nombre d'espèces de plantes décrites de 1500 à nos jours," *Revue d'Histoire des Sciences* 6 (1953): 42–9.

22 Brian W. Ogilvie, "Insects in John Ray's Natural History and Natural Theology," in *Zoology in Early Modern Culture: Intersections of Science, Theology, Philology, and Political and Religious Education*, edited by Karl A. E. Enenkel and Paul J. Smith, 234–60 (Leiden: Brill, 2014), 246–9.

23 Nicholas Jardine, James A. Secord, and Emma C. Spary, eds., *Cultures of Natural History* (Cambridge: Cambridge University Press, 1996), 127–96; Helen A. Curry, Nicholas Jardine, James A. Secord, and Emma C. Spary, eds., *Worlds of Natural History* (Cambridge: Cambridge University Press, 2018), 149–285.

24 Mary Terrall, *Catching Nature in the Act: Natural History in the Eighteenth Century* (Chicago: University of Chicago Press, 2014); Jacques Roger, *Buffon: A Life in Natural History* (Ithaca, NY: Cornell University Press, 1997).

25 *Encyclopédie: Dictionnaire raisonné des sciences, des arts et des métiers*, edited by Denis Diderot and Jean le Ronde d'Alembert (Paris: Briasson, 1751–1772), 2:489.

26 *Encyclopédie*, 2:490.

27 *Encyclopédie*, 2:492.

28 See Jonathan Sheehan, "Enlightenment, Religion, and the Enigma of Secularization: A Review Essay," *American Historical Review* 108, no. 4 (2003): 1061–80.

29 Jan Schröder, "The Concept of (Natural) Law in the Doctrine of Law and Natural Law of the Early Modern Era," in *Natural Law and Laws of Nature In Early Modern Europe: Jurisprudence, Theology, Moral and Natural Philosophy*, edited by Lorraine Daston and Michael Stolleis, 57–71 (Farnham, UK: Ashgate, 2008), 59, including the quotation.

30 Tim J. Hochstrasser, "Natural Law," in *Dictionary of the History of Ideas*, edited by Maryanne Cline Horowitz (Detroit: Thomson Gale, 2005), 4:1607–10.

31 Francis Oakley, *Natural Law, Laws of Nature, Natural Rights: Continuity and Discontinuity in the History of Ideas* (New York: Continuum, 2005); Annabel S. Brett, *Changes of State: Nature and the Limits of the City in Early Modern Natural Law* (Princeton, NJ: Princeton University Press, 2011).

32 See Rafael Alvira and Alfredo Cruz, "The Controversy Between Las Casas and Sepúlveda at Valladolid," in *Hispanic Philosophy in the Age of Discovery*, edited by Kevin White, 88–110 (Washington, DC: Catholic University of America Press, 1997).

33 Oakley, *Natural Law*, 79–80.

34 See Brett, *Changes of State*.

35 Richard Tuck, *Natural Rights Theories: Their Origin and Development* (Cambridge: Cambridge University Press, 1979).

36 Thomas Hobbes, *Leviathan* (Oxford: Oxford University Press, 2012), ch. 14, p. 198.

37 Hobbes, *Leviathan*, ch. 15, p. 240.

38 Oakley, *Natural Law*, 63–6.

39 Brian Tierney, *Liberty and Law: The Idea of Permissive Natural Law, 1100–1800*, Studies in Medieval and Early Modern Canon Law (Washington, DC: Catholic University of America Press, 2014), 305–25.

40 Derham, *Physico-theology*, 176 n. 8.

41 See Peter Gay, *The Enlightenment: An Interpretation* (New York: Knopf, 1966–1969), 2:455–8, and Paul Hazard, *The European Mind, 1680–1715*, trans. J. Lewis May (Cleveland, OH: World Publishing Co., 1953), 266–70. I thank Jack Censer for the references.

42 *Encyclopédie*, 11:46; cf. 9:665.

43 John Henry, "Metaphysics and the Origins of Modern Science: Descartes and the Importance of Laws of Nature," *Early Science and Medicine* 9, no. 2 (2004): 73–114; Mauro Dorato, *The Software of the Universe: An Introduction to the History and Philosophy of Laws of Nature* (Aldershot, UK: Ashgate, 2005), ix.

44 Cf. Nancy Cartwright, *How the Laws of Physics Lie* (Oxford: Oxford University Press, 1983).

45 For example, Edward Grant, *The Foundations of Modern Science in the Middle Ages* (Cambridge: Cambridge University Press, 1996).

46 Henry, "Metaphysics and the Origins," 79.

47 Henry, "Metaphysics and the Origins," 73–114.

48 Helen Thornton, *State of Nature or Eden? Thomas Hobbes and his Contemporaries on the Natural State of Human Beings* (Rochester, NY: University of Rochester Press, 2005), 10.

49 Boyle, *Works*, 10:457.

50 Sophie Roux, "Les lois de la nature à l'âge classique: La question terminologique," *Revue de synthèse*, 4th ser., nos. 2–4 (2001): 554–68.

51 Isaac Newton, *Philosophiae naturalis principia mathematica* (Londini: Jussu Societatis Regiae ac Typis Josephi Streater, 1687), 12.

52 Roux, "Lois de la nature," 564–65, 568.

53 *Encyclopédie*, 9:119. D'Alembert wrote that Kepler had two laws, properly speaking, but the term was principally used to refer to what we now call the third law.

54 A search of the text corpora for Early English Books Online and Eighteenth Century Texts Online turned up no examples of the term before 1800.

55 See Roux, "Lois de la nature"; Henry, "Metaphysics and the Origins"; Dorato, *Software*; and Lorraine Daston and Michael Stolleis, eds., *Natural Law and Laws of Nature in Early Modern Europe: Jurisprudence, Theology, Moral and Natural Philosophy* (Farnham, UK: Ashgate, 2008).

56 Campagne, "Witchcraft."

57 Michael R. Lynn, *Popular Science and Public Opinion in Eighteenth-Century France* (Manchester: Manchester University Press, 2006); Bernadette Bensaude-Vincent and Christine Blondel, eds., *Science and Spectacle in the European Enlightenment* (Farnham, UK: Ashgate, 2008).

58 See Andrea Reichenberger, "Émilie Du Châtelet's Interpretation of the Laws of Motion in the Light of 18th Century Mechanics," *Studies in History and Philosophy of Science Part A* 69 (2018): 1–11.

59 Thierry Hoquet, "History Without Time: Buffon's Natural History as a Nonmathematical Physique," *Isis* 101, no. 1 (2010): 30–61.

60 For the range of reactions in the Enlightenment and afterward, see Theodore E. D. Braun and John B. Radner, eds., *The Lisbon Earthquake of 1755: Representations and Reactions* (Oxford: Voltaire Foundation, 2005). On Lisbon as the first modern catastrophe, see Jörg Trempler, "Catastrophes and their Images: Event and Pictorial Act," *RES: Anthropology and Aesthetics* 63/64 (2013): 201–14.

61 Alexandra Walsham, *Providence in Early Modern England* (Oxford: Oxford University Press, 1999), 332.

62 Voltaire, *Poèmes sur le désastre de Lisbonne et sur la loi naturelle, avec des préfaces des notes &c.* (Geneva: [Cramer], 1766); Voltaire, "The Lisbon Earthquake," *New England Review* 26, no. 3 (2005): 183–93. In the French original Voltaire mocked the maxim, "tout est bien" (all is good), but his preface refers explicitly to Pope's *Essay on Man*, source of the English line, "Whatever is, is Right."

63 Voltaire, "Lisbon Earthquake," 185.

64 See several of the essays in Braun and Radner, *Lisbon Earthquake.*

65 William H. Gass, "The Story of the State of Nature," *Salmagundi* 94/95 (Spring–Summer 1992): 122.

66 Cicero, *De inventione* 1.2, *De oratore* 1.33, my translations.

67 See Alison Brown, *The Return of Lucretius to Renaissance Florence* (Cambridge, MA: Harvard University Press, 2010).

68 Tuck, *Natural Rights Theories*, ch. 2.

69 Hobbes, *Leviathan*, ch. 13.

70 Thornton, *State of Nature*, 3.

71 A. John Simmons, *On the Edge of Anarchy: Locke, Consent, and the Limits of Society* (Princeton, NJ: Princeton University Press, 1993), 15–16.

72 Frank Palmeri, *State of Nature, Stages of Society: Enlightenment Conjectural History And Modern Social Discourse* (New York: Columbia University Press, 2016), ch. 1.

73 Robin Douglass, "Rousseau's Debt to Burlamaqui: The Ideal of Nature and the Nature of Things," *Journal of the History of Ideas* 72, no. 2 (April 2011): 215.

74 Nicholas Dent, *Rousseau* (London: Routledge, 2005), 96–101.

75 John Locke, *Two Treatises of Government*, edited by Peter Laslett, Student edition, Cambridge Texts in the History of Political Thought (Cambridge: Cambridge University Press, 1988), 288.

76 Dugald Stewart, *Philosophical Essays* (Edinburgh: Printed by George Ramsay and Company for William Creech, and Archibald Constable and Company, Edinburgh; T. Cadell and W. Davies, Strand, John Murray, Fleet-Street, and Constable, Hunter, Park, and Hunter, London, 1810), 511.

77 Eric Wolf, *Europe and the People Without History* (Berkeley: University of California Press, 1982); Anthony Pagden, *Lords of All the World: Ideologies of Empire in Spain, Britain and France c. 1500–c. 1800* (New Haven, CT: Yale University Press, 1995).

78 The classic study is Stephen Jay Gould, *The Mismeasure of Man* (New York: Norton, 1981). For the seventeenth-century origins of such views, see Justin E. H. Smith, *Nature, Human Nature, and Human Difference: Race in Early Modern Philosophy* (Princeton, NJ: Princeton University Press, 2015).

Chapter 6

1 Nicholas Hudson, "What is the Enlightenment? Investigating the Origins and Ideological Uses of an Historical Category," *Érudit* 25 (2006): 168–9.

2 See, e.g., Peter Gay's review of Becker, "Carl Becker's Heavenly City," *Political Science Quarterly* 72, no. 2 (June 1957): 182–99.

3 Important recent work includes: David Sorkin, *The Religious Enlightenment: Protestants, Jews, and Catholics from London to Vienna* (Princeton, NJ: Princeton University Press, 2008); Jeffrey Burson, *The Rise and Fall of Theological Enlightenment: Jean-Martin de Prades and*

Ideological Polarization in Eighteenth-Century France (Notre Dame, IN: University of Notre Dame Press, 2010); Ulrich Lehner, *Enlightened Monks: The German Benedictines, 1740–1803* (Oxford: Oxford University Press, 2011); Charly Coleman, *The Virtues of Abandon: An Anti-Individualist History of the French Enlightenment* (Stanford, CA: Stanford University Press, 2014); William J. Bulman, *Anglican Enlightenment: Orientalism, Religion, and Politics in England and its Empire, 1648–1715* (Cambridge: Cambridge University Press, 2015); William J. Bulman and Robert G. Ingram, eds., *God in the Enlightenment* (Oxford: Oxford University Press, 2016); Alexander Bevilacqua, *The Republic of Arabic Letters: Islam and the European Enlightenment* (Cambridge, MA: Harvard University Press, 2018); Thomas Wallnig, *Critical Monks: The German Benedictines* (Leiden: Brill, 2019).

4   Simon Grote, "Religion and Enlightenment," *Journal of the History of Ideas* 75, no. 1 (January 2014): 147.

5   Sorkin, *Religious Enlightenment*, 11–13.

6   Amos Funkenstein, *Theology and the Scientific Imagination from the Middle Ages to the Seventeenth Century* (Princeton, NJ: Princeton University Press, 1986), 3.

7   Bulman, "Enlightenment for the Culture Wars," in Bulman and Ingram, *God in the Enlightenment*, 28 and 29.

8   See, e.g., Martin Gierl, *Pietismus und Aufklärung: Theologische Polemik und die Kommunikationsreform der Wissenschaft am Ende des 17. Jahrhunderts* (Göttingen: Vandenhoeck & Ruprecht, 1997); Jonathan Sheehan, *The Enlightenment Bible: Translation, Scholarship, Culture* (Princeton, NJ: Princeton University Press, 2005).

9   [D'Alembert], "Discours préliminaire des editeurs," in *Encyclopédie: Dictionnaire raisonné des sciences, des arts et des métiers* (Paris: Briasson, 1751), 1:xxxviii. When possible, and for convenience for English readers, further references to the preliminary discourse will come from d'Alembert, *Preliminary Discourse to the Encyclopedia of Diderot*.

10 Eva Dorothea Marcu, "Un Encyclopédiste oublié: Formey," *Revue d'Histoire littéraire de la France* 53, no. 3 (1953): 296–305; François Moureau, "L'*Encyclopédie* d'après les correspondants de Formey," *Recherches sur Diderot et sur l'Encyclopédie* 3 (1987): 125–45.

11 Johann Samuel Formey, *La belle Wolfienne* (La Haye: Charles le Vier, 1741), 5.

12 On Algarotti, see Massimo Mazzotti, "Newton for Ladies: Gentility, Gender, and Radical Culture," *British Journal for the History of Science* 37, no. 2 (June 2004): 119–46.

13 See, for example, Johan van der Zande, "The Microscope of Experience: Christian Garve's Translation of Cicero's *De Officiis* (1783)," *Journal of the History of Ideas* 59, no. 1 (January 1998): 75–94.

14 Annett Volmer, "Journalismus und Aufklärung: Jean Henri Samuel Formey und die Entwicklung der Zeitschrift zum Medium der Kritik," *Jahrbuch für Kommunikationsgeschichte* 9 (2007): 105–6. For the larger context and an excellent review of the relevant literature, see Thomas Broman, "Metaphysics for an Enlightened Public: The Controversy over Monads in Germany, 1746–1748," *Isis* 103, no. 1 (March 2012): 1–21.

15 D'Alembert, *Preliminary Discourse*, 110.

16 Louis Moréri, *Le grand dictionnaire historique* (Paris: Jean Baptiste Coignard, 1718), 2:750.

17 Ephraim Chambers, *Cyclopaedia: or, An Universal Dictionary of the Arts and Sciences* (London: James and John Knapton, 1728), s.v. "Definition," 1:176 [*sic*].

18 Chambers, *Cyclopaedia*, s.v. "God," 1:166 [*sic*].

19 D'Alembert, *Preliminary Discourse*, 47.

20 D'Alembert, *Preliminary Discourse*, 49.

21 *Encyclopédie*, s.v. "Dieu," 4:976.

22 *Encyclopédie*, s.v. "Dieu," 4:978.

23 Alan Charles Kors, "'A First Being, of Whom We Have No Proof': The Preamble of Atheism in Early Modern France," in *Anticipations of the Enlightenment in England, France, and Germany*, edited by Alan Charles Kors and Paul J. Korshin (Philadelphia: University of Pennsylvania Press, 1987), 18. Kors develops this argument fully in: *Atheism in France, 1650–1729* (Princeton, NJ: Princeton University Press, 1990).

24 Thomas Aquinas, *Summa Theologiae* (New York: Blackfriars, 1964), Ia. 2.3, p. 13.

25 Aquinas, *Summa Theologiae*, Ia. 2.3, p. 15.

26 Samuel Clarke, *Demonstration of the Being and Attributes of God* (London: William Botham, 1705), 25–6.

27 Clarke, *Demonstration of the Being and Attributes of God*, 27.

28 Clarke, *Demonstration of the Being and Attributes of God*, 75.

29 Clarke, *Demonstration of the Being and Attributes of God*, 264.

30 John J. Dahm, "Science and Apologetics in the Early Boyle Lectures," *Church History* 39, no. 2 (June 1970): 172.

31 s.v. "Encyclopédie," 5:642.

32 Zedler, *Grosses Vollständiges-Universal Lexicon aller Wissenschaften und Künste*, vol. 11, s.v. "Gott."

33 s.v. "Encyclopédie," 5:642a.

34 s.v. "Encyclopédie," 5:642a.

35 s.v. "création," 4:444.

36 On Naigeon, see Frank A. Kafker and Serena L. Kafker, *The Encyclopedists as Individuals: A Biographical Dictionary of the Authors of the Encyclopédie* (Oxford: Voltaire Foundatin, 1988), 278–83.

37 s.v. "Liberté," 9:463.

38 s.v. "demonstration," 4:822.

39 Samuel Clarke, "Answer to a Seventh Letter Concerning the Argument *a priori*," in *A Demonstration of the Being and Attributes of God*, edited by Ezio Vailati, 118–23 (Cambridge: Cambridge University Press, 1998), 118.

40 s.v. "demonstration," 4:823.

41 Anonymous, *La religion vengée, ou réfutation des auteurs impies* (Paris: Chaubert and Herissant, 1760), 10:310.

42 Anonymous, *La religion vengée*, 10:318.

43 Anonymous, *La religion vengée*, 10:319.

44 Abraham Joseph Chaumeix, *Préjugés légitimes contre l'Encyclopédie* (Brussels: Herissant, 1758), 1:59. See here John Lough, *The Encyclopédie* (New York: David McKay, 1971), 159–60.

45 s.v. "Dieu," 4:982.

46 s.v. "corruption," 4:278.

47 For la Mettrie, see Jonathan Sheehan and Dror Wahrman, *Invisible Hands: Self-Organization in the Eighteenth Century* (Chicago: University of Chicago Press, 2015), 168.

48 Anonymous, *La religion vengée*, 10:305, 338; emphasis in the original.

49 Sorkin, *Religious Enlightenment*, 6.

50 See especially Jonathan Israel, *Enlightenment Contested: Philosophy, Modernity, and the Emancipation of Man, 1670–1752* (Oxford: Oxford University Press, 2006).

51 For a related argument, see Robert Darnton, "Philosophers Trim the Tree of Knowledge: The Epistemological Strategy of the *Encyclopédie*," in *The Great Cat Massacre and Other Episodes in French Cultural History* (New York: Basic Books, 1984), 200.

52 See Alfred J. Bingham, "The Abbe Bergier: An Eighteenth-Century Catholic Apologist," *The Modern Language Review*, 54, no. 3 (July 1959): 337–50.

53 Nicolas Sylvestre Bergier, "Théologie," in *Encyclopédie méthodique* (Paris: Panckoucke, 1788), s.v. "Dieu," 1:534.

54 Avi Lifschitz, *Language and Enlightenment: The Berlin Debates of the Eighteenth Century* (Oxford: Oxford University Press, 2012), 149.

55 Bernard Fontenelle, "De l'Existence de Dieu," in *Oeuvres* (Amsterdam, 1754), 2:151.

56 See Israel, *Enlightenment Contested*, 497–9.

57 Fontenelle, "De l'origines des fables," in *Oeuvres*, 2:192.

58 Denis Diderot, "D'Alembert's Dream," in *Rameau's Nephew and Other Works*, trans. Jacques Barzun and Ralph H. Bowen (Indianapolis, IN: Bobbs-Merrill, 1956), 120. The rose reference is to the fifth evening of Fontenelle's *Entretiens sur la pluralité des mondes* (1686).

59 s.v. "paradis," 11:893.

60 s.v. "révélation," 14:225.

61 s.v. "anthropophages," 1:498.

62 See Robert Darnton, *The Business of Enlightenment: A Publishing History of the Encyclopédie, 1775–1800* (Cambridge, MA: Harvard University Press, 1979), 9–14; for a more polemical version of the story, see Jonathan Israel, "French Royal Censorship and the Battle to Suppress the Encyclopédie of Diderot and d'Alembert, 1751–1759," in *The Use Censorship in the Enlightenment*, edited by Mogens Laerke, 61–74 (Leiden: Brill, 2009). More generally on French censorship, see Raymond Birn, *Royal Censorship of Books in 18th-Century France* (Stanford, CA: Stanford University Press, 2012).

63 See Michael Kempe, *Wissenschaft, Theologie, Aufklärung: Johann Jakob Scheuchzer und die Sintfluttheorie* (Epfendorf: Bibliotheca Academica, 2003); Jonathan Sheehan, "From Philology to Fossils: The Biblical Encyclopedia in Early Modern Europe," *Journal of the History of Ideas* 64, no. 1 (January 2003): 41–60.

64 On Klopstock see, inter alia, Klaus Weimar, "Reading for Feeling," in *A New History of German Literature*, edited by David E. Wellbery, 356–60 (Cambridge, MA: Harvard University Press, 2004).

65 See Chad Wellmon, *Organizing Enlightenment: Information Overload and the Invention of the Modern Research University* (Baltimore: Johns Hopkins University Press, 2015).

Chapter 7

1 Jonathan Swift, *Gulliver's Travels* (London: George Bell and Sons, 1892), ch. 5.

2 Sophie Rosenfeld, *A Revolution in Language: The Problem of Signs in Late Eighteenth-Century France* (Stanford, CA: Stanford University Press, 2003), 19–21.

3 Francis Bacon, *The Advancement of Learning* (New York: the MacMillan Company 1898), 1:77.

4 Antoine Lilti, *The Invention of Celebrity* (Cambridge, UK: Polity, 2017), 109–59.

5 Clifford Siskin and William Warner, eds., *This is Enlightenment* (Chicago: University of Chicago Press, 2010), 17–18.

6 John K. Noyes, *Herder: Aesthetics Against Imperialism* (Toronto: University of Toronto Press, 2015), 4.

7 John Wilkins, *An Essay towards a Real Character, and a Philosophical Language* (Menston, UK: Scolar Press, 1968), 2.

8 Étienne de Condillac, *An Essay on the Origin of Human Knowledge*, trans. H. Aarsleff (Cambridge: Cambridge University Press, 2001), 114–15.

9 Condillac, *An Essay on the Origin of Human Knowledge*, 8, 6.

10 Jean-Jacques Rousseau, *Discourse on the Origin of Inequality*, trans. Donald A. Cress (Indianapolis, IN: Hackett Publishing, 1992), 30.

11 George Campbell, *The Works of George Campbell* (London: Thomas Tegg Campbell, 1840), 2:xvi.

12 George Campbell, *The Philosophy of Rhetoric* (New York: Jonathan Leavitt, 1834), 305.

13 Giambattista Vico, *The New Science of Giambattista Vico* (Ithaca, NY: Cornell University Press, 1984), 131.

14 Timothy Costelloe, "Giambattista Vico," in *The Stanford Encyclopedia of Philosophy* (Summer 2016), edited by Edward N. Zalta, available online: https://plato.stanford.edu/archives/sum2016/entries/vico/ (accessed November 15, 2017).

15 Jonathan Swift, "A Letter to a Young Clergyman," in *The Works of the Rev. Jonathan Swift* (London: Luke Hansard, 1720), 5:97–8.

16 Michel Le Faucheur, *Essay upon the Action of an Orator; as to his Pronunciation and Gesture* (London: N. Cox, 1702), 209.

17 Ange Goudar, *De Venise: Remarques sur la musique et la danse* (Venice: C. Palese, 1773), 67, 69 quoted in translation in Rosenfeld, *A Revolution in Language*, 80.

18 Thomas Sheridan, *A Course of Lectures on Elocution* (Troy: O. Penniman & Company, 1803), 106.

19 James Burgh, *The Art of Speaking: Containing, I. An Essay; in which are Given Rules for Expressing Properly the Principal Passions and Humours, … and II. Lessons, Taken from the Ancients and Moderns* (Dublin: Messrs. Price, Whitestone, Wilkinson, Chamberlaine, W. Watson, [and 12 others in Dublin], 1784), 19.

20 Edmund Burke, *The Writings and Speeches of Edmund Burke* (New York: Cosimo, 2008), 1:133.

21 Jean-Jacques Rousseau, *"The Discourses" and Other Early Political Writings* (Cambridge: Cambridge University Press, 1997), 251.

22 An extraordinary list of stalwarts of the Western canon of philosophy, rhetoric, and artistico-literary criticism expounded on these questions and their works merit exploration. In France, numerous treatises, periodicals, encyclopedia entries, and epistles were written by thinkers such as Boileau, Dominique Bouhours, Charles Batteux, Jean-Baptiste Dubos, Diderot, Fénelon, Friedrich Melchoir Grimm, Claude Hélvetius, René Rapin, Charles Rollin, Marivaux, Voltaire, Rousseau, the Encyclopédistes, and more. In England, Scotland, and Ireland, Joseph Addison, Archibald Alison, Hugh Blair, Edmund Burke, Lord Shaftesbury (Anthony Ashley Cooper), Alexander Gerard, William Gilpin, Lord Kames (Henry Home), David Hume, Francis Hucheson, Sir Uvedale Price, Thomas Reid, Adam Smith, and others wrote treatises and delivered lectures. German-speaking countries also made signal contributions to the discourse through writings by Baumgartner, Johann Jacob Bodmer, Johann Jacob Breitinger, Johann Christoph Gottsched, Johann Gottfried Herder, Immanuel Kant, Gotthold Ephraim Lessing, Georg Friedrich Meier, Moses Mendelssohn, Karl Philipp Moritz, Friedrich Riedel, Friedrich Wilhelm Joseph Schelling, Friedrich Schiller, Friedrich Schlegel, Johann Georg Sulzer, Johann Joachim Winckelmann, and Christian Wolff.

23 Burke, *The Writings and Speeches of Edmund Burke*, 134.

24 Paul Guyer, "18th Century German Aesthetics," in *The Stanford Encyclopedia of Philosophy* (Winter 2016), edited by Edward N. Zalta, available online: https://plato.stanford.edu/archives/win2016/entries/aesthetics-18th-german/ (accessed January 23, 2022).

25 Moses Mendelssohn, *Philosophical Writings*, trans. D. Dahlstrom, (Cambridge: Cambridge University Press, 1997), 178–9.

26 Gotthold Ephraim Lessing, *Laocoön: An Essay on the Limits of Painting and Poetry*, trans. E. McCormick (Baltimore: Johns Hopkins University Press, 1984), 85.

27 Johann Gottfried Herder, "First Grove," in *Kritische Wälder, oder Betrachtungen, die Wissenschaft und Kunst des Schönen betreffend* [Groves of Criticism, or Considerations concerning the Science and Art of the Beautiful], in *Johann Gottfried Herder, Schriften zur Ästhetik und Literatur 1767–1781*, edited by Gunter E. Grimm (Frankfurt: Deutscher Klassiker Verlag, 1993), translated in Guyer, "18th Century German Aesthetics."

28 Johann Gottfried Herder, "Herder: Extract from a Correspondence on Ossian and the Songs of Ancient People," trans. Joyce Crick, in *German Aesthetic and Literary Criticism: Winckelmann, Lessing, Hamann, Herder, Schiller, and Goethe*, edited by H. B. Nisbet, 151–76 (Cambridge: Cambridge University Press, 1985), 155–6.

Chapter 8

1 For Tupaia's role in Tahitian society and his engagement with the British see Anne Salmond, *The Trial of the Cannibal Dog: The Remarkable Story of Captain Cook's Encounters in the South Seas* (New Haven, CT: Yale University Press, 2003).

2 J. P. Malcolm, *An Historical Sketch of the Art of Caricaturing* (London, 1813), 3.

3 Thomas Crow, *Painters and Public Life in Eighteenth-Century Paris* (New Haven, CT: Yale University Press, 1985), 5.

4 See, for example, Malcolm Andrews, *Landscape and Western Art* (Oxford: Oxford University Press, 1999), and Martin Kemp, *The Oxford History of Western Art* (Oxford: Oxford University Press, 2000).

5 See David Summers, *Real Spaces: World Art History and the Rise of Western Modernism* (New York: Phaidon Press, 2003), and James Elkins, *Chinese Landscape Painting as Western Art History* (Hong Kong: Hong Kong University Press, 2010).

6 E. H. Gombrich established a foundation for understanding this component of European art in *Art and Illusion: A Study in the Psychology of Pictorial Presentation* (London: Phaidon, 1958). Bryson terms this approach "perspectivalism," in his critique of Gombrich, arguing against the presumption that Western artists were proto-scientists eagerly seeking new means to represent the world accurately. Norman Bryson, *Vision and Painting: The Logic of the Gaze* (New Haven, CT: Yale University Press, 1986).

7 See Paul Wood, *Western Art and the Wider World* (Chichester, UK: Wiley-Blackwell, 2013).

8 Cited in Matthew C. Hunter, *Wicked Intelligence: Visual Art and the Science of Experiment in Restoration London* (Chicago: University of Chicago, 2013), 41.

9 See Daniela Bleichmar, *Visible Empire: Botanical Expeditions and Visual Culture in the Hispanic Enlightenment* (Chicago: University of Chicago Press, 2012).

10 Bruno Latour, *Science in Action: How to Follow Scientists and Engineers through Society* (Cambridge, MA: Harvard University Press, 1987), 223.

11 Latour, *Science in Action*, 217.

12 Lorraine Daston and Peter Galison, *Objectivity* (New York: Zone Books, 2007), 58.

13 Michael Baxandall, *Patterns of Intention: On the Historical Explanation of Pictures* (New Haven, CT: Yale University Press, 1985), 102.

14 John Goodman, ed. and trans., *Diderot on Art: Volume 1, The Salon of 1765 and Notes on Painting* (New Haven, CT: Yale University Press, 1995), 22.

15 See Kay Dian Kriz, *Slavery, Sugar, and the Culture of Refinement* (New Haven, CT: Yale University Press, 2008), 71–115.

16 See Saree Makdisi, *Making England Western: Occidentalism, Race, and Imperial Culture* (Chicago: University of Chicago, 2014).

17 See David Bindman, *Ape to Apollo: Aesthetics and the Idea of Race in the 18th Century* (Ithaca, NY: Cornell University Press, 2002).

18 See Douglas Fordham, *British Art and the Seven Years' War: Allegiance and Autonomy* (Philadelphia: University of Pennsylvania Press, 2010), 201–48.

19 Philippe Bordes, *Le Serment du Jeu de paume de Jacques-Louis David. Le peintre, son milieu et son temps de 1789 à 1792* (Paris: Réunion des musées nationaux, 1983).

20 E. H. Gombrich, *The Story of Art* (New York: Phaidon, 1961), 358.

21 Ian McLean, *Rattling Spears: A History of Indigenous Australian Art* (London: Reaktion Books, 2016), 8.

22 See Howard Morphy, *Becoming Art: Exploring Cross-Cultural Categories* (Sydney: University of New South Wales Press, 2008).

Chapter 9

1 Harold A. Ellis, *Boulainvilliers and the French Monarchy: Aristocratic Politics in Early Eighteenth-Century France* (Ithaca, NY: Cornell University Press, 1988); Orest Ranum, *Artisans of Glory: Writers and Historical Thought in Seventeenth-Century France* (Chapel Hill: University of North Carolina Press, 1980).

2 For major overviews of this era, see (in a large literature) Karen O'Brien, *Narratives of Enlightenment: Cosmopolitan History from Voltaire to Gibbon* (Cambridge: Cambridge University Press, 1997); Hayden White, *Metahistory: The Historical Imagination in Nineteenth-Century Europe* (1973; repr. Baltimore: Johns Hopkins University Press, 2014), J. G. A. Pocock, *Barbarism and Religion*, 6 vols. (Cambridge: Cambridge University Press, 1999–2015); and Johnson Kent Wright, "Historical Thought in the Era of the Enlightenment," in *A Companion to Western Historical Thought*, edited by Lloyd Kramer and Sarah Maza, 123–42 (Oxford: Blackwell, 2006).

3 David Wootton, "David Hume, 'The Historian,'" in *The Cambridge Companion to Hume*, edited by David Fate Norton and Jacqueline Anne Taylor, 2nd edn., 447–79 (Cambridge: Cambridge University Press, 2009), 447.

4 White, *Metahistory*, xxix.

5 Edward Gibbon, *Memoirs of My Life*, edited by Georges A. Bonnard (London: Thomas A. Nelson & Sons, 1966), 157.

6 Gibbon, *Memoirs of My Life*, 159.

7 Henry St. John, Viscount Bolingbroke, *Letters on the Study and Use of History*, 2 vols. (London: A. Millar, 1752), 1:170.

8 Peter Whitefield, *London: A Life in Maps* (London: British Library, 2017), passim.

9 Whitefield, *London*, passim.

10 ArtUK, "Commerce, or the Triumph of the Thames (painting 4 of 6 in the series 'The Progress of Human Knowledge and Culture'): James Barry (1741–1806)," available online: https://artuk.org/discover/artworks/commerce-or-the-triumph-of-the-thames-218503 (accessed January 30, 2022).

11 Wootton, "David Hume, 'The Historian,'" 447–48.

12 Blanning, *The Culture of Power and the Power of Culture*, 142.

13 James Raven, *The Business of Books: Booksellers and the English Book Trade, 1450–1850* (New Haven, CT: Yale University Press, 2007); Sher, *The Enlightenment and the Book*; Alvin Kernan, *Printing Technology, Letters & Samuel Johnson* (Princeton, NJ: Princeton University Press, 1987), 62–117.

14 Daniel Rosenberg and Anthony Grafton, *Cartographies of Time: A History of the Timeline* (Princeton, NJ: Princeton Architectural Press, 2010), 97.

15 Blanning, *The Culture of Power*, 146.

16 *The Ambulator* (London: J. Bew, 1774), ii, 150. See also Elizabeth McKellar, *Landscapes of London: The City, the Country, and the Suburbs 1660–1840* (New Haven, CT: Paul Mellon Center for Studies in British Art, Yale University Press, 2013), 72.

17 Rosenberg and Grafton, *Cartographies of Time*, ch. 4.

18 John Brooke, "The Library of King George III," *Yale University Library Gazette* 52, no. 1 (July 1977): 33.

19 Blanning, *The Culture of Power*, 37.

20 Stuart Andrews, *The British Periodical Press and the French Revolution, 1789–99* (London: Palgrave Macmillan, 2000), 171.

21 Edmund Burke, *Reflections on the Revolution in France* (1790), edited and introduced by Conor Cruise O'Brien (New York: Penguin, 1986), 169.

22 *Encyclopaedia Britannica*, s.v. "Oliver Goldsmith," available online: https://www.britannica.com/biography/Oliver-Goldsmith-Anglo-Irish-author (accessed January 23, 2022).

23 Publius [James Madison, Alexander Hamilton, and John Jay], *The Federalist*, 2 vols. (New York: J. and A. M'Lean, 1788), 1:110.

24 Temple Stanyan, *The Grecian History*, 2 vols. (London: J. and R. Tonson and S. Draper, 1751), vol. 1, unpaginated preface; Giovanna Ceserani, "Modern Histories of Ancient Greece: Genealogies, Contexts and Eighteenth-Century Narrative Historiography," in *The Western Time of Ancient History: Historiographical Encounters with the Greek and Roman Pasts*, edited by Alexandra Lianeri, 138–55 (Cambridge: Cambridge University Press, 2011), 149.

25 Ceserani, "Modern Histories of Ancient Greece," 143, 152.

26 Caroline Winterer, *The Culture of Classicism: Ancient Greece and Rome in American Intellectual Life, 1780–1910* (Baltimore: Johns Hopkins University Press, 2002), 133–7.

27 Giovanna Ceserani, *Italy's Lost Greece: Magna Graecia and the Making of Modern Archaeology* (Oxford: Oxford University Press, 2012), 8, 42.

28 Winterer, *Culture of Classicism*, 82.

29 *OED Online*, s.v. "archive," (Oxford: Oxford University Press, 2018).

30 Wootton, "David Hume, 'The Historian,'" 454.

31 Voltaire, "History," in *The Encyclopedia of Diderot & d'Alembert Collaborative Translation Project*, trans. Jeremy Caradonna (Ann Arbor: Michigan Publishing, University of Michigan Library, 2006), available online: http://hdl.handle.net/2027/spo.did2222.0000.088 (accessed April 18, 2018). Originally published as "Histoire," in *Encyclopédie ou Dictionnaire raisonné des sciences, des arts et des métiers*, vol. 8, 220–5 (Paris, 1765).

32 Caroline Winterer, *American Enlightenments: Pursuing Happiness in the Age of Reason* (New Haven, CT: Yale University Press, 2016), 85.

33 Winterer, *American Enlightenments*, 85–6.

34 Louise Hollandine of the Palatinate, *Sophie von der Pfalz als Indianerin* (1644).

35 Henry St. John, Viscount Bolingbroke, *The Works of the Late Right Honorable Henry St. John, Viscount Bolingbroke*, 5 vols. (London: n.p., 1754), 5:152.

36 Barbara Mundy, *The Death of Aztec Tenochtitlan, the Life of Mexico City* (Austin: University of Texas Press, 2015); Elizabeth Yale, "The History of Archives: The State of the Discipline," *Book History* 18, no. 1 (2015): 332–59.

37 Richard Kagan, *Urban Images of the Hispanic World, 1493–1793* (New Haven, CT: Yale University Press, 2000), 50.

38 Winterer, *American Enlightenments*, 88–94.

39 Amber Brian, *Alva Ixtlilxochitl's Native Archive and the Circulation of Knowledge in Colonial Mexico* (Nashville, TN: Vanderbilt University Press, 2016), 23–5. See also Anna More, *Carlos*

de Sigüenza y Góngora and the Creole Archive of Colonial Mexico (Philadelphia: University of Pennsylvania Press, 2013).

40 Brian, *Alva Ixtlilxochitl's Native Archive*, 34.

41 Boturini Benaduci, *Catálogo del Museo histórico indiano del cavallero Lorenzo Boturini Benaduci* (Madrid: Juan de Zuñiga, 1746), 6, 48; John B. Glass, "The Boturini Collection and the Council of the Indies, 1780–1800," *Contributions to the Ethnohistory of Mexico*, no. 4 (Lincoln Center, MA: Conemex Associations, 1976); Jorge Cañizares-Esguerra, *How to Write the History of the New World: Histories, Epistemologies, and Identities in the Eighteenth-Century Atlantic World* (Stanford, CA: Stanford University Press, 2001), 135–55.

42 Winterer, *American Enlightenments*, 88–94.

43 Watt, *The Rise of the Novel*, 9–34.

44 Reinhart Koselleck, "Historical Criteria of the Modern Concept of Revolution," in *Futures Past: On the Semantics of Historical Time*, trans. Keith Tribe, 39–54 (Cambridge, MA: MIT Press, 1985).

45 *Encyclopaedia Britannica*, s.v. "Guillaume-Thomas Raynal, abbé de Raynal," available online: https://www.britannica.com/biography/Guillaume-Thomas-abbe-de-Raynal#ref206072 (accessed January 23, 2022).

46 John Adams to Thomas Cushing, July 25, 1778, in *The Adams Papers Digital Edition*, edited by Sara Martin (Charlottesville: University of Virginia Press, Rotunda, 2008–2018).

47 Raynal, *The Revolution of America*, 80.

48 Alexis de Tocqueville, *The Old Regime and the Revolution*, trans. John Bonner (New York: Harper and Brothers, 1856), 1.

49 Charles Dickens, *A Tale of Two Cities* (London: Chapman and Hall, 1859), 1.

50 Ernst Posner, "Some Aspects of Archival Development since the French Revolution," *American Archivist* 3, no. 3 (July 1940): 159–74.

51 Suzanne Marchand, *Down from Olympus: Archaeology and Philhellenism in Germany, 1750–1970* (Princeton, NJ: Princeton University Press, 1996), 4.

BIBLIOGRAPHY

PRIMARY SOURCES

The Aberdeen Magazine 3 (1788–1790).

The Adams Papers Digital Edition. Edited by Sara Martin. Charlottesville: University of Virginia Press, Rotunda, 2008–2018.

Adelung, Johann Christoph. *Grammatisch-kritisches Wörterbuch der hochdeutschen Mundart*. Vienna: Bauer, 1811.

Allgemeine Literatur-Zeitung. May 22, 1790.

The Ambulator. London: J. Bew, 1774.

Anonymous. *La religion vengée, ou réfutation des auteurs impies*. Paris, 1760.

Aquinas, Thomas. *Summa Theologiae*. New York: Blackfriars, 1964.

Bacon, Francis. *The Advancement of Learning*. Volume 1. New York: MacMillan, 1898.

Benaduci, Boturini. *Catálogo del Museo histórico indiano del cavallero Lorenzo Boturini Benaduci*. Madrid: Juan de Zuñiga, 1746.

Bergier, Nicolas Sylvestre. "Théologie." In *Encyclopédie méthodique*. Paris: Panckoucke, 1788.

Beutler, Johann Heinrich Christoph, and Johann Christoph Friedrich Gutsmuth, eds. *Allgemeines Sachregister ueber die wichstigsten deutschen Zeit- und Wochenschriften*. Leipzig, 1790.

Bolingbroke, Viscount Henry St. John. *Letters on the Study and Use of History*. 2 volumes. London: A. Millar, 1752.

Bolingbroke, Viscount Henry St. John. *The Works of the Late Right Honorable Henry St. John, Viscount Bolingbroke*. 5 volumes. London, 1754.

Boyle, Robert. *A Free Enquiry into the vulgarly receiv'd Notion of Nature; made in an essay address'd to a friend*. London: H. Clark, for John Taylor, 1685/6.

Boyle, Robert. *Works*. Edited by Michael Hunter and Edward B. Davis. 14 volumes. London: Pickering & Chatto, 1999–2000.

Burgh, James. *The Art of Speaking: Containing, I. An Essay; in which are Given Rules for Expressing Properly the Principal Passions and Humours, ... and II. Lessons, Taken from the Antients and Moderns*. Dublin: Messrs. Price, Whitestone, Wilkinson, Chamberlaine, W. Watson, [and 12 others in Dublin], 1784.

Burke, Edmund. *Reflections on the Revolution in France*. 1790. Edited and introduction by Conor Cruise O'Brien. New York: Penguin, 1986.

Burke, Edmund. *The Writings and Speeches of Edmund Burke*. Volume 1. New York: Cosimo, 2008.

Campbell, George. *The Philosophy of Rhetoric*. New York: Jonathan Leavitt, 1834.

Campbell, George. *The Works of George Campbell*. Volume 2. London: Thomas Tegg, 1840.

Chambers, Ephraim. *Cyclopaedia: or, An Universal Dictionary of the Arts and Sciences*. London, 1728.

Chaumeix, Abraham Joseph. *Préjugés légitimes contre l'Encyclopédie*. Brussels: Herissant, 1758.

Clarke, Samuel. *Demonstration of the Being and Attributes of God*. London, 1705.

Clarke, Samuel. "Answer to a Seventh Letter Concerning the Argument *a priori*." In *A Demonstration of the Being and Attributes of God*, edited by Ezio Vailati, 118–23. Cambridge: Cambridge University Press, 1998.

Condillac, Étienne de. *An Essay on the Origin of Human Knowledge*. Translated by Hans Aarsleff. Cambridge: Cambridge University Press, 2001.

d'Alembert, Jean le Rond. "Eulogy for President Montesquieu." In *Encyclopedic Liberty: Political Articles in the Dictionary of Diderot and d'Alembert*. Translated by Henry C. Clark and Christine Dunn Henderson, 122–38. Indianapolis, IN: Liberty Fund, 2016.

d'Alembert, Jean le Rond. *Preliminary Discourse to the Encyclopedia of Diderot*. Translated by Richard N. Schwab. Indianapolis, IN: Hackett, 1963.

de Ferrières, Charles Élie. *Correspondance inédite*. Paris: Armand Colin, 1932.

Denis, Michael. *Einleitung in die Bücherkunde*. Vienna: John Thomas von Trattner, 1778.

Derham, William. *Physico-theology: or, a Demonstration of the being and attributes of God, from his works of creation: Being the substance of sixteen sermons preached in St. Mary le Bow-Church, London, at the Hon.ble Mr. Boyle's Lectures, in the years 1711 and 1712: With large notes, and many curious observations*. 2nd edition. London: Printed for W. Innys, at the Princes Arms, in St. Paul's Church-Yard, 1714.

Dickens, Charles. *A Tale of Two Cities*. London: Chapman and Hall, 1859.

Diderot, Denis. *Oeuvres complètes*. Paris: Garnier, 1875–1877.

Diderot, Denis. "d'Alembert's Dream." In *Rameau's Nephew and Other Works*. Translated by Jacques Barzun and Ralph H. Bowen. Indianapolis, IN: Bobbs-Merrill, 1956.

Diderot, Denis. *Rameau's Nephew and d'Alembert's Dream*. Translated by Leonard Tancock. London: Penguin Books, 1966.

Diderot, Denis. "Encyclopédie." In Denis Diderot and Jean le Rond d'Alembert, eds., *L'Encyclopédie ou dictionnaire raisonné des sciences, des arts et des métiers*. Paris, 1780; reprint as compact edition, New York, 1969.

Du Pont de Nemours, Pierre-Samuel. "On the Origin and Progress of a New Science." In *Commerce, Culture and Liberty: Readings on Capitalism Before Adam Smith*, edited by Henry C. Clark, 564–97. Indianapolis, IN: Liberty Fund, 2003.

Ebert, Friedrich. *Ueber öffentliche Bibliotheken besonders deutsche Universitätsbibliotheken*. Freyberg: Commission der Craz und Gerlachisch buchhandlung, 1811.

Encyclopédie. ARTFL Project. Available online: https://artfl-project.uchicago.edu/ (accessed January 31, 2022).

Encyclopédie: Dictionnaire raisonné des sciences, des arts et des métiers. Edited by Denis Diderot and Jean le Rond d'Alembert. Paris: Briasson, 1751–1772.

Faucheur, Michel Le. *Essay upon the Action of an Orator; as to his Pronunciation and Gesture*. London: N. Cox, 1702.

Fontenelle, Bernard. *Œuvres*. Amsterdam, 1754.

Forbonnais, François Véron de. "Commerce." In *Encyclopedia of Diderot & d'Alembert Collaborative Translation Project*. Translated by Nelly S. Hoytand Thomas Cassirer. Ann Arbor: Michigan Publishing, University of Michigan Library, 2003.

Formey, Johann Samuel. *La belle Wolfienne*. La Haye, 1741.

Friedrich, Carl J., ed. *The Philosophy of Kant: Immanuel Kant's Moral and Political Writings*. New York: Modern Library, 1949.

Gedike, Friedrich. *"Der Universitäts-Bereiser": Friedrich Gedike und sein Bericht an Friedrich Wilhelm II*. Edited by Richard Fester. Berlin: Alexander Duncker, 1905.

Gibbon, Edward. *Memoirs of My Life*. Edited from the manuscripts by Georges A. Bonnard. London: Thomas A. Nelson & Sons, 1966.

Herder, Johann Gottfried. "Herder: Extract from a Correspondence on Ossian and the Songs of Ancient People." Translated by Joyce Crick. In *German Aesthetic and Literary Criticism: Winckelmann, Lessing, Hamann, Herder, Schiller, and Goethe*, edited by H. B. Nisbet, 151–76. Cambridge: Cambridge University Press, 1985.

Herder, Johann Gottfried. *Kritische Wälder, oder Betrachtungen, die Wissenschaft und Kunst des Schönen betreffend*. In *Johann Gottfried Herder Schriften zur Ästhetik und Literatur 1767–1781*, edited by Gunter Grimm. Frankfurt: Deutscher Klassiker Verlag, 1993.

Hobbes, Thomas. *Leviathan*. 3 volumes. Clarendon Edition of the Works of Thomas Hobbes. Oxford: Oxford University Press, 2012.

Humboldt, Wilhelm von. "Über die innere und äussere Organisation der höheren wissenschaftlichen Anstalten in Berlin." In *Wilhelm von Humboldts Gesammelte Schriften: Volume 10, Politische Denkschriften*, edited by Bruno Gebhardt, 250–6. Berlin: B. Behr, 1903.

Humboldt, Wilhelm von. "On the Internal Structure of the University in Berlin and Its Relationship to Other Organization." In *Rise of the Research University*, edited by Louis Menand, Paul Reitter, and Chad Wellmon, 108–19. Chicago: University of Chicago Press, 2017.

Hume, David. *Discours politiques*. Translated by Abbé Le Blanc. Amsterdam [Paris]: Lambert, 1754.

Jenaische Allgemeine Literatur-Zeitung, no. 70. April 1821: 73–80.

Jenaische Allgemeine Literatur-Zeitung, no. 71. April 1821: 81–5.

Jöcher, Christian Gottlieb. *Compendiöses Gelehrten-Lexicon*. Leipzig: Friedrich Gleditsch, 1733.

Jöcher, Christian Gottlieb. *Allgemeines Gelehrten-Lexicon*. 2 volumes. Leipzig: Friedrich Gleditsch, 1750.

Johnson, Samuel. *A Dictionary of the English Language: In Which the Words Are Deduced from Their Originals, and Illustrated in Their Different Significations by Examples from the Best Writers: To Which Are Prefixed, a History of the Language and an English Grammar*. London: Printed by W. Strahan, for J. and P. Knapton; T. and T. Longman; C. Hitch and L. Hawes; A. Millar; and R. and J. Dodsley, 1755.

Kant, Immanuel. *Gesammelte Schriften*. Edited by the Königlich Preussischen Akademie der Wissenschaften. 29 volumes. Berlin: Walter de Gruyter, 1902–.

Kayser, Albrecht Christoph. *Über die Manipulation bey der Einrichtung einer Bibliothek und der Verfertigung der Bücherverzeichnisse*. Bayreuth, 1790.

Köster, Heinrich, Martin Gottfried, and Johann Friedrich Roos, eds. *Deutsche Enzyklopädie, oder Allgemeines Real-Wörterbuch aller Künste und Wissenschaften*. 23 volumes. Frankfurt: Varrentrap Sohn & Wenner, 1778–1807.

Krug, Wilhelm Traugott. *Versuch einer systematischen Enzyklopädie der Wissenschaften*. Leipzig: Winckelmann & Barth, 1796.

Krug, Wilhelm Traugott. *Versuch einer neuen Eintheilung der Wissenschaften zur Begründung einer besseren Organization höheren gelehrten Bildungsanstalten*. Sulechów, Poland: Darnmann, 1805.

Leibniz, G. W. *Sämtliche Schriften und Briefe*. Berlin: Akademie Verlag, 1970.

Leibniz, G. W. *New Essays on Human Understanding*. Translated by Peter Remnant and Jonathan Bennett. Cambridge: Cambridge University Press, 1996.

Lessing, Gotthold Ephraim. *Laocoön: An Essay on the Limits of Painting and Poetry*. Translated by Edward Allen McCormick. Baltimore: Johns Hopkins University Press, 1984.

Lessius, Leonardus. *De providentia numinis et animi immortalitate libri duo adversus Atheos & Politicos*. Antverpiae: Ex Officina Plantiniana, apud Viduam & Filios Io. Moreti, 1613.

Les trois philosophes sur la nature de la monarchie. London, 1787.

Locke, John. *Two Treatises of Government.* Edited by Peter Laslett. Student edition. Cambridge Texts in the History of Political Thought. Cambridge: Cambridge University Press, 1988.

Malcolm, J. P. *An Historical Sketch of the Art of Caricaturing.* London, 1813.

Mendelssohn, Moses. *Philosophical Writings.* Translated by Daniel O. Dahlstrom. Cambridge: Cambridge University Press, 1997.

Mercier de la Rivière, Pierre-Paul Le. *L'Ordre naturel et essentiel des sociétés politiques.* London: Nourse and Densaint, 1767.

Mirabeau, Victor Riqueti, Marquis de. *l'Ami des hommes ou Traité de la population.* Nouvelle édition. 6 volumes. [Avignon], 1759.

Montesquieu. *Considerations on the Causes of the Greatness of the Romans and Their Decline.* Translated by David Lowenthal. Ithaca, NY: Cornell University Press, 1965.

Montesquieu. *The Spirit of the Laws.* Translated by Anne M. Cohler, Basia Carolyn Miller, and Harold Samuel Stone. Cambridge: Cambridge University Press, 1989.

Moréri, Louis. *Le grand dictionnaire historique.* Paris, 1718.

Newton, Isaac. *Philosophiae naturalis principia mathematica.* Londini: Jussu Societatis Regiae ac Typis Josephi Streater, 1687.

Nicolai, Friedrich. *Das Leben und die Meinungen des Herrn Magister Sebaldus Nothanker.* Volume 1. Berlin: Friedrich Nicolai, 1776.

Pluche, Noël-Antoine. *Le Spectacle de la Nature, ou Entretiens sur les particularités de l'histoire naturelle qui ont paru les plus propres à rendre les jeunes gens curieux et à leur former l'esprit.* 8 parts in 9 volumes. Paris: Vve Estienne, 1732–1750.

Pope, Alexander. *The Works of Alexander Pope, Esq: Volume 2, Containing His Epistles and Satires.* London: printed for L. Gilliver, 1735.

Pope, Alexander. *The Dunciad: Variorum 1729.* Leeds: Scolar Press, 1966.

Publius [James Madison, Alexander Hamilton, and John Jay]. *The Federalist.* 2 volumes. New York: J. and A. M'Lean, 1788.

[Quesnay, François]. "Remarques sur l'opinion de l'auteur de l'Esprit des Loix concernant les Colonies." Book 21. Chapter 17. *Journal de l'agriculture, du commerce, et des finances.* 5 April 1766.

Raynal, Abbé Guillaume Thomas. *The Revolution of America.* London: Lockyer Davis, 1781.

Raynal, Abbé Guillaume Thomas. *A Philosophical and Political History of the Settlements and Trade of the Europeans in the East and West Indies,* 8 volumes. London: Strahan and Cadell, 1788.

Rousseau, Jean-Jacques. *Discourse on the Origin of Inequality.* Translated by Donald A. Cress. Indianapolis, IN: Hackett Publishing, 1992.

Rousseau, Jean-Jacques. *"The Discourses" and Other Early Political Writings.* Cambridge: Cambridge University Press, 1997.

Rousseau, Jean-Jacques. *Discourse on Political Economy.* In *The Basic Political Writings.* 2nd edition. Translated by Donald Cress, 123–52. Indianapolis, IN: Hackett, 2011.

Rousseau, Jean-Jacques. *Les Confessions: Texte du manuscrit de Genéve.* 1782. Ebooks libre et gratuit, 2004. Available online: https://ebooks-bnr.com/ebooks/pdf4/rousseau_les_confessions.pdf (accessed February 5, 2022).

Schrettinger, Martin. *Versuch eines vollständigen Lehrbuchs der Bibliothek-Wissenschaften oder Anleitung zur vollkommenenen Geschäftsführung eines Bibliothekars in wissenschaftlicher Form.* 2 volumes. Munich: Lindauer, 1829.

Sheridan, Thomas. *A Course of Lectures on Elocution.* Troy: O. Penniman & Company, 1803.

Smith, Adam. *An Inquiry into the Nature and Causes of the Wealth of Nations,* 2 volumes. London: Strahan and Cadell, 1776.

Stanyan, Temple. *The Grecian History*. 2 volumes. London: J. and R. Tonson and S. Draper, 1751.

Stewart, Dugald. *Philosophical Essays*. Edinburgh: Printed by George Ramsay and Company for William Creech, and Archibald Constable and Company, Edinburgh; T. Cadell and W. Davies, Strand, John Murray, Fleet-Street, and Constable, Hunter, Park, and Hunter, London, 1810.

Sultzer, J. G. *Versuch einiger moralischen Betrachtungen über die Werke der Natur*. Berlin, 1745.

Swammerdam, Jan. *Historia insectorum generalis, ofte Algemeene Verhandeling van de Bloedeloose Dierkens*. Utrecht: by Meinardus van Drevnen, Ordinaris Drucker van d'Academie, 1669.

Swammerdam, Jan. *Historia insectorum generalis, in qua verissimae mutationem, seu lentae in membra epigeneseos rationes, duce experentia, redduntur, recepta vulgo insectorum metamorphosis solide refutatur*. Utrecht: Ex officina Otthonis de Vries, 1685.

Swift, Jonathan. "A Letter to a Young Clergyman." In *The Works of the Rev. Jonathan Swift*. Volume 5. London: Luke Hansard, 1720.

Swift, Jonathan, *Gulliver's Travels*. London: George Bell and Sons, 1892.

Tocqueville, Alexis de. *The Old Regime and the Revolution*. Translated by John Bonner. New York: Harper and Brothers, 1856.

Uffenbach, Herrn Zacharias Conrad von. *Merkwürdige Reise durch Niedersachsen, Holland und Engelland*. Ulm, 1754.

Venuti, Felippo. *Il trionfo letterario della Francia*. Avignon: Alessandro Giroud, 1750.

Vico, Giambattista. *The New Science of Giambattista Vico*. Ithaca, NY: Cornell University Press, 1984.

Voltaire. *Poèmes sur le désastre de Lisbonne et sur la loi naturelle, avec des préfaces des notes &c*. Geneva: [Cramer], 1766.

Voltaire. *Candide*. Translated and edited by Daniel Gordon. Boston: Bedford/St. Martin's, 1999.

Voltaire. "The Lisbon Earthquake." *New England Review* 26, no. 3 (2005): 183–93.

Voltaire. "History." In *The Encyclopedia of Diderot & d'Alembert Collaborative Translation Project*. Translated by Jeremy Caradonna. Ann Arbor: Michigan Publishing, University of Michigan Library, 2006. Available online: http://hdl.handle.net/2027/spo.did2222.0000.088 (accessed April 18, 2018).

Wilkins, John. *An Essay towards a Real Character, and a Philosophical Language*. Menston, UK: Scholar Press, 1968.

Witherspoon, John. *Lectures on Moral Philosophy*. Edited by Jack Scott. Newark: University of Delaware Press, 1982.

Zedler, Johann Heinrich. *Grosses Vollständiges-Universal Lexicon aller Wissenschaften und Künste*. Leipzig: Johann Heinrich Zedler, 1746.

SECONDARY SOURCES

Adam, Ulrich. *The Political Economy of J.H.G. Justi*. Bern: Peter Lang, 2006.

Alvira, Rafael, and Alfredo Cruz. "The Controversy Between Las Casas and Sepúlveda at Valladolid." In *Hispanic Philosophy in the Age of Discovery*, edited by Kevin White, 88–110. Washington, DC: Catholic University of America Press, 1997.

Andrews, Malcolm. *Landscape and Western Art*. Oxford: Oxford University Press, 1999.

Andrews, Stuart. *The British Periodical Press and the French Revolution, 1789–99*. London: Palgrave Macmillan, 2000.

Andries, Lise. "Récits de survie: les mémoires d'autodéfense pendant l'an II et l'an III." In *La Carmagnole des Muses: L'homme de lettres et l'artiste dans la Révolution*, edited by Jean-Claude Bonnet, 261–73. Paris: Colin, 1988.

Arch, Stephen Carl. "Benjamin Franklin's *Autobiography*, Then and Now." In *The Cambridge Companion to Benjamin Franklin*, edited by Carla Mumford, 159–71. Cambridge: Cambridge University Press, 2008.

ArtUK. "Commerce, or the Triumph of the Thames (painting 4 of 6 in the series 'The Progress of Human Knowledge and Culture'): James Barry (1741–1806)." Available online: https://artuk.org/discover/artworks/commerce-or-the-triumph-of-the-thames-218503 (accessed January 30, 2022).

Ashcraft, Richard. *Revolutionary Politics and Locke's Two Treatises of Government*. Princeton, NJ: Princeton University Press, 1986.

Baker, Keith Michael. "Defining the Public Sphere in Eighteenth-Century France: Variations on a Theme by Habermas." In *Habermas and the Public Sphere*, edited by Craig Calhoun, 181–211. Cambridge, MA: MIT Press, 1993.

Baker, Keith Michael. "Enlightenment and the Institution of Society: Notes for a Conceptual History." In *Main Trends in Cultural History: Ten Essays*, edited by Willem Melching and Wyger Velema, 96–108. Amsterdam: Rodopi, 1994.

Barker, Emma. *Greuze and the Painting of Sentiment*. Cambridge: Cambridge University Press, 2005.

Bartlett, Robert. *The Natural and the Supernatural in the Middle Ages*. Cambridge: Cambridge University Press, 1980.

Baxandall, Michael. *Patterns of Intention: On the Historical Explanation of Pictures*. New Haven, CT: Yale University Press, 1985.

Bennett, Tony. *The Birth of the Museum: History, Theory, Politics*. London: Routledge, 1995.

Bensaude-Vincent, Bernadette, and Christine Blondel, eds. *Science and Spectacle in the European Enlightenment*. Farnham, UK: Ashgate, 2008.

Berg, Maxine. *Luxury and Pleasure in Eighteenth-Century Britain*. Oxford: Oxford University Press, 2007.

Berti, Silvia, Françoise Charles-Daubert, and Richard H. Popkin, eds. *Heterodoxy, Spinozism, and Free Thought in Early-Eighteenth-Century Europe: Studies on the Traité des Trois Imposteurs*. International Archives of the History of Ideas/Archives internationales d'histoire des idées, 148. Dordrecht: Springer Netherlands, 1996.

Bevilacqua, Vincent. "Baconian Influences in the Development of Scottish Rhetorical Theory." *Proceedings of the American Philosophical Society* 111, no. 4 (1967): 212–18.

Bevilacqua, Vincent. "Campbell, Vico, and the Rhetorical Science of Human Nature." *Philosophy & Rhetoric* 18, no. 1 (1985): 23–30.

Bevilacqua, Alexander. *The Republic of Arabic Letters: Islam and the European Enlightenment*. Cambridge, MA: Harvard University Press, 2018.

Bindman, David. *Ape to Apollo: Aesthetics and the Idea of Race in the 18th Century*. Ithaca, NY: Cornell University Press, 2002.

Bingham, Alfred J. "The Abbe Bergier: An Eighteenth-Century Catholic Apologist." *Modern Language Review* 54, no. 3 (July 1959): 337–50.

Birn, Raymond. *Royal Censorship of Books in 18th-Century France*. Stanford, CA: Stanford University Press, 2012.

Blair, Ann. *Too Much to Know: Managing Scholarly Information before the Modern Age*. New Haven, CT: Yale University Press, 2010.

Blair, Ann. "Noël-Antoine Pluche as a Jansenist Natural Theologian." *Intellectual History Review* 26, no. 1 (2016): 91–9.

Blanning, T. C. W. *The Culture of Power and the Power of Culture: Old Regime Europe, 1660–1789*. Oxford: Oxford University Press, 2002.

Blanning, T. C. W. *The Pursuit of Glory: Europe 1648–1815*. London: Viking, 2007.

Bleichmar, Daniela. *Visible Empire: Botanical Expeditions and Visual Culture in the Hispanic Enlightenment*. Chicago: University of Chicago Press, 2012.

Blum, Carol. *Strength in Numbers: Population, Reproduction, and Power in Eighteenth-Century France*. Baltimore: Johns Hopkins University Press, 2002.

Bod, Rens, Jaap Maat, and Thijs Weststeijn, eds. *The Making of the Humanities*. Volumes 1–2. Amsterdam: Amsterdam University Press, 2010.

Bordes, Philippe. *Le Serment du Jeu de paume de Jacques-Louis David. Le peintre, son milieu et son temps de 1789 à 1792*. Paris: Réunion des musées nationaux, 1983.

Braun, Theodore E. D., and John B. Radner, eds. *The Lisbon Earthquake of 1755: Representations and Reactions*. Oxford: Voltaire Foundation, 2005.

Brett, Annabel S. *Changes of State: Nature and the Limits of the City in Early Modern Natural Law*. Princeton, NJ: Princeton University Press, 2011.

Brian, Amber. *Alva Ixtlilxochitl's Native Archive and the Circulation of Knowledge in Colonial Mexico*. Nashville, TN: Vanderbilt University Press, 2016.

Broman, Thomas. "Metaphysics for an Enlightened Public: The Controversy over Monads in Germany, 1746–1748." *Isis* 103, no. 1 (March 2012): 1–21.

Brooke, John. "The Library of King George III." *Yale University Library Gazette* 52, no. 1 (July 1977): 33–45.

Brot, Muriel. "Montesquieu dans l'Histoire des Deux Indes." *Revue Française d'Histoire des Idées Politiques* 35 (2012): 123–33.

Brown, Alison. *The Return of Lucretius to Renaissance Florence*. I Tatti Studies in Renaissance History. Cambridge, MA: Harvard University Press, 2010.

Bryson, Norman. *Vision and Painting: The Logic of the Gaze*. New Haven, CT: Yale University Press, 1986.

Buckley, Michael J., SJ. *At the Origins of Modern Atheism*. New Haven, CT: Yale University Press, 1987.

Buckley, Michael J., SJ. *Denying and Disclosing God: The Ambiguous Progress of Modern Atheism*. New Haven, CT: Yale University Press, 2004.

Bulman, William J. *Anglican Enlightenment: Orientalism, Religion, and Politics in England and Its Empire, 1648–1715*. Cambridge: Cambridge University Press, 2015.

Bulman, William J., and Robert G. Ingram, eds. *God in the Enlightenment*. Oxford: Oxford University Press, 2016.

Burson, Jeffrey. *The Rise and Fall of Theological Enlightenment: Jean-Martin de Prades and Ideological Polarization in Eighteenth-Century France*. Notre Dame, IN: University of Notre Dame Press, 2010.

Cailleux, André. "Progression du nombre d'espèces de plantes décrites de 1500 à nos jours." *Revue d'Histoire des Sciences* 6 (1953): 42–9.

Campagne, Fabián Alejandro. "Witchcraft and the Sense-of-the-Impossible in Early Modern Spain: Some Reflections Based on the Literature of Superstition (ca. 1500–1800)." *Harvard Theological Review* 96, no. 1 (2003): 25–62.

Cañizares-Esguerra, Jorge. *How to Write the History of the New World: Histories, Epistemologies, and Identities in the Eighteenth-Century Atlantic World*. Stanford, CA: Stanford University Press, 2001.

Carcassone, Elie. *Montesquieu et le problème de la constitution française au XVIIIe siècle*. Paris: Presses universitaires de France, 1927.

Carson, Cary. "The Consumer Revolution in Colonial British America: Why Demand?" In *Of Consuming Interests: The Style of Life in the Eighteenth Century*, edited by Cary Carson,

Ronald Hoffman, and Peter J. Albert, 483–697. Charlottesville: University of Virginia Press, 1994.

Cartwright, Nancy. *How the Laws of Physics Lie*. Oxford: Oxford University Press, 1983.

Censer, Jack. *The French Press in the Age of Enlightenment*. London: Routledge, 1994.

Ceserani, Giovanna. "Modern Histories of Ancient Greece: Genealogies, Contexts and Eighteenth-Century Narrative Historiography." In *The Western Time of Ancient History: Historiographical Encounters with the Greek and Roman Pasts*, edited by Alexandra Lianeri, 138–55. Cambridge: Cambridge University Press, 2011.

Ceserani, Giovanna. *Italy's Lost Greece: Magna Graecia and the Making of Modern Archaeology*. Oxford: Oxford University Press, 2012.

Charles, Loïc, and Philippe Steiner. "Entre Montesquieu et Rousseau: La physiocratie parmi les origines intellectuelles de la Révolution Française." *Etudes Jean-Jacques Rousseau* 11 (1999): 83–160.

Charles, Loïc, and Christine Théré. "The Writing Workshop of François Quesnay and the Making of Physiocracy." *History of Political Economy* 40 (2008): 1–42.

Charles, Loïc, Frédéric Lefebvre, and Christine Théré, eds. *Le Cercle de Vincent de Gournay: saviors économiques et pratiques administratives en France au milieu du XVIIIe siècle*s. Paris: Institut National d'Etudes Démographiques, 2011.

Chartier, Roger. *The Order of Books: Readers, Authors, and Libraries in Europe Between the Fourteenth and Eighteenth Centuries*. Palo Alto, CA: Stanford University Press, 1994.

Cheney, Paul. *Revolutionary Commerce: Globalization and the French Monarchy*. Cambridge, MA: Harvard University Press, 2010.

Clark, Henry C. *Compass of Society: Commerce and Absolutism in Old Regime France*. Lanham, MD: Lexington, 2007.

Clark, Henry C. "Montesquieu in Smith's Method of 'Theory and History.'" *Adam Smith Review* 4 (2008): 132–57.

Clark, William. "On the Bureaucratic Plots of the Research Library." In *Books and Sciences in History*, edited by Marina Frasca-Spada and Nick Jardine, 190–206. Cambridge: Cambridge University Press, 2000.

Clark, William. *Academic Charisma and the Origins of the Research University*. Chicago: University of Chicago Press, 2006.

Coleman, Charly. *The Virtues of Abandon: An Anti-Individualist History of the French Enlightenment*. Stanford, CA: Stanford University Press, 2014.

Costelloe, Timothy. "Giambattista Vico." *The Stanford Encyclopedia of Philosophy* (Summer 2016). Available online: https://plato.stanford.edu/archives/sum2016/entries/vico/ (accessed November 15, 2017).

Courtney, Cecil Patrick. "L'Esprit des lois dans la perspective de l'histoire du livre (1748–1800)." In *Le Temps de Montesquieu*, edited by Michel Porret and Catherine Volpilhac-Auger, 65–96. Geneva: Droz, 2002.

Cram, David, and Jaap Maat, eds. *George Dalgarno on Universal Language*. Oxford: Oxford University Press, 2001.

Cranston, Maurice. *The Solitary Self: Jean-Jacques Rousseau in Exile and Adversity*. Chicago: University of Chicago Press, 1997.

Cron, Adelaïde. *Mémoires féminins de la fin du XVIIe siècle à la période révolutionnaire: Enquête sur la constitution d'un genre et d'une identité*. Paris: Presses Sorbonne Nouvelle, 2016.

Crow, Thomas. *Painters and Public Life in Eighteenth-Century Paris*. New Haven, CT: Yale University Press, 1985.

Curry, Helen A., Nicholas Jardine, James A. Secord, and Emma C. Spary, eds. *Worlds of Natural History*. Cambridge: Cambridge University Press, 2018.

Dahm, John J. "Science and Apologetics in the Early Boyle Lectures." *Church History* 39, no. 2 (June 1970): 172–86.

Darnton, Robert. *The Business of Enlightenment: A Publishing History of the Encyclopédie, 1775–1800*. Cambridge, MA: Harvard University Press, 1979.

Darnton, Robert. *The Great Cat Massacre and Other Episodes in French Cultural History*. New York: Basic Books, 1984.

Daston, Lorraine, and Peter Galison. *Objectivity*. New York: Zone Books, 2007.

Daston, Lorraine, and Katharine Park. *Wonders and The Order of Nature, 1150–1750*. New York: Zone Books, 1998.

Daston, Lorraine, and Michael Stolleis, eds. *Natural Law and Laws of Nature in Early Modern Europe: Jurisprudence, Theology, Moral and Natural Philosophy*. Farnham, UK: Ashgate, 2008.

Denby, David. *Sentimental Narrative and the Social Order in France, 1760–1820*. Cambridge: Cambridge University Press, 1994.

Dent, Nicholas. *Rousseau*. Routledge Philosophers. London: Routledge, 2005.

de Vries, Jan. *The Industrious Revolution: Consumer Behavior and the Household Economy, 1650 to the Present*. Cambridge: Cambridge University Press, 2008.

Dierse, Ulrich. *Encyklopädie. Zur Geschichte eines philosophischen und wissenschaftlichen Begriffs*. Bonn: Bouvier Verlag, 1977.

Dorato, Mauro. *The Software of the Universe: An Introduction to the History and Philosophy of Laws of Nature*. Translated by Rachel Marshall. Ashgate New Critical Thinking in Philosophy. Aldershot, UK: Ashgate, 2005.

Douglass, Robin. "Rousseau's Debt to Burlamaqui: The Ideal of Nature and the Nature of Things." *Journal of the History of Ideas* 72, no. 2 (April 2011): 209–30.

Doyle, William. *Origins of the French Revolution*. 3rd edition. Oxford: Oxford University Press, 1999.

Duby, Georges. *The Three Orders: Feudal Society Imagined*. Translated by Arthur Goldhammer. Chicago: University of Chicago Press, 1980.

Edelstein, Dan, Robert Morissey, and Glenn Roe. "To Quote or Not to Quote: Citation Strategies in the *Encyclopédie*." *Journal of the History of Ideas* 74 (2013): 223–4.

Elkins, James. *Chinese Landscape Painting as Western Art History*. Hong Kong: Hong Kong University Press, 2010.

Ellis, Harold A. *Boulainvilliers and the French Monarchy: Aristocratic Politics in Early Eighteenth-Century France*. Ithaca, NY: Cornell University Press, 1988.

Encyclopaedia Britannica. Available online: https://www.britannica.com/ (accessed January 23, 2022).

Febvre, Lucien, and Henri-Jean Martin. *The Coming of the Book: The Impact of Printing 1450–1800*. Translated by David Gerard. New York: Verso Classics, 1997.

Feilla, Cecilia. *The Sentimental Theater of the French Revolution*. Farnham, UK: Ashgate, 2013.

Fordham, Douglas. *British Art and the Seven Years' War: Allegiance and Autonomy*. Philadelphia: University of Pennsylvania Press, 2010.

Forster, Antonia. "Review Journals and the Reading Public." In *Books and their Readers in Eighteenth-Century England: New Essays*, edited by Isabel Rivers, 171–90. London: Continuum, 2001.

Funkenstein, Amos. *Theology and the Scientific Imagination from the Middle Ages to the Seventeenth Century*. Princeton, NJ: Princeton University Press, 1986.

Garberson, Eric. *Eighteenth-Century Monastic Libraries in Southern Germany and Austria: Architecture and Decorations*. Baden-Baden: Valentin Koerner, 1998.

Garrett, Jeffrey. "Redefining Order in the German Library, 1775–1825." *Eighteenth-Century Studies* 33, no. 1 (1999): 103–23.

Gass, William H. "The Story of the State of Nature." *Salmagundi* 94/95 (Spring–Summer 1992): 114–35.

Gay, Peter. "Carl Becker's Heavenly City." *Political Science Quarterly* 72, no. 2 (June 1957): 182–99.

Gay, Peter. *The Enlightenment: An Interpretation*. New York: Knopf, 1966–1969.

Gierl, Martin. *Pietismus und Aufklärung: Theologische Polemik und die Kommunikationsreform der Wissenschaft am Ende des 17. Jahrhunderts*. Göttingen: Vandenhoeck & Ruprecht, 1997.

Ginsborg, Hannah. "Kant's Aesthetics and Teleology." *The Stanford Encyclopedia of Philosophy* (Winter 2019). Available online: https://plato.stanford.edu/archives/fall2014/entries/kant-aesthetics/ (accessed February 8, 2022).

Glacken, Clarence J. *Traces on the Rhodian Shore: Nature and Culture in Western Thought from Ancient Times to the End of the Eighteenth Century*. Berkeley: University of California Press, 1967.

Glass, John B. "The Boturini Collection and the Council of the Indies, 1780–1800." In *Contributions to the Ethnohistory of Mexico*, no. 4. Lincoln Center, MA: Conemex Associations, 1976.

Goldgar, Anne. *Impolite Learning: Conduct and Community in the Republic of Letters, 1680–1750*. New Haven, CT: Yale University Press, 1995.

Goldstein, Jan. *The Post-Revolutionary Self: Politics and Psyche in France, 1750–1850*. Cambridge, MA: Harvard University Press, 2005.

Gombrich, E. H. *Art and Illusion: A Study in the Psychology of Pictorial Presentation*. London: Phaidon, 1958.

Gombrich, E. H. *The Story of Art*. New York: Phaidon, 1961.

Goodman, Dena. *The Republic of Letters: A Cultural History of the French Enlightenment*. Ithaca, NY: Cornell University Press, 1994.

Goodman, John, ed. and trans. *Diderot on Art: Volume 1, The Salon of 1765 and Notes on Painting*. New Haven, CT: Yale University Press, 1995.

"Google Receives $25 Million in Equity Funding." Google Press, June 7, 1999. Available online: http://googlepress.blogspot.com/1999/06/google-receives-25-million-in-equity.html (accessed January 23, 2022).

Gordon, Daniel. *Citizens Without Sovereignty: Equality and Sociability in French Thought, 1670–1789*. Princeton, NJ: Princeton University Press, 1994.

Gould, Stephen Jay. *The Mismeasure of Man*. New York: Norton, 1981.

Goulemot, Jean Marie. "Literary Practices: Publicizing the Private." In *A History of Private Life: Volume 3, Passions of the Renaissance*, edited by Roger Chartier, 363–95. Translated by Arthur Goldhammer. Cambridge, MA: Harvard University Press, 1989.

Grant, Edward. *The Foundations of Modern Science in the Middle Ages*. Cambridge: Cambridge University Press, 1996.

Grant, Edward. *God and Reason in the Middle Ages*. Cambridge: Cambridge University Press, 2001.

Grote, Simon. "Religion and Enlightenment." *Journal of the History of Ideas* 75, no. 1 (January 2014): 137–60.

Gutwirth, Madelyn. *The Twilight of the Goddesses: Women and Representation in the French Revolutionary Era*. New Brunswick, NJ: Rutgers University Press, 1992.

Guyer, Paul. "18th Century German Aesthetics," *The Stanford Encyclopedia of Philosophy*. (Winter 2016). Available online: https://plato.stanford.edu/archives/win2016/entries/aesthetics-18th-german/ (accessed January 23, 2022).

Habermas, Jürgen. *The Structural Transformation of the Public Sphere: An Inquiry into a Category of Bourgeois Society*. Translated by Thomas Burger and Frederick Lawrence. Cambridge, MA: MIT Press, 1989.

Hanley, Ryan Patrick. "Political Economy and Liberty." In *The Challenge of Rousseau*, edited by Eve Grace and Christopher Kelly, 34–56. Cambridge: Cambridge University Press, 2013.

Hazard, Paul. *The European Mind, 1680–1715*. Translated by J. Lewis May. Cleveland, OH: World Publishing Co., 1953.

Henry, John. "Metaphysics and the Origins of Modern Science: Descartes and the Importance of Laws of Nature." *Early Science and Medicine* 9, no. 2 (2004): 73–114.

Hertz, Deborah. *Jewish High Society in Old Regime Berlin*. New Haven, CT: Yale University Press, 1988.

Hesse, Carla. "Revolutionary Rousseau's: The Story of His Editions." In *Media and Political Culture in the Eighteenth Century*, edited by Marie-Christine Skuncke, 107–28. Stockholm: Kungl. Vitterhets Historie och Antikvitets Akademien, 2005.

"Heynes Bericht von 1810." In *Vier Dokumente zur Geschichte der Universitäts-Bibliothek Göttingen*, edited by Karl Julius Hartmann, 14–18. Göttingen: Häntzchel & Co., 1937.

Hirschman, Albert. *The Passions and the Interests: Political Arguments for Capitalism Before Its Triumph*. Princeton, NJ: Princeton University Press, 1977.

Hochstrasser, Tim J. "Natural Law." In *Dictionary of the History of Ideas*, edited by Maryanne Cline Horowitz, Volume 4, 1607–10. Detroit: Thomson Gale, 2005.

Hont, Istvan. "The Early Enlightenment Debate on Commerce and Luxury." In *The Cambridge History of Eighteenth-Century Political Thought*, edited by Mark Goldie and Robert Walker, 379–418. Cambridge: Cambridge University Press, 2006.

Hont, Istvan. *Politics in Commercial Society: Jean-Jacques Rousseau and Adam Smith*. Edited by Béla Kapossy and Michael Sonenscher. Cambridge, MA: Harvard University Press, 2015.

Hoquet, Thierry. "History Without Time: Buffon's Natural History as a Nonmathematical Physique." *Isis* 101, no. 1 (2010): 30–61.

Hortzschansky, Adalbert. *Die Königliche Bibliothek zu Berlin: Ihre Geschichte und Ihre Organization*. Berlin: Behrend, 1908.

Howell, Wilbur Samuel. *Logic and Rhetoric in England, 1500–1700*. Princeton, NJ: Princeton University Press, 1956.

Howell, Wilbur Samuel. *Eighteenth-Century British Logic and Rhetoric*. Princeton, NJ: Princeton University Press, 1971.

Hudson, Nicholas. "What is the Enlightenment? Investigating the Origins and Ideological Uses of an Historical Category." *Lumen* 25 (2006): 163–74.

Hundert, Edward. *The Enlightenment's Fable: Bernard Mandeville and the Discovery of Society*. Cambridge: Cambridge University Press, 1994.

Hunt, Lynn. *The Family Romance of the French Revolution*. Berkeley: University of California Press, 1992.

Hunt, Lynn. *Inventing Human Rights: A History*. New York: W. W. Norton, 2007.

Hunter, Matthew C. *Wicked Intelligence: Visual Art and the Science of Experiment in Restoration London*. Chicago: University of Chicago Press, 2013.

Hunter, Michael, and Edward B. Davis. "The Making of Robert Boyle's 'Free enquiry into the vulgarly receiv'd notion of nature' (1686)." *Early Science and Medicine* 1, no. 2 (June 1996): 204–71.

Israel, Jonathan. *Enlightenment Contested: Philosophy, Modernity, and the Emancipation of Man 1670–1752*. Oxford: Oxford University Press, 2006.

Israel, Jonathan. "French Royal Censorship and the Battle to Suppress the Encyclopédie of Diderot and d'Alembert, 1751–1759." In *The Use of Censorship in the Enlightenment*, edited by Mogens Laerke, 61–74. Leiden: Brill, 2009.

Ives, Robin J. "Political Publicity and Political Economy in Eighteenth-Century France." *French History* 17 (2003): 1–18.

Jacob, Margaret. *Living the Enlightenment: Freemasonry and Politics in Eighteenth-Century Europe*. Oxford: Oxford University Press, 1991.

Jardine, Nicholas, James A. Secord, and Emma C. Spary, eds. *Cultures of Natural History*. Cambridge: Cambridge University Press, 1996.

Jentzsch, Rudolf. *Der deutsch-lateinische Büchermarkt nach den Leipziger Ostermeßkatalogen von 1740, 1770 und 1800 in seiner Gliederung und Wandlung*. Leipzig: Voigtländer, 1912.

Johns, Adrian. *The Nature of the Book: Print and Knowledge in the Making*. Chicago: University of Chicago Press, 1998.

Jones, Colin. "Bourgeois Revolution Revivified: 1789 and Social Change." In *Rewriting the French Revolution*, edited by Colin Lucas, 69–118. Oxford: Clarendon Press, 1991.

Jones, Colin. "The Great Chain of Buying: Medical Advertisement, the Bourgeois Public Sphere, and the Origins of the French Revolution." *American Historical Review* 101 (1996): 13–40.

Kafker, Frank A., and Serena L. Kafker. *The Encyclopedists as Individuals: A Biographical Dictionary of the Authors of the Encyclopédie*. Oxford: Voltaire Foundation, 1988.

Kagan, Richard. *Urban Images of the Hispanic World, 1493–1793*. New Haven, CT: Yale University Press, 2000.

Kaminski, John P., Gaspare J. Saladino, Richard Leffler, Charles H. Schoenleber, and Margaret A. Hogan, eds. *The Documentary History of the Ratification of the Constitution*. Digital edition. Charlottesville: University of Virginia Press, 2009. Available online: http://rotunda. upress.virginia.edu/founders/RNCN (accessed May 16, 2014).

Kaufmann, Jean-Claude. *L'invention de soi: une théorie de l'identité*. Paris: Armand Colin, 2004.

Kemp, Martin. *The Oxford History of Western Art*. Oxford: Oxford University Press, 2000.

Kempe, Michael. *Wissenschaft, Theologie, Aufklärung: Johann Jakob Scheuchzer und die Sintfluttheorie*. Epfendorf: Bibliotheca Academica, 2003.

Kernan, Avin. *Printing Technology, Letters & Samuel Johnson*. Princeton, NJ: Princeton University Press, 1987.

Keynes, John Maynard. "Preface to the French Edition." In *The Collected Writings of John Maynard Keynes: Volume 7, The General Theory*, edited by Elizabeth Johnson and Donald Moggridge, xv–xvii. Cambridge: Cambridge University Press, 1978.

Knott, Sarah. *Sensibility and the American Revolution*. Chapel Hill: University of North Carolina Press, 2009.

Kors, Alan Charles. "'A First Being, of Whom We Have No Proof': The Preamble of Atheism in Early Modern France." In *Anticipations of the Enlightenment in England, France, and Germany*, edited by Alan Charles Kors and Paul J. Korshin, 17–68. Philadelphia: University of Pennsylvania Press, 1987.

Kors, Alan Charles. *Atheism in France, 1650–1729*. Princeton, NJ: Princeton University Press, 1990.

Koselleck, Reinhart. "Historical Criteria of the Modern Concept of Revolution." In *Futures Past: On the Semantics of Historical Time*. Translated by Keith Tribe, 39–54. Cambridge, MA: MIT Press, 1985.

Krajewski, Markus. "Zwischen Häusern und Büchern: Die Domestiken der Bibliotheken." In *Museum, Bibliothek, Stadtraum: Räumliche Wissensordnungen 1600–1900*, edited by Robert Felfe and Kirsten Wagner, 141–52. Berlin: Lit Verlag, 2010.

Kriz, Kay Dian. *Slavery, Sugar, and the Culture of Refinement*. New Haven, CT: Yale University Press, 2008.

Kunoff, Hugo. *The Foundations of the German Academic Library*. Chicago: American Library Association, 1982.

Kwass, Michael. "Consumption and the World of Ideas: Consumer Revolution and the Moral Economy of the Marquis de Mirabeau." *Eighteenth-Century Studies* 37 (2004): 187–213.

Land, Stephen K. "Adam Smith's 'Considerations Concerning the First Formation of Languages.'" *Journal of the History of Ideas* 38, no. 4 (Fall 1977): 677–90.

Laqueur, Thomas. "Bodies, Details, and the Humanitarian Narrative." In *The New Cultural History*, edited by Lynn Hunt, 176–204. Berkeley: University of California Press, 1989.

Laqueur, Thomas. *Making Sex: Body and Gender from the Greeks to Freud*. Cambridge, MA: Harvard University Press, 1990.

Larrère, Catherine. *L'Invention de l'economie au XVIIIe siècle: Du droit naturel à la physiocratie*. Paris: Presses universitaires de France, 1992.

Latour, Bruno. *Science in Action: How To Follow Scientists And Engineers through Society*. Cambridge, MA: Harvard University Press,1987.

Ledbury, Mark. *Sedaine, Greuze, and the Boundaries of Genre*. Oxford: The Voltaire Foundation, 2000.

Lehner, Ulrich. *Enlightened Monks: The German Benedictines, 1740–1803*. Oxford: Oxford University Press, 2011.

Levin, Jerome David. *Theories of the Self*. Washington, DC: Taylor & Francis, 1992.

Lewis, C. S. *Studies in Words*. Cambridge: Cambridge University Press, 1960.

Leyh, Georg. "Die Deutschen Bibliotheken von der Aufklärung bis zur Gegenwart." In *Handbuch der Bibliothekswissenschaft*, vol. 3, pt. 2, edited by Georg Leyh, 1–491. Wiesbaden: Otto Harrassowitz, 1957.

Lifschitz, Avi. *Language and Enlightenment: The Berlin Debates of the Eighteenth Century*. Oxford: Oxford University Press, 2012.

Lilti, Antoine. *The Worlds of the Salons: Sociability and Wordliness in Eighteenth-Century Paris*. Translated by Lydia Cochrane. Oxford: Oxford University Press, 2015.

Lilti, Antoine. *The Invention of Celebrity*. Cambridge, UK: Polity, 2017.

Lougee, Carolyn Chappell. *Le Paradis des Femmes: Women, Salons, and Social Stratification in Seventeenth-Century France*. Princeton, NJ: Princeton University Press, 1976.

Lougee, Carolyn Chappell. "Emigration and Memory: After 1685 and After 1789." In *Egodocuments and History: Autobiographical Writing in its Social Context since the Middle Ages*, edited by Rudolf Dekker, 89–106. Hilversum: Verloren, 2002.

Lough, John. *The Encyclopédie*. New York: David McKay, 1971.

Lynn, Michael R. *Popular Science and Public Opinion in Eighteenth-Century France*. Manchester: Manchester University Press, 2006.

Maat, Jaap. "Language and Semiotics." In *The Oxford Handbook of Philosophy in Early Modern Europe*, edited by Desmond M. Clarke and Catherine Wilson, 272–94. Oxford: Oxford University Press, 2013.

Maatsch, Jonas. *Naturgeschichte der Philosopheme: Frühromantische Wissensordnungen im Kontext.* Heidelberg: Universitätsverlag Winter, 2008.

Maier, Pauline. *Ratification: The People Debate the Constitution, 1787–1788.* New York: Simon and Schuster, 2010.

Makdisi, Saree. *Making England Western: Occidentalism, Race, and Imperial Culture.* Chicago: University of Chicago Press, 2014.

Marchand, Suzanne. *Down from Olympus: Archaeology and Philhellenism in Germany, 1750–1970.* Princeton, NJ: Princeton University Press, 1996.

Marcu, Eva Dorothea. "Un encyclopédiste oublié: Formey." *Revue d'Histoire Littéraire de la France* 53, no. 3 (1953): 296–305.

Markus, Gygory. "Changing Images of Science." *Thesis Eleven* 33, no. 1 (August 1992): 1–56.

Marshall, Colin. "Kant's Metaphysics of the Self." *Philosopher's Imprint* 10, no. 8 (August 2010): 1–21.

Marshall, David L. "Literature Survey Early Modern Rhetoric: Recent Research in German, Italian, French, and English." *Intellectual History Review* 17, no. 1 (January 2007): 107–35.

Marshall, David L. *Vico and the Transformation of Rhetoric in Early Modern Europe.* Cambridge: Cambridge University Press, 2010.

Martin, Andy. *Napoleon the Novelist.* Cambridge, UK: Polity, 2001.

Martin, John J. *Myths of the Renaissance Individualism.* London: Palgrave, 2004.

Martin, Raymond, and John Barresi. *Naturalization of the Soul: Self and Personal Identity in the Eighteenth Century.* London: Routledge, 2000.

Martin, Raymond, and John Barresi. *The Rise and Fall of Soul and Self.* New York: Columbia University Press, 2006.

Mascuch, Michael. *Origins of the Individualist Self: Autobiography and Self-Identity in England, 1591–1791.* Stanford, CA: Stanford University Press, 1996.

Maza, Sarah. *The Myth of the French Bourgeoisie: An Essay on the Social Imaginary, 1750–1850.* Cambridge, MA: Harvard University Press, 2003.

Maza, Sarah. "The Cultural Origins of the French Revolution." In *A Companion to the French Revolution*, edited by Peter McPhee, 42–56. Chichester, UK: Blackwell, 2013.

Mazzotti, Massimo. "Newton for Ladies: Gentility, Gender, and Radical Culture." *British Journal for the History of Science* 37, no. 2 (June 2004): 119–46.

McDowell, Paula. *The Invention of the Oral: Print Commerce and Fugitive Voices in Eighteenth-Century Britain.* Chicago: University of Chicago Press, 2017.

McKellar, Elizabeth. *Landscapes of London: The City, the Country, and the Suburbs 1660–1840.* New Haven, CT: Paul Mellon Center for Studies in British Art, Yale University Press, 2013.

McLean, Ian. *Rattling Spears: A History of Indigenous Australian Art.* London: Reaktion Books, 2016.

Melton, James Van Horn. *The Rise of the Public in Enlightenment Europe: New Approaches to European History.* Cambridge: Cambridge University Press, 2001.

Migon, Krystof. *Das Buch als Gegenstand wissenschaftlicher Forschung: Buchwissenschaft und Ihre Problematik.* Wiesbaden: Otto Harrassowitz, 1990.

Moran, Michael G., ed. *Eighteenth-Century British and American Rhetorics and Rhetoricians: Critical Studies and Sources.* Westport, CT: Greenwood Press, 1994.

More, Anna. *Carlos de Sigüenza y Góngora and the Creole Archive of Colonial Mexico.* Philadelphia: University of Pennsylvania Press, 2013.

Morizot, Jacques, "18th Century French Aesthetics," *The Stanford Encyclopedia of Philosophy.* (Summer 2013). Available online: https://plato.stanford.edu/archives/sum2013/entries/aesthetics-18th-french/ (accessed January 23, 2022).

Morphy, Howard. *Becoming Art: Exploring Cross-Cultural Categories*. Sydney: University of New South Wales Press, 2008.

Moureau, François. "L'*Encyclopédie* d'après les correspondants de Formey." *Recherches sur Diderot et sur l'Encyclopédie* 3 (1987): 125–45.

Mullan, John. "Feelings and Novels." In *Rewriting the Self: Histories from the Renaissance to the Present*, edited by Roy Porter, 119–34. London: Routledge, 1997.

Müller-Wille, Staffan. "Collection and Collation: Theory and Practice of Linnaean Botany." *Studies in History and Philosophy of Biological and Biomedical Sciences* 38 (January 2007): 541–62.

The Multigraph Collective. *Interacting with Print*. Chicago: University of Chicago Press, 2018.

Mundy, Barbara. *The Death of Aztec Tenochtitlan, the Life of Mexico City*. Austin: University of Texas Press, 2015.

Noyes, John K. *Herder: Aesthetics Against Imperialism*. Toronto: University of Toronto Press, 2015.

Oakley, Francis. *Natural Law, Laws of Nature, Natural Rights: Continuity and Discontinuity in the History of Ideas*. New York: Continuum, 2005.

O'Brien, Karen. *Narratives of Enlightenment: Cosmopolitan History from Voltaire to Gibbon*. Cambridge: Cambridge University Press, 1997.

OED Online. Oxford: Oxford University Press, 2018.

Ogilvie, Brian W. "Insects in John Ray's Natural History and Natural Theology." In *Zoology in Early Modern Culture: Intersections of Science, Theology, Philology, and Political and Religious Education*, edited by Karl A. E. Enenkel and Paul J. Smith, 234–60. Leiden: Brill, 2014.

Ogilvie, Brian W. "Stoics, Neoplatonists, Atheists, Politicians: Sources and Uses of Early Modern Jesuit Natural Theology." In *For the Sake of Learning: Essays in Honor of Anthony Grafton*, edited by Ann Blair and Anja-Silvia Goeing, Volume 2, 761–79. Leiden: Brill, 2016.

Pagden, Anthony. *Lords of All the World: Ideologies of Empire in Spain, Britain and France c. 1500–c. 1800*. New Haven, CT: Yale University Press, 1995.

Paige, Nicholas D. *Being Interior: Autobiography and the Contradictions of Modernity in Seventeenth-Century France*. Philadelphia: University of Pennsylvania Press, 2001.

Palmeri, Frank. *State of Nature, Stages of Society: Enlightenment Conjectural History and Modern Social Discourse*. Columbia Studies in Political Thought/Political History. New York: Columbia University Press, 2016.

Pardailhé-Galabrun, Annick. *The Birth of Intimacy: Privacy and Domestic Life in Eighteenth-Century Paris*. Translated by Jocelyn Phelps. Philadelphia: University of Pennsylvania Press, 1992.

Pasanek, Bradley, and Chad Wellmon, "The Enlightenment Index." *Eighteenth Century Theory and Interpretation* 56, no. 3 (Fall 2015): 357–80.

Pearsall, Sarah. *Atlantic Families: Lives and Letters in the Later Eighteenth Century*. Oxford: Oxford University Press, 2008.

Philippe, Audegean. "Genovesi, Antonio." Translated by Philip Stewart. In *A Montesquieu Dictionary* [online]. Directed by Catherine Volpilhac-Auger. ENS Lyon, September 2013. Available online: http://dictionnaire-montesquieu.ens-lyon.fr/en/article/1367160245/en (accessed January 23, 2022).

Pocock, J. G. A. *The Machiavellian Moment: Florentine Political Thought and the Atlantic Republican Tradition*. Princeton, NJ: Princeton University Press, 1975.

Pocock, J. G. A. *Barbarism and Religion*. 6 volumes. Cambridge: Cambridge University Press, 1999–2015.

Porter, Roy, ed. *Rewriting the Self: Histories from the Renaissance to the Present*. London: Routledge, 1997.

Porter, Roy. *Flesh in the Age of Reason: The Modern Foundations of Body and Soul*. New York: W. W. Norton, 2003.

Posner, Ernst. "Some Aspects of Archival Development since the French Revolution." *American Archivist* 3 (July 1940): 159–74.

Rahe, Paul A. "The Enlightenment Indicted: Rousseau's Response to Montesquieu." *Journal of the Historical Society* 8 (2008): 273–302.

Ranum, Orest. *Artisans of Glory: Writers and Historical Thought in Seventeenth-Century France*. Chapel Hill: University of North Carolina Press, 1980.

Raven, James. *The Business of Books: Booksellers and the English Book Trade, 1450–1850*. New Haven, CT: Yale University Press, 2007.

Reddy, William. *The Navigation of Feeling: A Framework for the History of Emotions*. Cambridge: Cambridge University Press, 2001.

Reichenberger, Andrea. "Émilie Du Châtelet's Interpretation of the Laws of Motion in the Light of 18th Century Mechanics." *Studies in History and Philosophy of Science Part A* 69 (2018): 1–11.

"Review of Le Mercier de la Rivière, *L'Ordre naturel*." *Journal de l'agriculture, du commerce, et des finances* (September 1767): 102.

Riley, James C. *The Seven Years War and the Old Regime in France: The Economic and Financial Toll*. Princeton, NJ: Princeton University Press, 1986.

Riley, Patrick. "Fénelon's Republican Monarchism in *Telemachus*." In *Monarchisms in the Age of Enlightenment: Liberty, Patriotism, and the Common Good*, edited by Hans W. Blom, John Christian Laursen, and Luisa Simonuttti, 78–100. Toronto: University of Toronto Press, 2007.

Robertson, John. *The Case for Enlightenment: Scotland and Naples 1680–1760*. Cambridge: Cambridge University Press, 2005.

Roche, Daniel. *The People of Paris: An Essay in Popular Culture in the 18th Century*. Translated by Marie Evans. Berkeley: University of California Press, 1987.

Roche, Daniel. *The Culture of Clothing: Dress and Fashion in the Ancien Régime*. Translated by Jean Birrell. Cambridge: Cambridge University Press, 1997.

Roche, Daniel. *A History of Everyday Things: The Birth of Consumption in France, 1600–1800*. Translated by Brian Pearce. Cambridge: Cambridge University Press, 2000.

Roger, Jacques. *Buffon: A Life in Natural History*. Translated by Sarah Lucille Bonnefoi. Cornell History of Science. Ithaca, NY: Cornell University Press, 1997.

Rosenberg, Daniel. "An 18th-Century Time Machine: The *Encyclopédie* of Denis Diderot." In *Postmodernism and the Enlightenment*, edited by Daniel Gordon, 45–67. London: Routledge, 2001.

Rosenberg, Daniel, and Anthony Grafton. *Cartographies of Time: A History of the Timeline*. Princeton, NJ: Princeton Architectural Press, 2010.

Rosenfeld, Sophia. *A Revolution in Language: The Problem of Signs in Late Eighteenth-Century France*. Stanford, CA: Stanford University Press, 2003.

Ross, Ellen. "The Debate on Luxury in Eighteenth-Century France: A Study in the Language of Opposition." PhD diss., University of Chicago, 1975.

Rothschild, Emma. *Economic Sentiments: Adam Smith, Condorcet, and the Enlightenment*. Cambridge, MA: Harvard University Press, 2001.

Roux, Sophie. "Les lois de la nature à l'âge classique: La question terminologique." *Revue de synthèse*, 4th ser., nos. 2–4 (2001): 531–76.

Russo, Elena. "The Self, Real and Imaginary: Social Sentiment in Marivaux and Hume." *Yale French Studies* 92 (1997): 126–48.

Salmond, Anne. *The Trial of the Cannibal Dog: The Remarkable Story of Captain Cook's Encounters in the South Seas*. New Haven, CT: Yale University Press, 2003.

Samurin, E. I. *Geschichte der bibliothekarisch-bibliographischen Klassifikation*. 2 volumes. Leipzig: VEB Bibliographisches Institut, 1964–1967.

Saunders, David. "The Natural Jurisprudence of Jean Barbeyrac: Translation as an Art of Political Adjustment." *Eighteenth-Century Studies* 36 (2003): 473–90.

Schiebinger, Londa. *The Mind Has No Sex? Women in the Origins of Modern Science*. Cambridge, MA: Harvard University Press, 1991.

Schröder, Jan. "The Concept of (Natural) Law in the Doctrine of Law and Natural Law of the Early Modern Era." In *Natural Law and Laws of Nature in Early Modern Europe: Jurisprudence, Theology, Moral and Natural Philosophy*, edited by Lorraine Daston and Michael Stolleis, 57–71. Farnham, UK: Ashgate, 2008.

Schulte-Albert, Hans. "Leibniz and Literary Classification." *Journal of Library History* 6, no. 2 (1971): 133–52.

Seigel, Jerrold. *The Idea of the Self: Thought and Experience in Western Europe since the Seventeenth Century*. Cambridge: Cambridge University Press, 2005.

Sekora, John. *Luxury: The Concept in Western Thought, Eden to Smollett*. Baltimore: Johns Hopkins University Press, 1977.

Sewell, William H., Jr. *A Rhetoric of Bourgeois Revolution: The Abbé Sieyes and What is the Third Estate?* Durham, NC: Duke University Press, 1994.

Sheehan, Colleen A. "Madison and the French Enlightenment: The Authority of Public Opinion." *William and Mary Quarterly* 59 (2002): 925–56.

Sheehan, Colleen A. *The Mind of James Madison: The Legacy of Classical Republicanism*. Cambridge: Cambridge University Press, 2015.

Sheehan, Jonathan. "From Philology to Fossils: The Biblical Encyclopedia in Early Modern Europe." *Journal of the History of Ideas* 64, no. 1 (January 2003): 41–60.

Sheehan, Jonathan. "Enlightenment, Religion, and the Enigma of Secularization: A Review Essay," *American Historical Review* 108, no. 4 (2003): 1061–80.

Sheehan, Jonathan. *The Enlightenment Bible: Translation, Scholarship, Culture*. Princeton, NJ: Princeton University Press, 2005.

Sheehan, Jonathan, and Dror Wahrman. *Invisible Hands: Self-Organization and the Eighteenth Century*. Chicago: University of Chicago Press, 2015.

Shelley, James. "18th Century British Aesthetics." *The Stanford Encyclopedia of Philosophy*. (Winter 2020). Available online: https://plato.stanford.edu/archives/fall2014/entries/aesthetics-18th-british/ (accessed February 8, 2022).

Sher, Richard B. *The Enlightenment and the Book: Scottish Authors and Their Publishers in Eighteenth-Century Britain, Ireland, and America*. Chicago: University of Chicago Press, 2006.

Shovlin, John. *The Political Economy of Virtue: Luxury, Patriotism, and the Origins of the French Revolution*. Ithaca, NY: Cornell University Press, 2006.

Simmons, A. John. *On the Edge of Anarchy: Locke, Consent, and the Limits of Society*. Princeton, NJ: Princeton University Press, 1993.

Siskin, Clifford, and William Warner, eds., *This is Enlightenment*. Chicago: University of Chicago Press, 2010.

Skinner, Quentin. *Reason and Rhetoric in the Philosophy of Hobbes*. Cambridge: University of Cambridge Press, 1996.

Sluhovsky, Moshe. *Becoming a New Self: Practices of Belief in Early Modern Catholicism.* Chicago: University of Chicago Press, 2017.

Smith, Justin E. H. *Nature, Human Nature, and Human Difference: Race in Early Modern Philosophy.* Princeton, NJ: Princeton University Press, 2015.

Sonenscher, Michael. *Before the Deluge: Public Debt, Inequality, and the Intellectual Origins of the French Revolution.* Princeton, NJ: Princeton University Press, 2007.

Sorkin, David. *The Religious Enlightenment: Protestants, Jews, and Catholics from London to Vienna.* Princeton, NJ: Princeton University Press, 2008.

Spector, Céline. *Montesquieu et l'émergence de l'économie politique.* Paris: Champion, 2006.

Steinbrugge, Liselotte. *The Moral Sex: Woman's Nature in the French Enlightenment.* Translated by Pamela E. Selwyn. Oxford: Oxford University Press, 1995.

Stewart, Philip. *L'invention du sentiment: roman et économie affective au XVIIIe siècle.* Oxford: Voltaire Foundation, 2010.

Stone, Lawrence. *The Family, Sex, and Marriage in England, 1500–1800.* New York: Harper & Row, 1977.

Summers, David. *Real Spaces: World Art History and the Rise of Western Modernism.* New York: Phaidon Press, 2003.

Susato, Ryu. "Hume's Nuanced Defense of Luxury." *Hume Studies* 32 (2006): 167–86.

Sutherland, Christine M., and Rebecca Sutcliffe, eds. *The Changing Tradition: Women in the History of Rhetoric.* Calgary: University of Calgary Press, 1999.

Taylor, Charles. *Sources of the Self: The Making of the Modern Identity.* Cambridge: Cambridge University Press, 1989.

Taylor, Charles. *A Secular Age.* Cambridge, MA: Harvard University Press, 2007.

Terrall, Mary. *Catching Nature in the Act: Natural History in the Eighteenth Century.* Chicago: University of Chicago Press, 2014.

Théré, Christine. "Economic Publishing and Authors, 1566–1789." In *Studies in the History of French Political Economy from Bodin to Walras*, edited by Gilbert Faccarello, 1–56. New York: Routledge, 1998.

Thomas, Downing A. *Music and the Origins of Language: Theories from the French Enlightenment.* Cambridge: Cambridge University Press, 1995.

Thompson, Dennis F. "Bibliography: The Education of a Founding Father. The Reading List for John Witherspoon's Course in Political Theory, as Taken by James Madison." *Political Theory* 4 (1976): 523–9.

Thornton, Helen. *State of Nature or Eden? Thomas Hobbes and His Contemporaries on the Natural State of Human Beings.* Rochester Studies in Philosophy. Rochester, NY: University of Rochester Press, 2005.

Tierney, Brian. *Liberty and Law: The Idea of Permissive Natural Law, 1100–1800.* Studies in Medieval and Early Modern Canon Law. Washington, DC: Catholic University of America Press, 2014.

Tillet, Edouart. "Jean Barbeyrac, or the Ambiguities of Political Radicality at the Dawn of the Enlightenment." In *The Internationalization of Intellectual Exchange in a Globalizing Europe 1636–1780*, edited by Robert Mankin, 31–54. Lewisburg, PA: Bucknell University Press, 2018.

Trempler, Jörg. "Catastrophes and their Images: Event and Pictorial Act." *RES: Anthropology and Aesthetics* 63/64 (2013): 201–14.

Tuck, Richard. *Natural Rights Theories: Their Origin and Development.* Cambridge: Cambridge University Press, 1979.

van der Zande, Johan. "The Microscope of Experience: Christian Garve's Translation of Cicero's *De Officiis* (1783)." *Journal of the History of Ideas* 59, no. 1 (January 1998): 75–94.

Vardi, Liana. *The Physiocrats and the World of the Enlightenment*. Cambridge: Cambridge University Press, 2012.

Volmer, Annett. "Journalismus und Aufklärung: Jean Henri Samuel Formey und die Entwicklung der Zeitschrift zum Medium der Kritik." *Jahrbuch für Kommunikationsgeschichte* 9 (2007): 101–29.

Wahnbaeck, Till. *Luxury and Public Happiness: Political Economy in the Italian Enlightenment*. Oxford: Oxford University Press, 2004.

Wahrman, Dror. "On Queen Bees and Being Queens: A Late Eighteenth-Century 'Cultural Revolution'?" In *The Age of Cultural Revolutions*, edited by Colin Jones and Dror Wahrman, 251–80. Berkeley: University of California Press, 2002.

Wahrman, Dror. *The Making of the Modern Self: Identity and Culture in Eighteenth-Century England*. New Haven, CT: Yale University Press, 2004.

Wallnig, Thomas. *Critical Monks: The German Benedictines*. Leiden: Brill, 2019.

Walsham, Alexandra. *Providence in Early Modern England*. Oxford: Oxford University Press, 1999.

Watt, Ian. *The Rise of the Novel: Studies in Defoe, Richardson, and Fielding*. Berkeley: University of California Press, 1957.

Weatherill, Lorna. *Consumer Behaviour and Material Culture in Britain 1660–1760*. 2nd edition. London: Routledge, 1996.

Weimar, Klaus. "Reading for Feeling." In *A New History of German Literature*, edited by David E. Wellbery, 356–60. Cambridge, MA: Harvard University Press, 2004.

Wellmon, Chad. *Organizing Enlightenment: Information Overload and the Invention of the Modern Research University*. Baltimore: Johns Hopkins University Press, 2015.

Wellmon, Chad. "The Future of Search." *Hedgehog Review* 18, no. 2 (Summer 2016): 110–13.

White, Hayden. *Metahistory: The Historical Imagination in Nineteenth-Century Europe*. Reprint. Baltimore: Johns Hopkins University Press, 2014.

Whitefield, Peter. *London: A Life in Maps*. London: British Library, 2017.

Winterer, Caroline. *The Culture of Classicism: Ancient Greece and Rome in American Intellectual Life, 1780–1910*. Baltimore: Johns Hopkins University Press, 2002.

Winterer, Caroline. *American Enlightenments: Pursuing Happiness in the Age of Reason*. New Haven, CT: Yale University Press, 2016.

Wolf, Eric. *Europe and the People Without History*. Berkeley: University of California Press, 1982.

Womack, William R. "Eighteenth-Century Themes in the *Histoire philosophique et politique des deux Indes* of Guillaume Raynal." *Studies on Voltaire and the Eighteenth Century* 96 (1972): 129–65.

Wood, Paul. *Western Art and the Wider World*. Chichester, UK: Wiley-Blackwell, 2013.

Wootton, David. "Unhappy Voltaire, or 'I shall never get over it as long as I live.'" *History Workshop Journal* 50 (2000): 137–55.

Wootton, David. "David Hume, 'The Historian.'" In *The Cambridge Companion to Hume*, 2nd edition, edited by David Fate Norton and Jacqueline Anne Taylor, 447–79. Cambridge: Cambridge University Press, 2009.

Wright, Johnson Kent. "Historical Thought in the Era of the Enlightenment." In *A Companion to Western Historical Thought*, edited by Lloyd Kramer and Sarah Maza, 123–42. Oxford: Blackwell, 2006.

Wright, Johnson Kent. "Rousseau and Montesquieu." In *Thinking with Rousseau, from Machiavelli to Schmitt*, edited by Helena Rosenblatt and Paul Schweigert, 63–91. Cambridge: Cambridge University Press, 2017.

Yale, Elizabeth. "The History of Archives: The State of the Discipline." *Book History* 18, no. 1 (2015): 332–59.

Zedelmaier, Helmut. *Werkstatten des Wissens zwischen Renaissance und Aufklärung*. Tubingen: Mohr Siebeck, 2015.

Zedelmaier, Helmut. "Suchen und Finden vor Google: Zur Metadatenproduktion im 16. Jahrhundert." In *For the Sake of Learning: Essays in Honor of Anthony Grafton*, volume 18, edited by Ann Blair and Anja-Silvia Goeing, 423–40. Leiden: Brill, 2016.

CONTRIBUTORS

Howard G. Brown is Professor of History at Binghamton University (State University of New York), USA. He is the author of *War, Revolution and the Bureaucratic State: Politics and Army Administration in France, 1791–1799* (1995) and the prize-winning *Ending the French Revolution: Violence, Justice, and Repression from the Terror to Napoleon* (2006), as well as the co-editor, with Judith A. Miller, of *Taking Liberties: Problems of a New Order from the French Revolution to Napoleon* (2002). His most recent book is *Mass Violence and the Self: From the French Wars of Religion to the Paris Commune* (2018).

Jack R. Censer is Emeritus Professor of History at George Mason University, USA. He earned his doctorate at Johns Hopkins University, USA in 1973 and spent most of his academic career at George Mason University (1977–2015). His most recent publications include *Debating Modern Revolution: The Evolution of Revolutionary Ideas* (2016) and, with Lynn Hunt, *The French Revolution and Napoleon: Crucible of the Modern World* (2017), both published by Bloomsbury Academic.

Douglas Fordham is Professor of Art History at the University of Virginia, USA. He is the author of *British Art and the Seven Years' War: Allegiance and Autonomy* (2007) and, most recently, *Aquatint Worlds: Travel, Print, and Empire, 1770–1820* (2019), which examines printed representations from Western India, Southern Africa, and China; and co-editor of *Art and the British Empire* (2010) and *Boomalli Prints and Paper: Making Space as an Art Collective* (2022).

Gary Kates is H. Russell Smith Foundation Chair in the Social Sciences and Professor of History at Pomona College, USA. He is the author of *Monsieur d'Eon is a Woman: A Tale of Gender Confusion and Sexual Masquerade* (1995), *The Cercle Social, the Girondins, and the French Revolution* (2014), *The Books that Made the European Enlightenment: A History in 12 Case Studies* (2022), and the editor of *The French Revolution: Recent Debates and New Controversies* (2005).

Sarah Maza is Jane Long Professor in the Arts and Sciences and Professor of History at Northwestern University, USA. Her books include *Servants and Masters in Eighteenth-Century France* (1983), *Private Lives and Public Affairs: The Causes Célèbres of Prerevolutionary France* (1993), *The Myth of the French Bourgeoisie: An Essay on the Social Imaginary* (2003), *Violette Nozière: A Story of Murder in 1930s Paris* (2011), and most recently, *Thinking About History* (2017).

Brian W. Ogilvie is Professor of History at the University of Massachusetts Amherst, USA. His research addresses the history of science and scholarship in early modern Europe. He is the author of *The Science of Describing: Natural History in Renaissance Europe* (2006).

Christy Pichichero is Associate Professor of French and History at George Mason University, USA. She is the author of *The Military Enlightenment: War and Culture in the French Empire from Louis XIV to Napoleon* (2017), which was a finalist for the Oscar Kenshur Book Prize, and the co-editor, with Emily Marker, of the *H-France Salon* special issue "Race, Racism & the Study of France and the Francophone World Today" (2019).

Jonathan Sheehan is Professor of History at the University of California, Berkeley, USA. Most recently, he is co-author, with Dror Wahrman, of *Invisible Hands: Self-Organization and the Eighteenth Century* (2015). His previous book, *The Enlightenment Bible: Translation, Scholarship, Culture* (2005), won the George Mosse Prize from the American Historical Association and was a Choice Outstanding Academic Title.

Chad Wellmon is Professor of German Studies and History at the University of Virginia, USA. His work includes *Organizing Enlightenment: Information Overload and the Invention of the Modern Research University* (2015). His more recent work, including essays, can be found at https://chadwellmon.com.

Caroline Winterer is William Roberston Coe Professor of History at Stanford University, USA. Her books include *The Culture of Classicism: Ancient Greece and Rome in American Intellectual Life, 1780–1910* (2002), *The Mirror of Antiquity: American Women and the Classical Tradition, 1750–1900* (2007), *American Enlightenments: Pursuing Happiness in the Age of Reason* (2016), *and Time in Maps: From the Age of Discovery to our Digital Era*, edited with Karen Wigen (2020).

INDEX